SHONEN JUMP MANGA

ONE PIECE

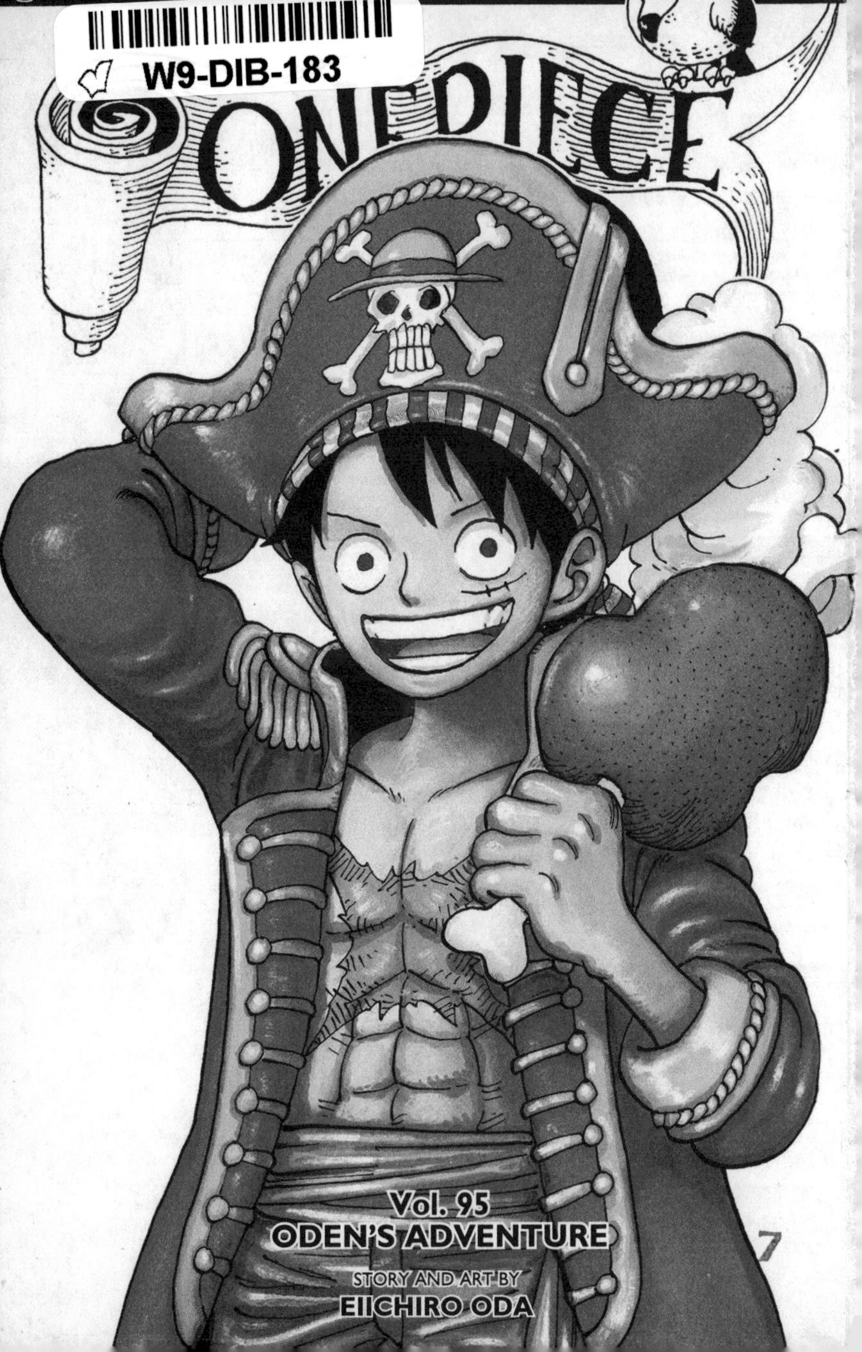

Vol. 95

ODEN'S ADVENTURE

STORY AND ART BY

EIICHIRO ODA

The Straw Hat Crew

Chopperemon [Ninja]
Tony Tony Chopper

Studied powerful medicines in the Birdie Kingdom as he waited to rejoin the crew.

Ship's Doctor, Bounty: 100 berries

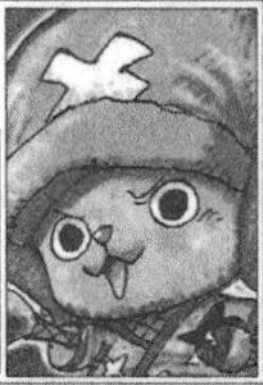

Luffytaro [Ronin]
Monkey D. Luffy

A young man dreaming of being the Pirate King. After two years of training he rejoins his friends in search of the New World!

Captain, Bounty: 1.5 billion berries

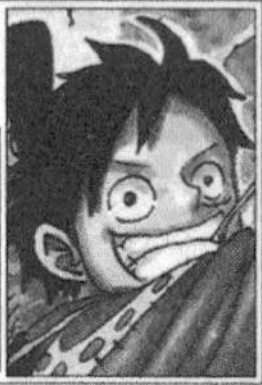

Orobi [Geisha]
Nico Robin

Spent time on the island of Baltigo with Dragon, Luffy's father and leader of the Revolutionary Army.

Archeologist, Bounty: 130 million berries

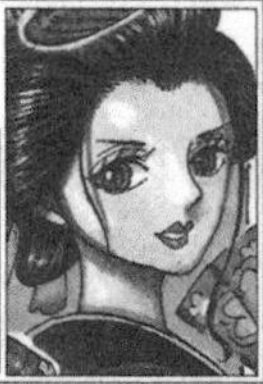

Zolojuro [Ronin]
Roronoa Zolo

Swallowed his pride on Gloom Island and trained under Mihawk before rejoining Luffy.

Fighter, Bounty: 320 million berries

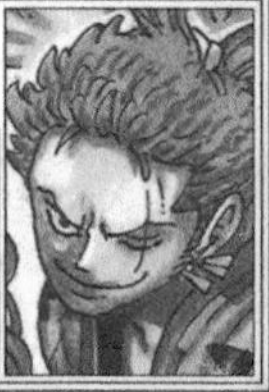

Franosuke [Carpenter]
Franky

Upgraded himself into "Armored Franky" in the Future Land, Baldimore.

Shipwright, Bounty: 94 million berries

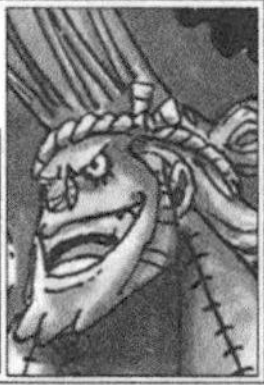

Onami [Kunoichi]
Nami

Learned about the climates of the New World on Weatheria, a Sky Island that studies the atmosphere.

Navigator, Bounty: 66 million berries

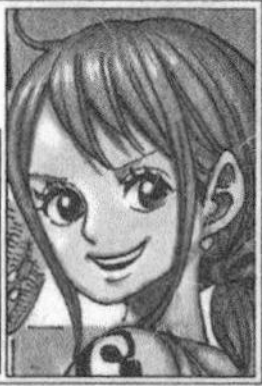

Bonekichi [Ghost]
Brook

Originally captured by Long-Arm bandits for a freak show, he is now the mega-star "Soul King" Brook.

Musician, Bounty: 83 million berries

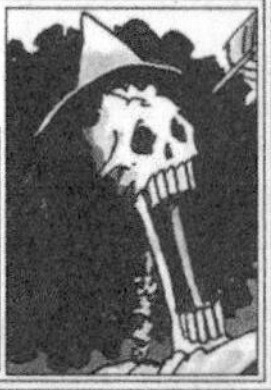

Usohachi [Toad Oil Salesman]
Usopp

Received Heraclesun's lessons on the Bowin Islands in his quest to be the "king of the snipers."

Sniper, Bounty: 200 million berries

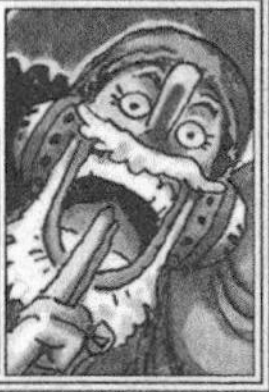

Shanks

One of the Four Emperors. Waits for Luffy in the "New World," the second half of the Grand Line.

Captain of the Red-Haired Pirates

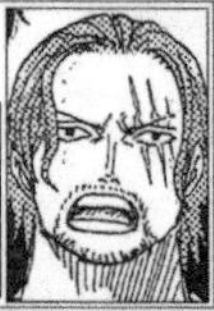

Sangoro [Soba Cook]
Sanji

Honed his skills fighting with the masters of Newcomer Kenpo in the Kamabakka Kingdom.

Cook, Bounty: 330 million berries

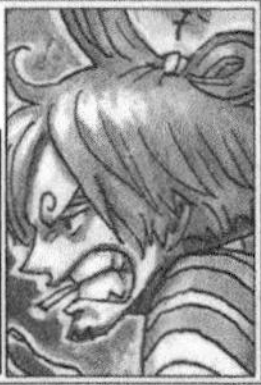

The story of ONE PIECE 1»95

Kozuki Momonosuke

Daimyo (Heir) to Kuri in Wano

Akazaya Nine

Foxfire Kin'emon

Samurai of Wano

Raizo of the Mist

Ninja of Wano

Evening Shower Kanjuro

Samurai of Wano

Okiku

Samurai of Wano

Kozuki Hiyori

Momonosuke's Little Sister

Ashura Doji (Shutenmaru)

Chief, Atamayama Thieves Brigade

Kawamatsu

Samurai of Wano

Duke Dogstorm

King of the Day, Mokomo

Cat Viper

King of the Night, Mokomo

People of Wano

Shinobu

Veteran Kunoichi

Otsuru (Kin'emon's Wife)

Tea Shop Owner

Gyukimaru

Bandit Warrior-monk, Koma Fox

Tonoyasu

Daimyo of the Kozuki Clan

Toko

Kamuro, Yasuie's Daughter

Tenguyama Hitetsu

Katana Blacksmith

Otama

Child of Kuri in Wano

Hyogoro the Flower

Senior Yakuza Boss

Blood-Writing Ohmasa

Yakuza Boss of Udon

Split-Hat Tsunagoro

Yakuza Boss of Hakumai

Ocho the Bottle Gourd

Yakuza Boss of Ringo

Snake-Eyes Yatappe

Yakuza Boss of Kibi

Heart Pirates

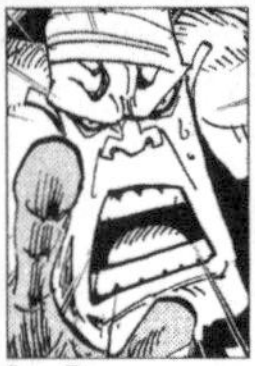
Jean Bart
Crew, Heart Pirates

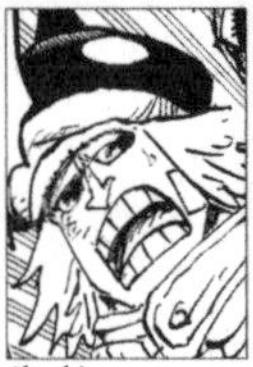
Shachi
Crew, Heart Pirates

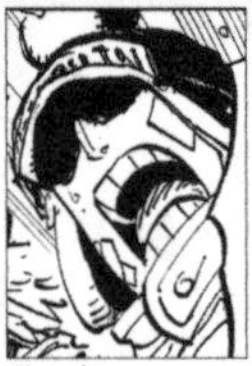
Penguin
Crew, Heart Pirates

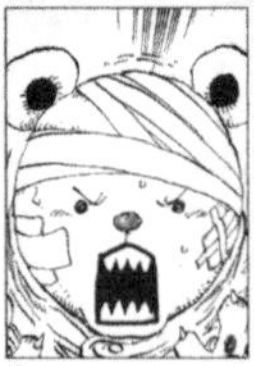
Bepo
Navigator, Heart Pirates

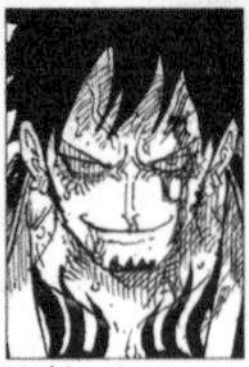
Trafalgar Law
Captain, Heart Pirates

Mokomo Dukedom

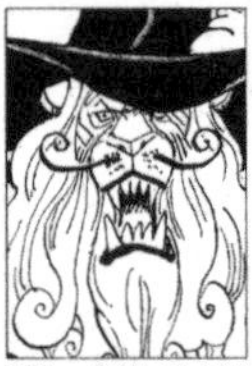
Full-Power Shishilian (Lion Mink)
Captain, Dogstorm Musketeers

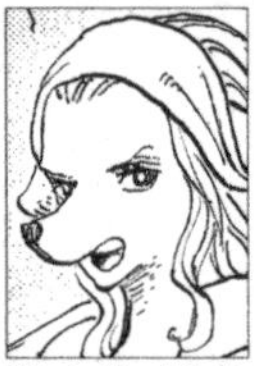
Wanda (Dog Mink)
Battlebeast Tribe, Kingsbird

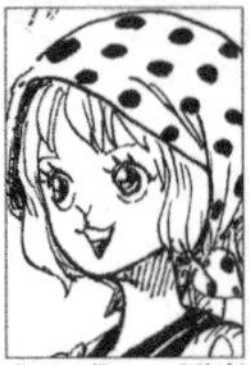
Carrot (Bunny Mink)
Battlebeast Tribe, Kingsbird

Kid Pirates

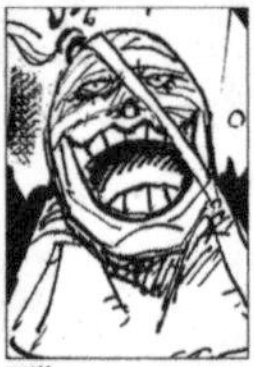
Killer
Fighter, Kid Pirates

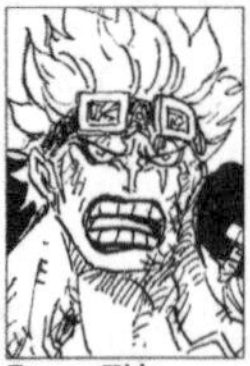
Eustass Kid
Captain, Kid Pirates

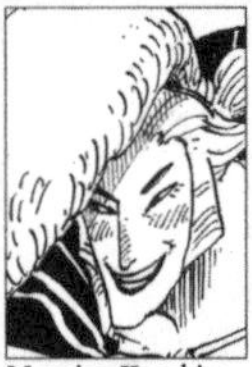
Napping Kyoshiro
Money Changer for the Kurozumi Clan

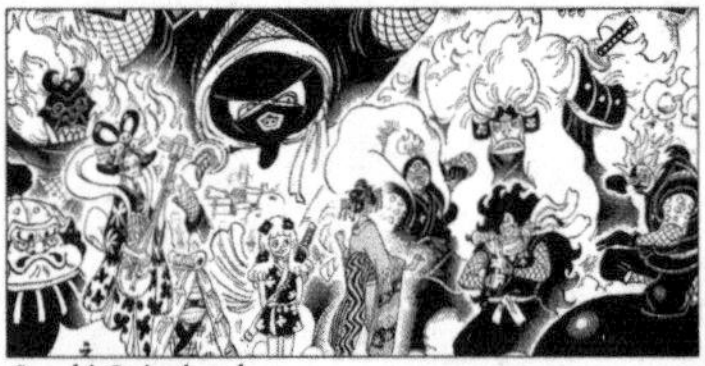
Orochi Oniwabanshu
Shogun of Wano's Private Ninja Squad

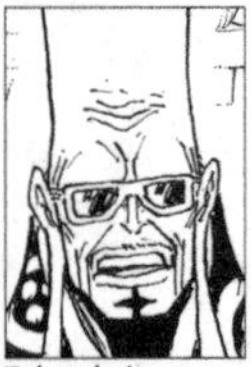
Fukurokuju
Leader, Orochi Oniwabanshu

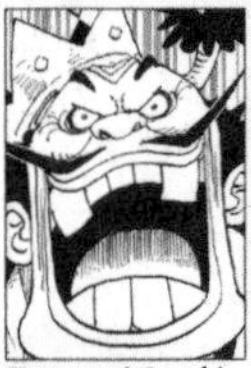
Kurozumi Orochi
Shogun of Wano

Kaido's side learns about the raid plan, but thanks to Yasuie's sacrifice, the plans are successfully changed. Kin'emon and his fellow samurai must rebuild the plan without time to mourn their fallen friend. Meanwhile, Luffy succeeds in taking over the excavation camp, adding Hyogoro and the other yakuza to his side before the big battle. By that point, Big Mom has recovered her memories and started to fight with Kaido...

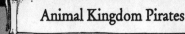

Animal Kingdom Pirates

Kaido, King of the Beasts
(Emperor of the Sea)

A pirate known as the "strongest creature alive." Despite numerous tortures and death sentences, none have been able to kill him.

Captain, Animal Kingdom Pirates

Big Mom
(Emperor of the Sea)

One of the Four Emperors, a.k.a. Big Mom. Uses the Soul-Soul Fruit that extracts life span from others.

Captain, Big Mom Pirates

Lead Performers

King the Wildfire

Queen the Plague

Jack the Drought

Tobi Roppo

X. (Diez) Drake

Page One

Headliners

Basil Hawkins

Holdem

Babanuki

Daifugo

Solitaire

Speed

Dobon

Story

After two years of hard training, the Straw Hat pirates are back together, first at the Sabaody Archipelago and then through Fish-Man Island to their next stage: the New World!!

Luffy and crew disembark on Wano for the purpose of defeating Kaido, one of the Four Emperors. They begin to recruit allies for a raid in two weeks' time, but Kaido's sudden appearance leads to Luffy's defeat. Luffy is sent to the excavation labor camp while the rest of the crew is spotted by Kaido's underlings and have to go on the run!

Vol. 95
ODEN'S ADVENTURE

CONTENTS

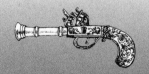

Chapter 954:

LIKE A DRAGON GIVEN WINGS

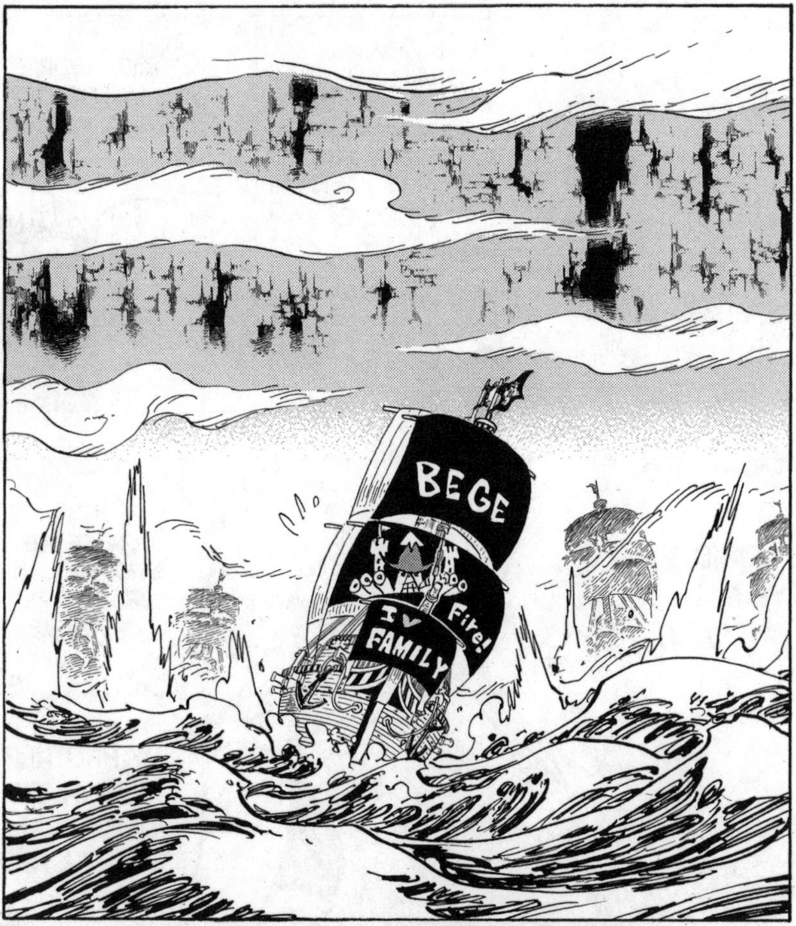
BEGE
I ♥ FAMILY
Fire!

GANG BEGE'S OH MY FAMILY
VOL. 5: "CAN'T GET PAST THE RED LINE WITH ALL THE HUBBUB AT THE REVERIE!!"

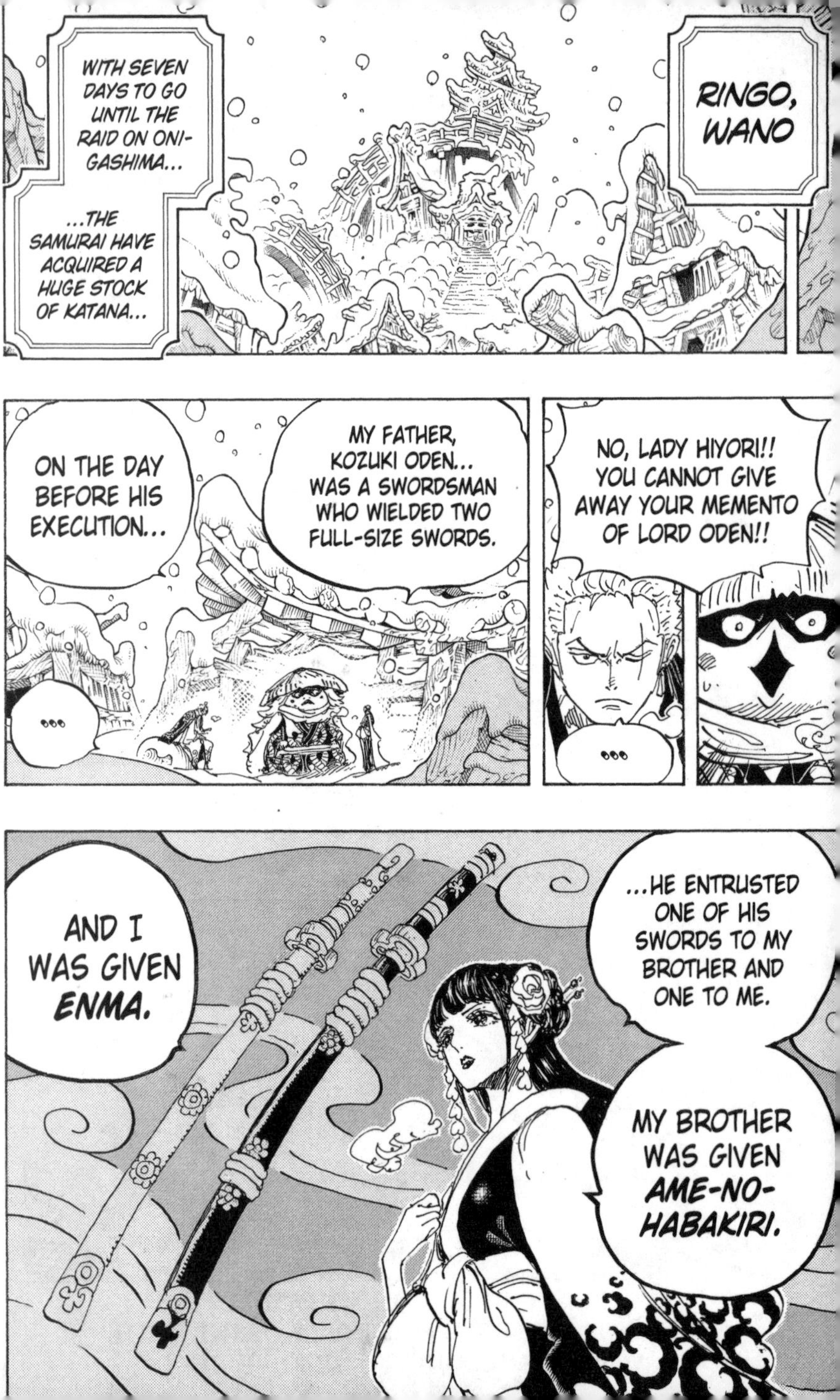
RINGO, WANO
WITH SEVEN DAYS TO GO UNTIL THE RAID ON ONIGASHIMA...
...THE SAMURAI HAVE ACQUIRED A HUGE STOCK OF KATANA...
NO, LADY HIYORI!! YOU CANNOT GIVE AWAY YOUR MEMENTO OF LORD ODEN!!
...
MY FATHER, KOZUKI ODEN... WAS A SWORDSMAN WHO WIELDED TWO FULL-SIZE SWORDS.
ON THE DAY BEFORE HIS EXECUTION...
...
...HE ENTRUSTED ONE OF HIS SWORDS TO MY BROTHER AND ONE TO ME.
MY BROTHER WAS GIVEN AME-NO-HABAKIRI.
AND I WAS GIVEN ENMA.

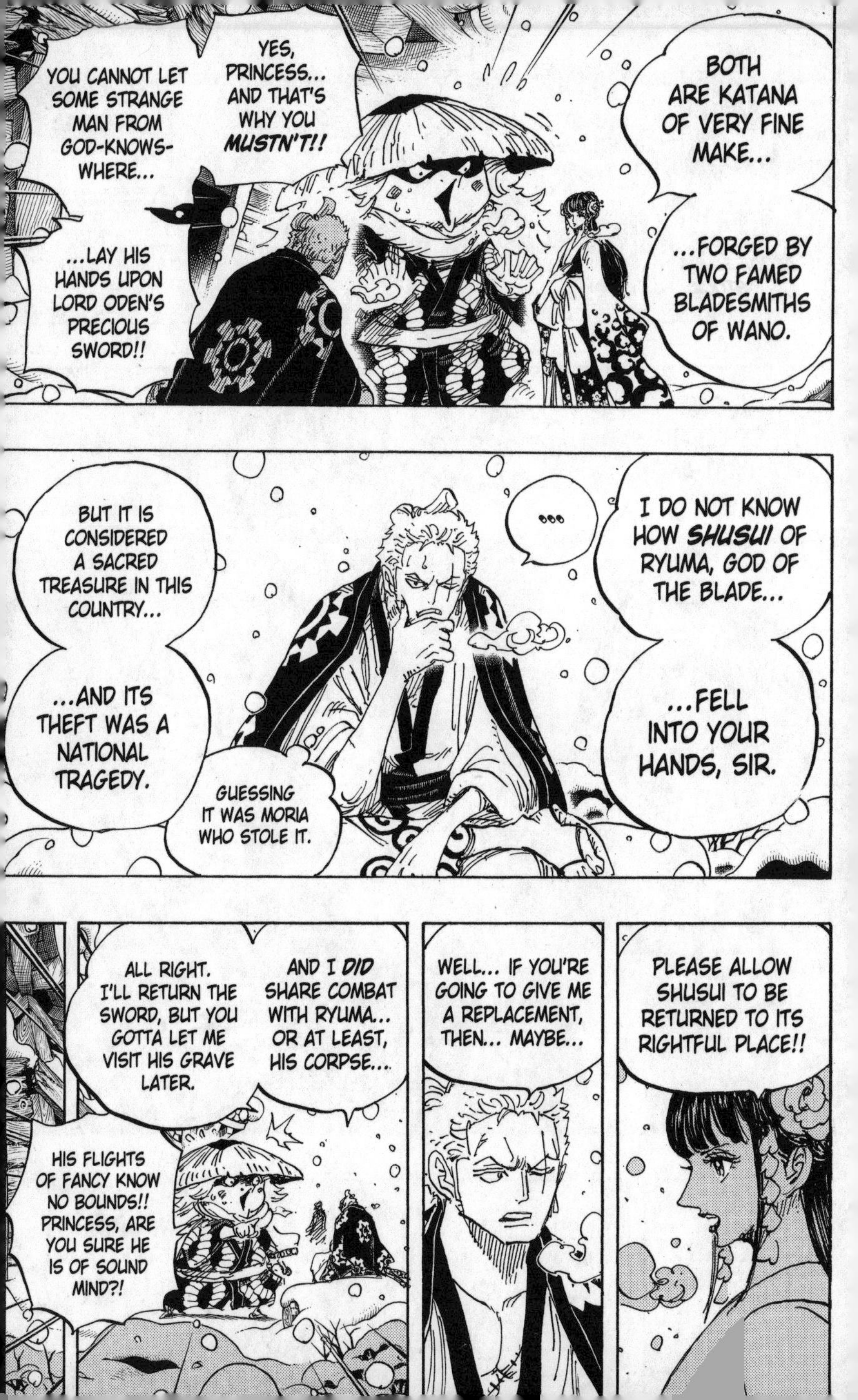
BOTH ARE KATANA OF VERY FINE MAKE...
...FORGED BY TWO FAMED BLADESMITHS OF WANO.
YES, PRINCESS... AND THAT'S WHY YOU *MUSTN'T!!*
YOU CANNOT LET SOME STRANGE MAN FROM GOD-KNOWS-WHERE...
...LAY HIS HANDS UPON LORD ODEN'S PRECIOUS SWORD!!
I DO NOT KNOW HOW *SHUSUI* OF RYUMA, GOD OF THE BLADE...
...FELL INTO YOUR HANDS, SIR.
...
BUT IT IS CONSIDERED A SACRED TREASURE IN THIS COUNTRY...
...AND ITS THEFT WAS A NATIONAL TRAGEDY.
GUESSING IT WAS MORIA WHO STOLE IT.
PLEASE ALLOW SHUSUI TO BE RETURNED TO ITS RIGHTFUL PLACE!!
WELL... IF YOU'RE GOING TO GIVE ME A REPLACEMENT, THEN... MAYBE...
AND I *DID* SHARE COMBAT WITH RYUMA... OR AT LEAST, HIS CORPSE....
ALL RIGHT. I'LL RETURN THE SWORD, BUT YOU GOTTA LET ME VISIT HIS GRAVE LATER.
HIS FLIGHTS OF FANCY KNOW NO BOUNDS!! PRINCESS, ARE YOU SURE HE IS OF SOUND MIND?!

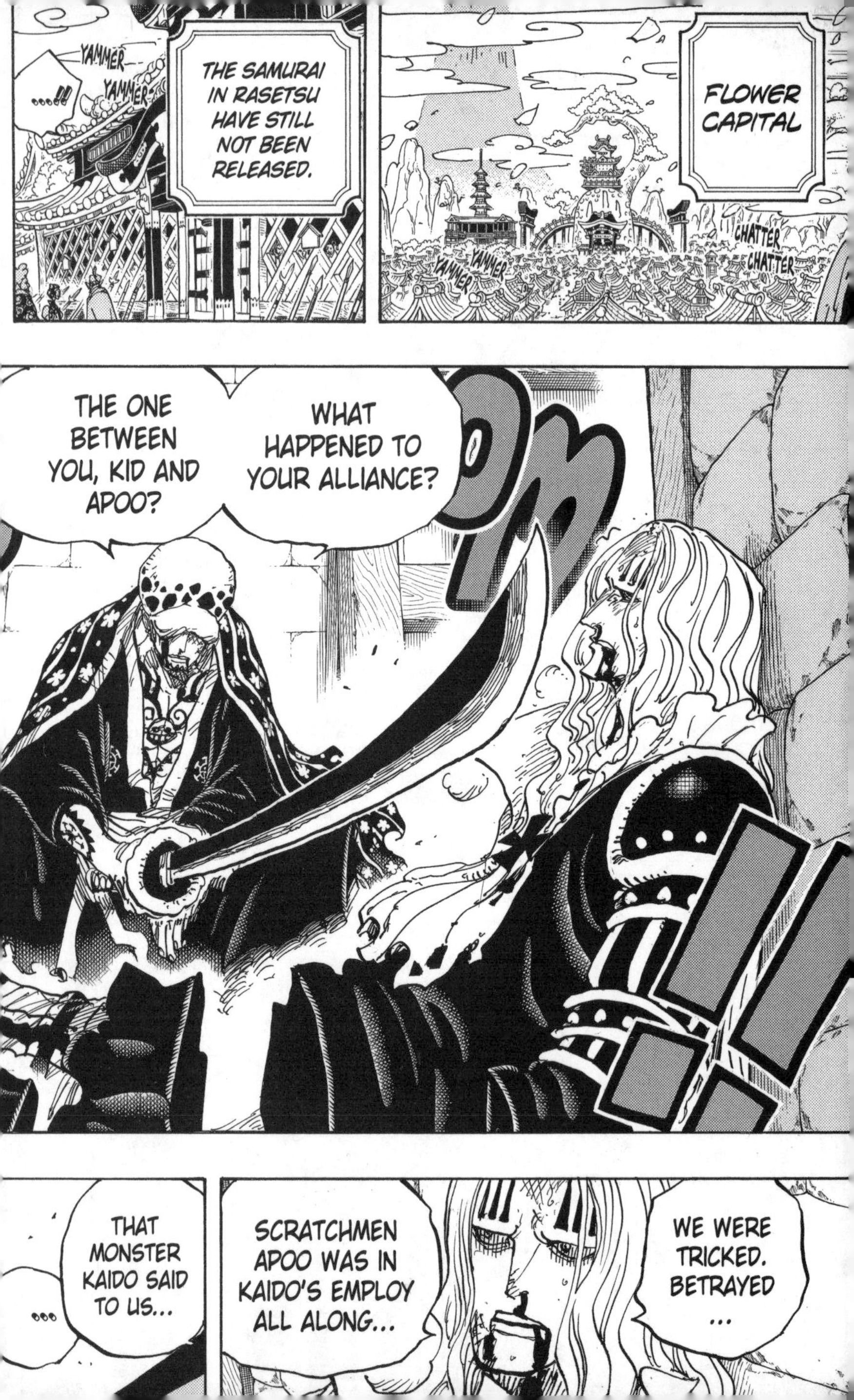
FLOWER CAPITAL
CHATTER CHATTER
YAMMER YAMMER
THE SAMURAI IN RASETSU HAVE STILL NOT BEEN RELEASED.
YAMMER YAMMER
...!!
WHAT HAPPENED TO YOUR ALLIANCE?
THE ONE BETWEEN YOU, KID AND APOO?
WE WERE TRICKED. BETRAYED ...
SCRATCHMEN APOO WAS IN KAIDO'S EMPLOY ALL ALONG...
THAT MONSTER KAIDO SAID TO US...
...

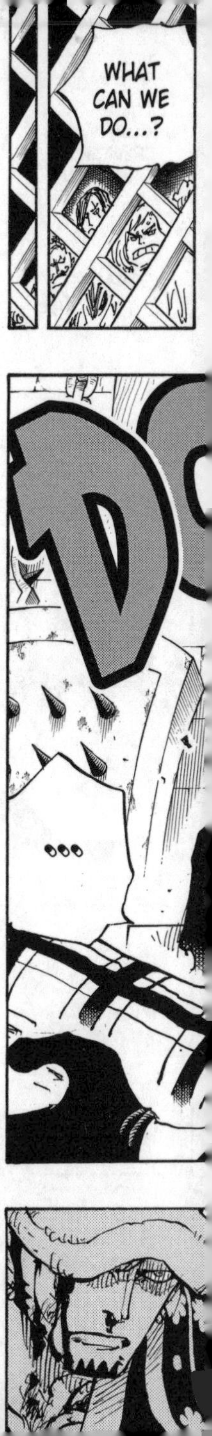
WHAT CAN WE DO...?
...

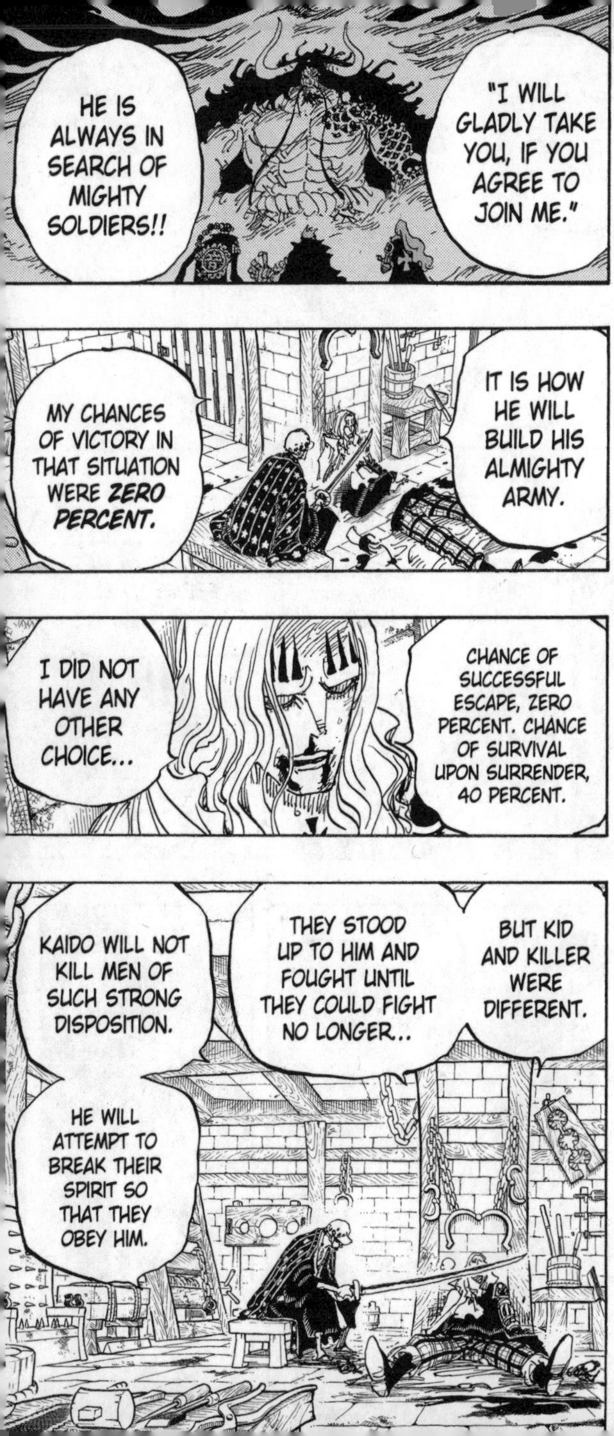
"I WILL GLADLY TAKE YOU, IF YOU AGREE TO JOIN ME."
HE IS ALWAYS IN SEARCH OF MIGHTY SOLDIERS!!
IT IS HOW HE WILL BUILD HIS ALMIGHTY ARMY.
MY CHANCES OF VICTORY IN THAT SITUATION WERE ZERO PERCENT.
CHANCE OF SUCCESSFUL ESCAPE, ZERO PERCENT. CHANCE OF SURVIVAL UPON SURRENDER, 40 PERCENT.
I DID NOT HAVE ANY OTHER CHOICE...
BUT KID AND KILLER WERE DIFFERENT.
THEY STOOD UP TO HIM AND FOUGHT UNTIL THEY COULD FIGHT NO LONGER...
KAIDO WILL NOT KILL MEN OF SUCH STRONG DISPOSITION.
HE WILL ATTEMPT TO BREAK THEIR SPIRIT SO THAT THEY OBEY HIM.

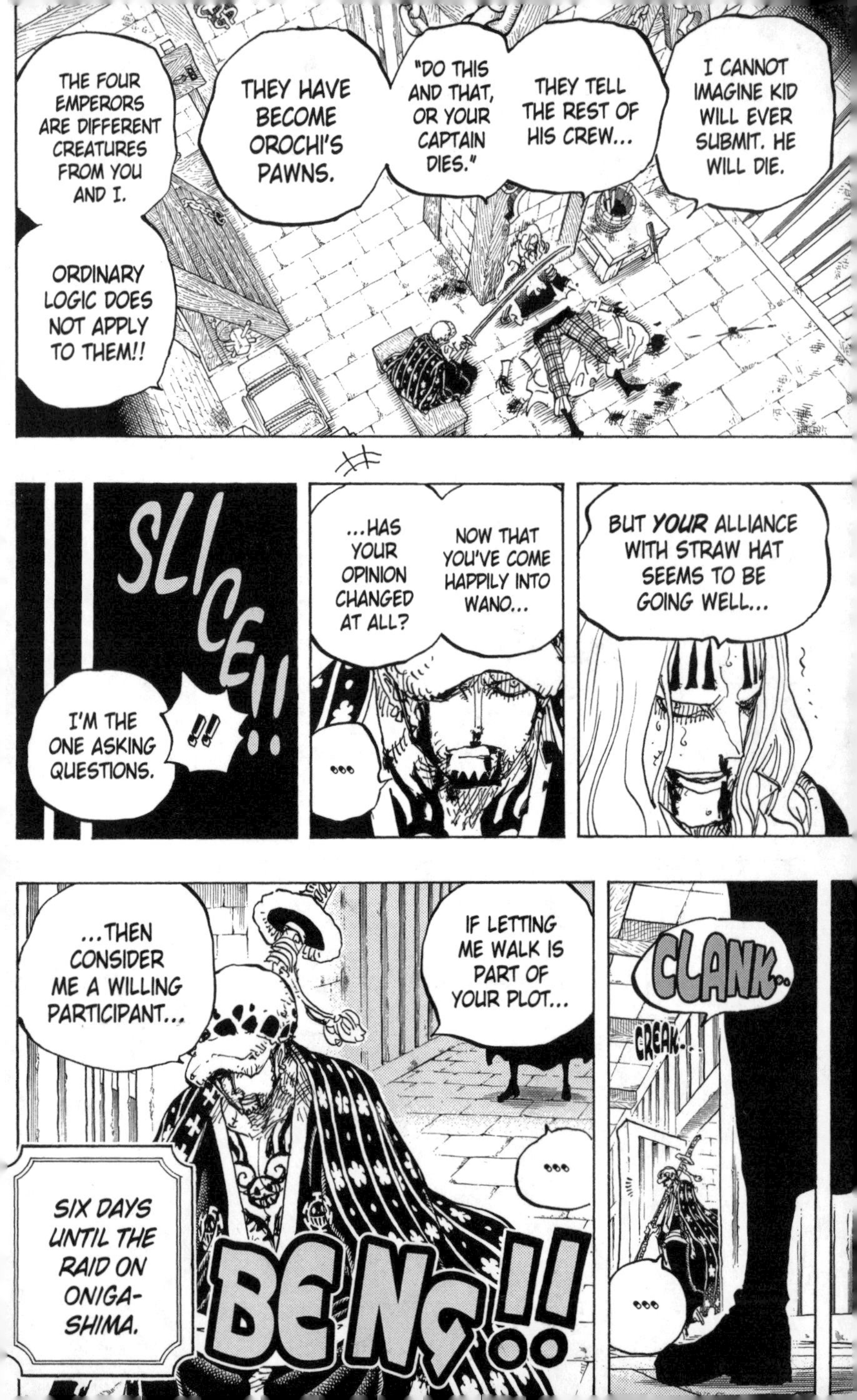
I CANNOT IMAGINE KID WILL EVER SUBMIT. HE WILL DIE.
THEY TELL THE REST OF HIS CREW...
"DO THIS AND THAT, OR YOUR CAPTAIN DIES."
THEY HAVE BECOME OROCHI'S PAWNS.
THE FOUR EMPERORS ARE DIFFERENT CREATURES FROM YOU AND I.
ORDINARY LOGIC DOES NOT APPLY TO THEM!!
BUT *YOUR* ALLIANCE WITH STRAW HAT SEEMS TO BE GOING WELL...
NOW THAT YOU'VE COME HAPPILY INTO WANO...
...HAS YOUR OPINION CHANGED AT ALL?
...
SLICE!!
!!
I'M THE ONE ASKING QUESTIONS.
CLANK..
CREAK...
...
IF LETTING ME WALK IS PART OF YOUR PLOT...
...THEN CONSIDER ME A WILLING PARTICIPANT...
...
BENG!!
SIX DAYS UNTIL THE RAID ON ONIGA-SHIMA.

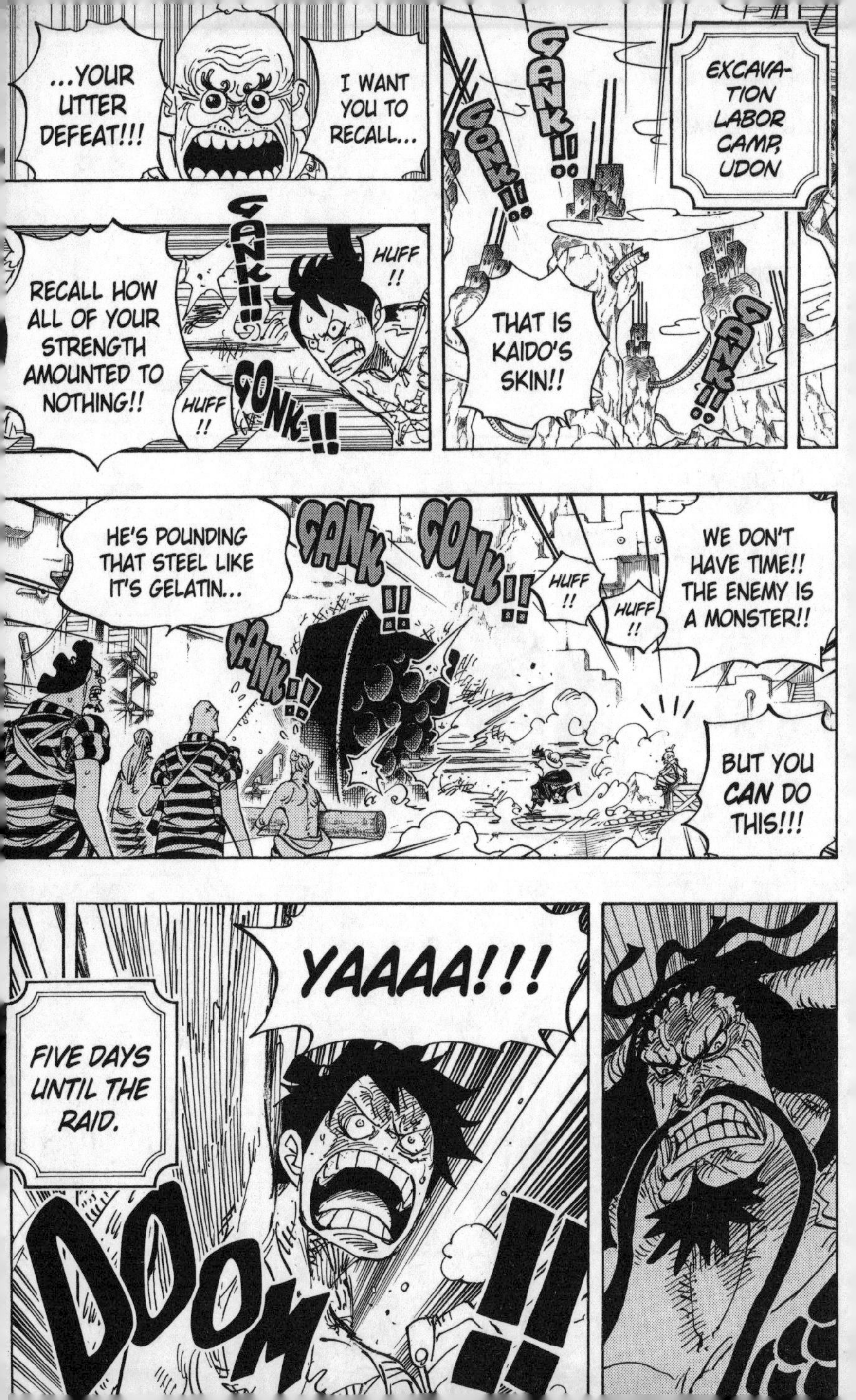
EXCAVATION LABOR CAMP, UDON
GANK!!
GONK!!
THAT IS KAIDO'S SKIN!!
GANK!!
I WANT YOU TO RECALL...
...YOUR UTTER DEFEAT!!!
GANK!!
HUFF!!
RECALL HOW ALL OF YOUR STRENGTH AMOUNTED TO NOTHING!!
GONK!!
HUFF!!
WE DON'T HAVE TIME!! THE ENEMY IS A MONSTER!!
HUFF!!
HUFF!!
GONK!!
GANK!!
HE'S POUNDING THAT STEEL LIKE IT'S GELATIN...
GANK!!
BUT YOU CAN DO THIS!!!
YAAAA!!!
FIVE DAYS UNTIL THE RAID.
DOOM!!

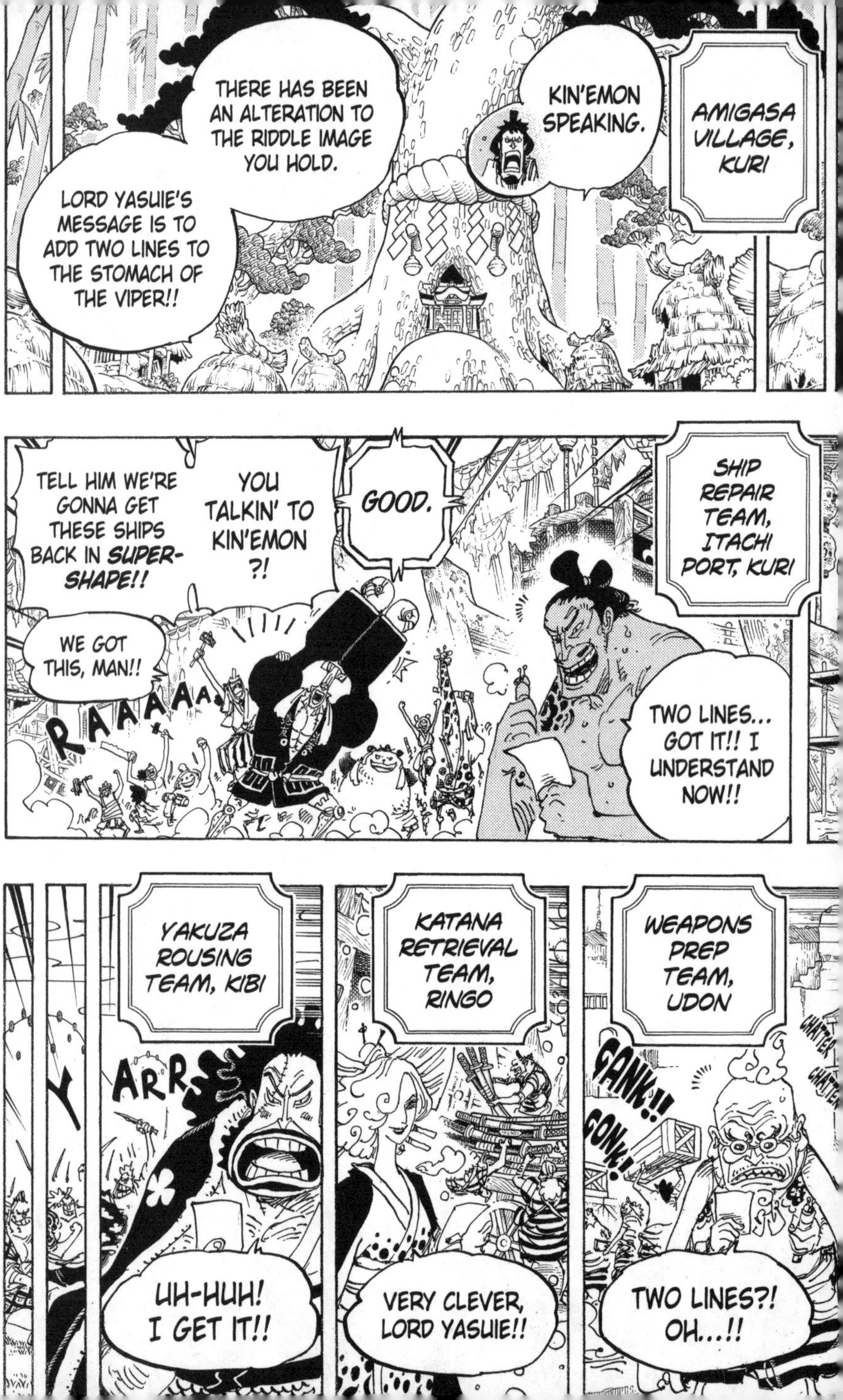
AMIGASA VILLAGE, KURI
KIN'EMON SPEAKING.
THERE HAS BEEN AN ALTERATION TO THE RIDDLE IMAGE YOU HOLD.
LORD YASUIE'S MESSAGE IS TO ADD TWO LINES TO THE STOMACH OF THE VIPER!!
SHIP REPAIR TEAM, ITACHI PORT, KURI
TWO LINES... GOT IT!! I UNDERSTAND NOW!!
GOOD.
YOU TALKIN' TO KIN'EMON ?!
TELL HIM WE'RE GONNA GET THESE SHIPS BACK IN SUPER-SHAPE!!
WE GOT THIS, MAN!!
RAAAAA
WEAPONS PREP TEAM, UDON
CHATTER CHATTER
GANK!! GONK!!
TWO LINES?! OH...!!
KATANA RETRIEVAL TEAM, RINGO
VERY CLEVER, LORD YASUIE!!
YAKUZA ROUSING TEAM, KIBI
ARR
UH-HUH! I GET IT!!

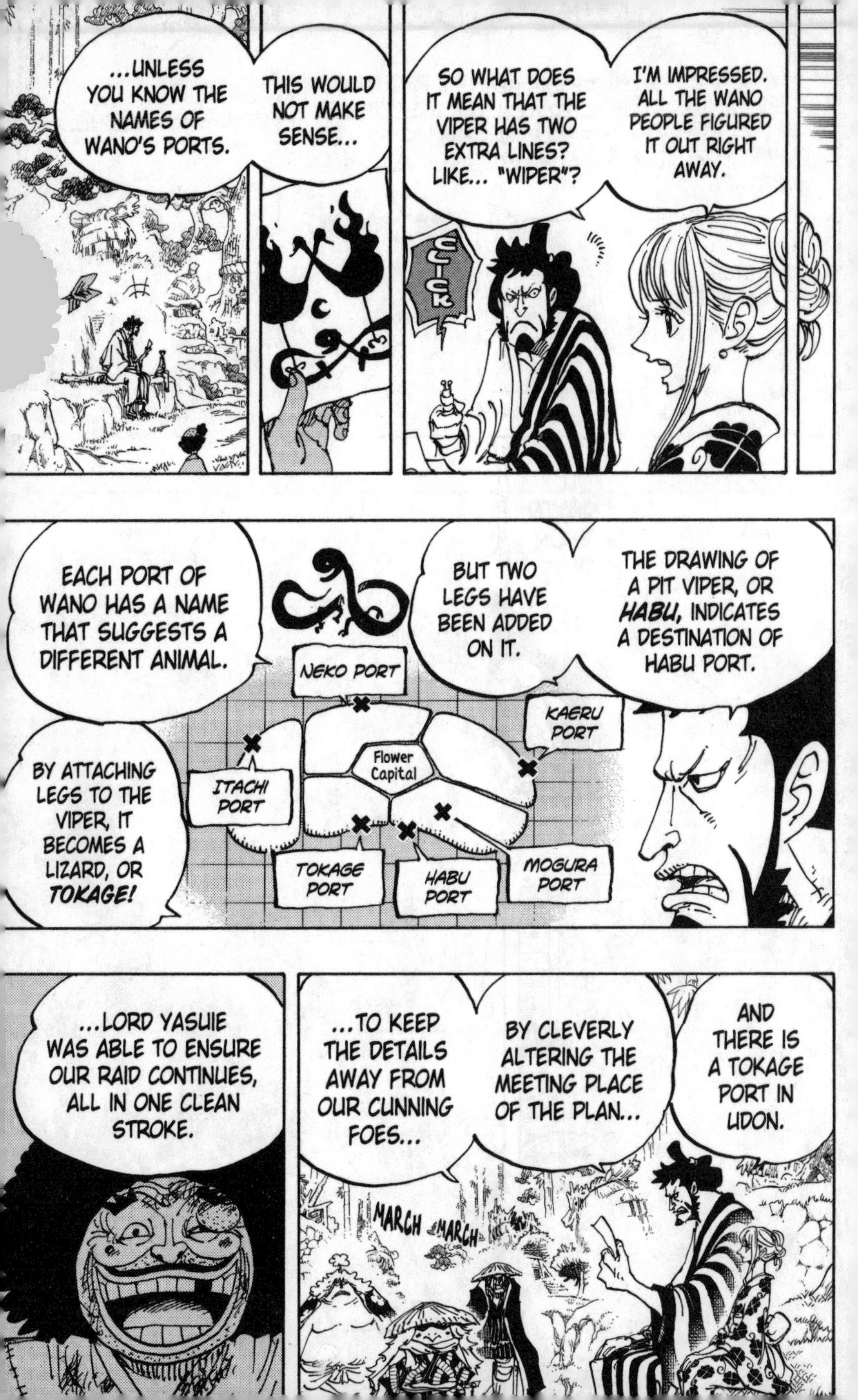
I'M IMPRESSED. ALL THE WANO PEOPLE FIGURED IT OUT RIGHT AWAY.
SO WHAT DOES IT MEAN THAT THE VIPER HAS TWO EXTRA LINES? LIKE... "WIPER"?
CLICK
THIS WOULD NOT MAKE SENSE...
...UNLESS YOU KNOW THE NAMES OF WANO'S PORTS.
THE DRAWING OF A PIT VIPER, OR HABU, INDICATES A DESTINATION OF HABU PORT.
BUT TWO LEGS HAVE BEEN ADDED ON IT.
EACH PORT OF WANO HAS A NAME THAT SUGGESTS A DIFFERENT ANIMAL.
NEKO PORT
KAERU PORT
Flower Capital
ITACHI PORT
MOGURA PORT
HABU PORT
TOKAGE PORT
BY ATTACHING LEGS TO THE VIPER, IT BECOMES A LIZARD, OR TOKAGE!
AND THERE IS A TOKAGE PORT IN UDON.
BY CLEVERLY ALTERING THE MEETING PLACE OF THE PLAN...
...TO KEEP THE DETAILS AWAY FROM OUR CUNNING FOES...
MARCH
MARCH
...LORD YASUIE WAS ABLE TO ENSURE OUR RAID CONTINUES, ALL IN ONE CLEAN STROKE.

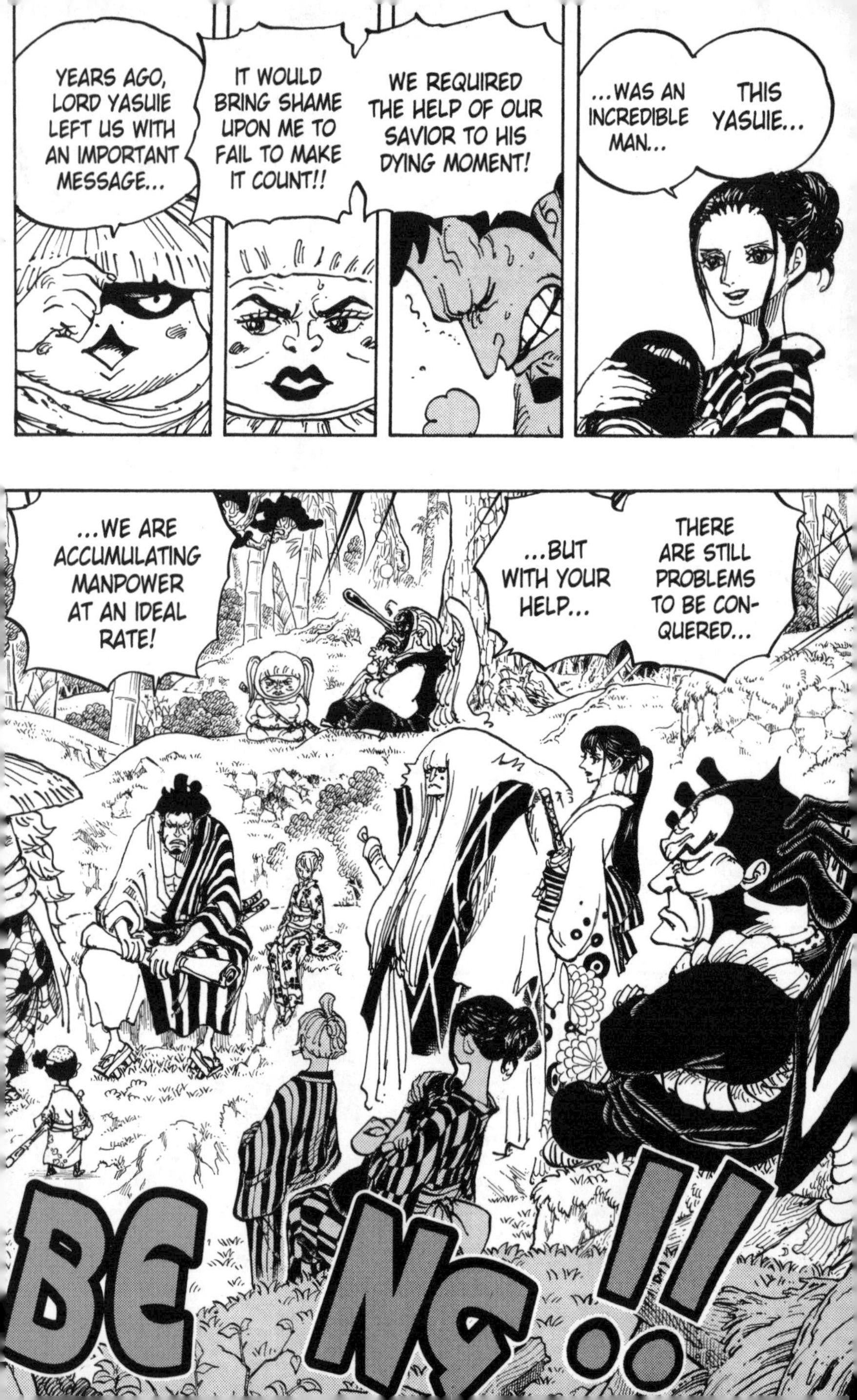
THIS YASUIE...
...WAS AN INCREDIBLE MAN...
WE REQUIRED THE HELP OF OUR SAVIOR TO HIS DYING MOMENT!
IT WOULD BRING SHAME UPON ME TO FAIL TO MAKE IT COUNT!!
YEARS AGO, LORD YASUIE LEFT US WITH AN IMPORTANT MESSAGE...
THERE ARE STILL PROBLEMS TO BE CON-QUERED...
...BUT WITH YOUR HELP...
...WE ARE ACCUMULATING MANPOWER AT AN IDEAL RATE!

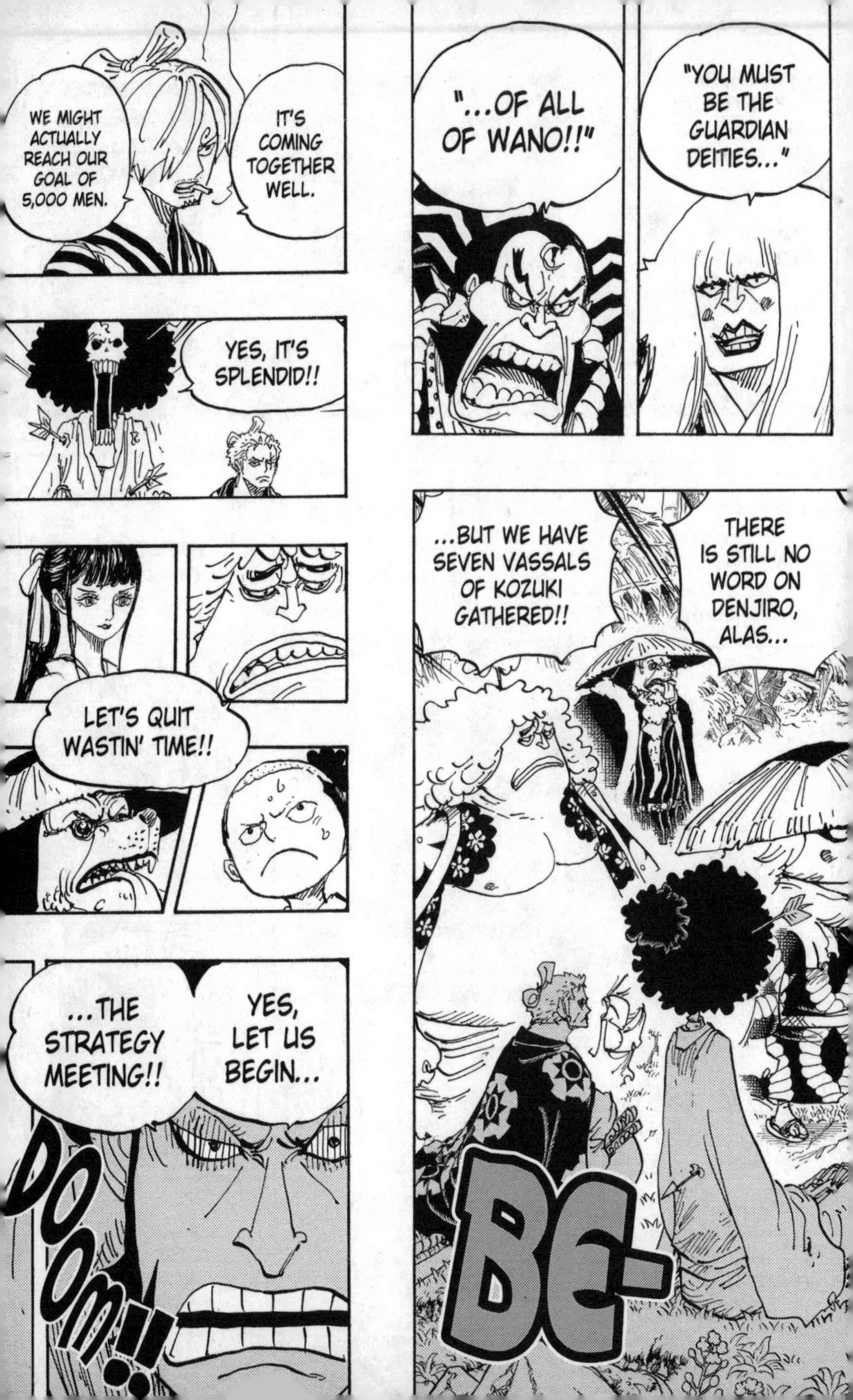
"YOU MUST BE THE GUARDIAN DEITIES..."
"...OF ALL OF WANO!!"
THERE IS STILL NO WORD ON DENJIRO, ALAS...
...BUT WE HAVE SEVEN VASSALS OF KOZUKI GATHERED!!
BC-
IT'S COMING TOGETHER WELL.
WE MIGHT ACTUALLY REACH OUR GOAL OF 5,000 MEN.
YES, IT'S SPLENDID!!
LET'S QUIT WASTIN' TIME!!
YES, LET US BEGIN...
...THE STRATEGY MEETING!!
DOOOM!!

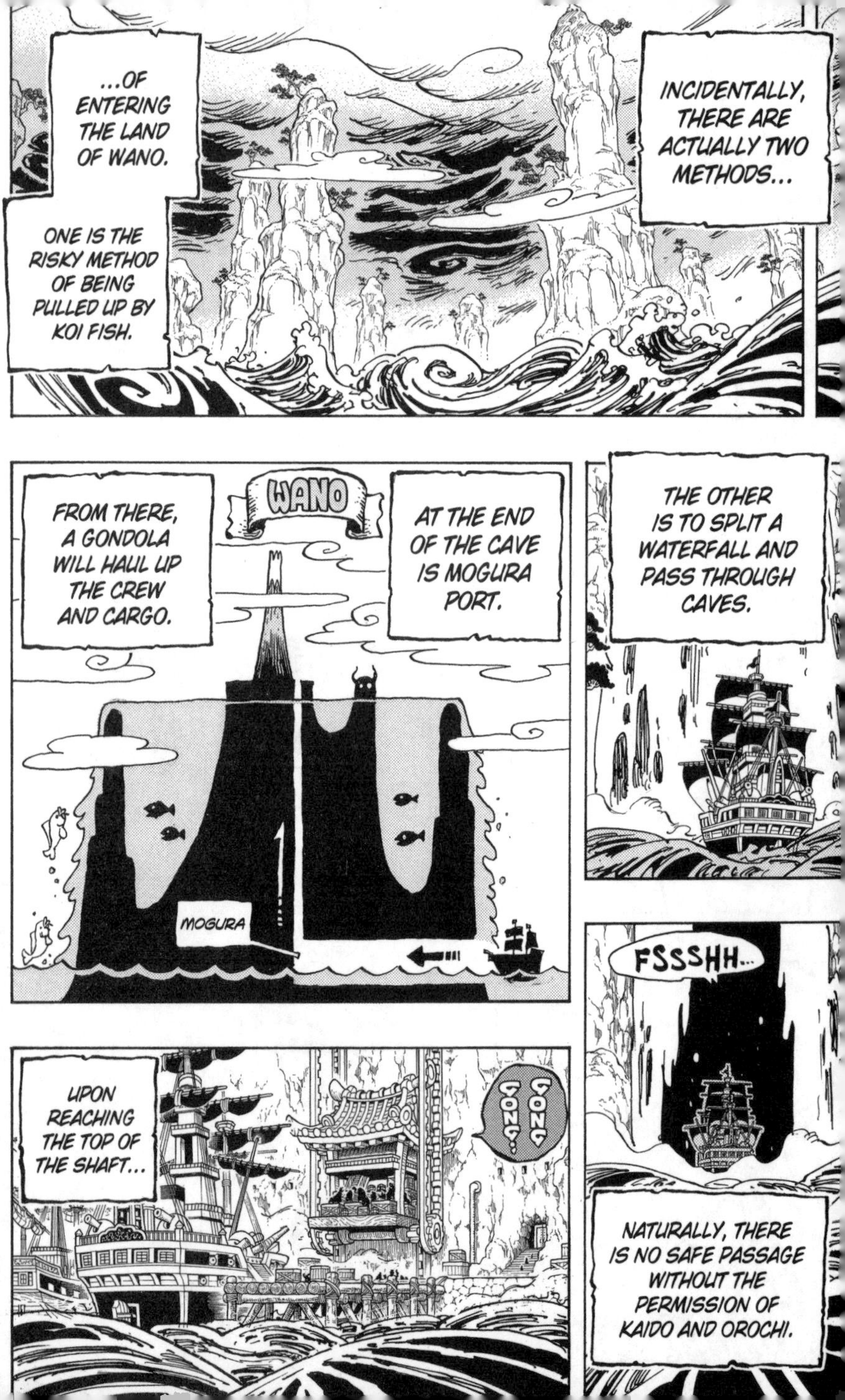
INCIDENTALLY, THERE ARE ACTUALLY TWO METHODS...
...OF ENTERING THE LAND OF WANO.
ONE IS THE RISKY METHOD OF BEING PULLED UP BY KOI FISH.
THE OTHER IS TO SPLIT A WATERFALL AND PASS THROUGH CAVES.
FSSSHH...
NATURALLY, THERE IS NO SAFE PASSAGE WITHOUT THE PERMISSION OF KAIDO AND OROCHI.
AT THE END OF THE CAVE IS MOGURA PORT.
WANO
FROM THERE, A GONDOLA WILL HAUL UP THE CREW AND CARGO.
MOGURA
UPON REACHING THE TOP OF THE SHAFT...
GONG GONG

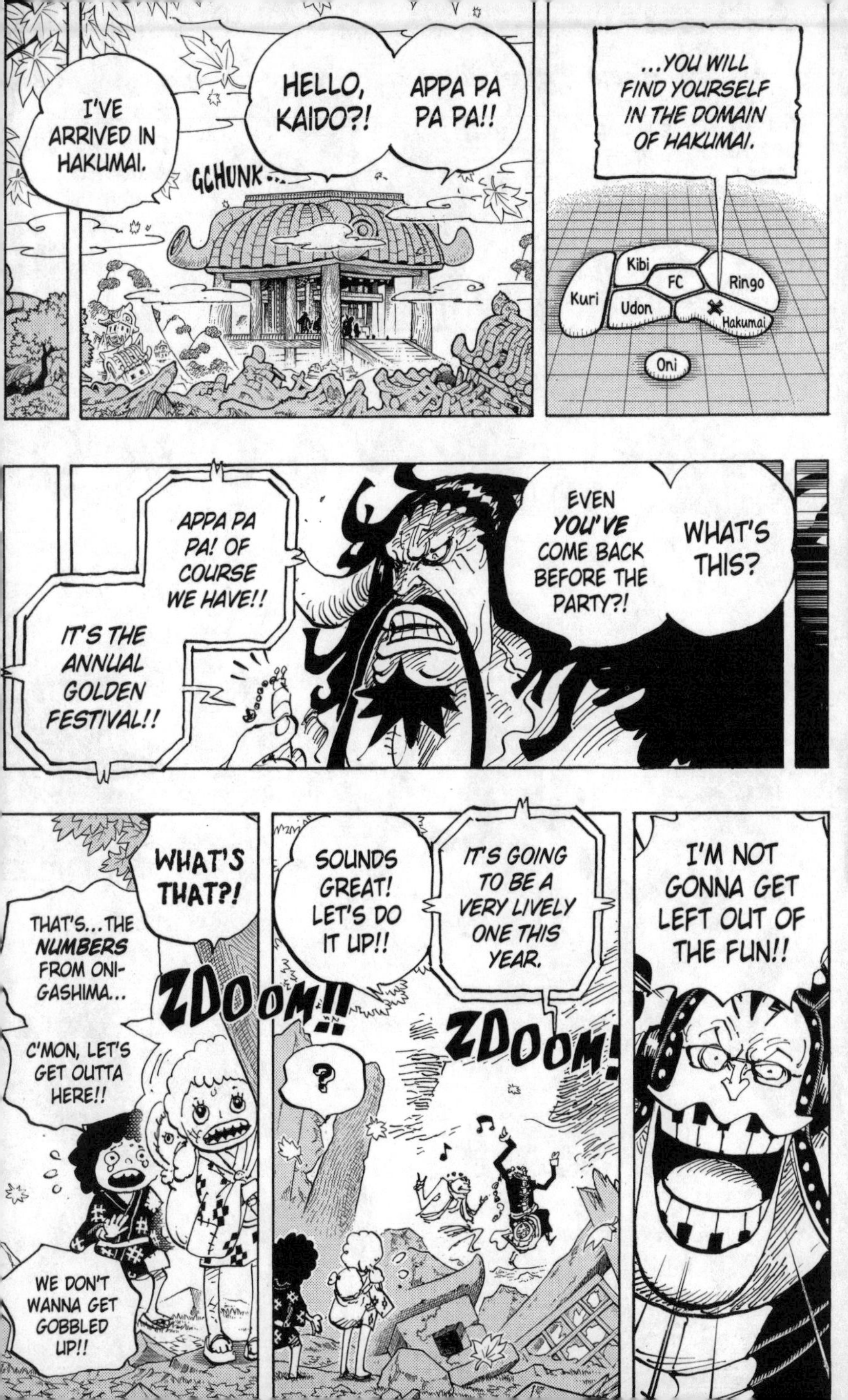
...YOU WILL FIND YOURSELF IN THE DOMAIN OF HAKUMAI.
Kibi
FC
Ringo
Kuri
Udon
Hakumai
Oni
HELLO, KAIDO?!
APPA PA PA PA!!
GCHUNK...
I'VE ARRIVED IN HAKUMAI.
WHAT'S THIS?
EVEN YOU'VE COME BACK BEFORE THE PARTY?!
APPA PA PA! OF COURSE WE HAVE!!
IT'S THE ANNUAL GOLDEN FESTIVAL!!
I'M NOT GONNA GET LEFT OUT OF THE FUN!!
IT'S GOING TO BE A VERY LIVELY ONE THIS YEAR.
SOUNDS GREAT! LET'S DO IT UP!!
ZDOOM!
?
WHAT'S THAT?!
THAT'S...THE NUMBERS FROM ONI-GASHIMA...
ZDOOM!!
C'MON, LET'S GET OUTTA HERE!!
WE DON'T WANNA GET GOBBLED UP!!

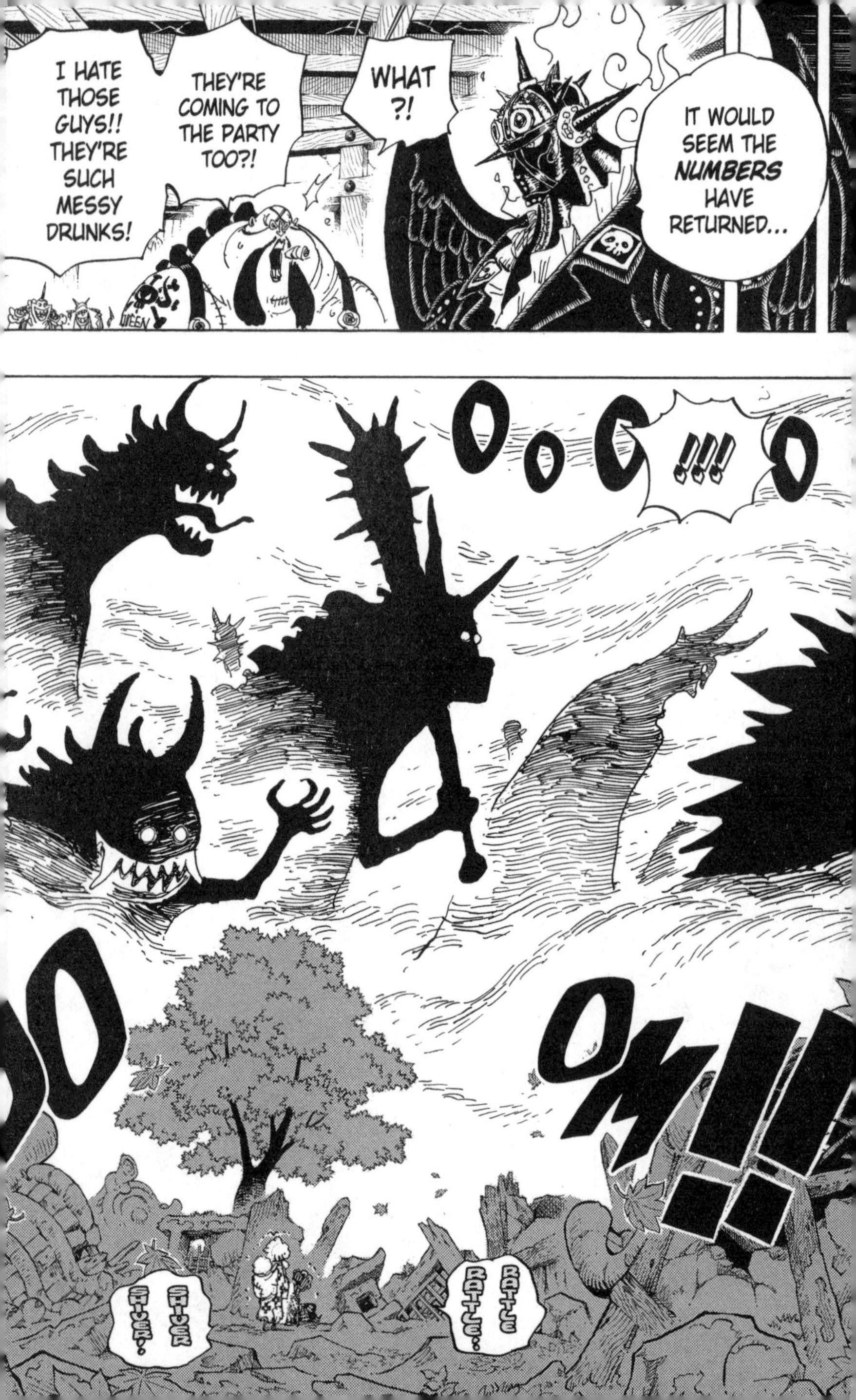
IT WOULD SEEM THE **NUMBERS** HAVE RETURNED...
WHAT?!
THEY'RE COMING TO THE PARTY TOO?!
I HATE THOSE GUYS!! THEY'RE SUCH MESSY DRUNKS!
O O O !!! O
DO
OM!!!
RATTLE RATTLE
SHIVER SHIVER

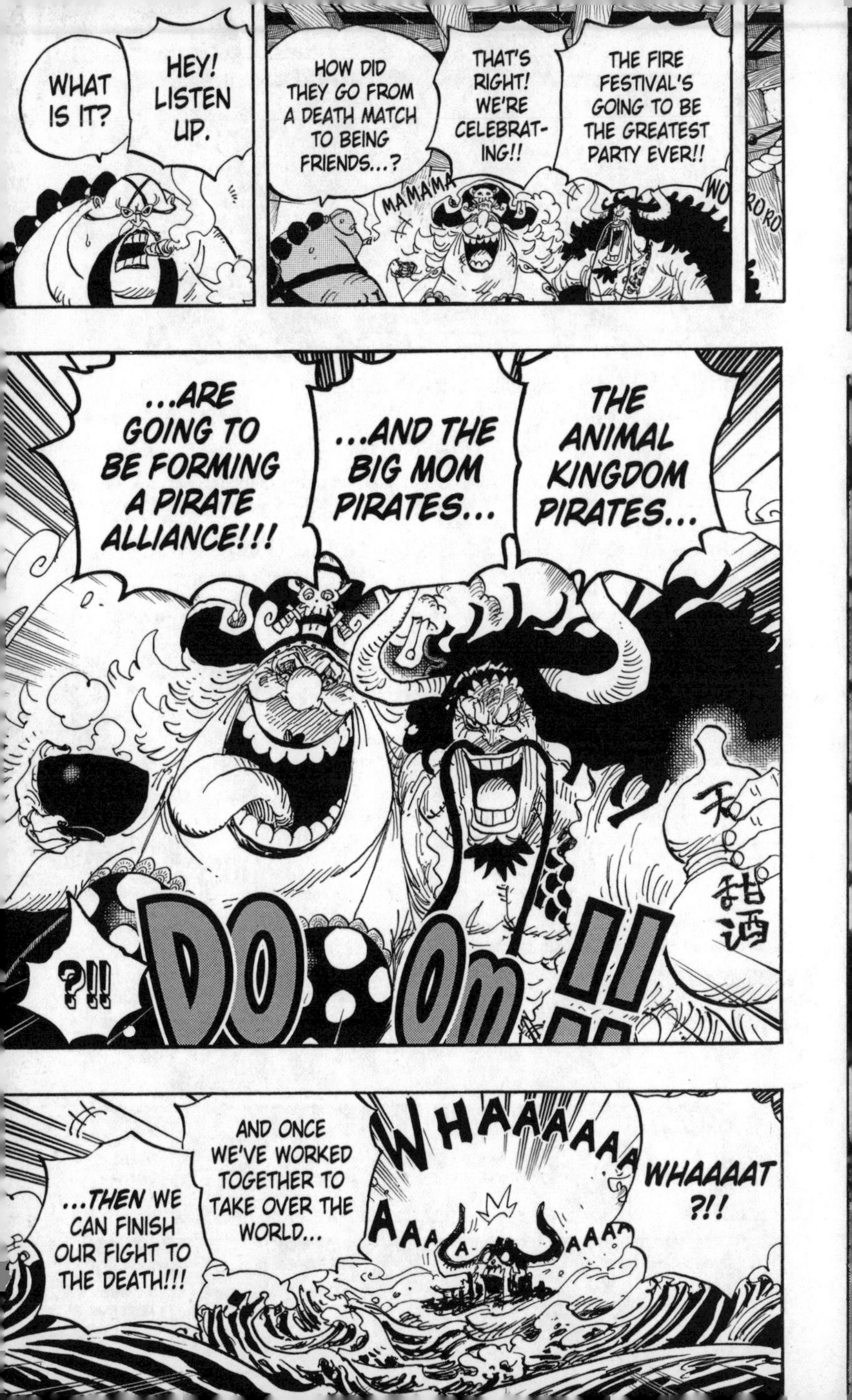
THE FIRE FESTIVAL'S GOING TO BE THE GREATEST PARTY EVER!!
WOROROROR
THAT'S RIGHT! WE'RE CELEBRAT-ING!!
MAMAMA
HOW DID THEY GO FROM A DEATH MATCH TO BEING FRIENDS...?
HEY! LISTEN UP.
WHAT IS IT?
THE ANIMAL KINGDOM PIRATES...
...AND THE BIG MOM PIRATES...
...ARE GOING TO BE FORMING A PIRATE ALLIANCE!!!
甘酒
DO:OM!!
?!!
WHAAAAT?!!
WHAAAAAAAAAAAAA
AND ONCE WE'VE WORKED TOGETHER TO TAKE OVER THE WORLD...
...THEN WE CAN FINISH OUR FIGHT TO THE DEATH!!!

SBS Question Corner

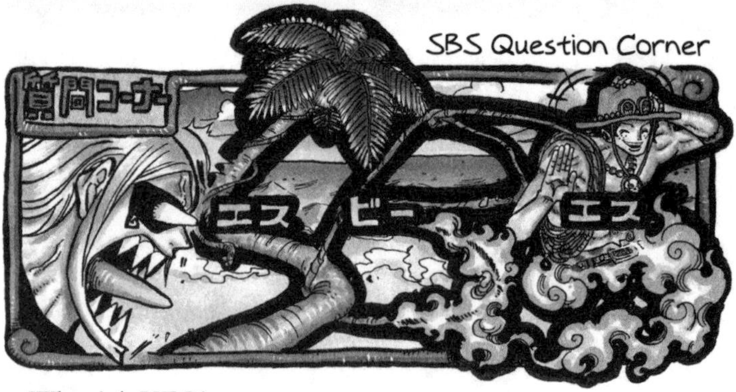

質問コーナー
エス ビー エス

(Hamane, Tokyo)

Q: Whoa! A UFO! (*While Odacchi is distracted*) Ready, set… Start the SBS!!

--Tomo and Isshi

A: Huh?! Where?! I wanna see a UFO! I've never seen one!! I'll take my bike to check it out!! Which way did it go?! Oh! I see something shining! And spinning! No, that's just an idol fan waving glowsticks...
Wait a second, the SBS started without me!!

Q: Question for Odacchi! Does the teacher with the elongated neck have Devil Fruit powers? Or is she part of a special race?

--Masajuro the Ronin

A: Ah yes, that would be Miss Sarahebi. She's a very popular teacher with the children, but of course, she's a henchman of Orochi and Kaido, and is filling the kids' heads with anti-Kozuki lies. Her neck is a snake's neck because of a Smile fruit.

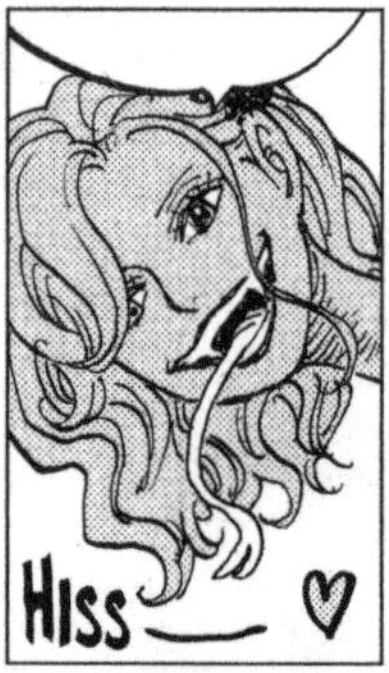

HISS ♡

Q: Hello, Oda Sensei. I would like to know the flower and animal that you associate with each member of the Worst Generation.

--Takusai

A: Okay. I don't know much about flowers, so I'm not looking up their special flower meanings or anything!

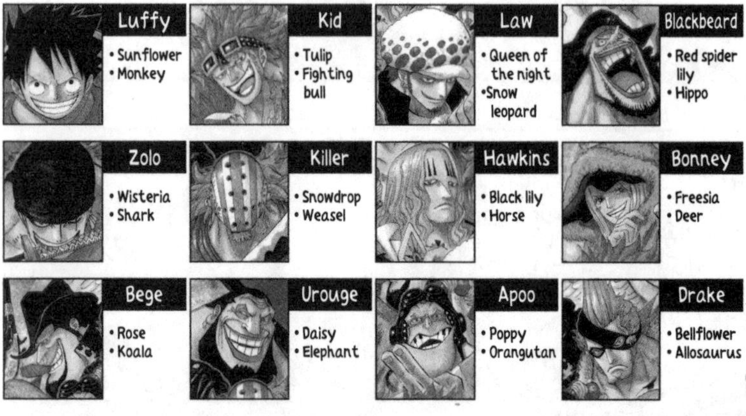

Luffy
• Sunflower
• Monkey
Kid
• Tulip
• Fighting bull
Law
• Queen of the night
• Snow leopard
Blackbeard
• Red spider lily
• Hippo
Zolo
• Wisteria
• Shark
Killer
• Snowdrop
• Weasel
Hawkins
• Black lily
• Horse
Bonney
• Freesia
• Deer
Bege
• Rose
• Koala
Urouge
• Daisy
• Elephant
Apoo
• Poppy
• Orangutan
Drake
• Bellflower
• Allosaurus

Chapter 955:
ENMA

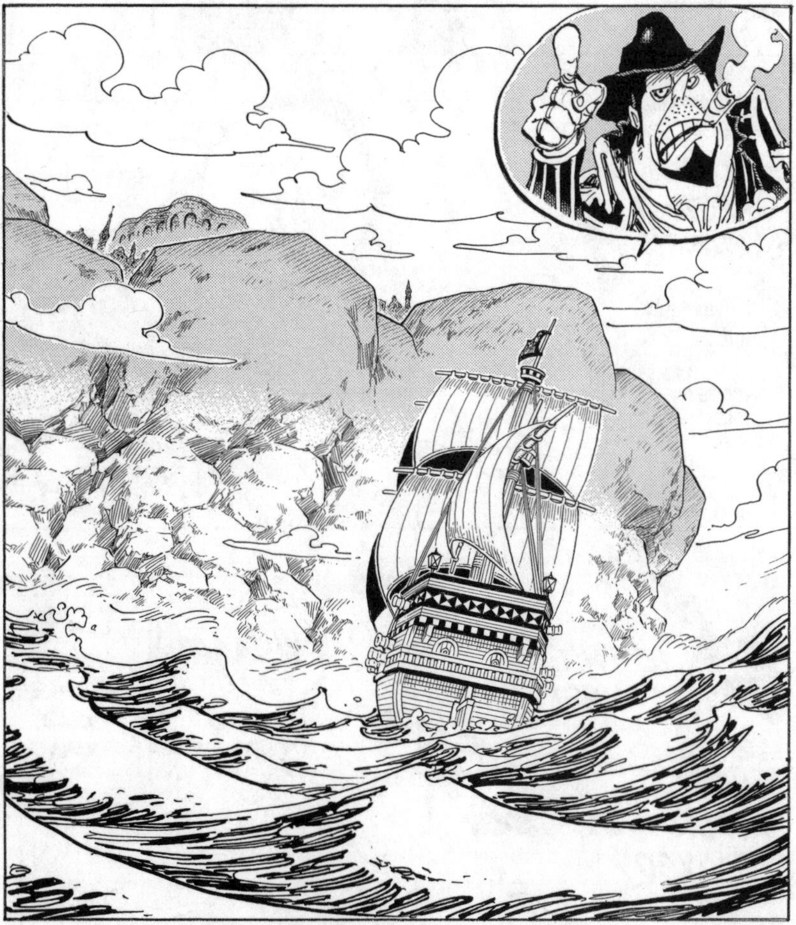

GANG BEGE'S OH MY FAMILY
VOL. 6: "STOPPING AT THIS ISLAND TO STOCK UP ON FOOD"

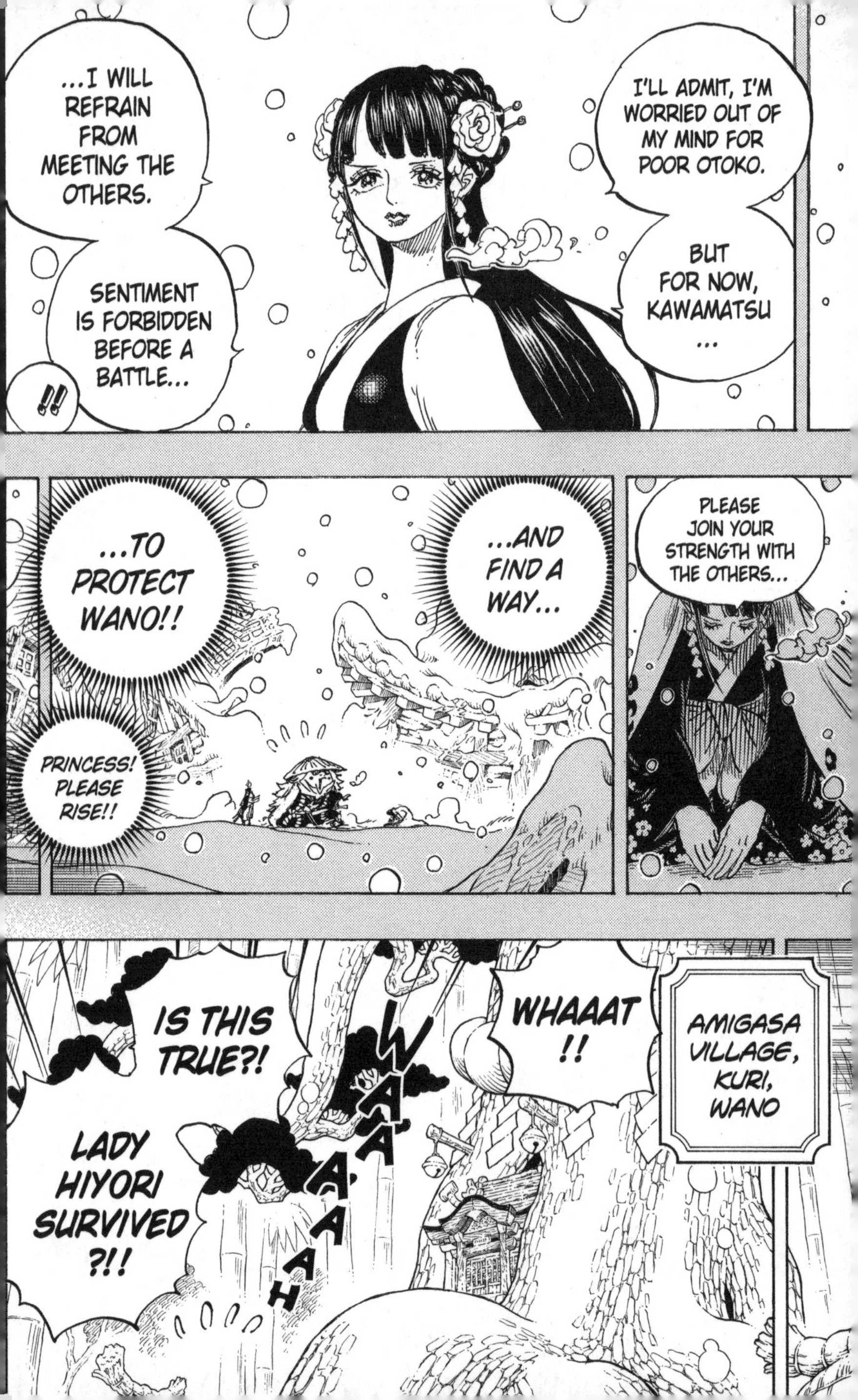
I'LL ADMIT, I'M WORRIED OUT OF MY MIND FOR POOR OTOKO.
BUT FOR NOW, KAWAMATSU ...
...I WILL REFRAIN FROM MEETING THE OTHERS.
SENTIMENT IS FORBIDDEN BEFORE A BATTLE...
!!
PLEASE JOIN YOUR STRENGTH WITH THE OTHERS...
...AND FIND A WAY...
...TO PROTECT WANO!!
PRINCESS! PLEASE RISE!!
AMIGASA VILLAGE, KURI, WANO
WHAAAT !!
WAAAAAH
IS THIS TRUE?!
LADY HIYORI SURVIVED ?!!

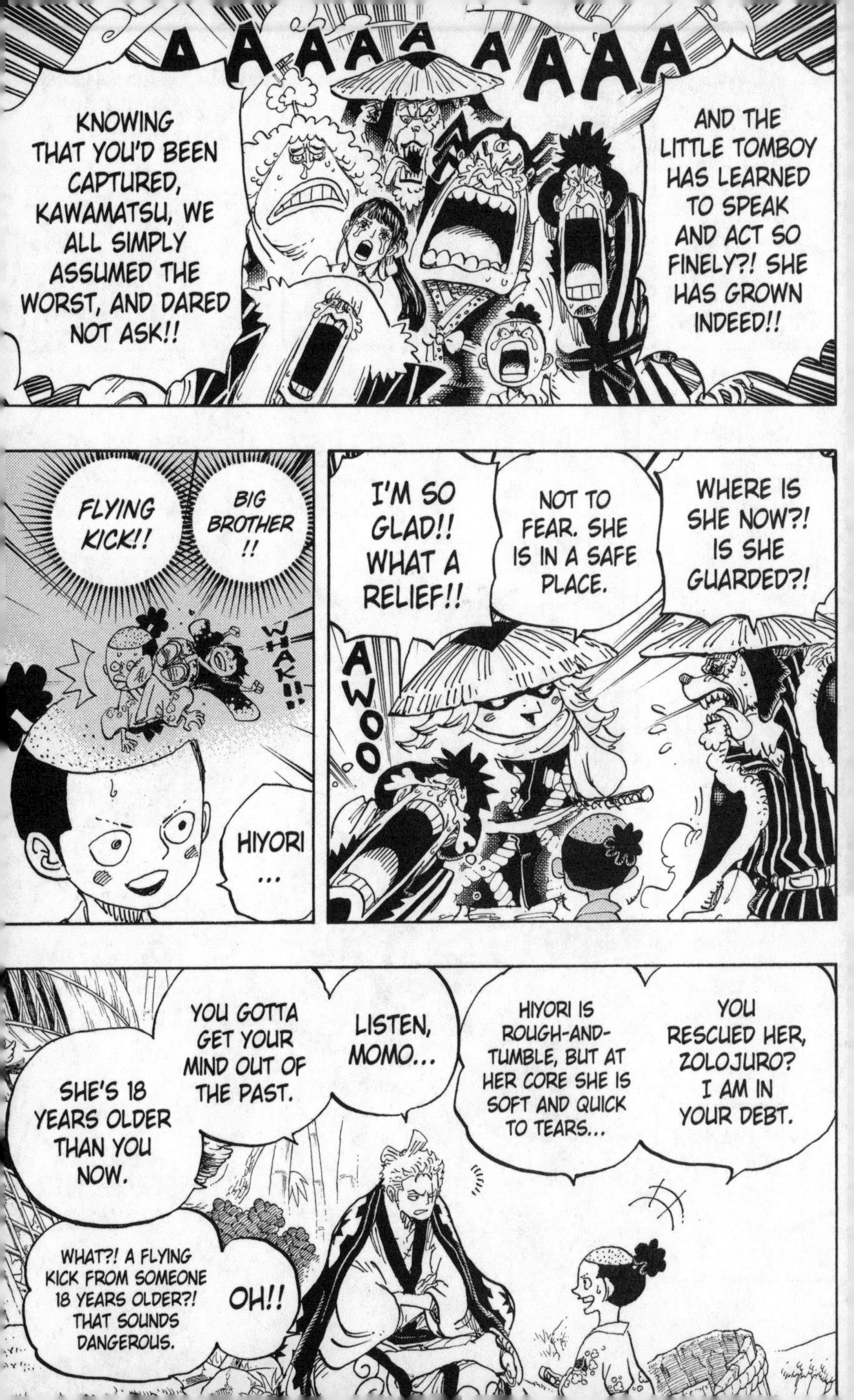
AAAAAAAAA
AND THE LITTLE TOMBOY HAS LEARNED TO SPEAK AND ACT SO FINELY?! SHE HAS GROWN INDEED!!
KNOWING THAT YOU'D BEEN CAPTURED, KAWAMATSU, WE ALL SIMPLY ASSUMED THE WORST, AND DARED NOT ASK!!
WHERE IS SHE NOW?! IS SHE GUARDED?!
NOT TO FEAR. SHE IS IN A SAFE PLACE.
I'M SO GLAD!! WHAT A RELIEF!!
AWOOO
BIG BROTHER!!
FLYING KICK!!
WHAK!!
HIYORI...
YOU RESCUED HER, ZOLOJURO? I AM IN YOUR DEBT.
HIYORI IS ROUGH-AND-TUMBLE, BUT AT HER CORE SHE IS SOFT AND QUICK TO TEARS...
LISTEN, MOMO...
YOU GOTTA GET YOUR MIND OUT OF THE PAST.
SHE'S 18 YEARS OLDER THAN YOU NOW.
OH!!
WHAT?! A FLYING KICK FROM SOMEONE 18 YEARS OLDER?! THAT SOUNDS DANGEROUS.

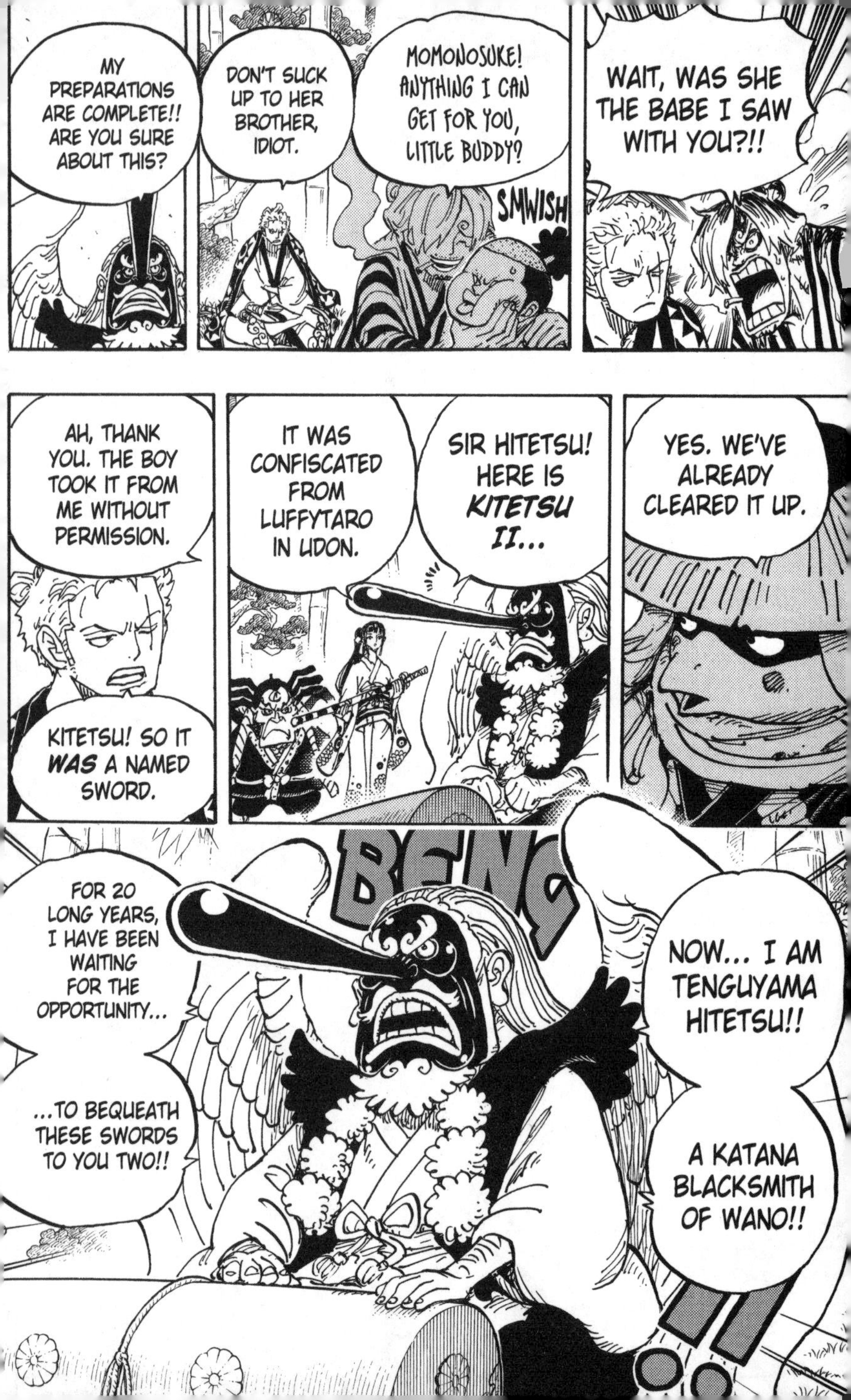
WAIT, WAS SHE THE BABE I SAW WITH YOU?!!
MOMONOSUKE! ANYTHING I CAN GET FOR YOU, LITTLE BUDDY?
SMWISH
DON'T SUCK UP TO HER BROTHER, IDIOT.
MY PREPARATIONS ARE COMPLETE!! ARE YOU SURE ABOUT THIS?
YES. WE'VE ALREADY CLEARED IT UP.
SIR HITETSU! HERE IS *KITETSU II*...
IT WAS CONFISCATED FROM LUFFYTARO IN UDON.
AH, THANK YOU. THE BOY TOOK IT FROM ME WITHOUT PERMISSION.
KITETSU! SO IT *WAS* A NAMED SWORD.
BENG
NOW... I AM TENGUYAMA HITETSU!!
A KATANA BLACKSMITH OF WANO!!
FOR 20 LONG YEARS, I HAVE BEEN WAITING FOR THE OPPORTUNITY...
...TO BEQUEATH THESE SWORDS TO YOU TWO!!

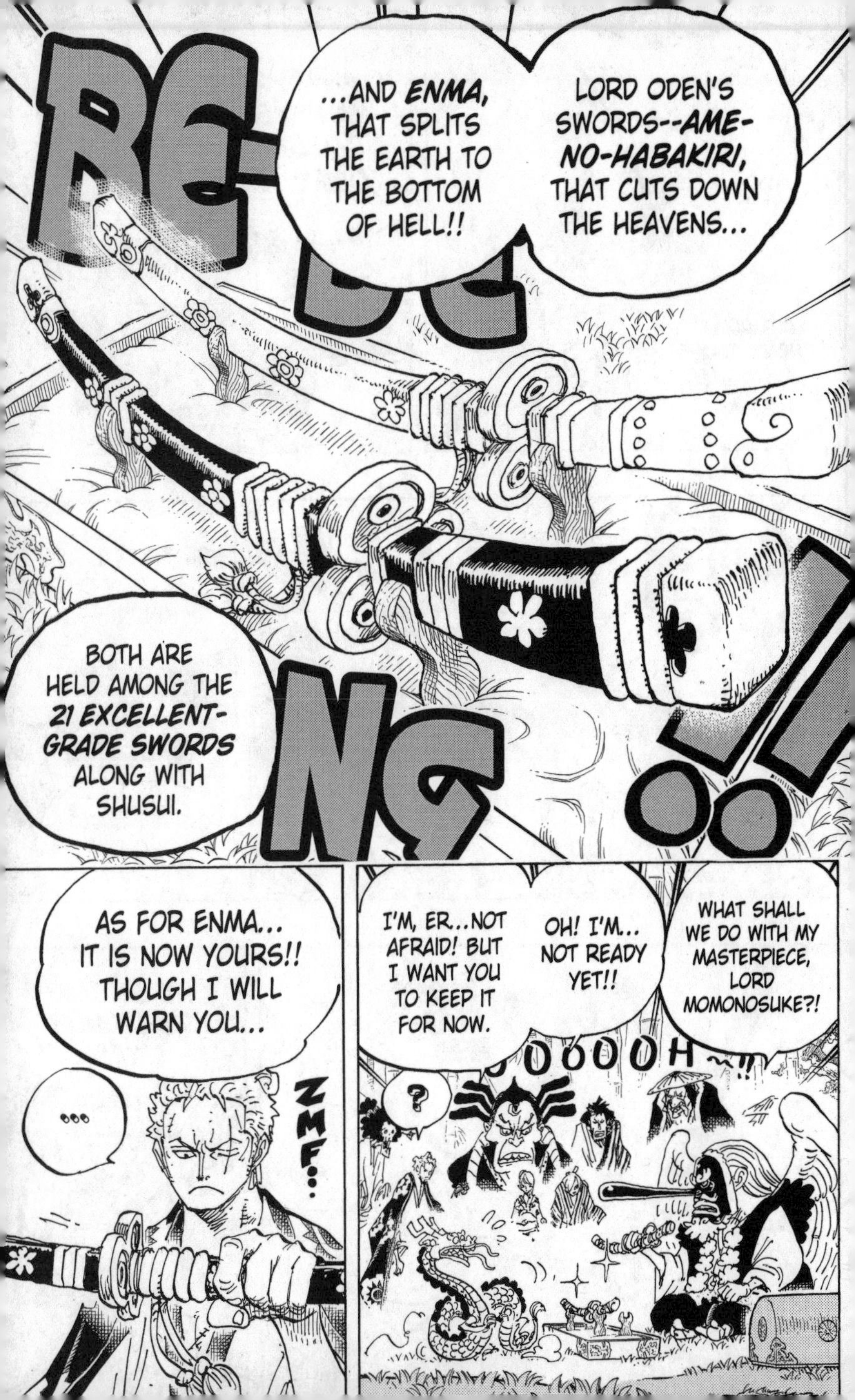
LORD ODEN'S SWORDS--AME-NO-HABAKIRI, THAT CUTS DOWN THE HEAVENS...
...AND ENMA, THAT SPLITS THE EARTH TO THE BOTTOM OF HELL!!
BOTH ARE HELD AMONG THE 21 EXCELLENT-GRADE SWORDS ALONG WITH SHUSUI.
WHAT SHALL WE DO WITH MY MASTERPIECE, LORD MOMONOSUKE?!
OH! I'M... NOT READY YET!!
I'M, ER...NOT AFRAID! BUT I WANT YOU TO KEEP IT FOR NOW.
?
AS FOR ENMA... IT IS NOW YOURS!! THOUGH I WILL WARN YOU...
...
ZMF..

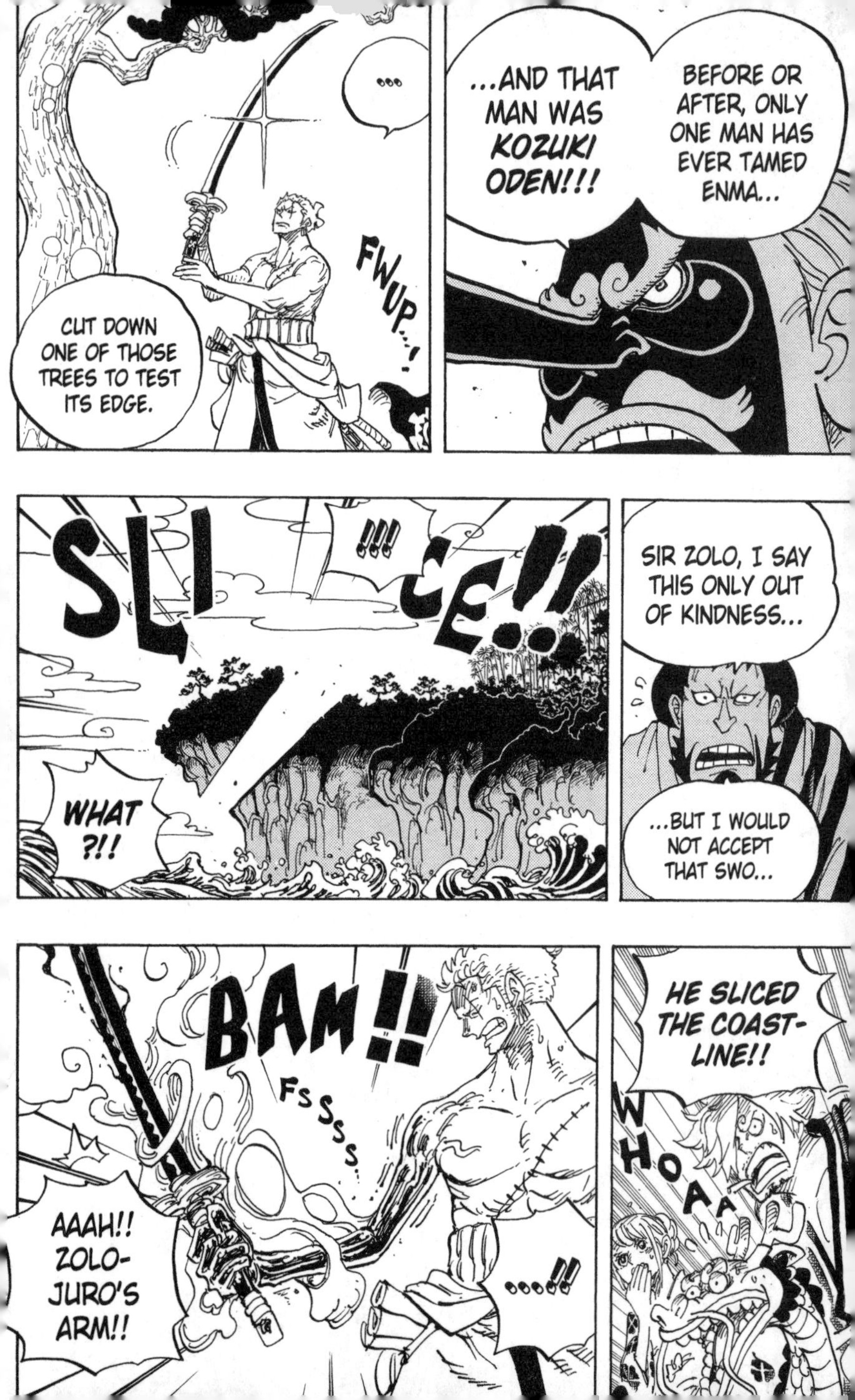
BEFORE OR AFTER, ONLY ONE MAN HAS EVER TAMED ENMA...
...AND THAT MAN WAS KOZUKI ODEN!!!
...
FWUP...!
CUT DOWN ONE OF THOSE TREES TO TEST ITS EDGE.
SIR ZOLO, I SAY THIS ONLY OUT OF KINDNESS...
...BUT I WOULD NOT ACCEPT THAT SWO...
!!!
SLICE!!
WHAT?!!
HE SLICED THE COAST-LINE!!
WHOAA
BAM!!
FSSSS...
....!!
AAAH!! ZOLO-JURO'S ARM!!

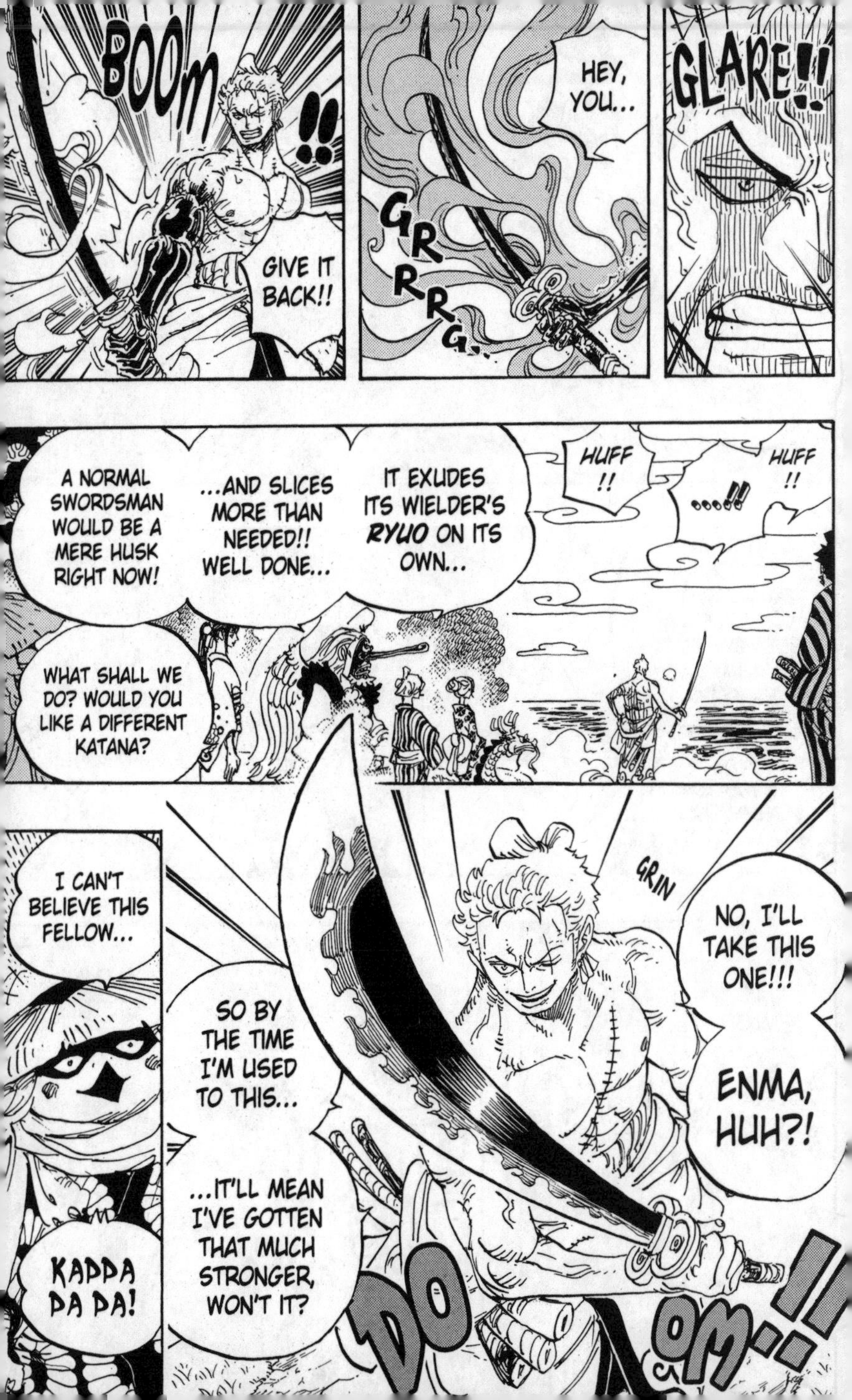
GLARE!!
HEY, YOU...
GRRRG
BOOM!!
GIVE IT BACK!!
HUFF!!
...!!
HUFF!!
IT EXUDES ITS WIELDER'S *RYUO* ON ITS OWN...
...AND SLICES MORE THAN NEEDED!! WELL DONE...
A NORMAL SWORDSMAN WOULD BE A MERE HUSK RIGHT NOW!
WHAT SHALL WE DO? WOULD YOU LIKE A DIFFERENT KATANA?
GRIN
NO, I'LL TAKE THIS ONE!!!
ENMA, HUH?!
SO BY THE TIME I'M USED TO THIS...
...IT'LL MEAN I'VE GOTTEN THAT MUCH STRONGER, WON'T IT?
DOOM!!
I CAN'T BELIEVE THIS FELLOW...
KAPPA PA PA!

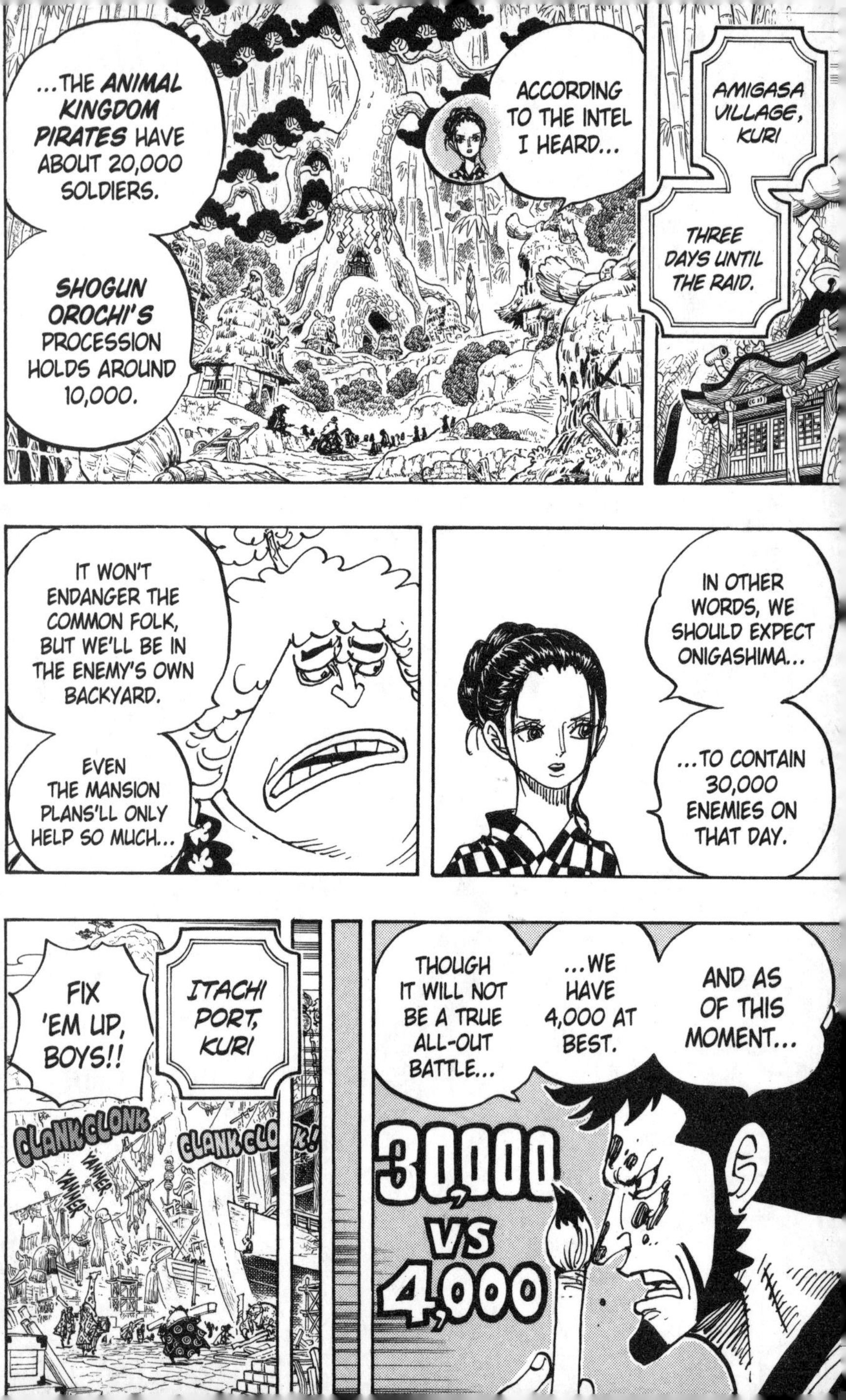
AMIGASA VILLAGE, KURI
THREE DAYS UNTIL THE RAID.
ACCORDING TO THE INTEL I HEARD...
...THE ANIMAL KINGDOM PIRATES HAVE ABOUT 20,000 SOLDIERS.
SHOGUN OROCHI'S PROCESSION HOLDS AROUND 10,000.
IN OTHER WORDS, WE SHOULD EXPECT ONIGASHIMA...
...TO CONTAIN 30,000 ENEMIES ON THAT DAY.
IT WON'T ENDANGER THE COMMON FOLK, BUT WE'LL BE IN THE ENEMY'S OWN BACKYARD.
EVEN THE MANSION PLANS'LL ONLY HELP SO MUCH...
AND AS OF THIS MOMENT...
...WE HAVE 4,000 AT BEST.
THOUGH IT WILL NOT BE A TRUE ALL-OUT BATTLE...
30,000 VS 4,000
ITACHI PORT, KURI
FIX 'EM UP, BOYS!!
CLANK CLONK
CLANK CLONK!
YAMMER
YAMMER

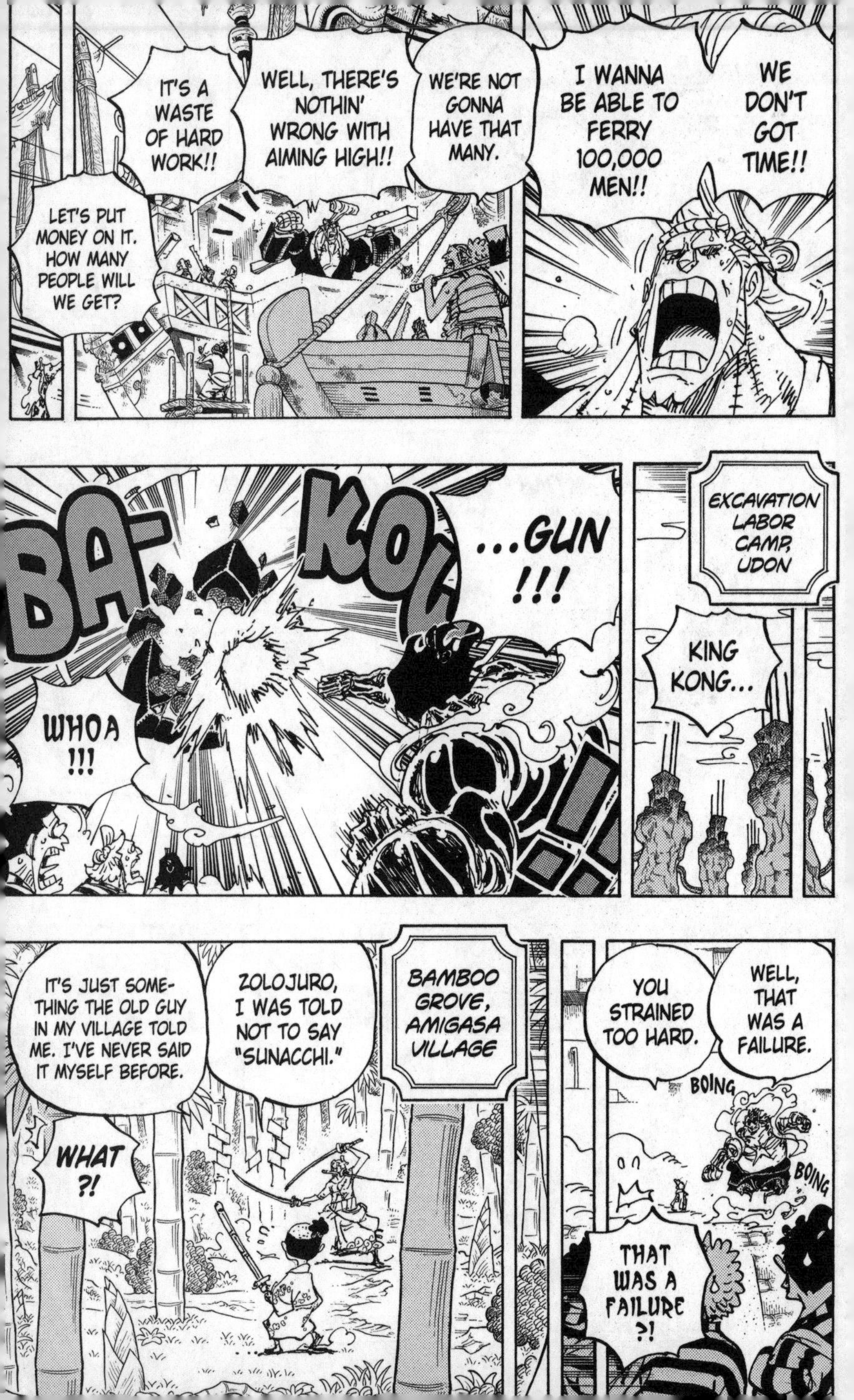
WE DON'T GOT TIME!!
I WANNA BE ABLE TO FERRY 100,000 MEN!!
WE'RE NOT GONNA HAVE THAT MANY.
WELL, THERE'S NOTHIN' WRONG WITH AIMING HIGH!!
IT'S A WASTE OF HARD WORK!!
LET'S PUT MONEY ON IT. HOW MANY PEOPLE WILL WE GET?
EXCAVATION LABOR CAMP, UDON
KING KONG...
BA-KO...GUN!!!
WHOA!!!
WELL, THAT WAS A FAILURE.
YOU STRAINED TOO HARD.
BOING
BOING
THAT WAS A FAILURE?!
BAMBOO GROVE, AMIGASA VILLAGE
ZOLOJURO, I WAS TOLD NOT TO SAY "SUNACCHI."
IT'S JUST SOME-THING THE OLD GUY IN MY VILLAGE TOLD ME. I'VE NEVER SAID IT MYSELF BEFORE.
WHAT?!

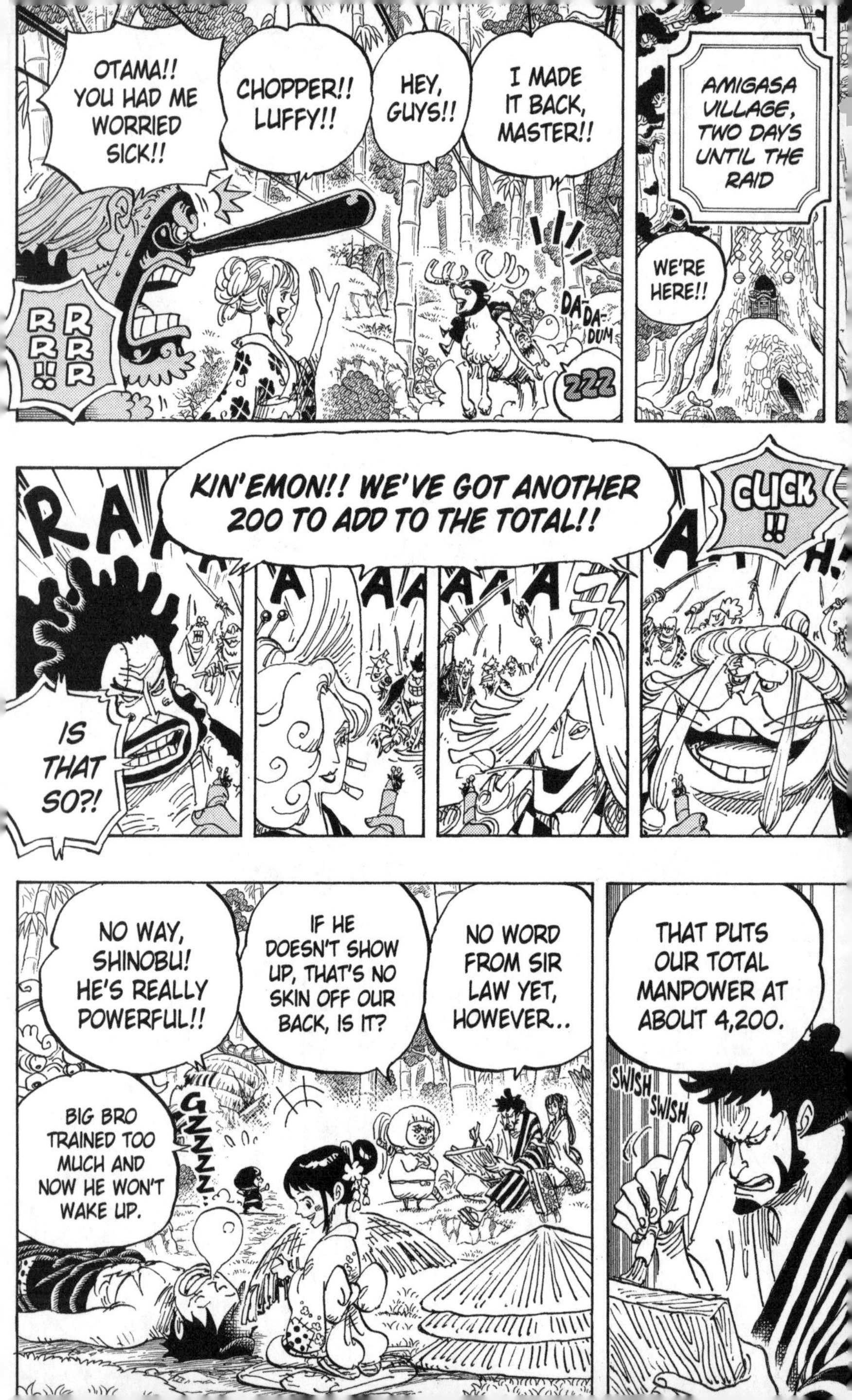
AMIGASA VILLAGE, TWO DAYS UNTIL THE RAID
WE'RE HERE!!
I MADE IT BACK, MASTER!!
HEY, GUYS!!
CHOPPER!! LUFFY!!
OTAMA!! YOU HAD ME WORRIED SICK!!
DA-DA-DUM
ZZZ
RRRRRR!!
CLICK!!
KIN'EMON!! WE'VE GOT ANOTHER 200 TO ADD TO THE TOTAL!!
IS THAT SO?!
SWISH SWISH
THAT PUTS OUR TOTAL MANPOWER AT ABOUT 4,200.
NO WORD FROM SIR LAW YET, HOWEVER...
IF HE DOESN'T SHOW UP, THAT'S NO SKIN OFF OUR BACK, IS IT?
NO WAY, SHINOBU! HE'S REALLY POWERFUL!!
GZZZZ...
BIG BRO TRAINED TOO MUCH AND NOW HE WON'T WAKE UP.

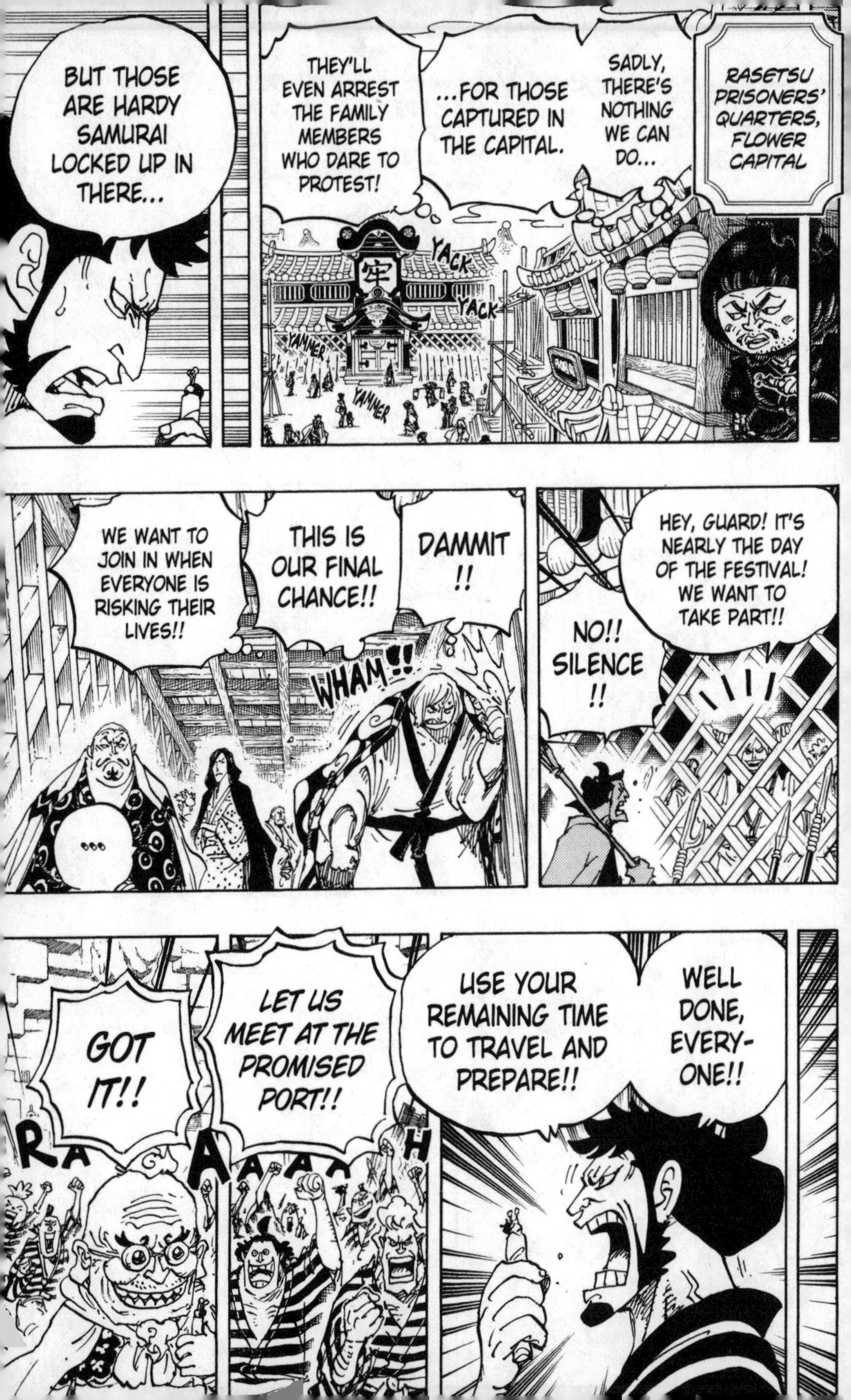
RASETSU PRISONERS' QUARTERS, FLOWER CAPITAL
SADLY, THERE'S NOTHING WE CAN DO...
...FOR THOSE CAPTURED IN THE CAPITAL.
THEY'LL EVEN ARREST THE FAMILY MEMBERS WHO DARE TO PROTEST!
YACK
YACK
YAMMER
YAMMER
BUT THOSE ARE HARDY SAMURAI LOCKED UP IN THERE...
HEY, GUARD! IT'S NEARLY THE DAY OF THE FESTIVAL! WE WANT TO TAKE PART!!
NO!! SILENCE!!
DAMMIT!!
THIS IS OUR FINAL CHANCE!!
WE WANT TO JOIN IN WHEN EVERYONE IS RISKING THEIR LIVES!!
WHAM!!
...
WELL DONE, EVERY-ONE!!
USE YOUR REMAINING TIME TO TRAVEL AND PREPARE!!
LET US MEET AT THE PROMISED PORT!!
GOT IT!!
RAAAAAH

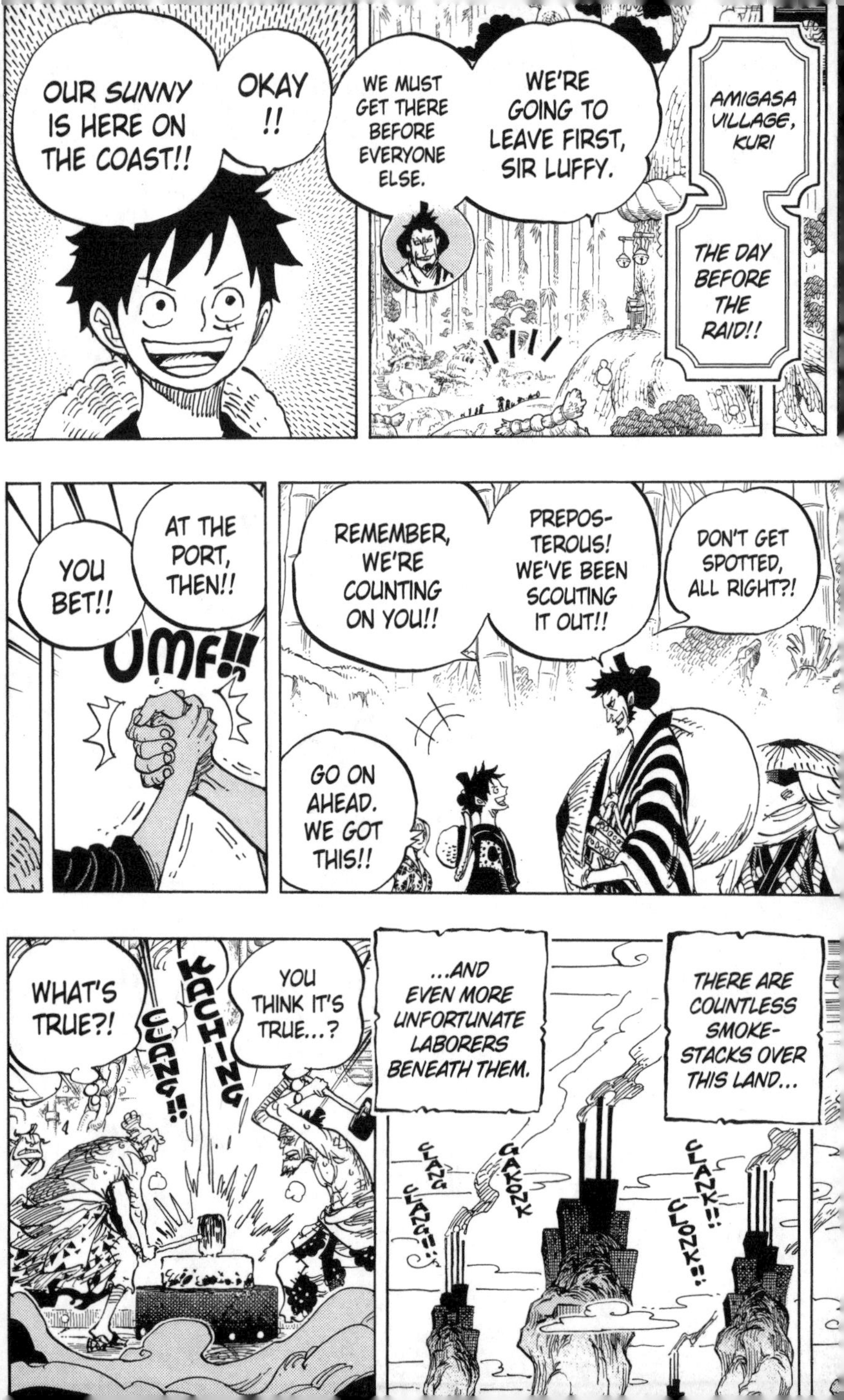
AMIGASA VILLAGE, KURI
THE DAY BEFORE THE RAID!!
WE'RE GOING TO LEAVE FIRST, SIR LUFFY.
WE MUST GET THERE BEFORE EVERYONE ELSE.
OKAY!!
OUR SUNNY IS HERE ON THE COAST!!
DON'T GET SPOTTED, ALL RIGHT?!
PREPOS-TEROUS! WE'VE BEEN SCOUTING IT OUT!!
REMEMBER, WE'RE COUNTING ON YOU!!
GO ON AHEAD. WE GOT THIS!!
AT THE PORT, THEN!!
YOU BET!!
UMF!!
THERE ARE COUNTLESS SMOKE-STACKS OVER THIS LAND...
CLANK!! CLONK!!
...AND EVEN MORE UNFORTUNATE LABORERS BENEATH THEM.
GAKONK
CLANG CLANG!!
YOU THINK IT'S TRUE...?
KACHING
CLANG!!
WHAT'S TRUE?!

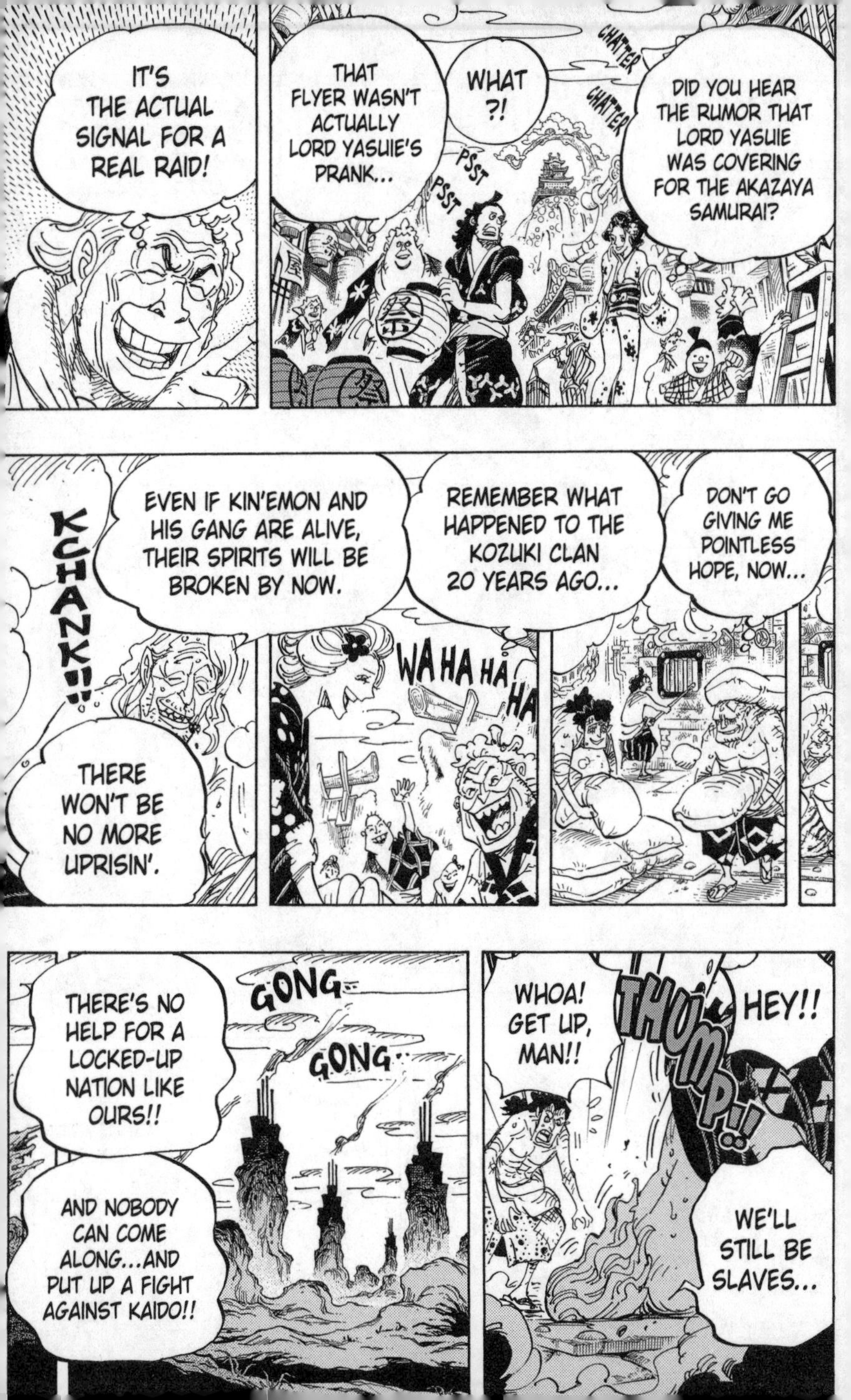
DID YOU HEAR THE RUMOR THAT LORD YASUIE WAS COVERING FOR THE AKAZAYA SAMURAI?
CHATTER
CHATTER
WHAT?!
PSST
PSST
THAT FLYER WASN'T ACTUALLY LORD YASUIE'S PRANK...
IT'S THE ACTUAL SIGNAL FOR A REAL RAID!
DON'T GO GIVING ME POINTLESS HOPE, NOW...
REMEMBER WHAT HAPPENED TO THE KOZUKI CLAN 20 YEARS AGO...
WA HA HA HA
EVEN IF KIN'EMON AND HIS GANG ARE ALIVE, THEIR SPIRITS WILL BE BROKEN BY NOW.
KCHANK!!
THERE WON'T BE NO MORE UPRISIN'.
HEY!!
THUMP!!
WHOA! GET UP, MAN!!
WE'LL STILL BE SLAVES...
GONG
GONG
THERE'S NO HELP FOR A LOCKED-UP NATION LIKE OURS!!
AND NOBODY CAN COME ALONG...AND PUT UP A FIGHT AGAINST KAIDO!!

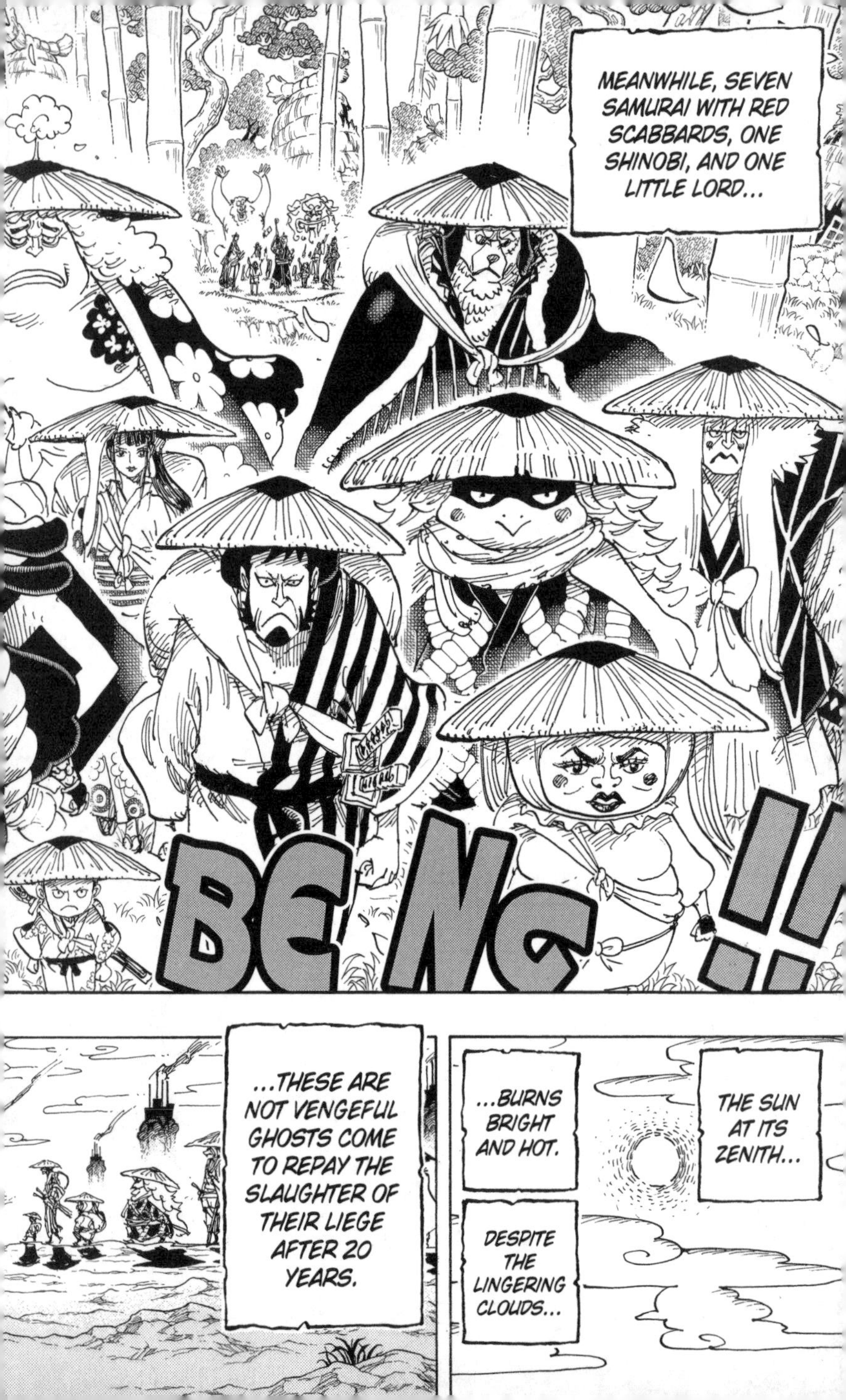
MEANWHILE, SEVEN SAMURAI WITH RED SCABBARDS, ONE SHINOBI, AND ONE LITTLE LORD...
BE NG!!
THE SUN AT ITS ZENITH...
...BURNS BRIGHT AND HOT.
DESPITE THE LINGERING CLOUDS...
...THESE ARE NOT VENGEFUL GHOSTS COME TO REPAY THE SLAUGHTER OF THEIR LIEGE AFTER 20 YEARS.

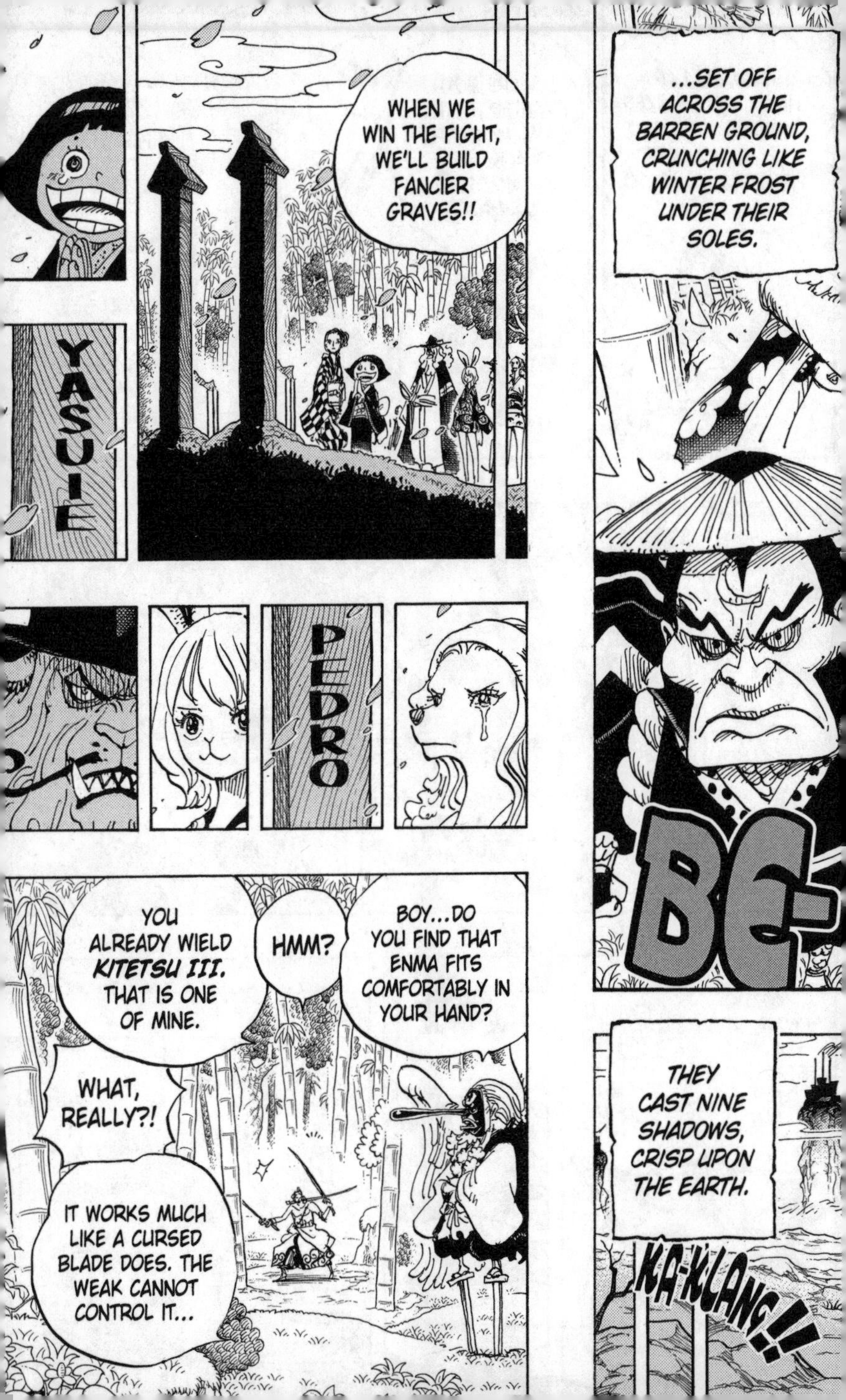
...SET OFF ACROSS THE BARREN GROUND, CRUNCHING LIKE WINTER FROST UNDER THEIR SOLES.
BO-
THEY CAST NINE SHADOWS, CRISP UPON THE EARTH.
KA-KLANG!!
WHEN WE WIN THE FIGHT, WE'LL BUILD FANCIER GRAVES!!
YASUIE
PEDRO
BOY...DO YOU FIND THAT ENMA FITS COMFORTABLY IN YOUR HAND?
HMM?
YOU ALREADY WIELD *KITETSU III*. THAT IS ONE OF MINE.
WHAT, REALLY?!
IT WORKS MUCH LIKE A CURSED BLADE DOES. THE WEAK CANNOT CONTROL IT...

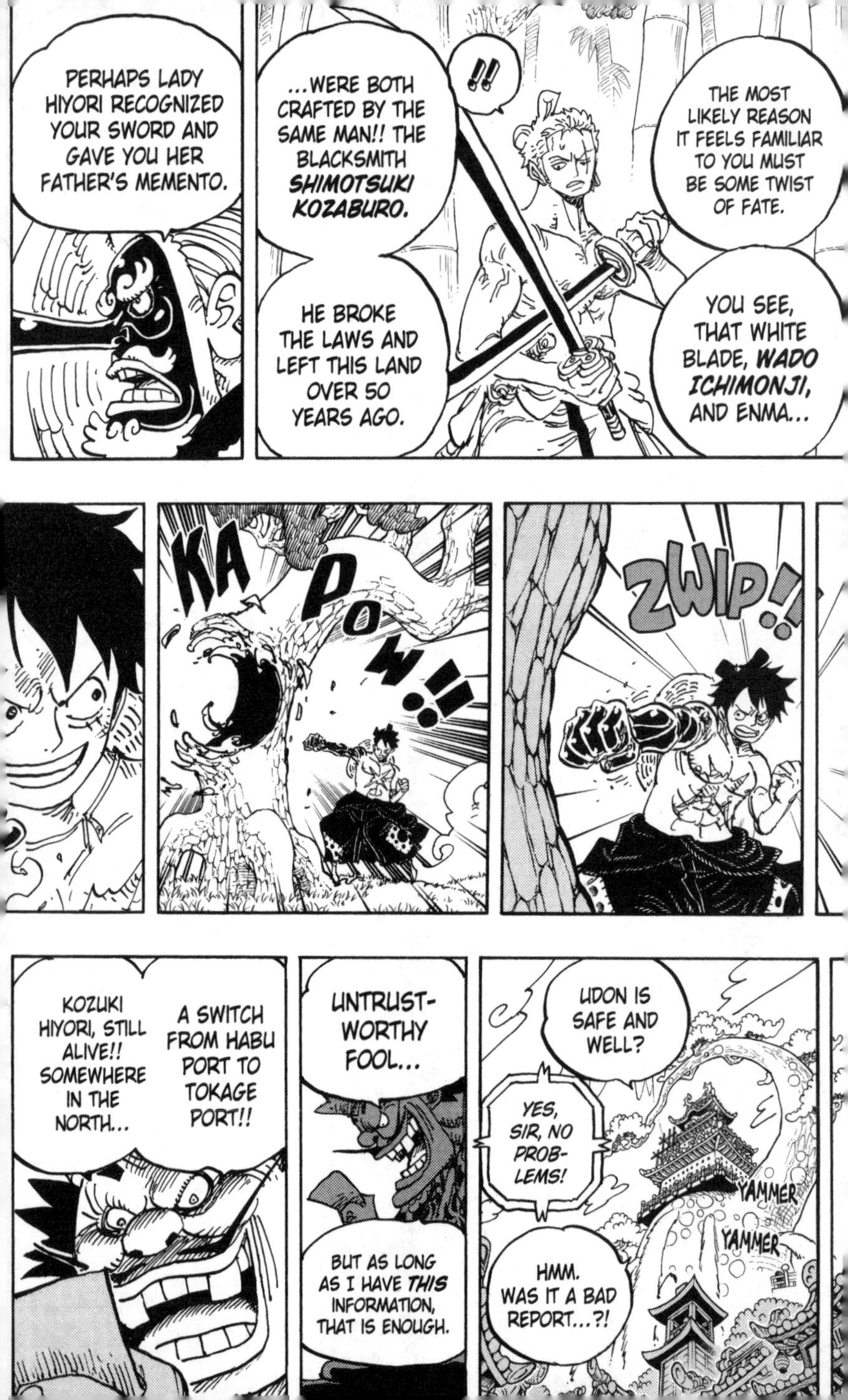
THE MOST LIKELY REASON IT FEELS FAMILIAR TO YOU MUST BE SOME TWIST OF FATE.
YOU SEE, THAT WHITE BLADE, *WADO ICHIMONJI*, AND ENMA...
!!
...WERE BOTH CRAFTED BY THE SAME MAN!! THE BLACKSMITH *SHIMOTSUKI KOZABURO.*
HE BROKE THE LAWS AND LEFT THIS LAND OVER 50 YEARS AGO.
PERHAPS LADY HIYORI RECOGNIZED YOUR SWORD AND GAVE YOU HER FATHER'S MEMENTO.
ZWIP!!
KA POW!!
UDON IS SAFE AND WELL?
YES, SIR, NO PROB-LEMS!
YAMMER
YAMMER
HMM. WAS IT A BAD REPORT...?!
UNTRUST-WORTHY FOOL...
BUT AS LONG AS I HAVE *THIS* INFORMATION, THAT IS ENOUGH.
A SWITCH FROM HABU PORT TO TOKAGE PORT!!
KOZUKI HIYORI, STILL ALIVE!! SOMEWHERE IN THE NORTH...

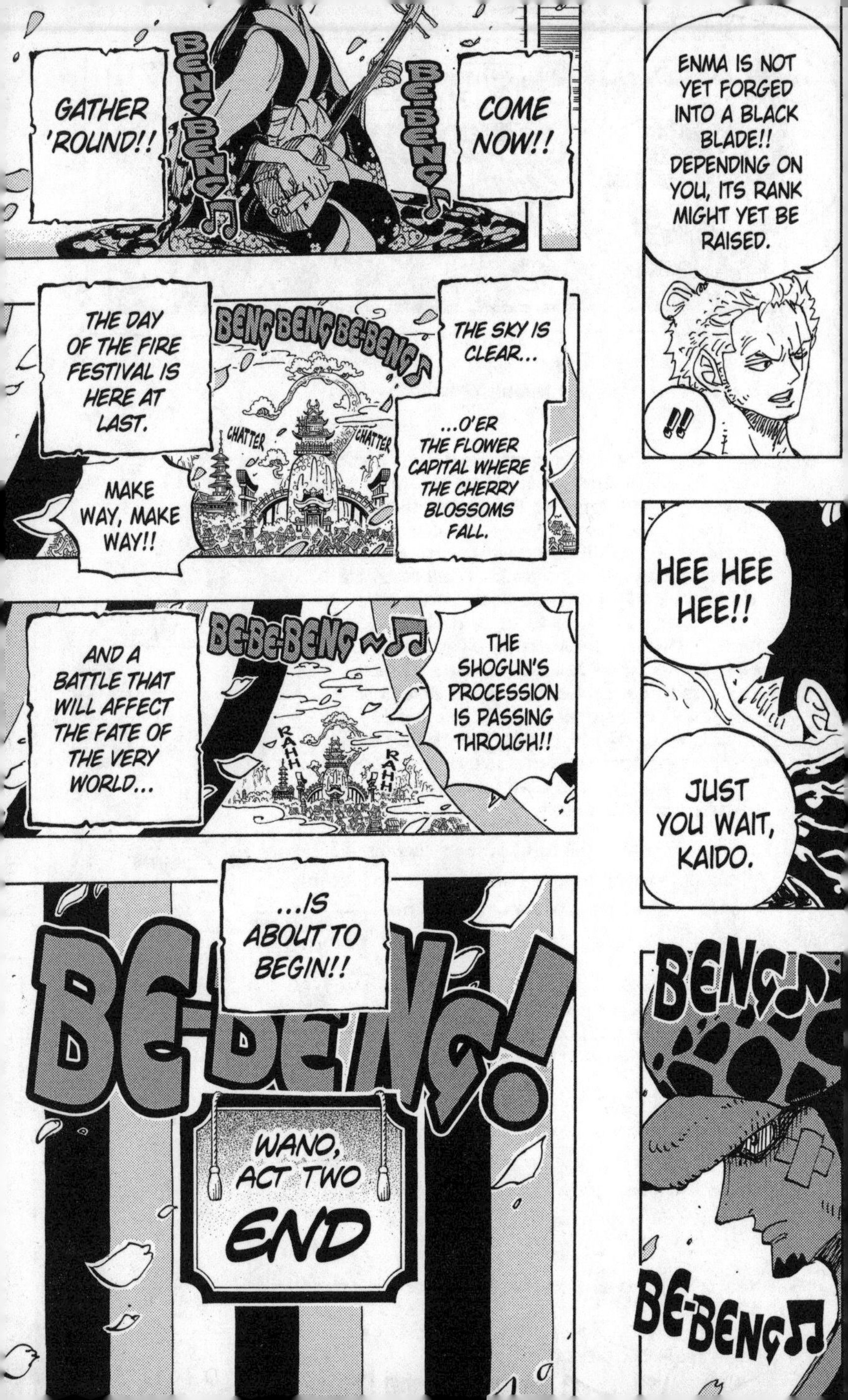
ENMA IS NOT YET FORGED INTO A BLACK BLADE!! DEPENDING ON YOU, ITS RANK MIGHT YET BE RAISED.
!!
HEE HEE HEE!!
JUST YOU WAIT, KAIDO.
BENG♫
BE-BENG♫
COME NOW!!
BEBENG♫
BENGBENG♫
GATHER 'ROUND!!
THE SKY IS CLEAR...
...O'ER THE FLOWER CAPITAL WHERE THE CHERRY BLOSSOMS FALL.
CHATTER
CHATTER
BENG BENG BE-BENG♫
THE DAY OF THE FIRE FESTIVAL IS HERE AT LAST.
MAKE WAY, MAKE WAY!!
THE SHOGUN'S PROCESSION IS PASSING THROUGH!!
RAHH
RAHH
BE-BE-BENG~♫
AND A BATTLE THAT WILL AFFECT THE FATE OF THE VERY WORLD...
...IS ABOUT TO BEGIN!!
BE-BENG!
WANO, ACT TWO
END

(1 ♡ OP, Ishikawa)

Q: Hello, Oda Sensei. I have a question to ask you. Zolo bites his sword. Doesn't that hurt his teeth? My favorite character is Zolo.

--Shunya N.

A: Ahh, Zolo's biggest fan, Shunya! That's a very kind concern. Yeah, I bet Zolo's teeth probably hurt. But he bites on the sword through the pain anyway! He does this because he made a promise with his old best friend when he was a kid. They promised that one of them would become the strongest in the world, and the sword he bites now is a memento of that friend after she died. Now Zolo uses three swords because he turns his friend's sorrow into strength! So he bites his sword even if his teeth hurt! He'll do it until he becomes the best in the world!! Thanks for your letter! Send them in whenever you want!

Q: You know how, in the bathhouse of chapter 935, someone is using the art of water escape to hide in the bath? As a matter of fact, that was me!

--Sanadacchi

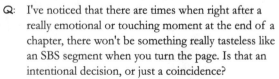

A: That was you?! ⚡
I was having a nice wholesome, heartwarming SBS with Shunya and you've ruined it all!!!

Q: I've noticed that there are times when right after a really emotional or touching moment at the end of a chapter, there won't be something really tasteless like an SBS segment when you turn the page. Is that an intentional decision, or just a coincidence?

--Hoshito

A: Yes! Sometimes I use a placeholder instead. I do pay close attention to that stuff! I mean, the last thing you want to see after a nice heartfelt moment is Sanada!

Chapter 956:
BIG NEWS

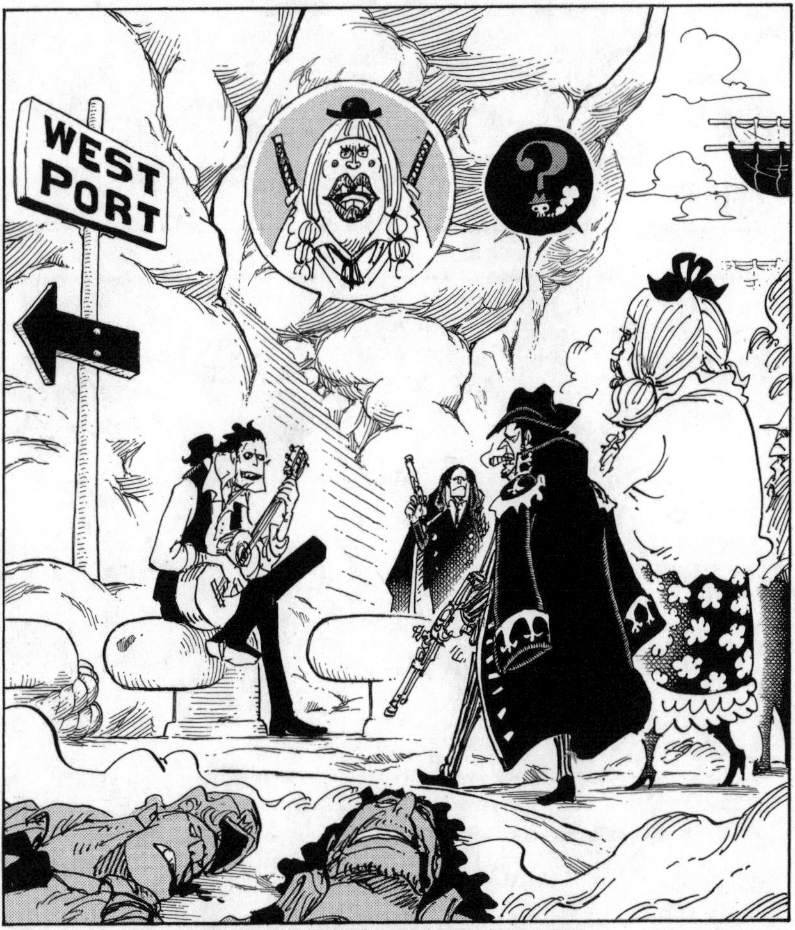
WEST PORT

GANG BEGE'S OH MY FAMILY
VOL. 7: "HEY, WHAT'S UP, LOLA? YOU FINALLY SNAGGED A HUBBY!!"

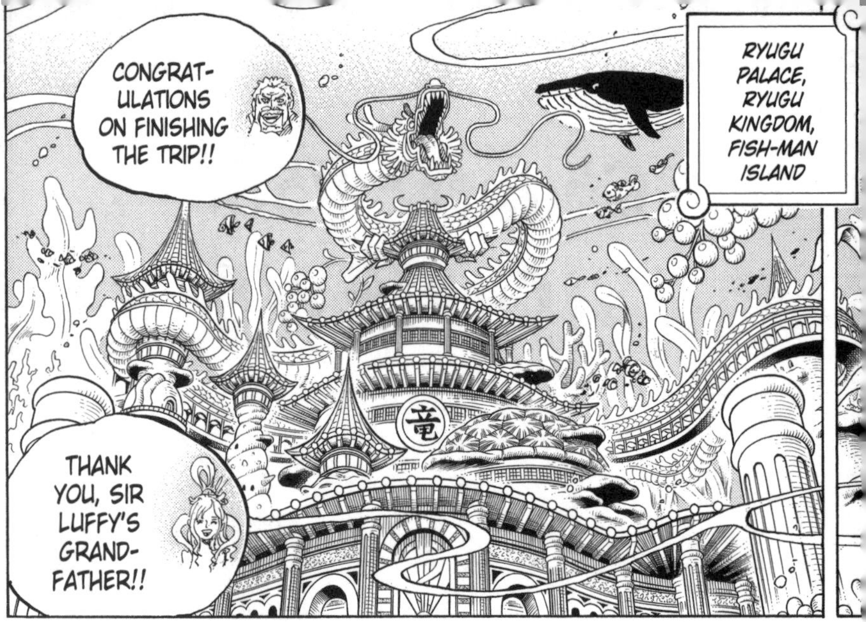
RYUGU PALACE, RYUGU KINGDOM, FISH-MAN ISLAND
CONGRAT-ULATIONS ON FINISHING THE TRIP!!
THANK YOU, SIR LUFFY'S GRAND-FATHER!!

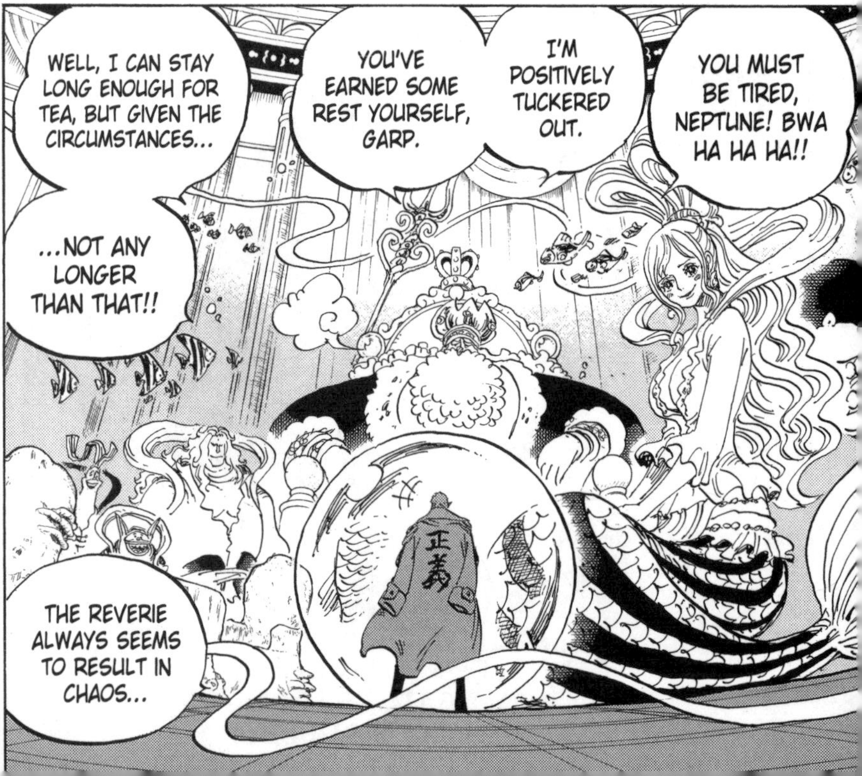
YOU MUST BE TIRED, NEPTUNE! BWA HA HA HA!!
I'M POSITIVELY TUCKERED OUT.
YOU'VE EARNED SOME REST YOURSELF, GARP.
WELL, I CAN STAY LONG ENOUGH FOR TEA, BUT GIVEN THE CIRCUMSTANCES...
...NOT ANY LONGER THAN THAT!!
THE REVERIE ALWAYS SEEMS TO RESULT IN CHAOS...

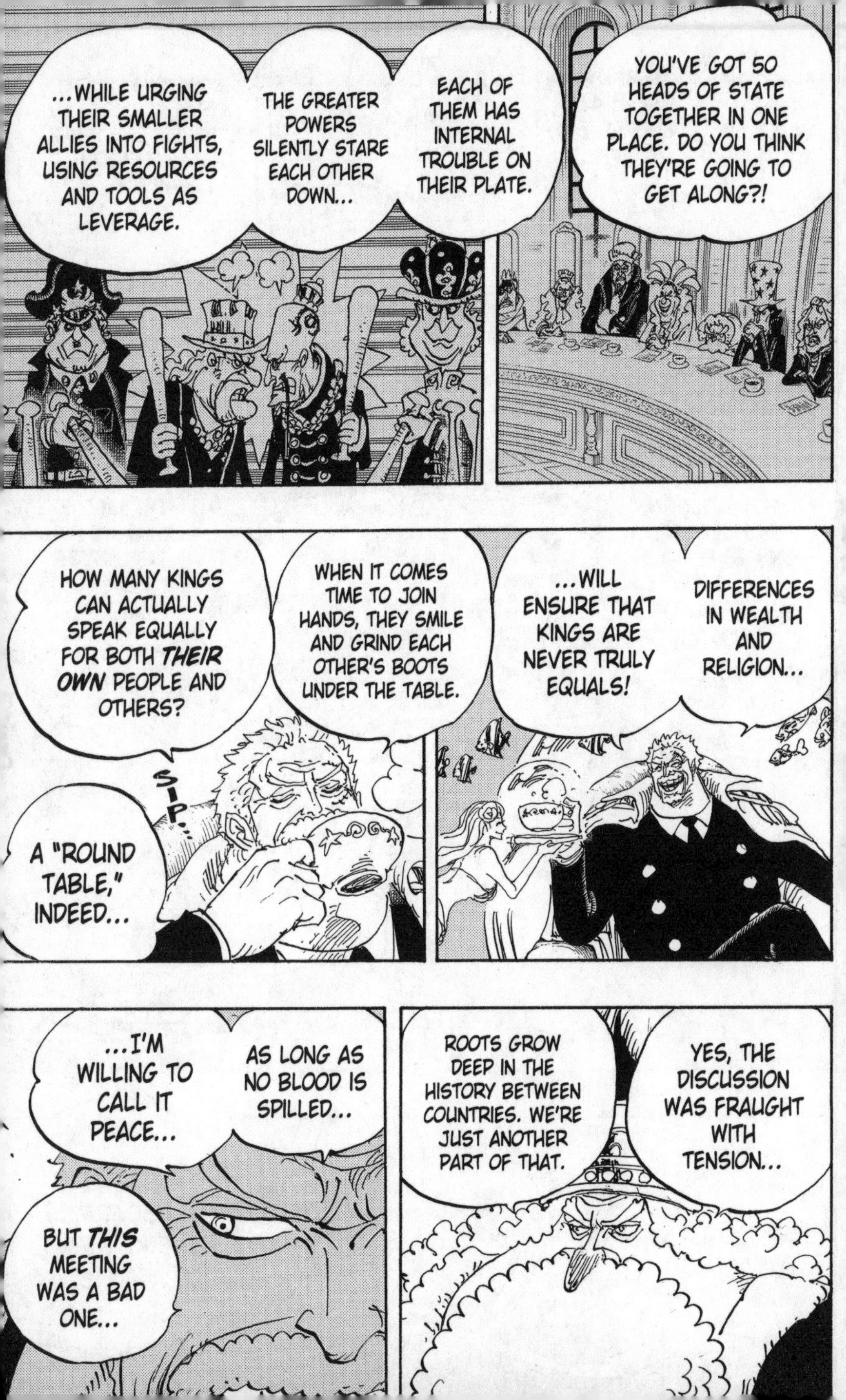
YOU'VE GOT 50 HEADS OF STATE TOGETHER IN ONE PLACE. DO YOU THINK THEY'RE GOING TO GET ALONG?!
EACH OF THEM HAS INTERNAL TROUBLE ON THEIR PLATE.
THE GREATER POWERS SILENTLY STARE EACH OTHER DOWN...
...WHILE URGING THEIR SMALLER ALLIES INTO FIGHTS, USING RESOURCES AND TOOLS AS LEVERAGE.
DIFFERENCES IN WEALTH AND RELIGION...
...WILL ENSURE THAT KINGS ARE NEVER TRULY EQUALS!
WHEN IT COMES TIME TO JOIN HANDS, THEY SMILE AND GRIND EACH OTHER'S BOOTS UNDER THE TABLE.
HOW MANY KINGS CAN ACTUALLY SPEAK EQUALLY FOR BOTH *THEIR OWN* PEOPLE AND OTHERS?
SIP...
A "ROUND TABLE," INDEED...
YES, THE DISCUSSION WAS FRAUGHT WITH TENSION...
ROOTS GROW DEEP IN THE HISTORY BETWEEN COUNTRIES. WE'RE JUST ANOTHER PART OF THAT.
AS LONG AS NO BLOOD IS SPILLED...
...I'M WILLING TO CALL IT PEACE...
BUT *THIS* MEETING WAS A BAD ONE...

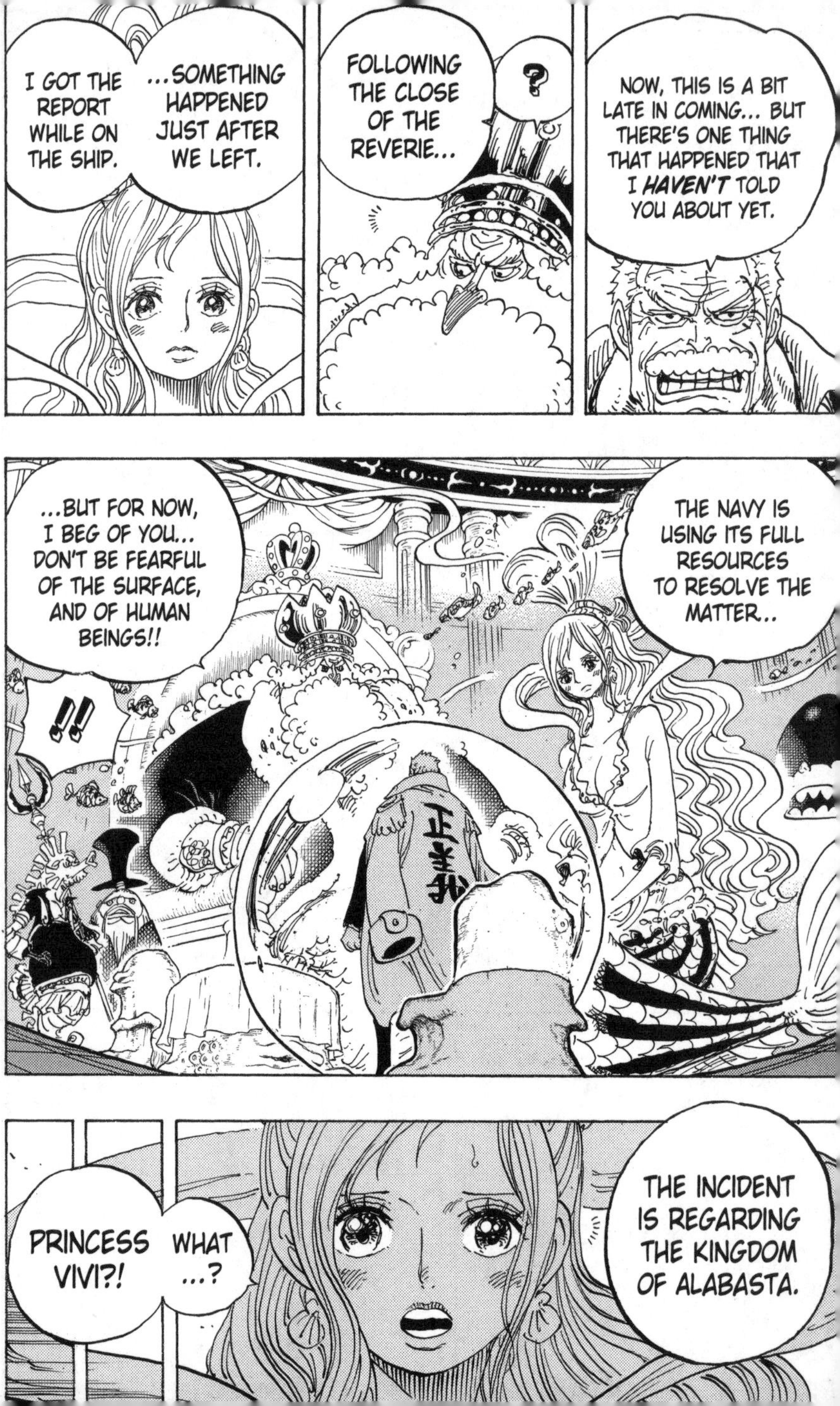
NOW, THIS IS A BIT LATE IN COMING... BUT THERE'S ONE THING THAT HAPPENED THAT I *HAVEN'T* TOLD YOU ABOUT YET.
?
FOLLOWING THE CLOSE OF THE REVERIE...
...SOMETHING HAPPENED JUST AFTER WE LEFT.
I GOT THE REPORT WHILE ON THE SHIP.
THE NAVY IS USING ITS FULL RESOURCES TO RESOLVE THE MATTER...
...BUT FOR NOW, I BEG OF YOU... DON'T BE FEARFUL OF THE SURFACE, AND OF HUMAN BEINGS!!
!!
正義
THE INCIDENT IS REGARDING THE KINGDOM OF ALABASTA.
WHAT ...?
PRINCESS VIVI?!

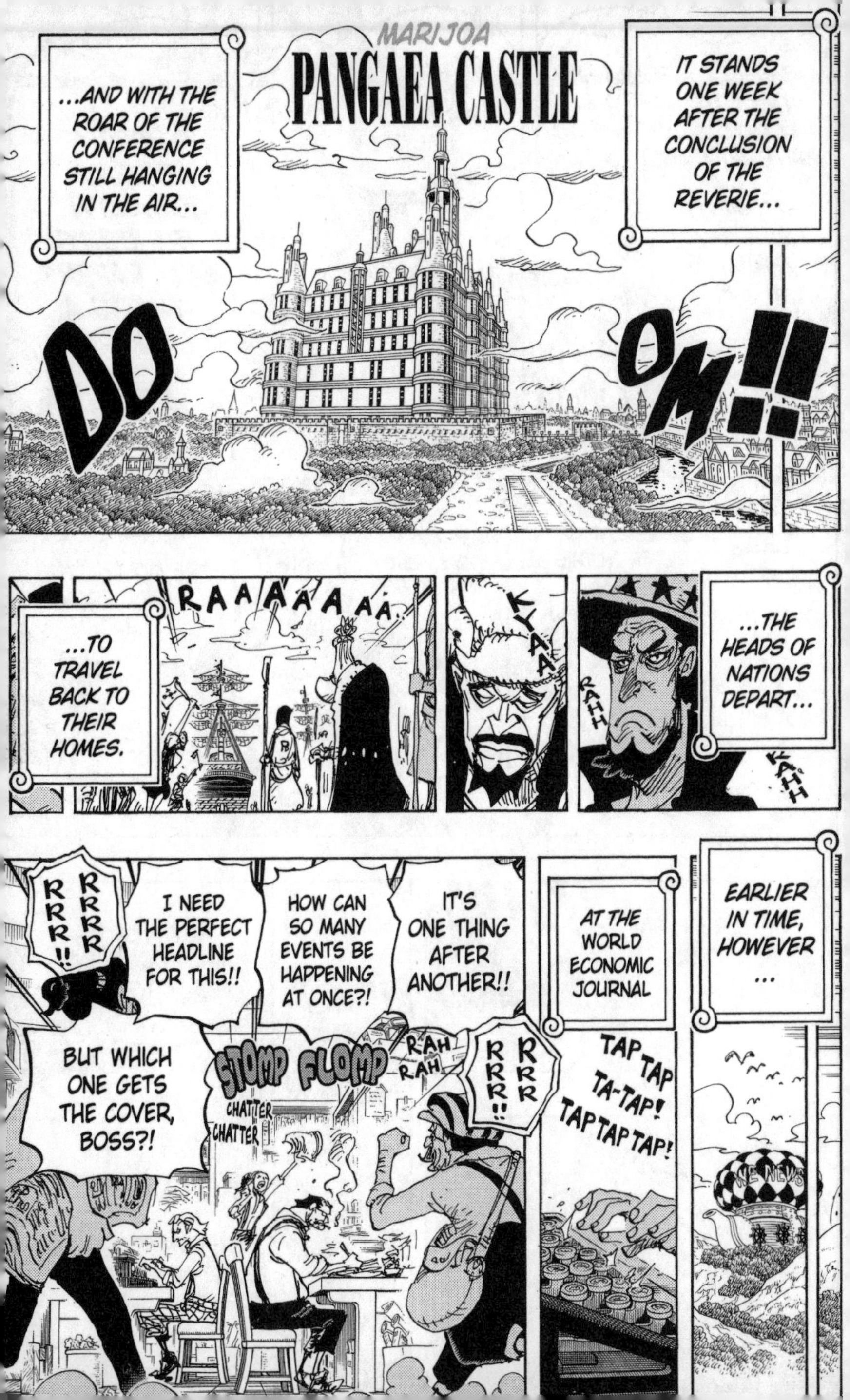
IT STANDS ONE WEEK AFTER THE CONCLUSION OF THE REVERIE...
MARIJOA
PANGAEA CASTLE
...AND WITH THE ROAR OF THE CONFERENCE STILL HANGING IN THE AIR...
DO
OM!!
...THE HEADS OF NATIONS DEPART...
RAHH
RAHH
KYAAA
RAAAAAAA
...TO TRAVEL BACK TO THEIR HOMES.
EARLIER IN TIME, HOWEVER ...
AT THE WORLD ECONOMIC JOURNAL
TAP TAP
TA-TAP!
TAPTAPTAP!
RRR RRR!!
IT'S ONE THING AFTER ANOTHER!!
HOW CAN SO MANY EVENTS BE HAPPENING AT ONCE?!
I NEED THE PERFECT HEADLINE FOR THIS!!
RRRR RRR!!
RAH
RAH
STOMP FLOMP
BUT WHICH ONE GETS THE COVER, BOSS?!
CHATTER
CHATTER

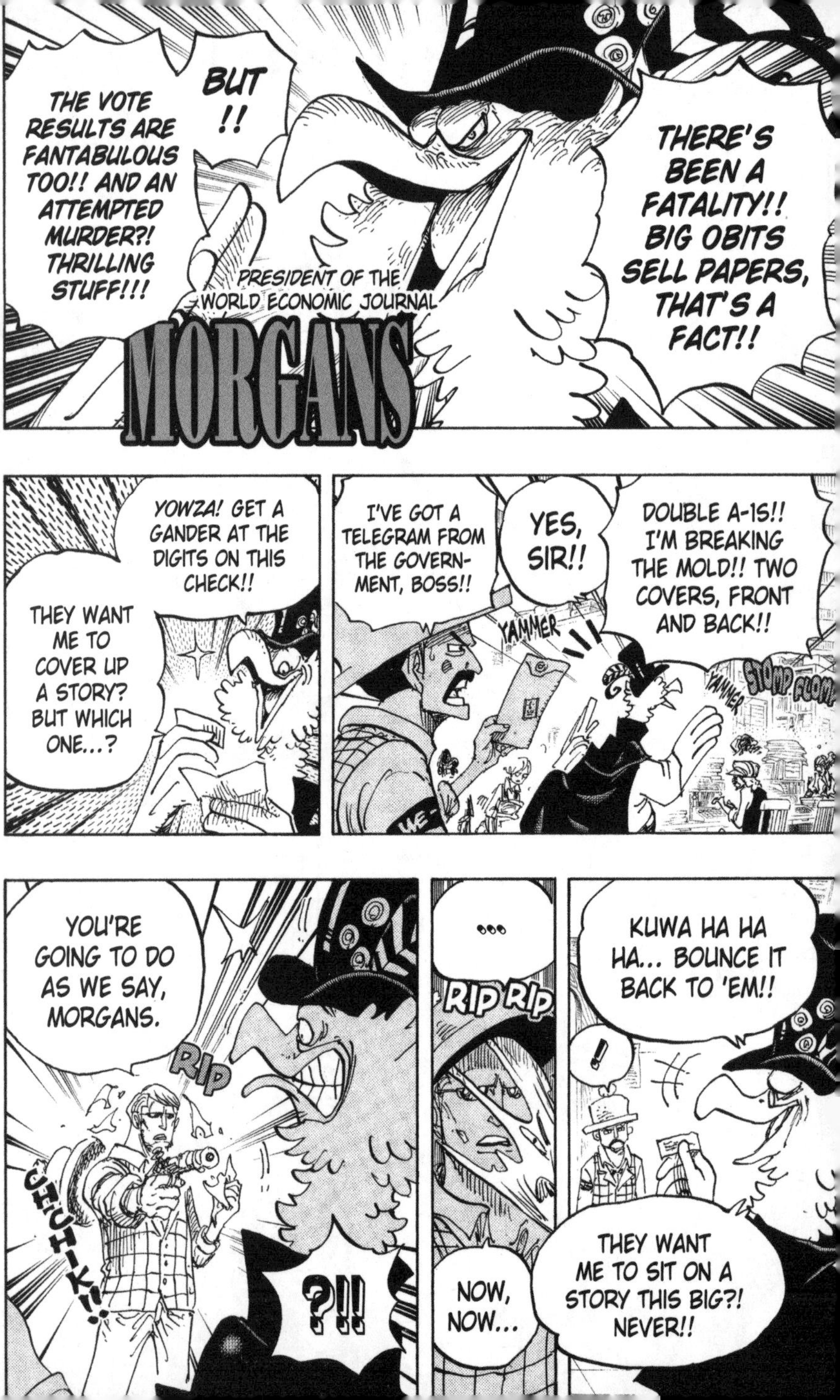
THERE'S BEEN A FATALITY!! BIG OBITS SELL PAPERS, THAT'S A FACT!!
BUT !!
THE VOTE RESULTS ARE FANTABULOUS TOO!! AND AN ATTEMPTED MURDER?! THRILLING STUFF!!!
PRESIDENT OF THE WORLD ECONOMIC JOURNAL
MORGANS
DOUBLE A-1S!! I'M BREAKING THE MOLD!! TWO COVERS, FRONT AND BACK!!
YES, SIR!!
I'VE GOT A TELEGRAM FROM THE GOVERNMENT, BOSS!!
YAMMER
YAMMER
YOWZA! GET A GANDER AT THE DIGITS ON THIS CHECK!!
THEY WANT ME TO COVER UP A STORY? BUT WHICH ONE...?
KUWA HA HA HA... BOUNCE IT BACK TO 'EM!!
!
THEY WANT ME TO SIT ON A STORY THIS BIG?! NEVER!!
...
RIP RIP
NOW, NOW...
YOU'RE GOING TO DO AS WE SAY, MORGANS.
RIP
CHICHIKI!!
?!!

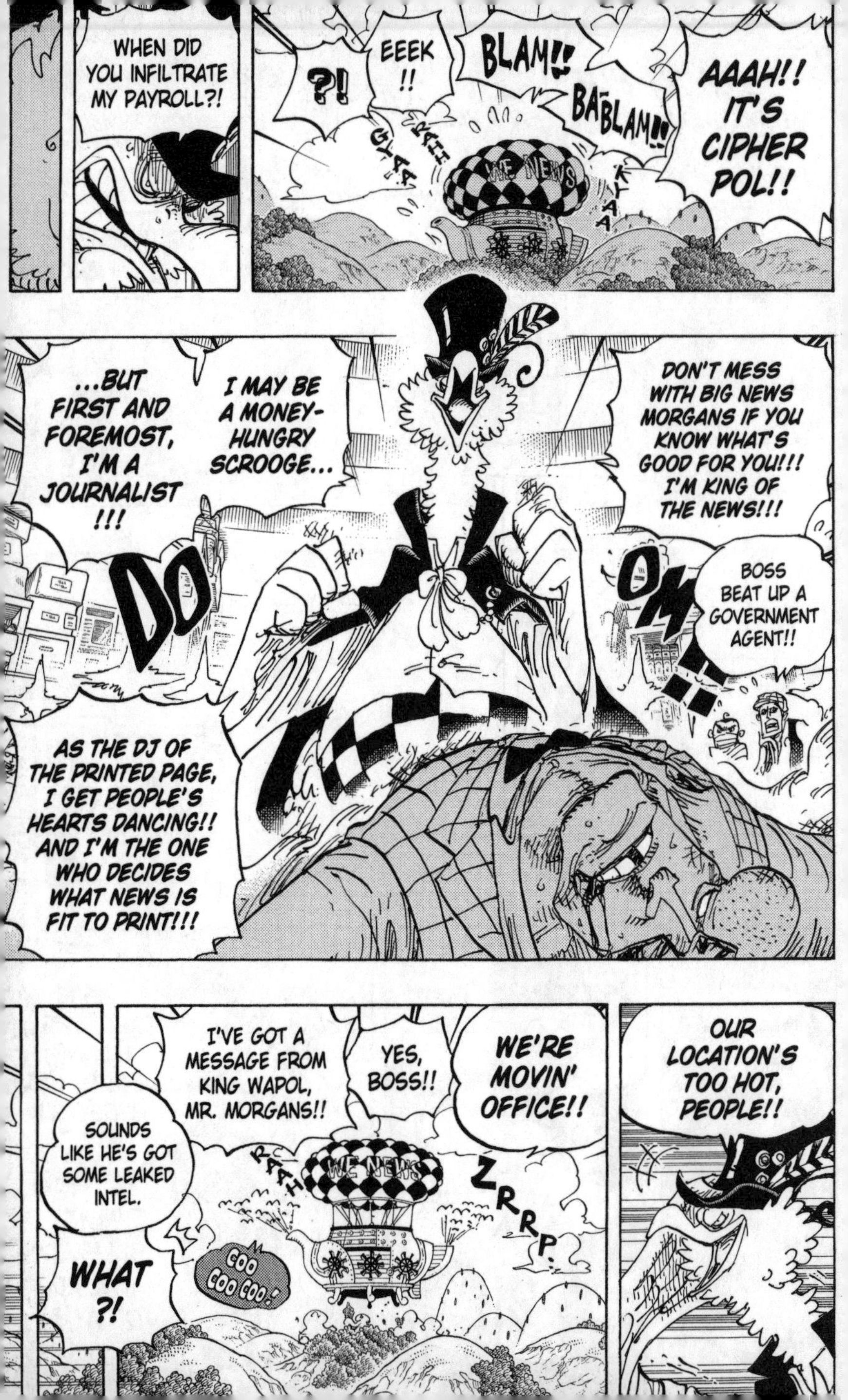
AAAH!! IT'S CIPHER POL!!
BLAM!!
BA-BLAM!!
EEEK !!
?!
WE NEWS
WHEN DID YOU INFILTRATE MY PAYROLL?!
DON'T MESS WITH BIG NEWS MORGANS IF YOU KNOW WHAT'S GOOD FOR YOU!!! I'M KING OF THE NEWS!!!
BOSS BEAT UP A GOVERNMENT AGENT!!
I MAY BE A MONEY-HUNGRY SCROOGE...
...BUT FIRST AND FOREMOST, I'M A JOURNALIST !!!
DOOM!!
AS THE DJ OF THE PRINTED PAGE, I GET PEOPLE'S HEARTS DANCING!! AND I'M THE ONE WHO DECIDES WHAT NEWS IS FIT TO PRINT!!!
OUR LOCATION'S TOO HOT, PEOPLE!!
WE'RE MOVIN' OFFICE!!
YES, BOSS!!
I'VE GOT A MESSAGE FROM KING WAPOL, MR. MORGANS!!
SOUNDS LIKE HE'S GOT SOME LEAKED INTEL.
WHAT ?!
ZRRRP
WE NEWS
COO COO COO

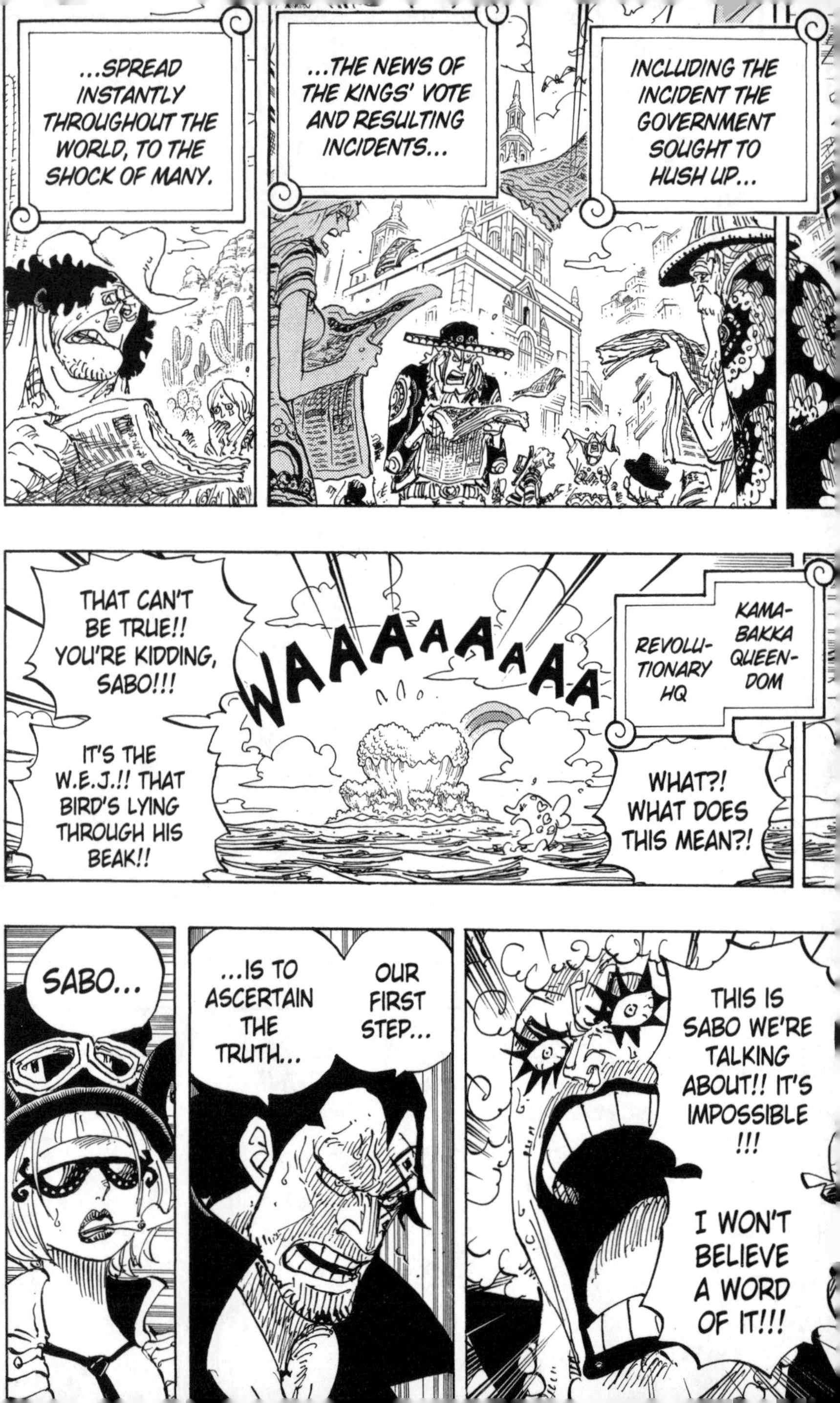
INCLUDING THE INCIDENT THE GOVERNMENT SOUGHT TO HUSH UP...
...THE NEWS OF THE KINGS' VOTE AND RESULTING INCIDENTS...
...SPREAD INSTANTLY THROUGHOUT THE WORLD, TO THE SHOCK OF MANY.
KAMA-BAKKA QUEEN-DOM
REVOLU-TIONARY HQ
WHAT?! WHAT DOES THIS MEAN?!
WAAAAAAAA
THAT CAN'T BE TRUE!! YOU'RE KIDDING, SABO!!!
IT'S THE W.E.J.!! THAT BIRD'S LYING THROUGH HIS BEAK!!
THIS IS SABO WE'RE TALKING ABOUT!! IT'S IMPOSSIBLE!!!
I WON'T BELIEVE A WORD OF IT!!!
OUR FIRST STEP...
...IS TO ASCERTAIN THE TRUTH...
SABO...

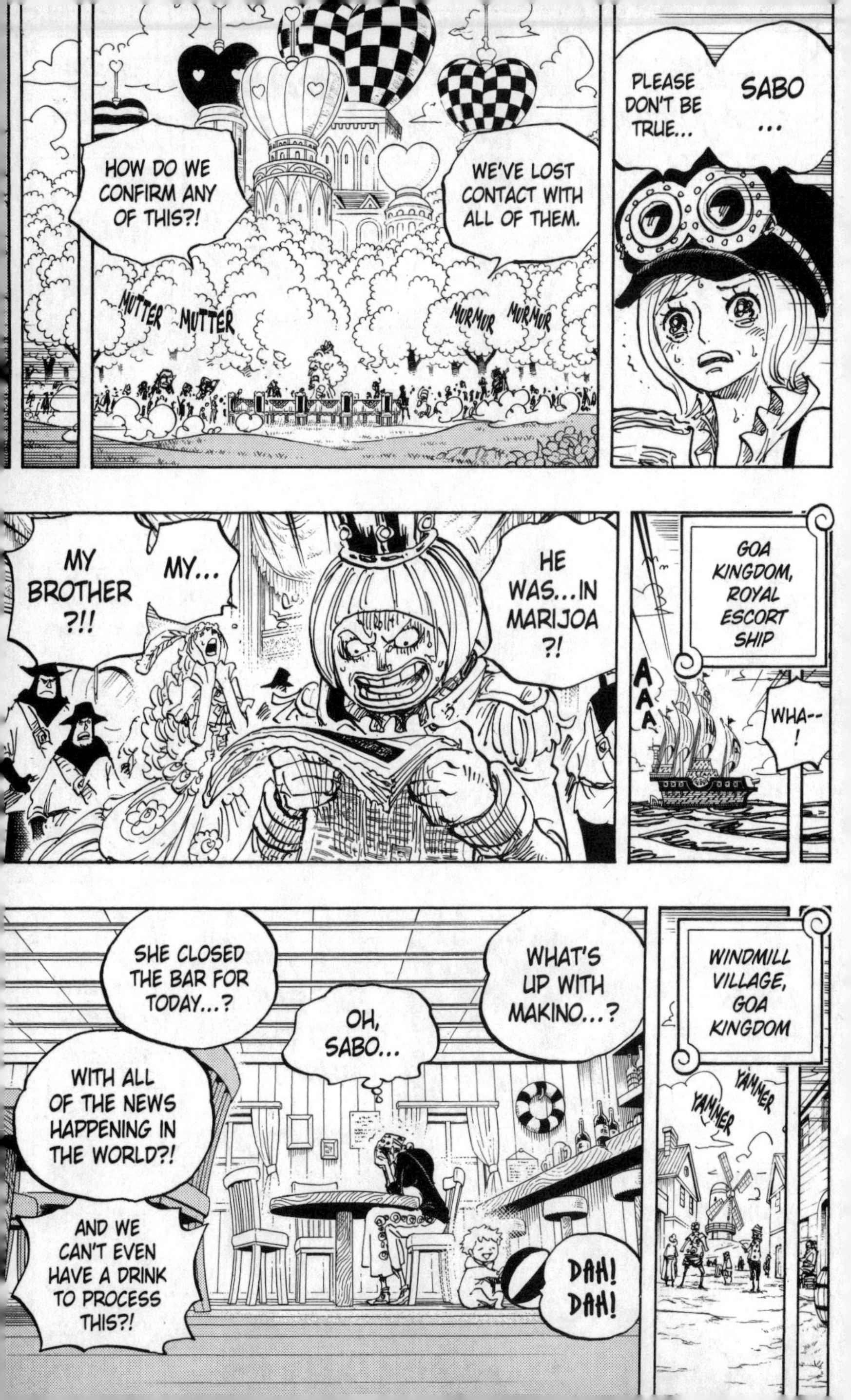
SABO...
PLEASE DON'T BE TRUE...
WE'VE LOST CONTACT WITH ALL OF THEM.
HOW DO WE CONFIRM ANY OF THIS?!
MURMUR MURMUR
MUTTER MUTTER
GOA KINGDOM, ROYAL ESCORT SHIP
WHA--!
AAA
HE WAS...IN MARIJOA ?!
MY...
MY BROTHER ?!!
WINDMILL VILLAGE, GOA KINGDOM
YAMMER YAMMER
WHAT'S UP WITH MAKINO...?
SHE CLOSED THE BAR FOR TODAY...?
OH, SABO...
WITH ALL OF THE NEWS HAPPENING IN THE WORLD?!
DAH! DAH!
AND WE CAN'T EVEN HAVE A DRINK TO PROCESS THIS?!

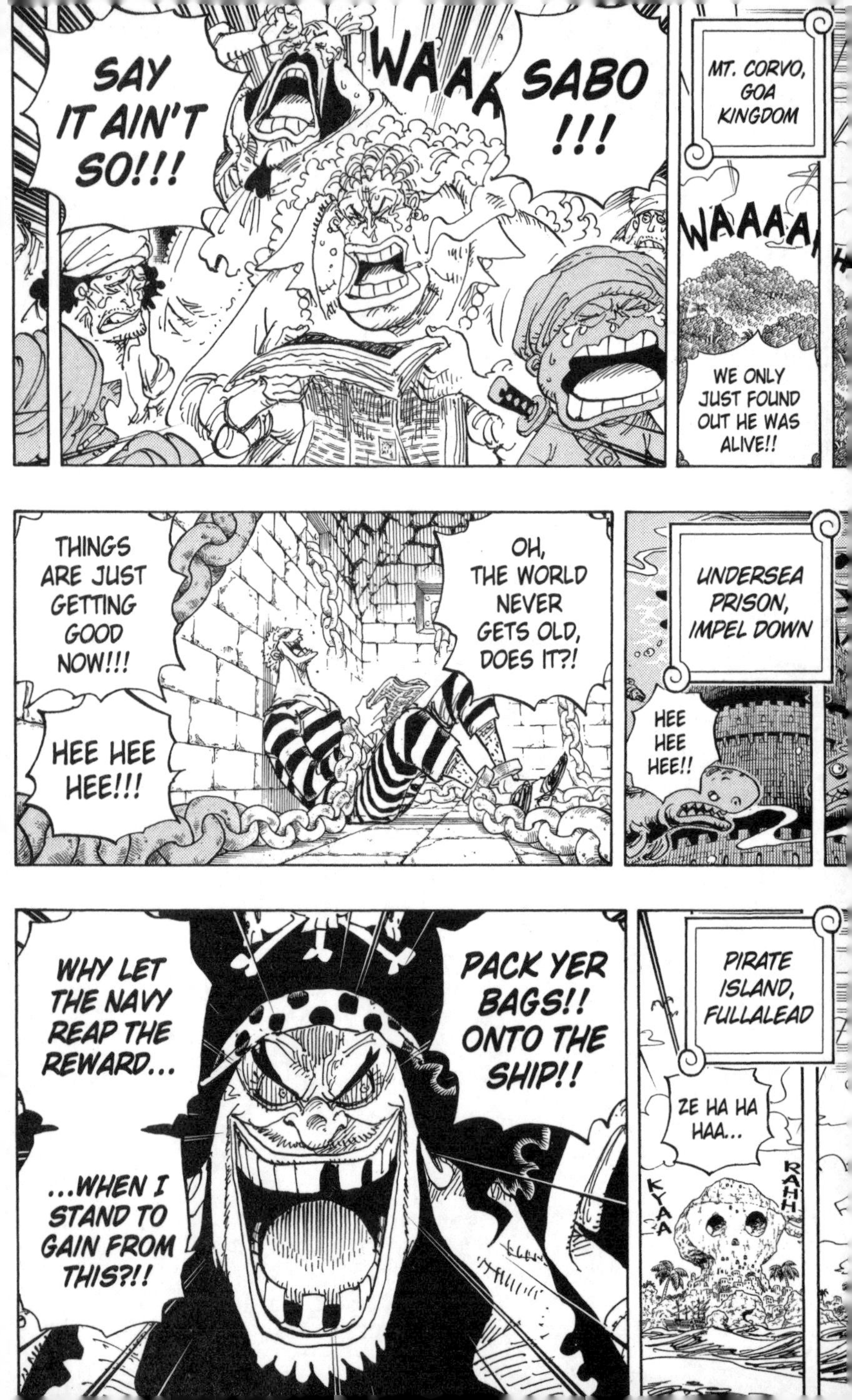
MT. CORVO, GOA KINGDOM
WAAAA
WE ONLY JUST FOUND OUT HE WAS ALIVE!!
SABO!!!
WAAA
SAY IT AIN'T SO!!!
UNDERSEA PRISON, IMPEL DOWN
HEE HEE HEE!!
OH, THE WORLD NEVER GETS OLD, DOES IT?!
THINGS ARE JUST GETTING GOOD NOW!!!
HEE HEE HEE!!!
PIRATE ISLAND, FULLALEAD
ZE HA HA HAA...
RAHH
KYAA
PACK YER BAGS!! ONTO THE SHIP!!
WHY LET THE NAVY REAP THE REWARD...
...WHEN I STAND TO GAIN FROM THIS?!!

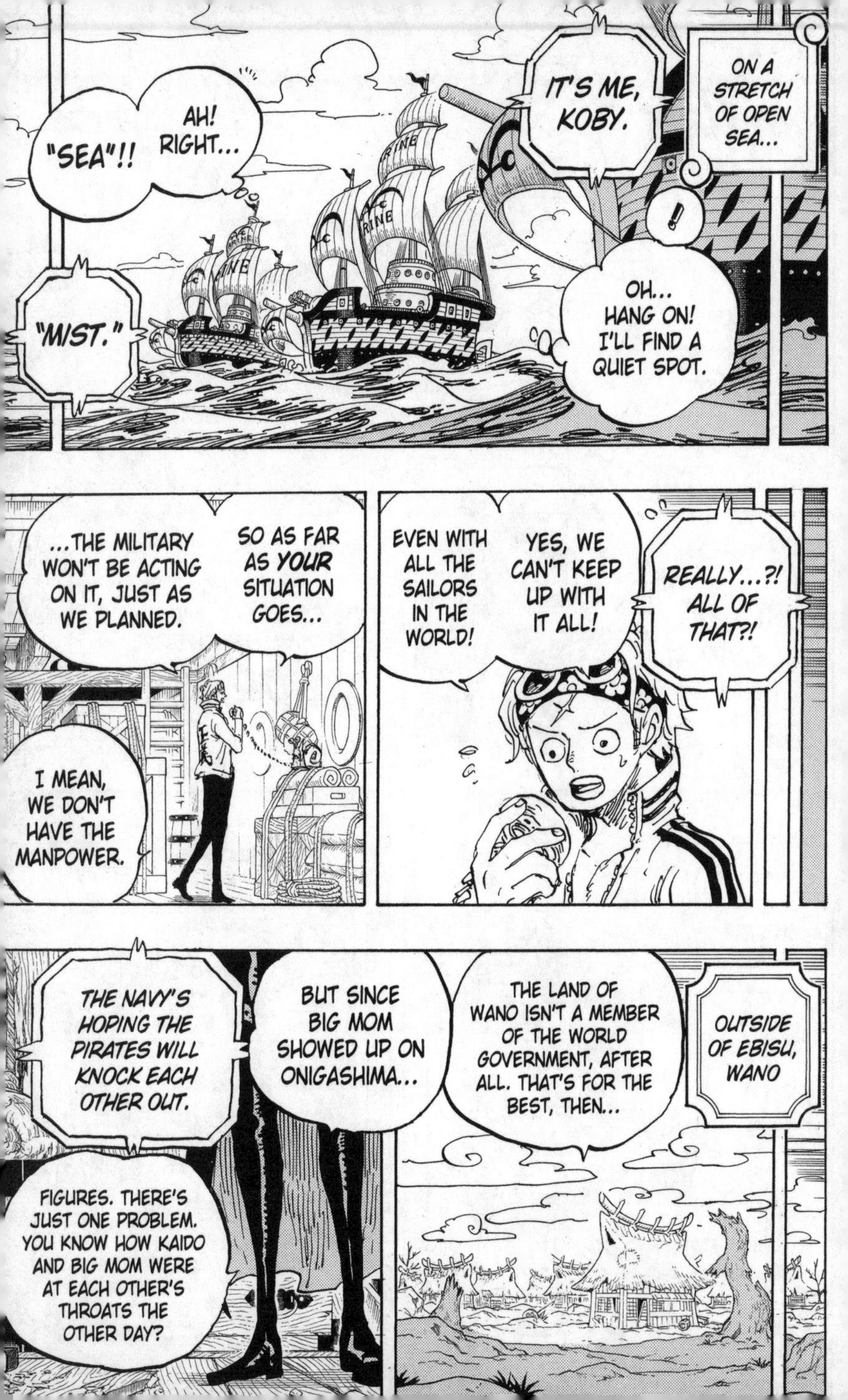
ON A STRETCH OF OPEN SEA...
IT'S ME, KOBY.
!
OH... HANG ON! I'LL FIND A QUIET SPOT.
"MIST."
AH! RIGHT...
"SEA"!!
REALLY...?! ALL OF THAT?!
YES, WE CAN'T KEEP UP WITH IT ALL!
EVEN WITH ALL THE SAILORS IN THE WORLD!
SO AS FAR AS YOUR SITUATION GOES...
...THE MILITARY WON'T BE ACTING ON IT, JUST AS WE PLANNED.
I MEAN, WE DON'T HAVE THE MANPOWER.
OUTSIDE OF EBISU, WANO
THE LAND OF WANO ISN'T A MEMBER OF THE WORLD GOVERNMENT, AFTER ALL. THAT'S FOR THE BEST, THEN...
BUT SINCE BIG MOM SHOWED UP ON ONIGASHIMA...
THE NAVY'S HOPING THE PIRATES WILL KNOCK EACH OTHER OUT.
FIGURES. THERE'S JUST ONE PROBLEM. YOU KNOW HOW KAIDO AND BIG MOM WERE AT EACH OTHER'S THROATS THE OTHER DAY?

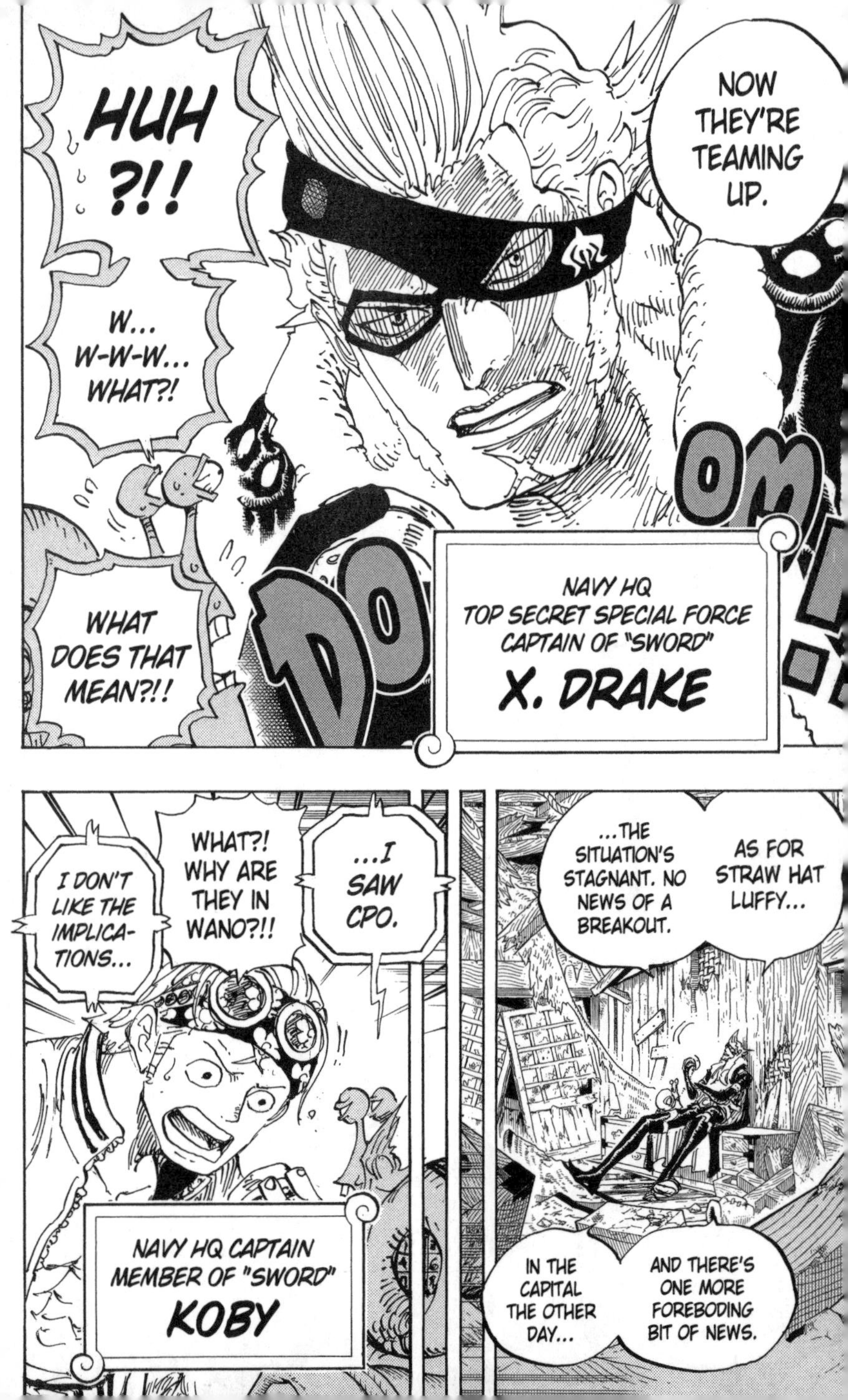
NOW THEY'RE TEAMING UP.
HUH ?!!
W... W-W-W... WHAT?!
WHAT DOES THAT MEAN?!!
NAVY HQ TOP SECRET SPECIAL FORCE CAPTAIN OF "SWORD" X. DRAKE
AS FOR STRAW HAT LUFFY...
...THE SITUATION'S STAGNANT. NO NEWS OF A BREAKOUT.
AND THERE'S ONE MORE FOREBODING BIT OF NEWS.
IN THE CAPITAL THE OTHER DAY...
...I SAW CP0.
WHAT?! WHY ARE THEY IN WANO?!!
I DON'T LIKE THE IMPLICATIONS...
NAVY HQ CAPTAIN MEMBER OF "SWORD" KOBY

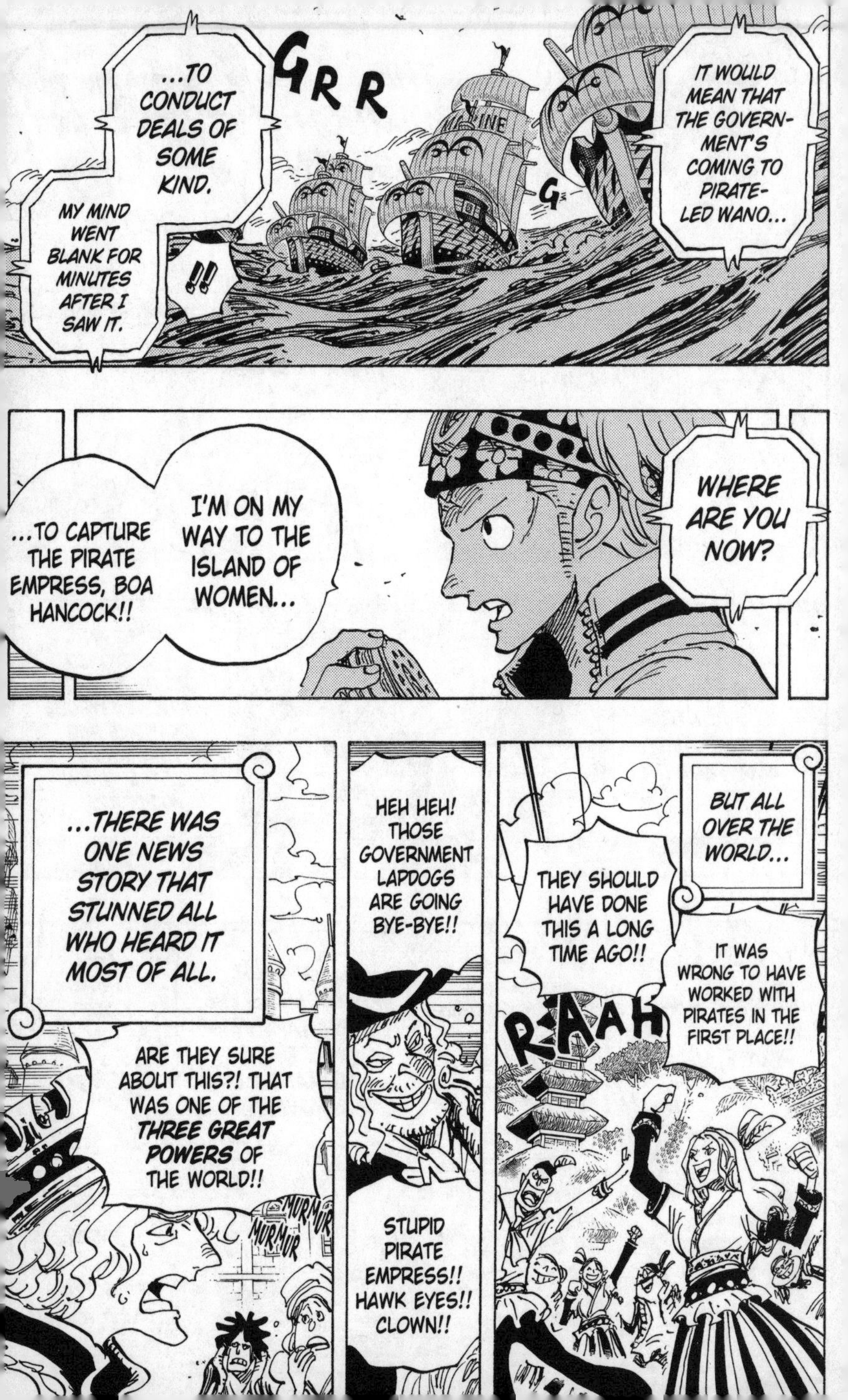
IT WOULD MEAN THAT THE GOVERNMENT'S COMING TO PIRATE-LED WANO...
GRR
G
...TO CONDUCT DEALS OF SOME KIND.
!!
MY MIND WENT BLANK FOR MINUTES AFTER I SAW IT.
WHERE ARE YOU NOW?
I'M ON MY WAY TO THE ISLAND OF WOMEN...
...TO CAPTURE THE PIRATE EMPRESS, BOA HANCOCK!!
BUT ALL OVER THE WORLD...
THEY SHOULD HAVE DONE THIS A LONG TIME AGO!!
IT WAS WRONG TO HAVE WORKED WITH PIRATES IN THE FIRST PLACE!!
RAAH
HEH HEH! THOSE GOVERNMENT LAPDOGS ARE GOING BYE-BYE!!
STUPID PIRATE EMPRESS!! HAWK EYES!! CLOWN!!
...THERE WAS ONE NEWS STORY THAT STUNNED ALL WHO HEARD IT MOST OF ALL.
ARE THEY SURE ABOUT THIS?! THAT WAS ONE OF THE THREE GREAT POWERS OF THE WORLD!!
MURMUR
MURMUR

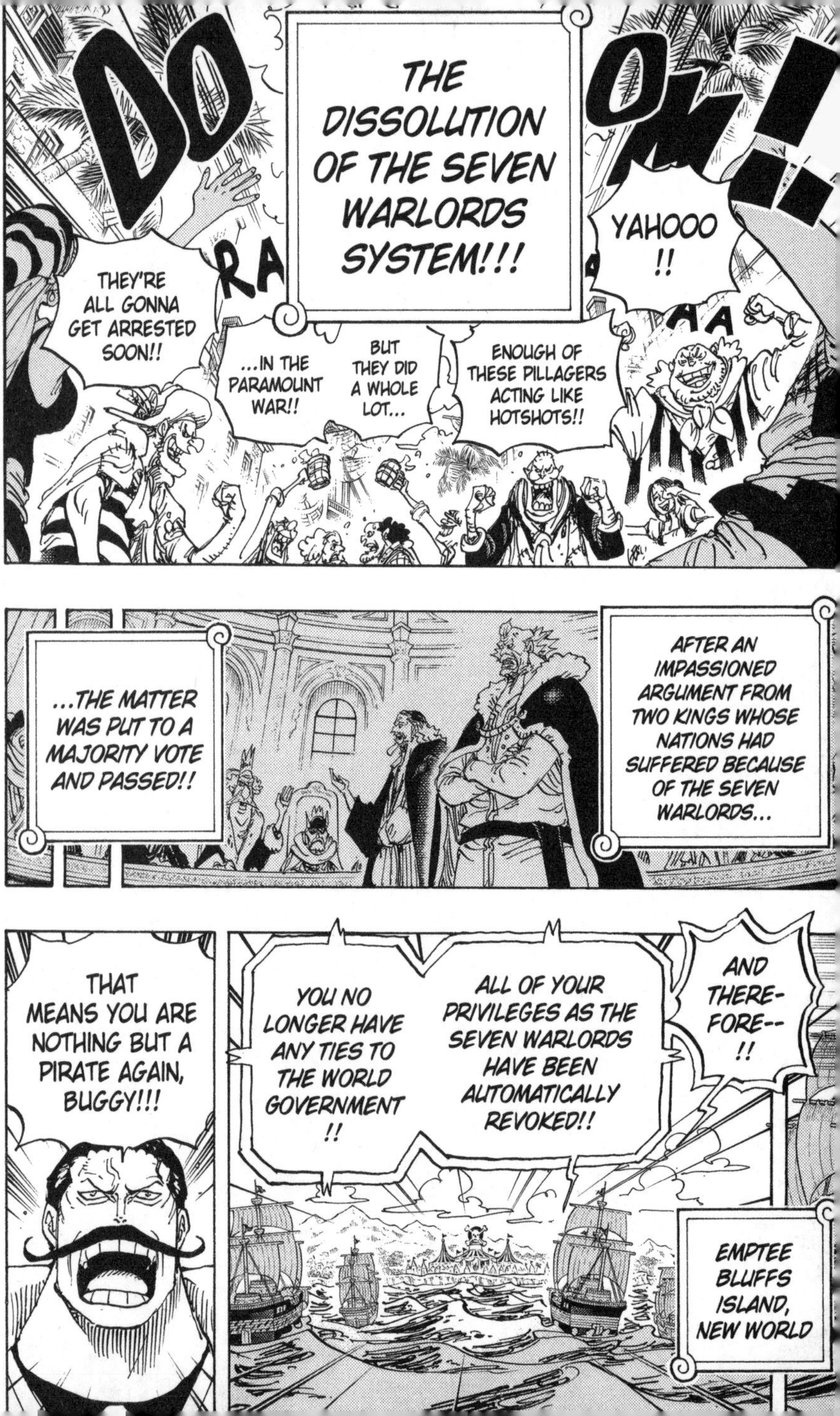
DOOM!!
THE DISSOLUTION OF THE SEVEN WARLORDS SYSTEM!!!
YAHOOO !!
AA
ENOUGH OF THESE PILLAGERS ACTING LIKE HOTSHOTS!!
BUT THEY DID A WHOLE LOT...
...IN THE PARAMOUNT WAR!!
RA
THEY'RE ALL GONNA GET ARRESTED SOON!!
AFTER AN IMPASSIONED ARGUMENT FROM TWO KINGS WHOSE NATIONS HAD SUFFERED BECAUSE OF THE SEVEN WARLORDS...
...THE MATTER WAS PUT TO A MAJORITY VOTE AND PASSED!!
AND THEREFORE--!!
ALL OF YOUR PRIVILEGES AS THE SEVEN WARLORDS HAVE BEEN AUTOMATICALLY REVOKED!!
YOU NO LONGER HAVE ANY TIES TO THE WORLD GOVERNMENT!!
EMPTEE BLUFFS ISLAND, NEW WORLD
THAT MEANS YOU ARE NOTHING BUT A PIRATE AGAIN, BUGGY!!!

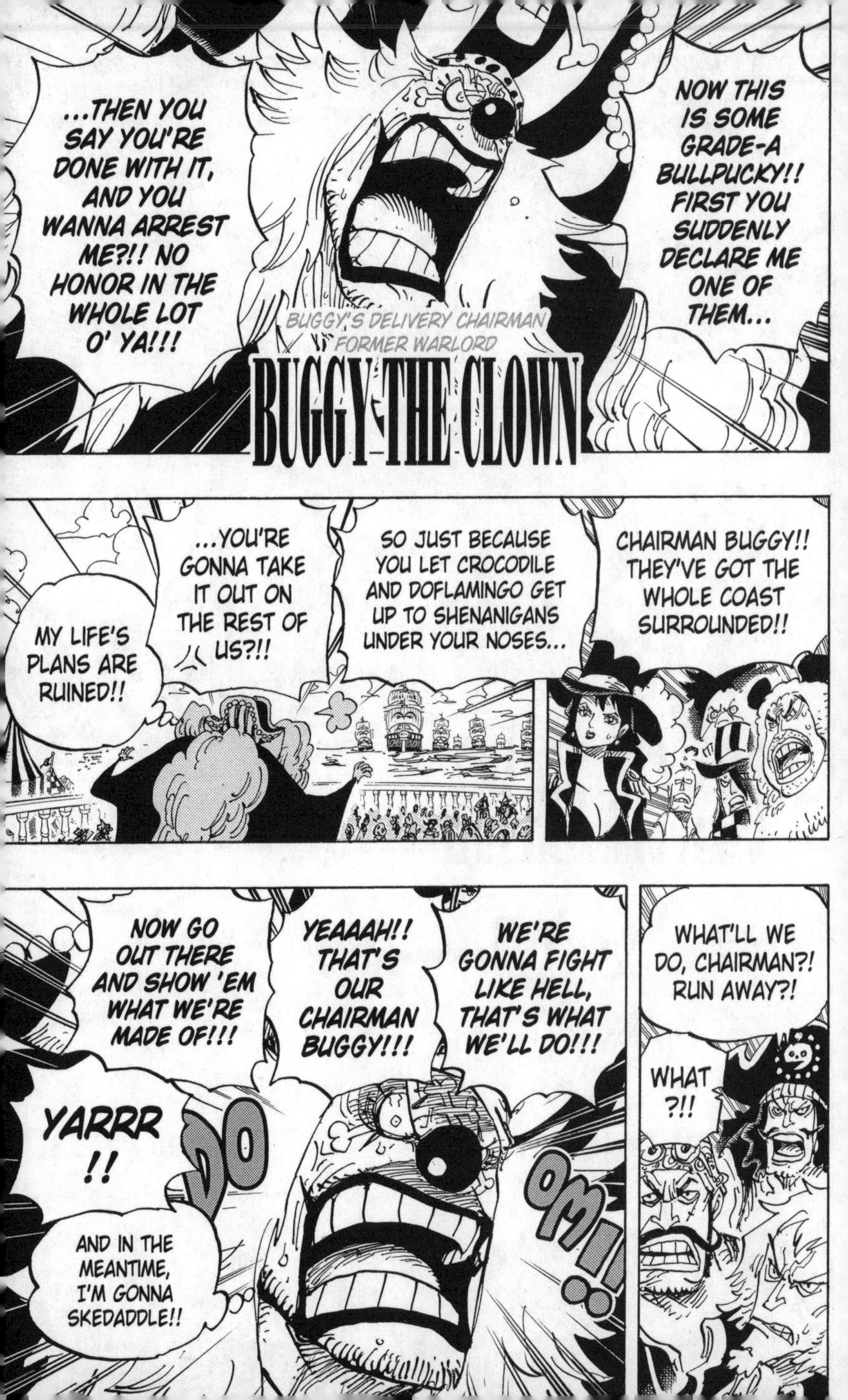
NOW THIS IS SOME GRADE-A BULLPUCKY!! FIRST YOU SUDDENLY DECLARE ME ONE OF THEM...
...THEN YOU SAY YOU'RE DONE WITH IT, AND YOU WANNA ARREST ME?!! NO HONOR IN THE WHOLE LOT O' YA!!!
BUGGY'S DELIVERY CHAIRMAN
FORMER WARLORD
BUGGY THE CLOWN
CHAIRMAN BUGGY!! THEY'VE GOT THE WHOLE COAST SURROUNDED!!
SO JUST BECAUSE YOU LET CROCODILE AND DOFLAMINGO GET UP TO SHENANIGANS UNDER YOUR NOSES...
...YOU'RE GONNA TAKE IT OUT ON THE REST OF US?!!
MY LIFE'S PLANS ARE RUINED!!
WHAT'LL WE DO, CHAIRMAN?! RUN AWAY?!
WHAT ?!!
WE'RE GONNA FIGHT LIKE HELL, THAT'S WHAT WE'LL DO!!!
YEAAAH!! THAT'S OUR CHAIRMAN BUGGY!!!
NOW GO OUT THERE AND SHOW 'EM WHAT WE'RE MADE OF!!!
YARRR !!
DOOM!!
AND IN THE MEANTIME, I'M GONNA SKEDADDLE!!

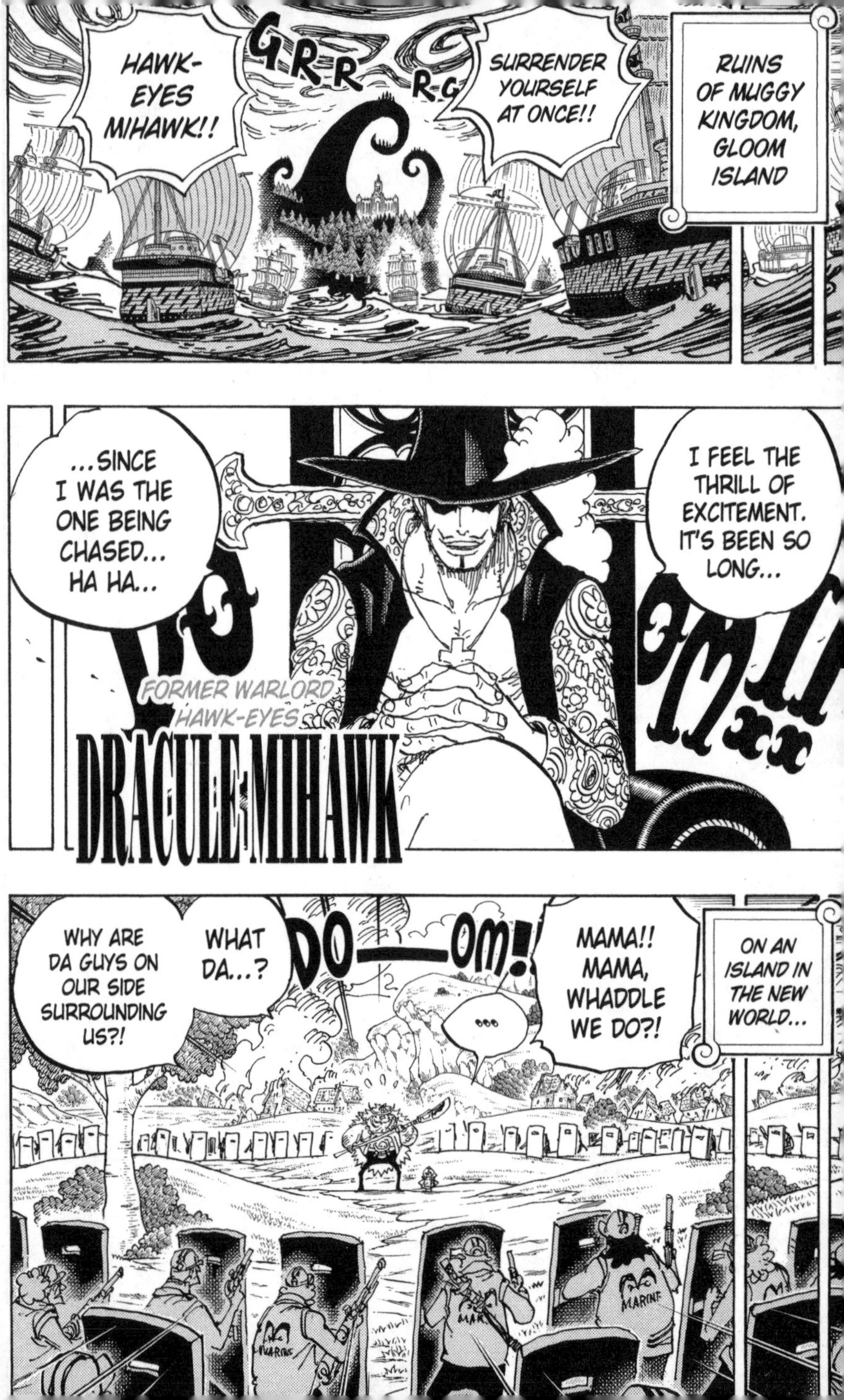
RUINS OF MUGGY KINGDOM, GLOOM ISLAND
SURRENDER YOURSELF AT ONCE!!
GRRR-RG
HAWK-EYES MIHAWK!!
I FEEL THE THRILL OF EXCITEMENT. IT'S BEEN SO LONG...
...SINCE I WAS THE ONE BEING CHASED... HA HA...
FORMER WARLORD HAWK-EYES
DRACULE MIHAWK
ON AN ISLAND IN THE NEW WORLD...
MAMA!! MAMA, WHADDLE WE DO?!
...
DO—OM!
WHAT DA...?
WHY ARE DA GUYS ON OUR SIDE SURROUNDING US?!

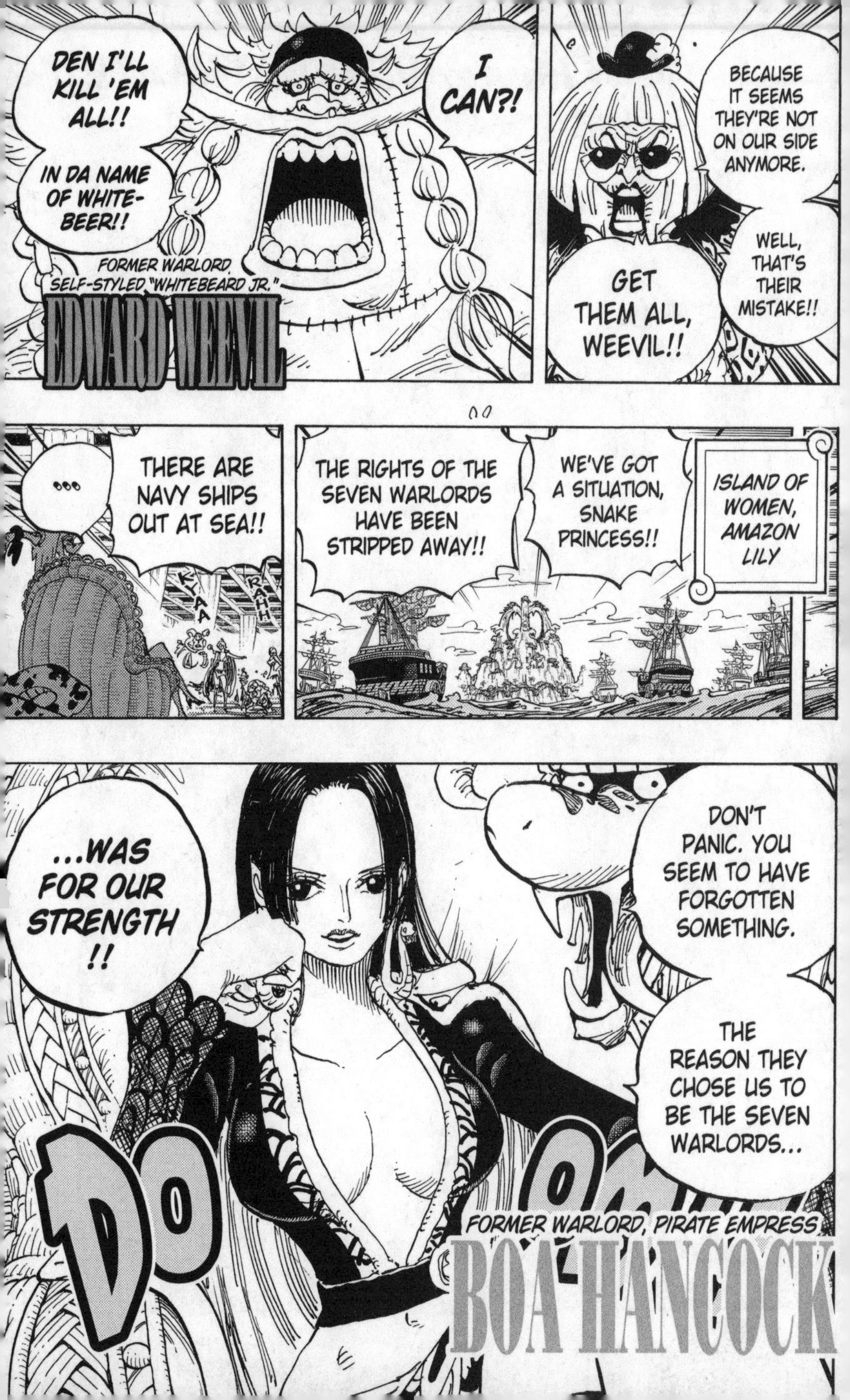
BECAUSE IT SEEMS THEY'RE NOT ON OUR SIDE ANYMORE.
WELL, THAT'S THEIR MISTAKE!!
GET THEM ALL, WEEVIL!!
I CAN?!
DEN I'LL KILL 'EM ALL!!
IN DA NAME OF WHITE-BEER!!
FORMER WARLORD, SELF-STYLED "WHITEBEARD JR."
EDWARD WEEVIL
ISLAND OF WOMEN, AMAZON LILY
WE'VE GOT A SITUATION, SNAKE PRINCESS!!
THE RIGHTS OF THE SEVEN WARLORDS HAVE BEEN STRIPPED AWAY!!
THERE ARE NAVY SHIPS OUT AT SEA!!
...
RAHH
KYAA
DON'T PANIC. YOU SEEM TO HAVE FORGOTTEN SOMETHING.
THE REASON THEY CHOSE US TO BE THE SEVEN WARLORDS...
...WAS FOR OUR STRENGTH!!
DO
FORMER WARLORD, PIRATE EMPRESS
BOA HANCOCK

Chapter 957: ULTIMATE

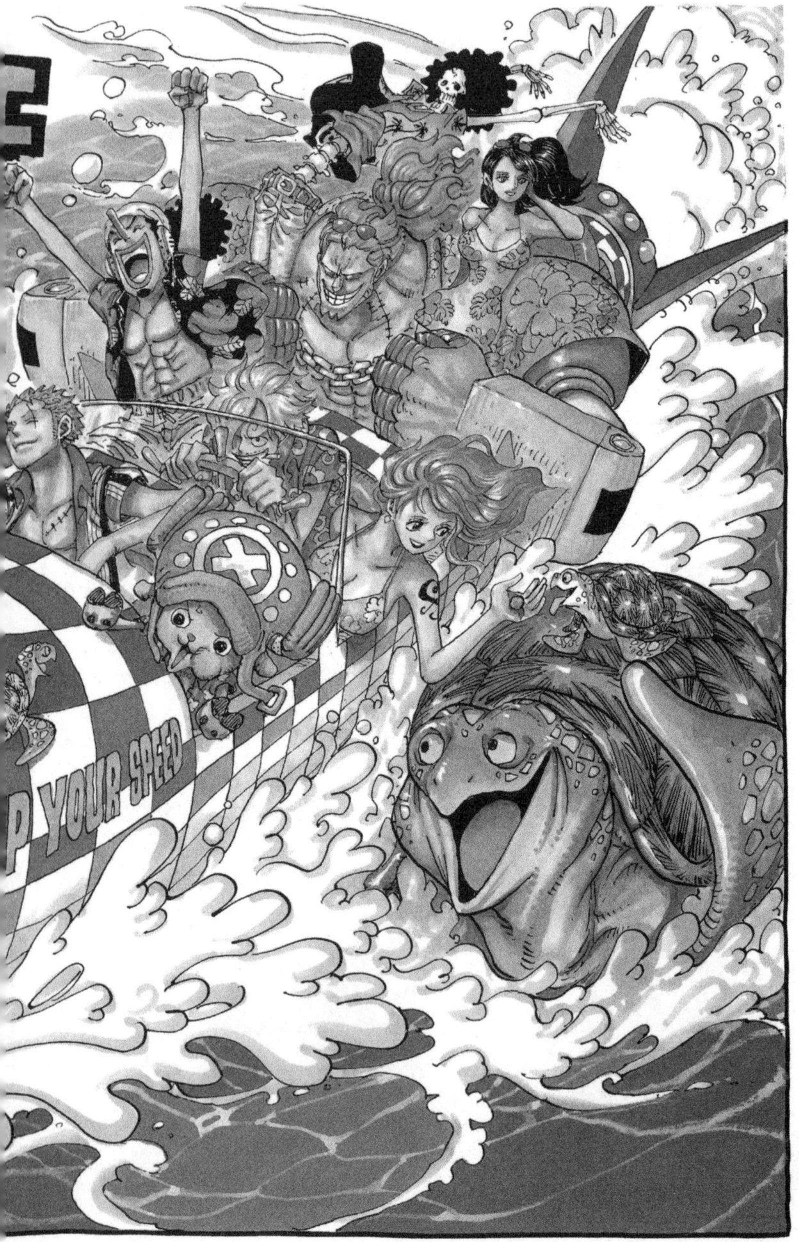
P YOUR SPEED

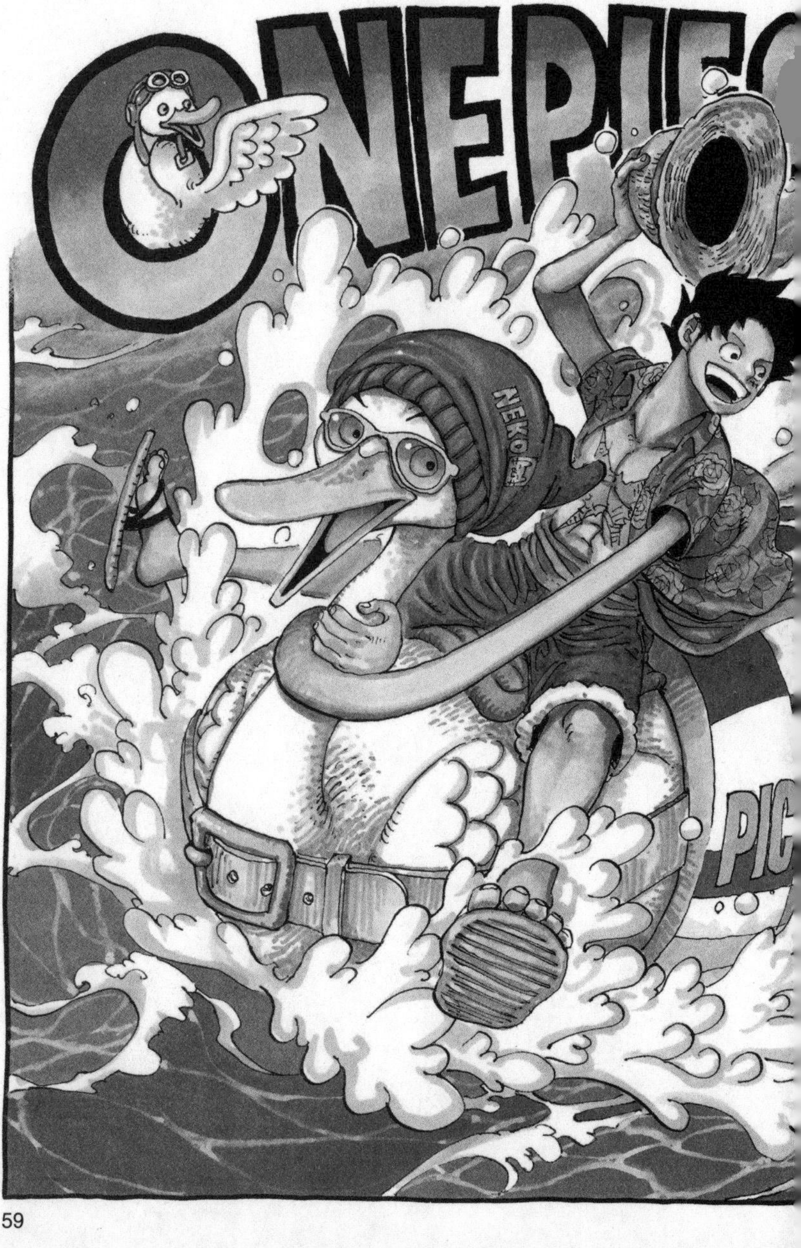
ONE PIE
NEKO
PIC

ONE PIECE vol.95

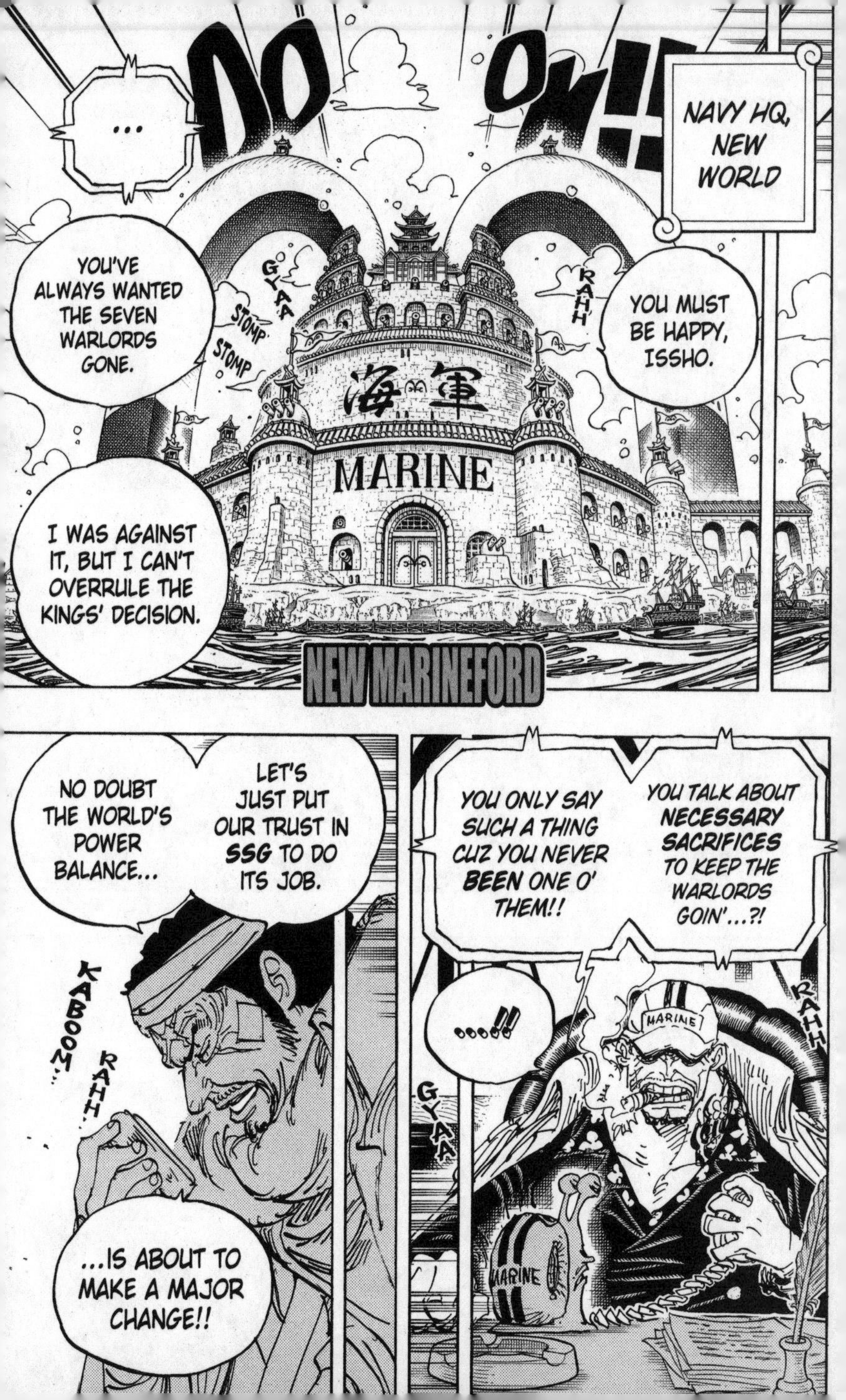
NAVY HQ, NEW WORLD
DOON!!
...
YOU MUST BE HAPPY, ISSHO.
RAHH
GYAA
STOMP
STOMP
YOU'VE ALWAYS WANTED THE SEVEN WARLORDS GONE.
I WAS AGAINST IT, BUT I CAN'T OVERRULE THE KINGS' DECISION.
海軍
MARINE
NEW MARINEFORD
YOU TALK ABOUT NECESSARY SACRIFICES TO KEEP THE WARLORDS GOIN'...?!
YOU ONLY SAY SUCH A THING CUZ YOU NEVER BEEN ONE O' THEM!!
RAHH
...!!
MARINE
GYAA
MARINE
LET'S JUST PUT OUR TRUST IN SSG TO DO ITS JOB.
NO DOUBT THE WORLD'S POWER BALANCE...
KABOOM!!
RAHH!!
...IS ABOUT TO MAKE A MAJOR CHANGE!!

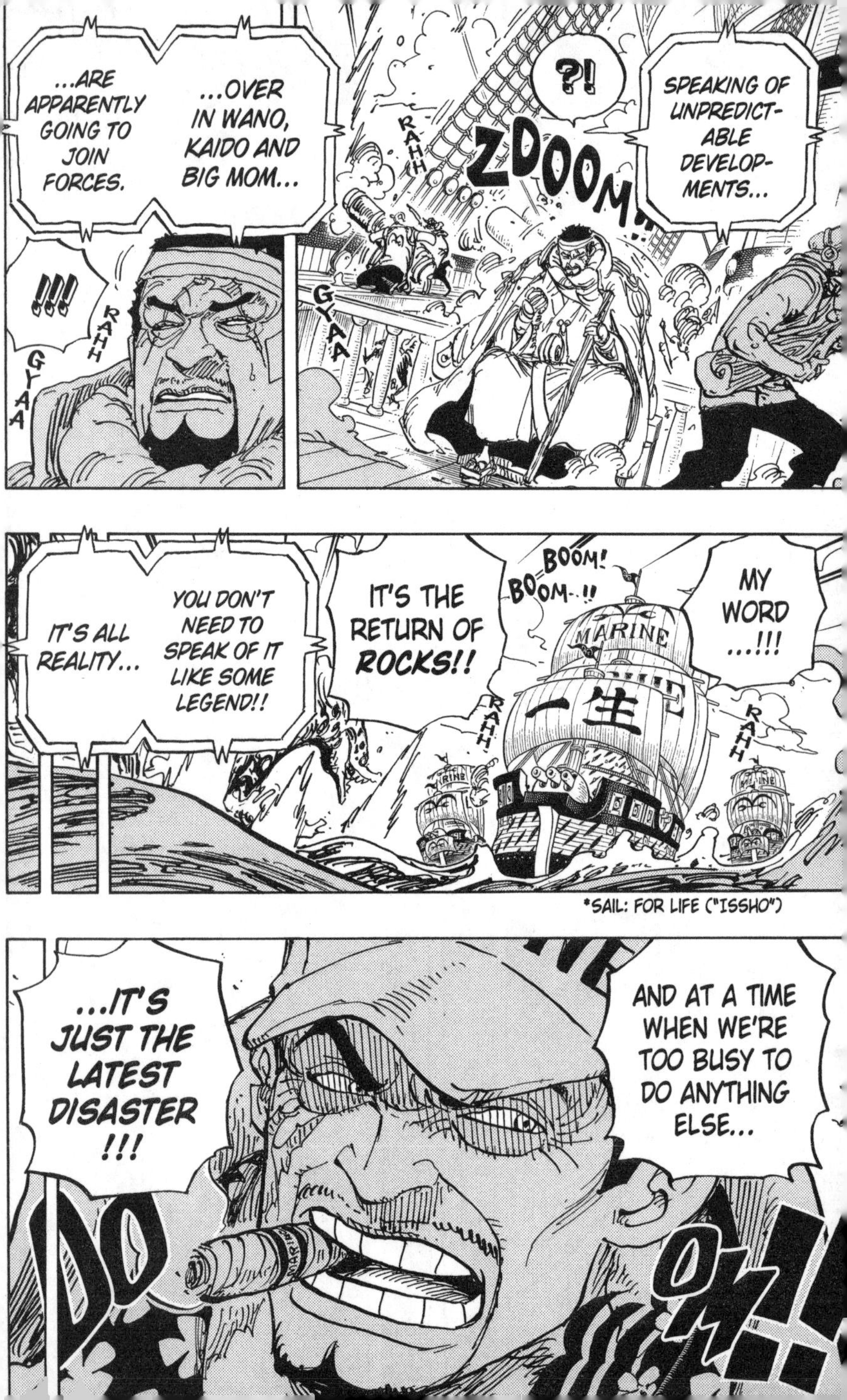

SPEAKING OF UNPREDICTABLE DEVELOPMENTS...
?!
ZDOOM!!
RAHH
GYAA
...OVER IN WANO, KAIDO AND BIG MOM...
...ARE APPARENTLY GOING TO JOIN FORCES.
!!!
RAHH
GYAA
MY WORD ...!!!
BOOM!
BOOM..!!
MARINE
一生
RAHH
RAHH
IT'S THE RETURN OF ROCKS!!
YOU DON'T NEED TO SPEAK OF IT LIKE SOME LEGEND!!
IT'S ALL REALITY...
*SAIL: FOR LIFE ("ISSHO")
AND AT A TIME WHEN WE'RE TOO BUSY TO DO ANYTHING ELSE...
...IT'S JUST THE LATEST DISASTER!!!
DO
ON!!

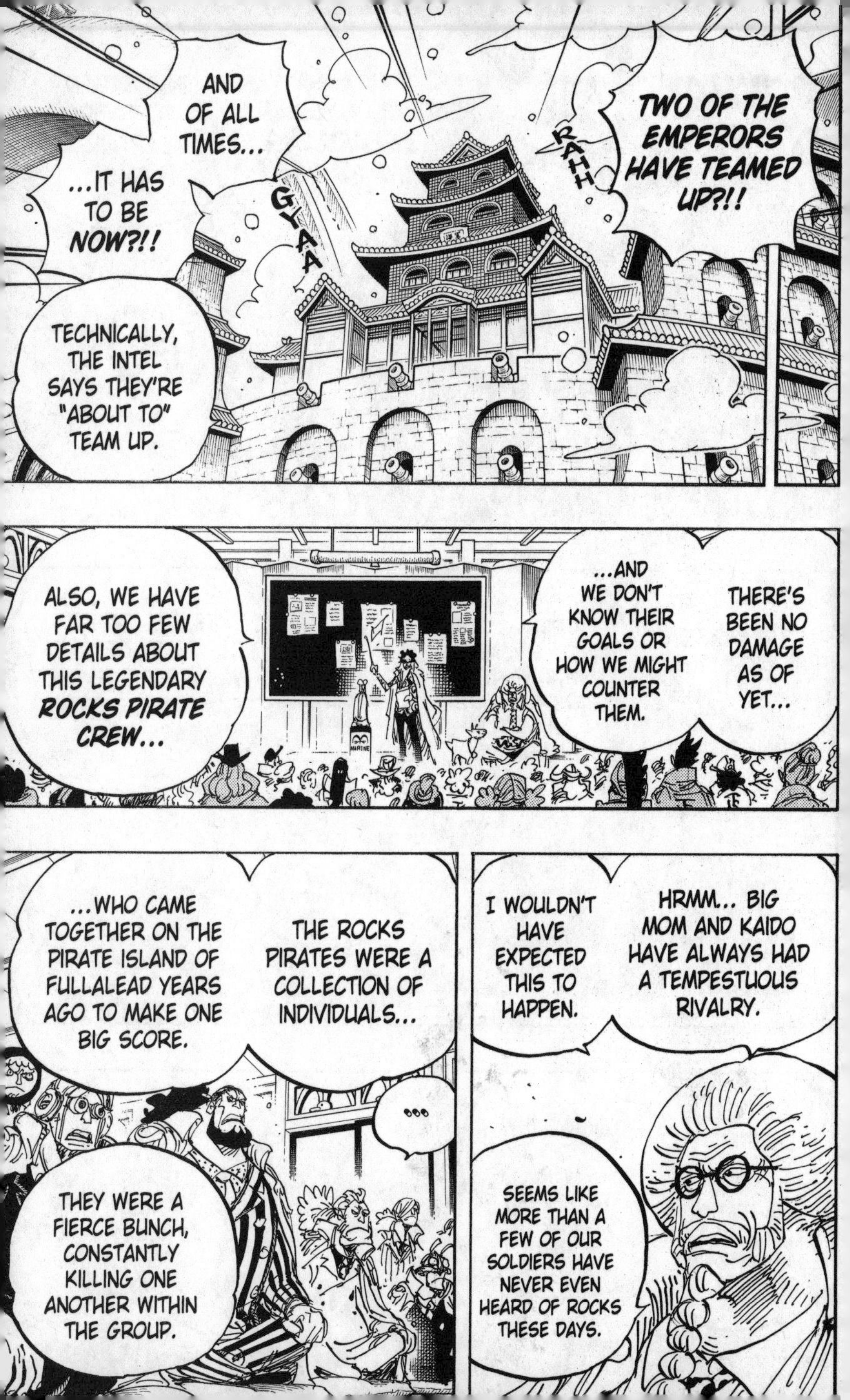
TWO OF THE EMPERORS HAVE TEAMED UP?!!
RAHH
GYAA
AND OF ALL TIMES...
...IT HAS TO BE NOW?!!
TECHNICALLY, THE INTEL SAYS THEY'RE "ABOUT TO" TEAM UP.
THERE'S BEEN NO DAMAGE AS OF YET...
...AND WE DON'T KNOW THEIR GOALS OR HOW WE MIGHT COUNTER THEM.
ALSO, WE HAVE FAR TOO FEW DETAILS ABOUT THIS LEGENDARY ROCKS PIRATE CREW...
MARINE
HRMM... BIG MOM AND KAIDO HAVE ALWAYS HAD A TEMPESTUOUS RIVALRY.
I WOULDN'T HAVE EXPECTED THIS TO HAPPEN.
SEEMS LIKE MORE THAN A FEW OF OUR SOLDIERS HAVE NEVER EVEN HEARD OF ROCKS THESE DAYS.
THE ROCKS PIRATES WERE A COLLECTION OF INDIVIDUALS...
...WHO CAME TOGETHER ON THE PIRATE ISLAND OF FULLALEAD YEARS AGO TO MAKE ONE BIG SCORE.
...
THEY WERE A FIERCE BUNCH, CONSTANTLY KILLING ONE ANOTHER WITHIN THE GROUP.

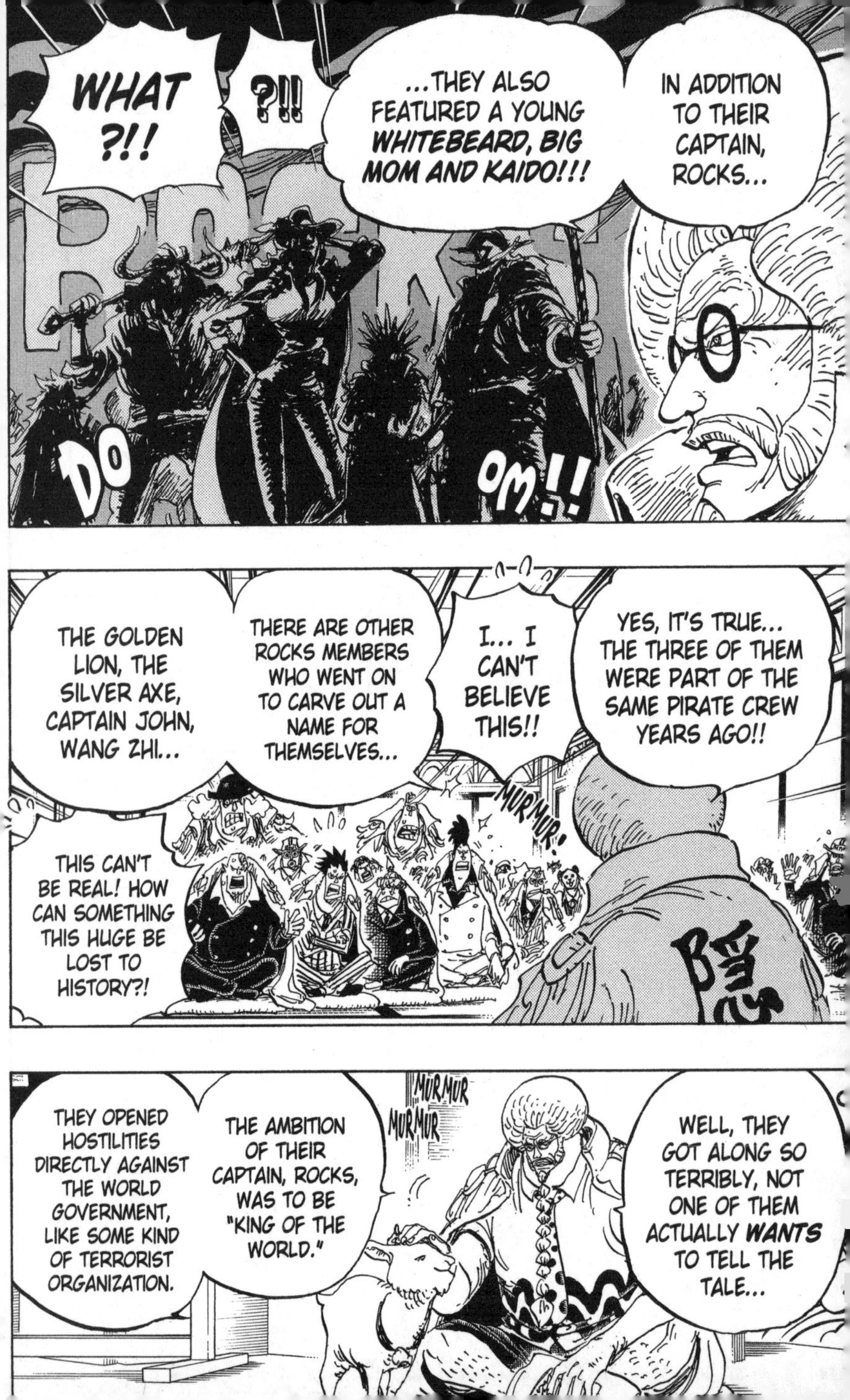

IN ADDITION TO THEIR CAPTAIN, ROCKS...
...THEY ALSO FEATURED A YOUNG **WHITEBEARD, BIG MOM AND KAIDO!!!**
?!!
WHAT ?!!
DOOM!!
YES, IT'S TRUE... THE THREE OF THEM WERE PART OF THE SAME PIRATE CREW YEARS AGO!!
I... I CAN'T BELIEVE THIS!!
MURMUR
THERE ARE OTHER ROCKS MEMBERS WHO WENT ON TO CARVE OUT A NAME FOR THEMSELVES...
THE GOLDEN LION, THE SILVER AXE, CAPTAIN JOHN, WANG ZHI...
THIS CAN'T BE REAL! HOW CAN SOMETHING THIS HUGE BE LOST TO HISTORY?!
WELL, THEY GOT ALONG SO TERRIBLY, NOT ONE OF THEM ACTUALLY ***WANTS*** TO TELL THE TALE...
MURMUR
MURMUR
THE AMBITION OF THEIR CAPTAIN, ROCKS, WAS TO BE "KING OF THE WORLD."
THEY OPENED HOSTILITIES DIRECTLY AGAINST THE WORLD GOVERNMENT, LIKE SOME KIND OF TERRORIST ORGANIZATION.

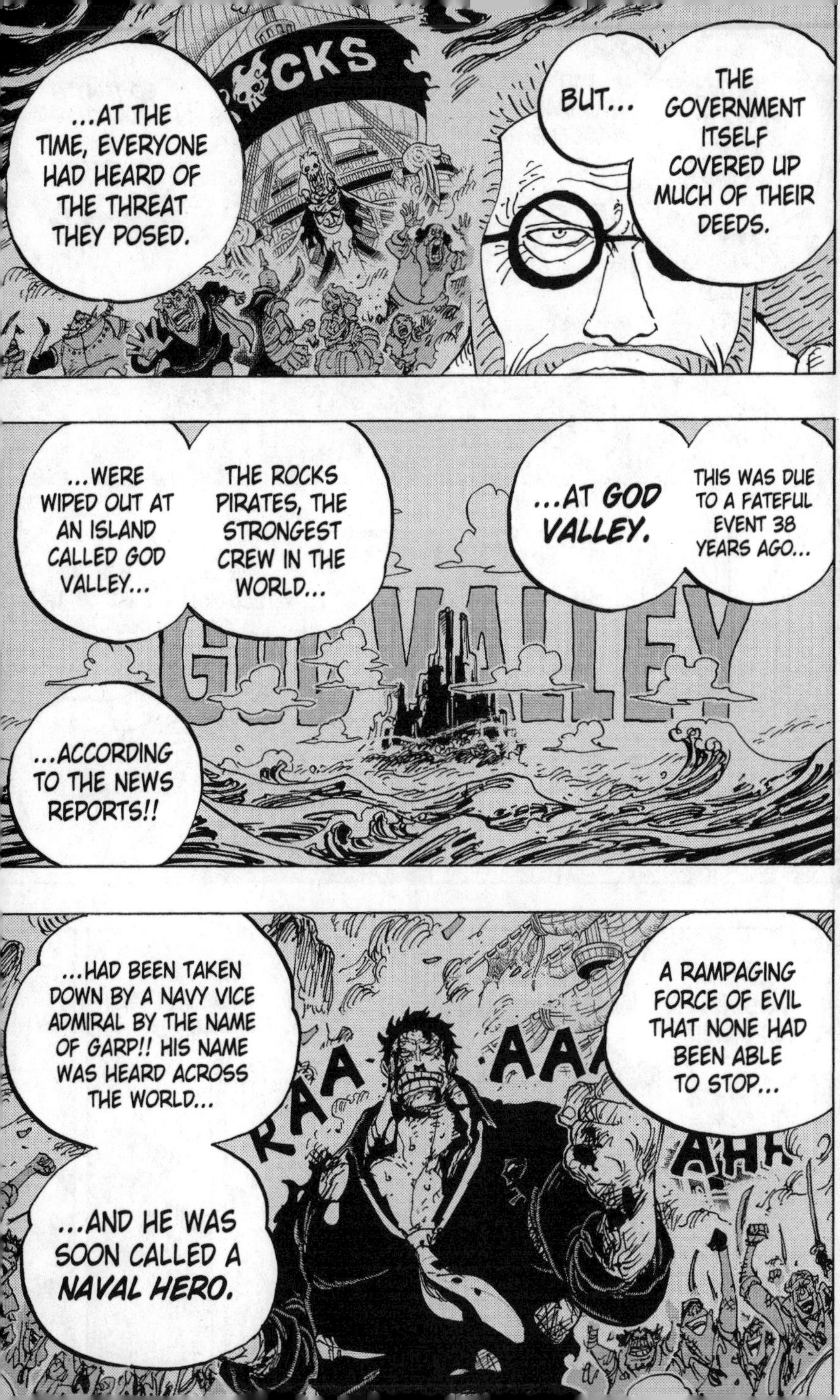
BUT... THE GOVERNMENT ITSELF COVERED UP MUCH OF THEIR DEEDS.
...AT THE TIME, EVERYONE HAD HEARD OF THE THREAT THEY POSED.
THIS WAS DUE TO A FATEFUL EVENT 38 YEARS AGO...
...AT ***GOD VALLEY.***
THE ROCKS PIRATES, THE STRONGEST CREW IN THE WORLD...
...WERE WIPED OUT AT AN ISLAND CALLED GOD VALLEY...
...ACCORDING TO THE NEWS REPORTS!!
A RAMPAGING FORCE OF EVIL THAT NONE HAD BEEN ABLE TO STOP...
...HAD BEEN TAKEN DOWN BY A NAVY VICE ADMIRAL BY THE NAME OF GARP!! HIS NAME WAS HEARD ACROSS THE WORLD...
...AND HE WAS SOON CALLED A ***NAVAL HERO.***

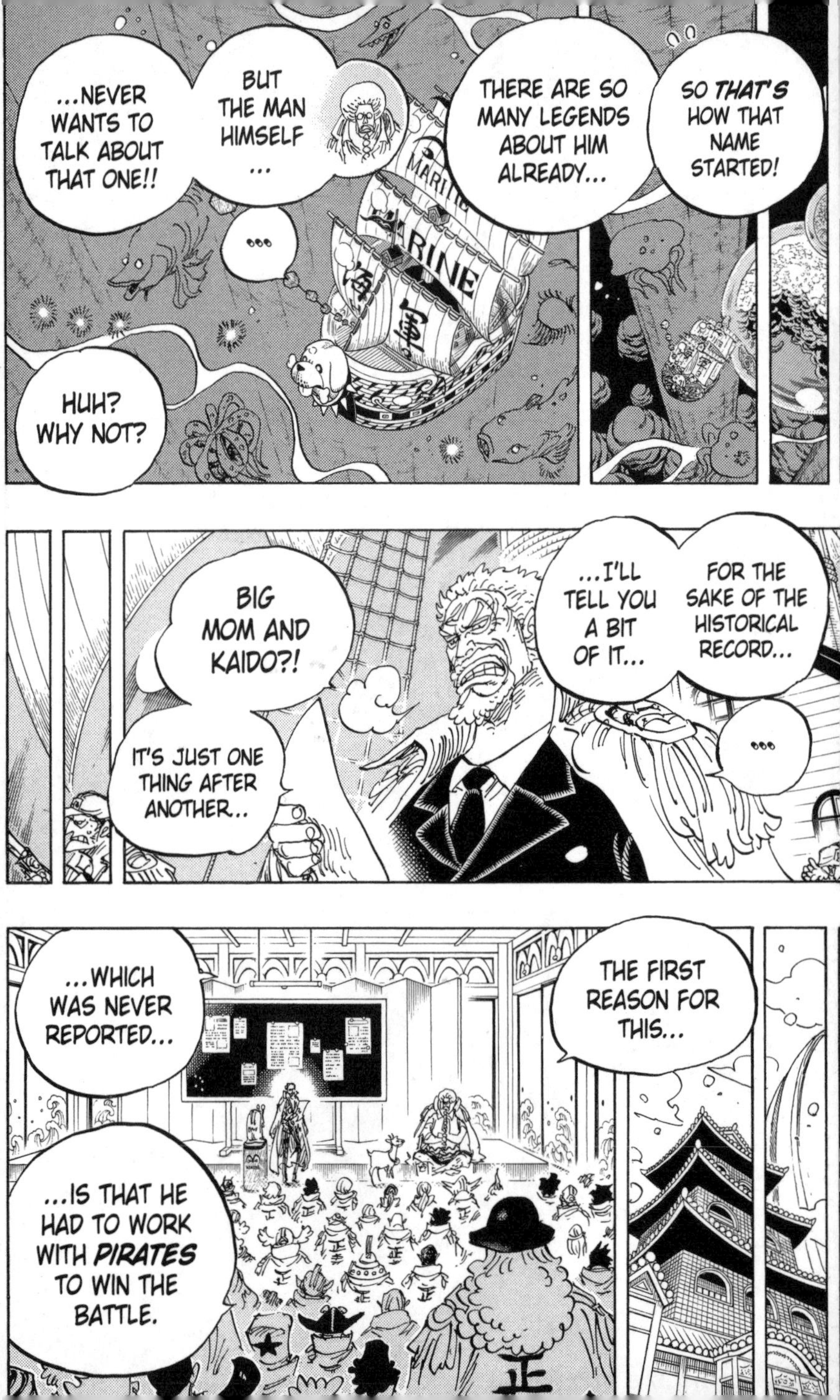
SO *THAT'S* HOW THAT NAME STARTED!
THERE ARE SO MANY LEGENDS ABOUT HIM ALREADY...
BUT THE MAN HIMSELF ...
...NEVER WANTS TO TALK ABOUT THAT ONE!!
...
HUH? WHY NOT?
FOR THE SAKE OF THE HISTORICAL RECORD...
...I'LL TELL YOU A BIT OF IT...
...
BIG MOM AND KAIDO?!
IT'S JUST ONE THING AFTER ANOTHER...
THE FIRST REASON FOR THIS...
...WHICH WAS NEVER REPORTED...
...IS THAT HE HAD TO WORK WITH *PIRATES* TO WIN THE BATTLE.

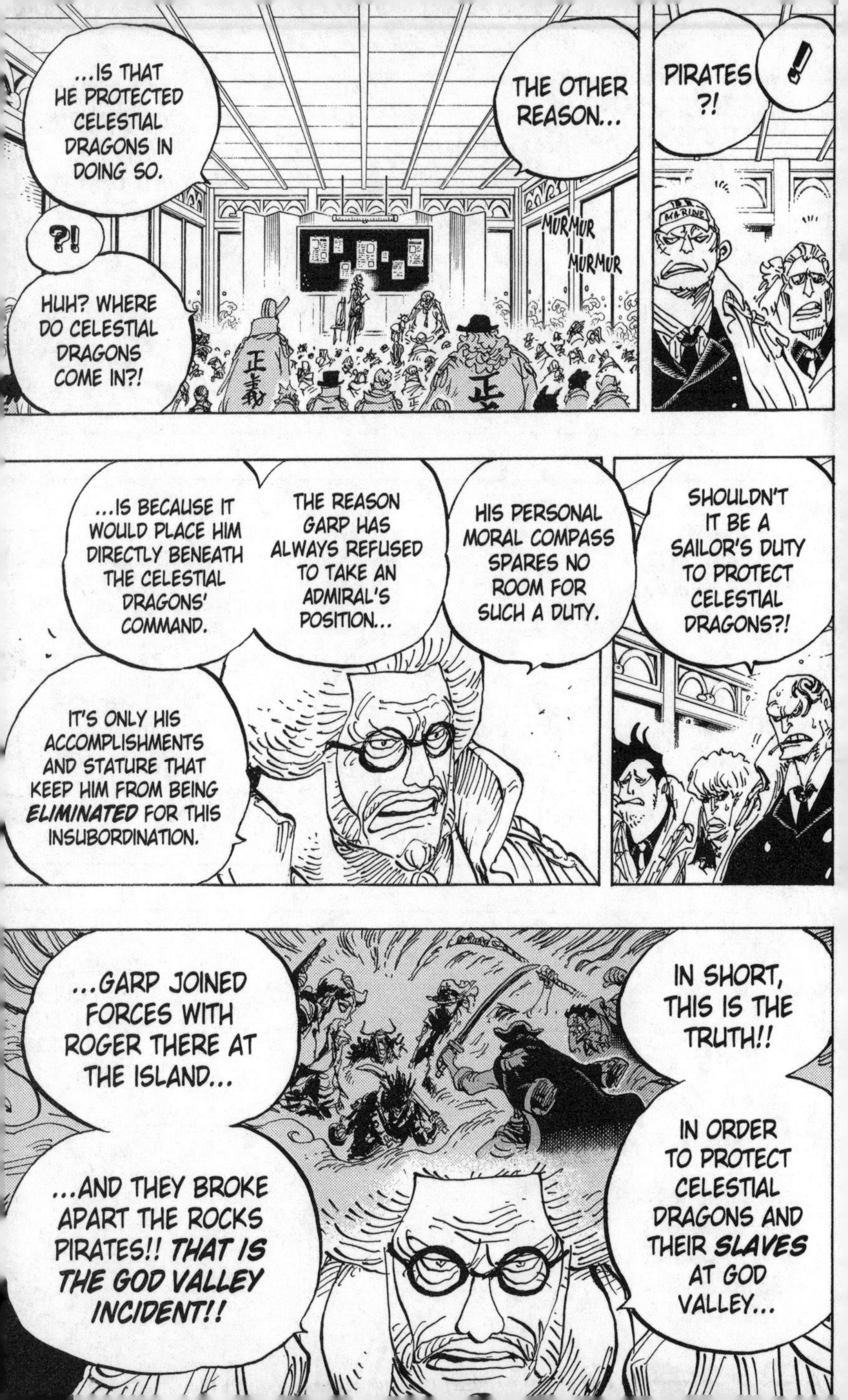
PIRATES ?!
!
THE OTHER REASON...
...IS THAT HE PROTECTED CELESTIAL DRAGONS IN DOING SO.
MURMUR
MURMUR
?!
HUH? WHERE DO CELESTIAL DRAGONS COME IN?!
SHOULDN'T IT BE A SAILOR'S DUTY TO PROTECT CELESTIAL DRAGONS?!
HIS PERSONAL MORAL COMPASS SPARES NO ROOM FOR SUCH A DUTY.
THE REASON GARP HAS ALWAYS REFUSED TO TAKE AN ADMIRAL'S POSITION...
...IS BECAUSE IT WOULD PLACE HIM DIRECTLY BENEATH THE CELESTIAL DRAGONS' COMMAND.
IT'S ONLY HIS ACCOMPLISHMENTS AND STATURE THAT KEEP HIM FROM BEING *ELIMINATED* FOR THIS INSUBORDINATION.
IN SHORT, THIS IS THE TRUTH!!
IN ORDER TO PROTECT CELESTIAL DRAGONS AND THEIR *SLAVES* AT GOD VALLEY...
...GARP JOINED FORCES WITH ROGER THERE AT THE ISLAND...
...AND THEY BROKE APART THE ROCKS PIRATES!! *THAT IS THE GOD VALLEY INCIDENT!!*

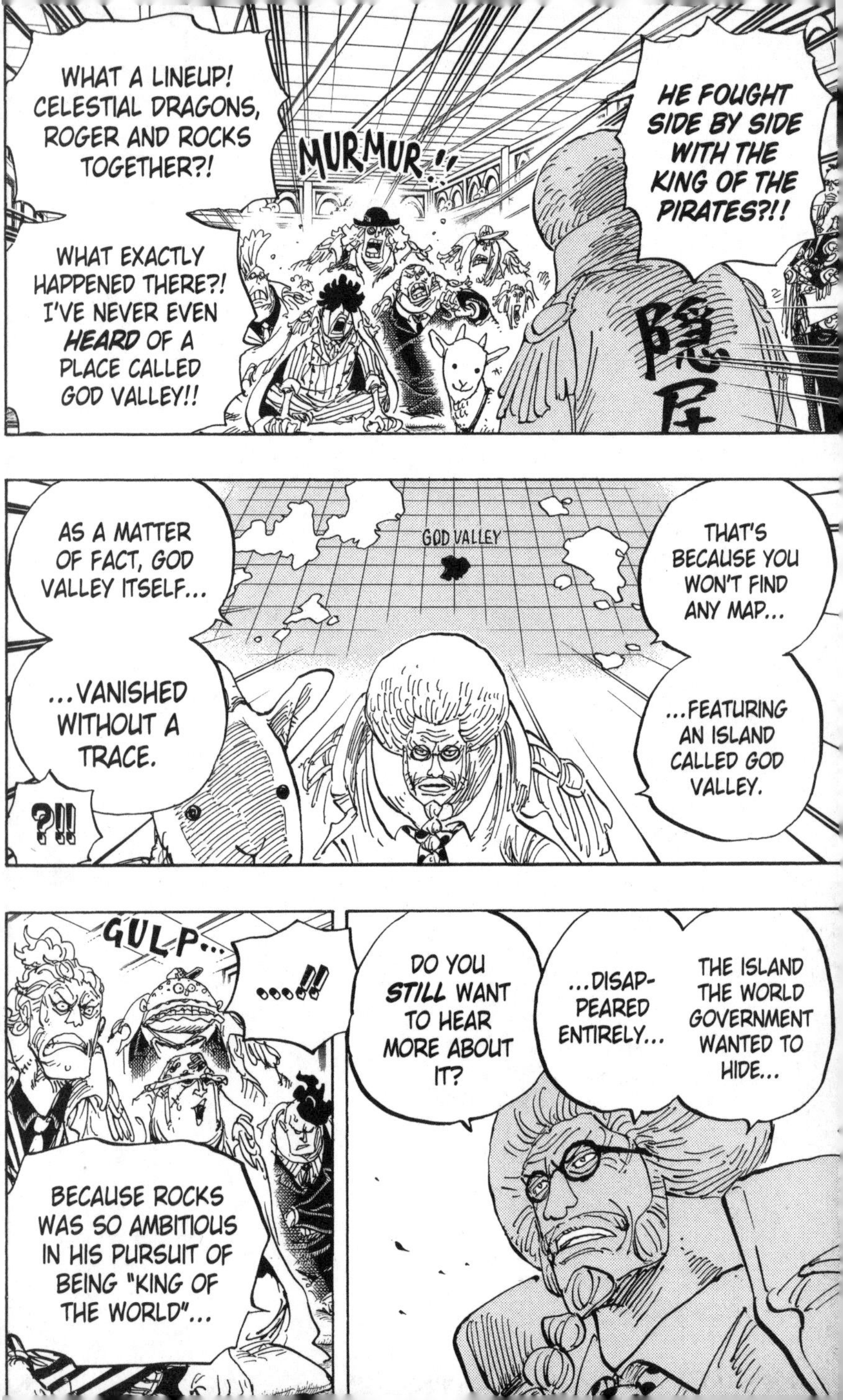
HE FOUGHT SIDE BY SIDE WITH THE KING OF THE PIRATES?!!
隠
MURMUR..
WHAT A LINEUP! CELESTIAL DRAGONS, ROGER AND ROCKS TOGETHER?!
WHAT EXACTLY HAPPENED THERE?! I'VE NEVER EVEN HEARD OF A PLACE CALLED GOD VALLEY!!
THAT'S BECAUSE YOU WON'T FIND ANY MAP...
...FEATURING AN ISLAND CALLED GOD VALLEY.
GOD VALLEY
AS A MATTER OF FACT, GOD VALLEY ITSELF...
...VANISHED WITHOUT A TRACE.
?!!
THE ISLAND THE WORLD GOVERNMENT WANTED TO HIDE...
...DISAP-PEARED ENTIRELY...
DO YOU STILL WANT TO HEAR MORE ABOUT IT?
....!!
GULP...
BECAUSE ROCKS WAS SO AMBITIOUS IN HIS PURSUIT OF BEING "KING OF THE WORLD"...

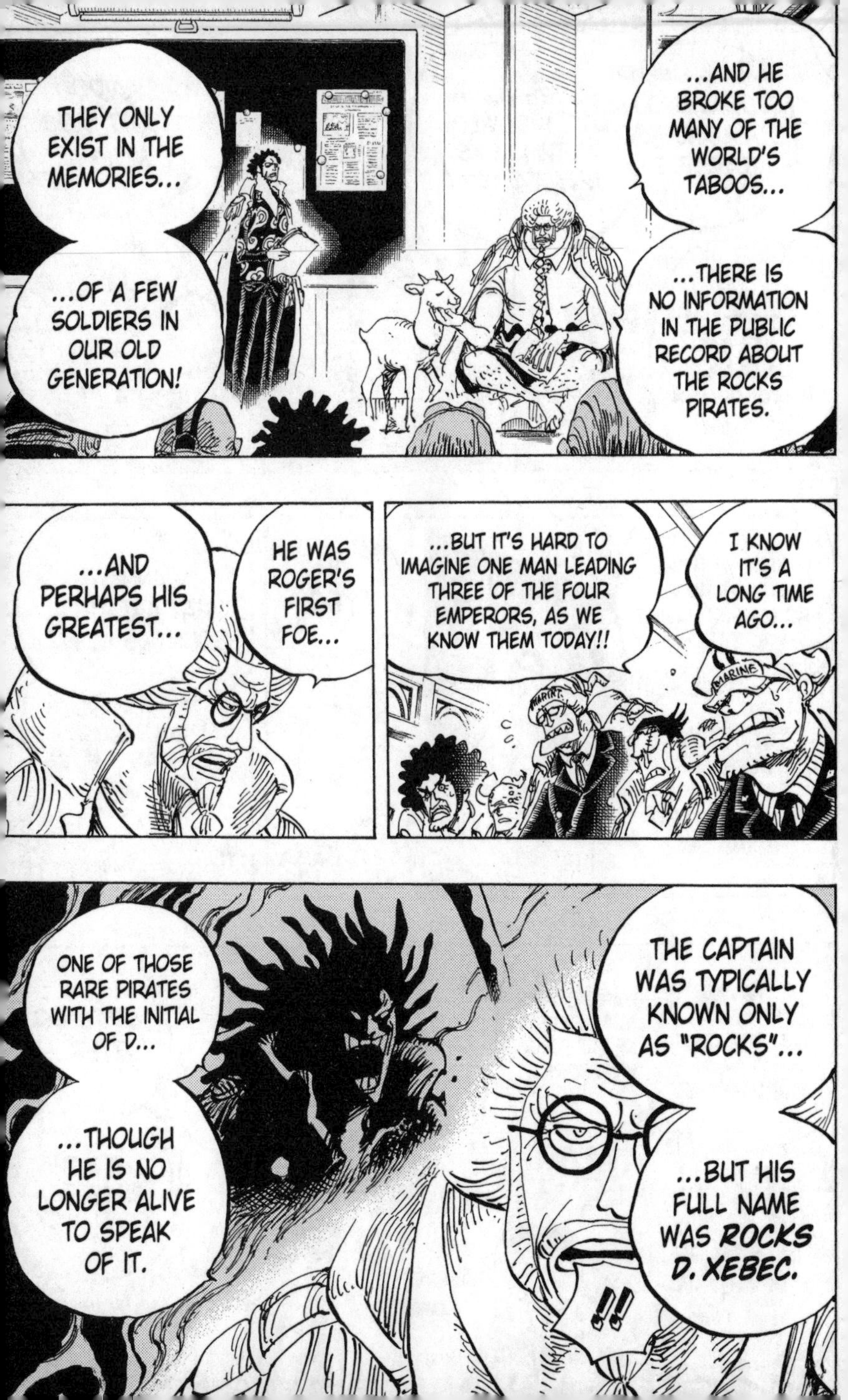
...AND HE BROKE TOO MANY OF THE WORLD'S TABOOS...
...THERE IS NO INFORMATION IN THE PUBLIC RECORD ABOUT THE ROCKS PIRATES.
THEY ONLY EXIST IN THE MEMORIES...
...OF A FEW SOLDIERS IN OUR OLD GENERATION!
I KNOW IT'S A LONG TIME AGO...
...BUT IT'S HARD TO IMAGINE ONE MAN LEADING THREE OF THE FOUR EMPERORS, AS WE KNOW THEM TODAY!!
MARINE
HE WAS ROGER'S FIRST FOE...
...AND PERHAPS HIS GREATEST...
THE CAPTAIN WAS TYPICALLY KNOWN ONLY AS "ROCKS"...
...BUT HIS FULL NAME WAS *ROCKS D. XEBEC.*
!!
ONE OF THOSE RARE PIRATES WITH THE INITIAL OF D...
...THOUGH HE IS NO LONGER ALIVE TO SPEAK OF IT.

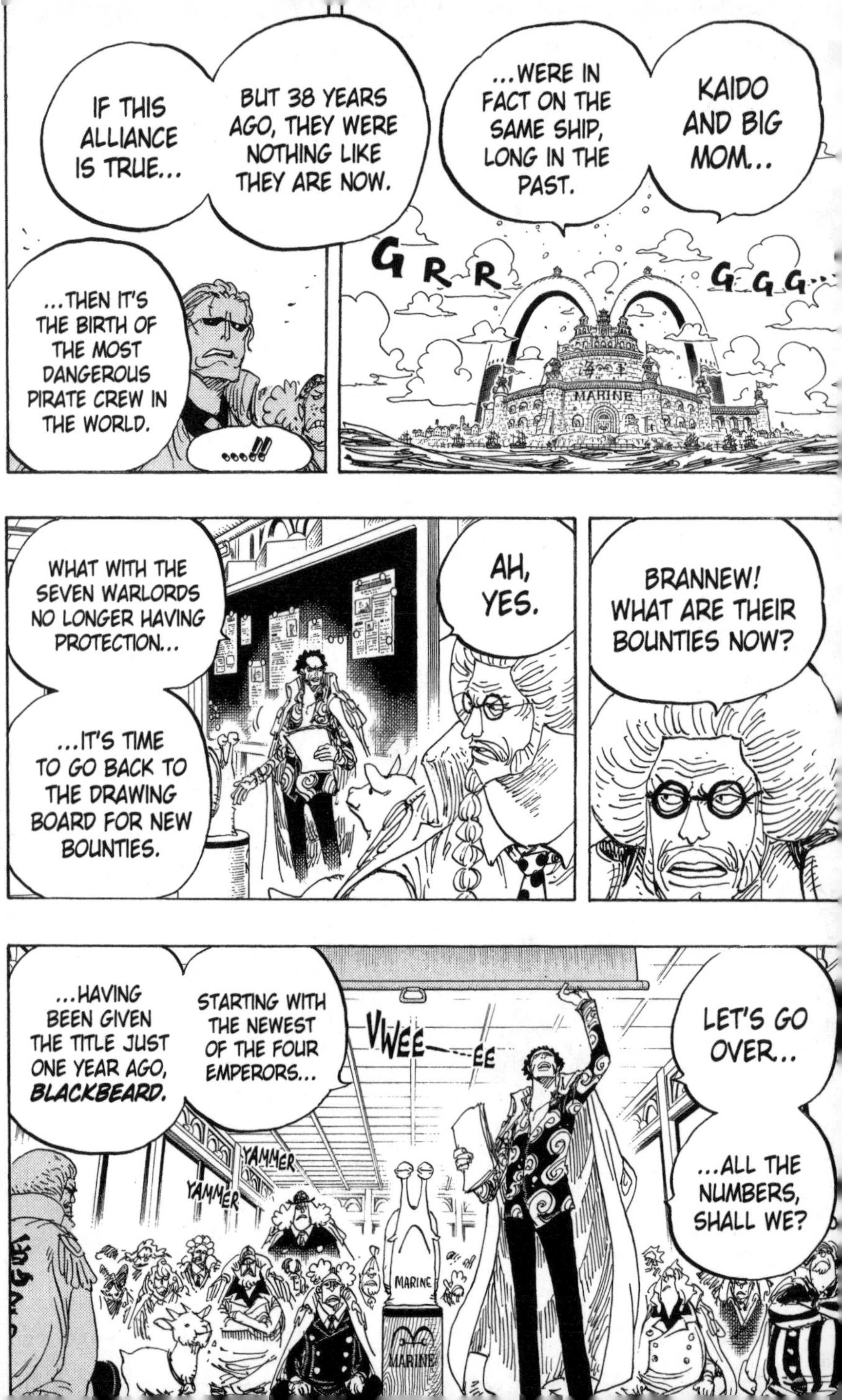
KAIDO AND BIG MOM...
...WERE IN FACT ON THE SAME SHIP, LONG IN THE PAST.
GRR
GGG...
MARINE
BUT 38 YEARS AGO, THEY WERE NOTHING LIKE THEY ARE NOW.
IF THIS ALLIANCE IS TRUE...
...THEN IT'S THE BIRTH OF THE MOST DANGEROUS PIRATE CREW IN THE WORLD.
....!!
BRANNEW! WHAT ARE THEIR BOUNTIES NOW?
AH, YES.
WHAT WITH THE SEVEN WARLORDS NO LONGER HAVING PROTECTION...
...IT'S TIME TO GO BACK TO THE DRAWING BOARD FOR NEW BOUNTIES.
LET'S GO OVER...
...ALL THE NUMBERS, SHALL WE?
VWEE--EE
STARTING WITH THE NEWEST OF THE FOUR EMPERORS...
...HAVING BEEN GIVEN THE TITLE JUST ONE YEAR AGO, *BLACKBEARD.*
YAMMER
YAMMER
MARINE
MARINE

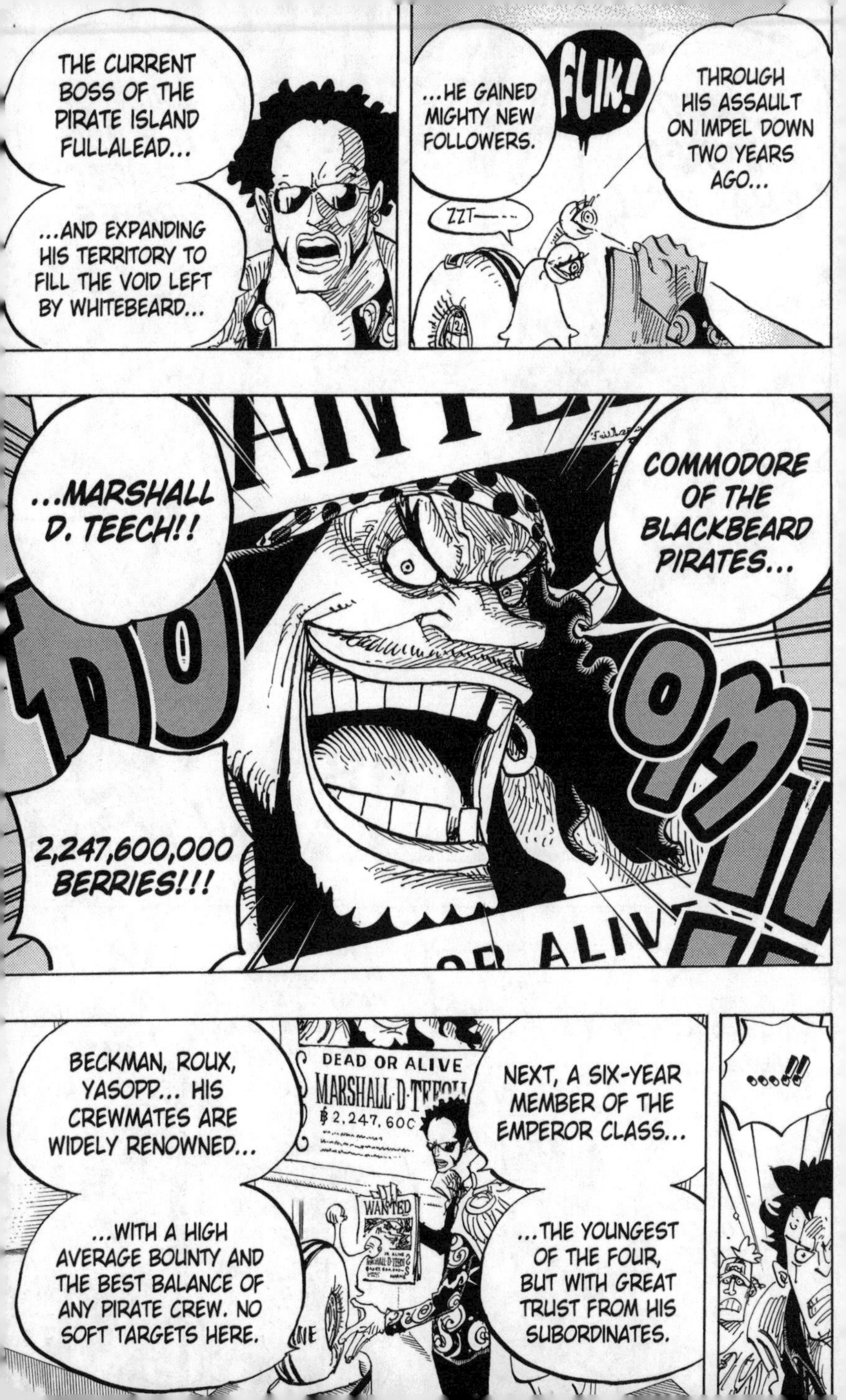
THROUGH HIS ASSAULT ON IMPEL DOWN TWO YEARS AGO...
FLIK!
...HE GAINED MIGHTY NEW FOLLOWERS.
ZZT---
THE CURRENT BOSS OF THE PIRATE ISLAND FULLALEAD...
...AND EXPANDING HIS TERRITORY TO FILL THE VOID LEFT BY WHITEBEARD...
COMMODORE OF THE BLACKBEARD PIRATES...
...MARSHALL D. TEECH!!
2,247,600,000 BERRIES!!!
...!!
NEXT, A SIX-YEAR MEMBER OF THE EMPEROR CLASS...
...THE YOUNGEST OF THE FOUR, BUT WITH GREAT TRUST FROM HIS SUBORDINATES.
DEAD OR ALIVE
WANTED
BECKMAN, ROUX, YASOPP... HIS CREWMATES ARE WIDELY RENOWNED...
...WITH A HIGH AVERAGE BOUNTY AND THE BEST BALANCE OF ANY PIRATE CREW. NO SOFT TARGETS HERE.

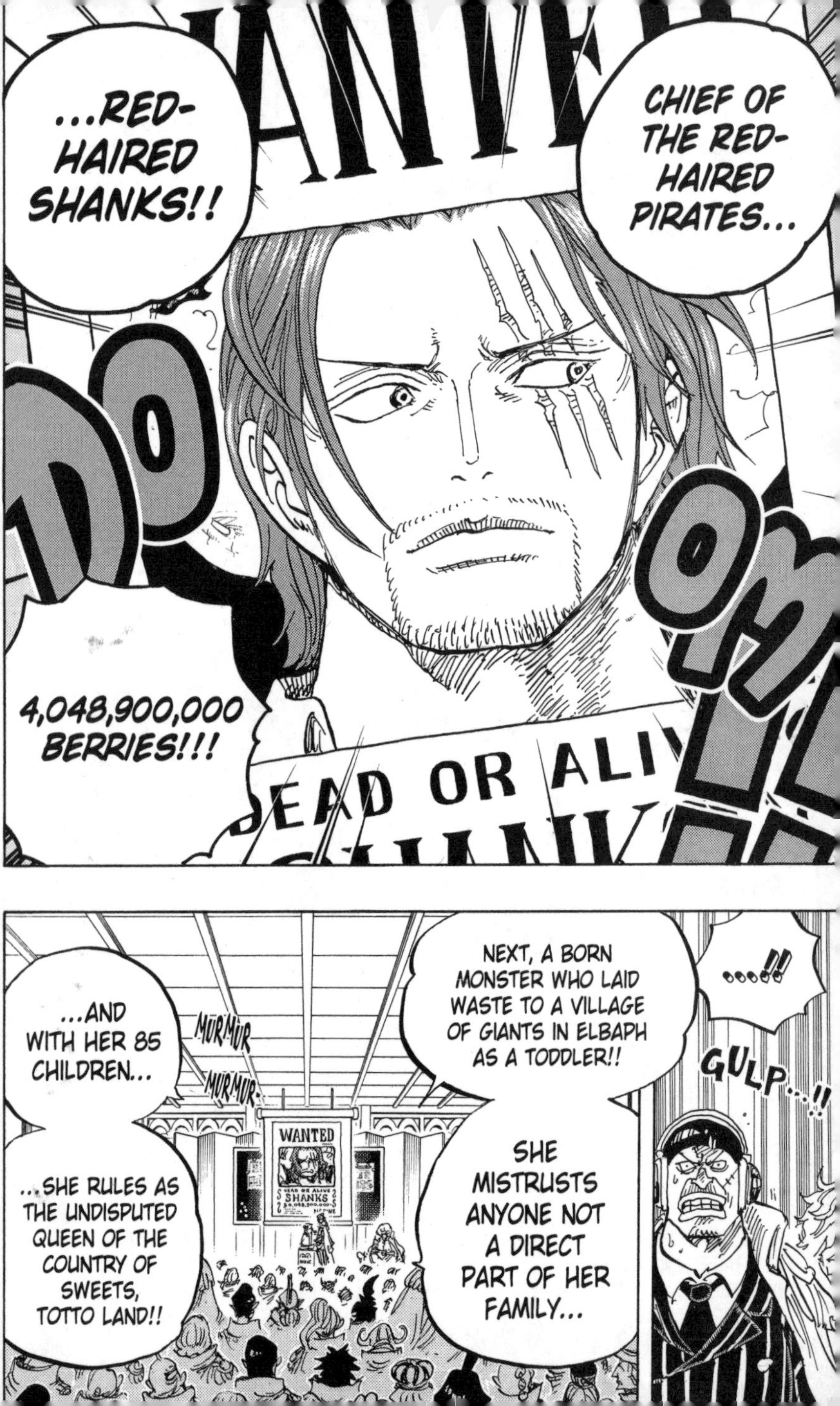
CHIEF OF THE RED-HAIRED PIRATES...
...RED-HAIRED SHANKS!!
4,048,900,000 BERRIES!!!
....!!
GULP...!!
NEXT, A BORN MONSTER WHO LAID WASTE TO A VILLAGE OF GIANTS IN ELBAPH AS A TODDLER!!
SHE MISTRUSTS ANYONE NOT A DIRECT PART OF HER FAMILY...
MURMUR
MURMUR
WANTED
SHANKS
...AND WITH HER 85 CHILDREN...
...SHE RULES AS THE UNDISPUTED QUEEN OF THE COUNTRY OF SWEETS, TOTTO LAND!!

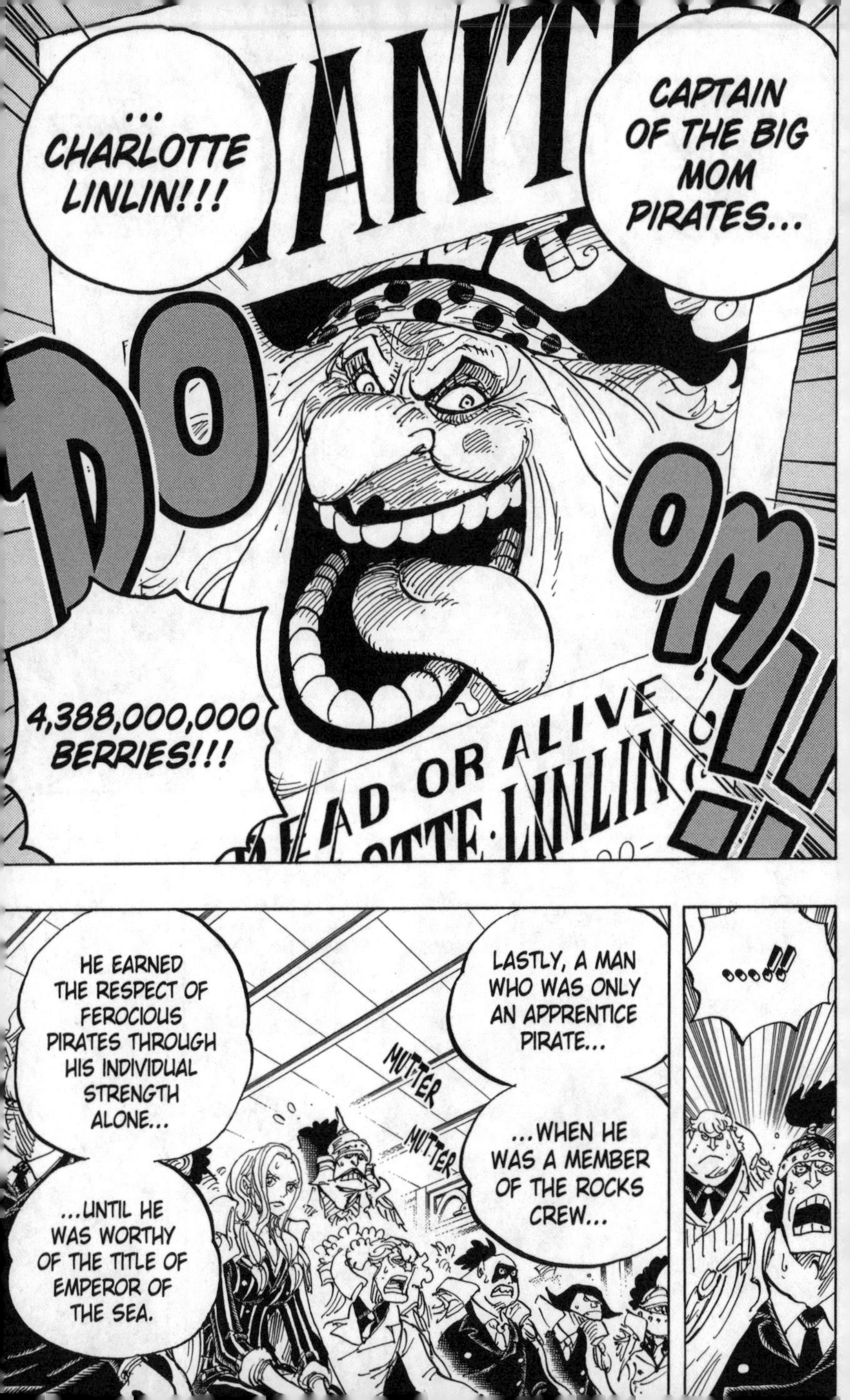
CAPTAIN OF THE BIG MOM PIRATES...
...CHARLOTTE LINLIN!!!
DOOM!!
4,388,000,000 BERRIES!!!
....!!
LASTLY, A MAN WHO WAS ONLY AN APPRENTICE PIRATE...
...WHEN HE WAS A MEMBER OF THE ROCKS CREW...
MUTTER
MUTTER
HE EARNED THE RESPECT OF FEROCIOUS PIRATES THROUGH HIS INDIVIDUAL STRENGTH ALONE...
...UNTIL HE WAS WORTHY OF THE TITLE OF EMPEROR OF THE SEA.

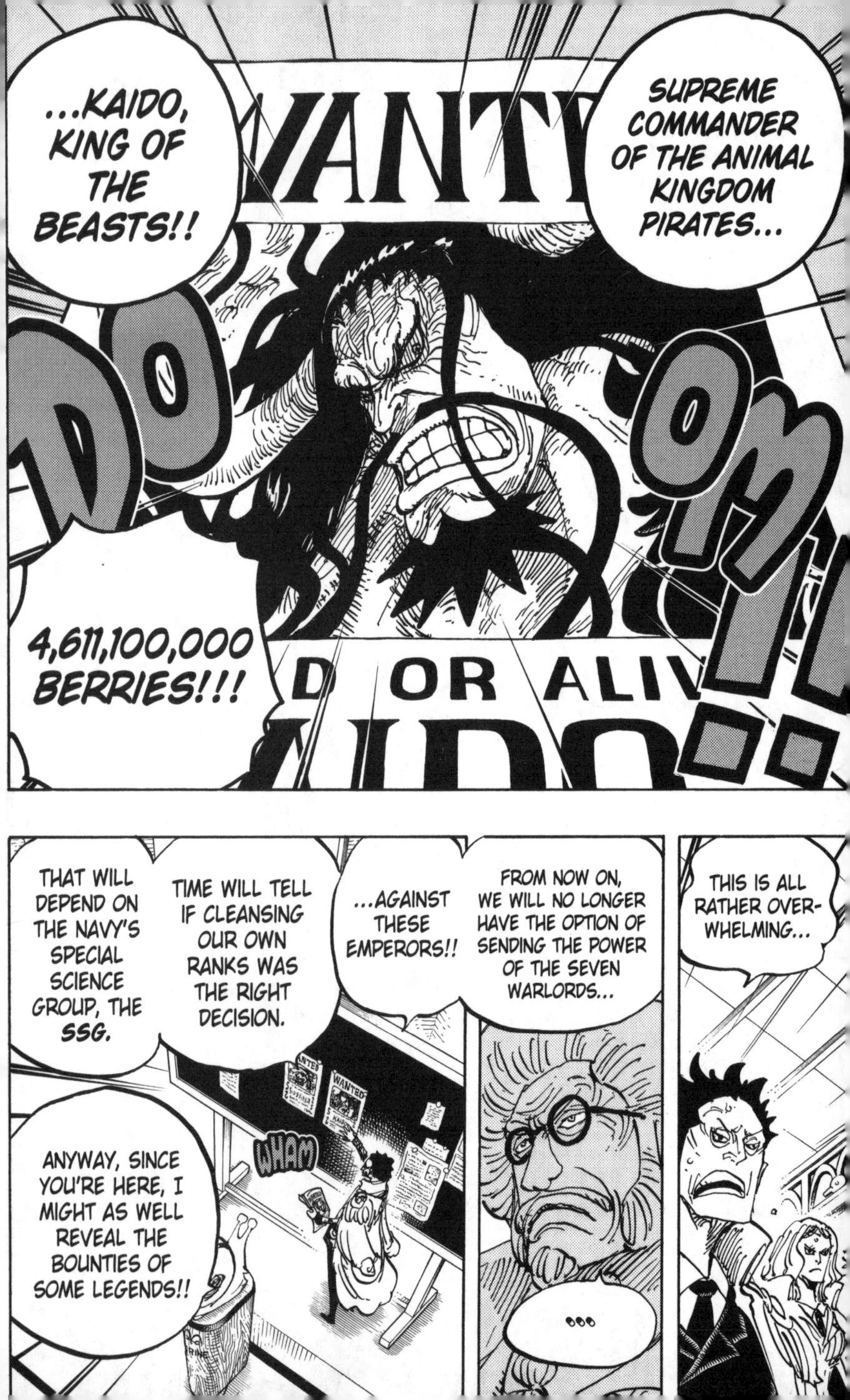
SUPREME COMMANDER OF THE ANIMAL KINGDOM PIRATES...
...KAIDO, KING OF THE BEASTS!!
DO OM
4,611,100,000 BERRIES!!!
THIS IS ALL RATHER OVER-WHELMING...
FROM NOW ON, WE WILL NO LONGER HAVE THE OPTION OF SENDING THE POWER OF THE SEVEN WARLORDS...
...AGAINST THESE EMPERORS!!
...
TIME WILL TELL IF CLEANSING OUR OWN RANKS WAS THE RIGHT DECISION.
THAT WILL DEPEND ON THE NAVY'S SPECIAL SCIENCE GROUP, THE SSG.
WHAM
ANYWAY, SINCE YOU'RE HERE, I MIGHT AS WELL REVEAL THE BOUNTIES OF SOME LEGENDS!!

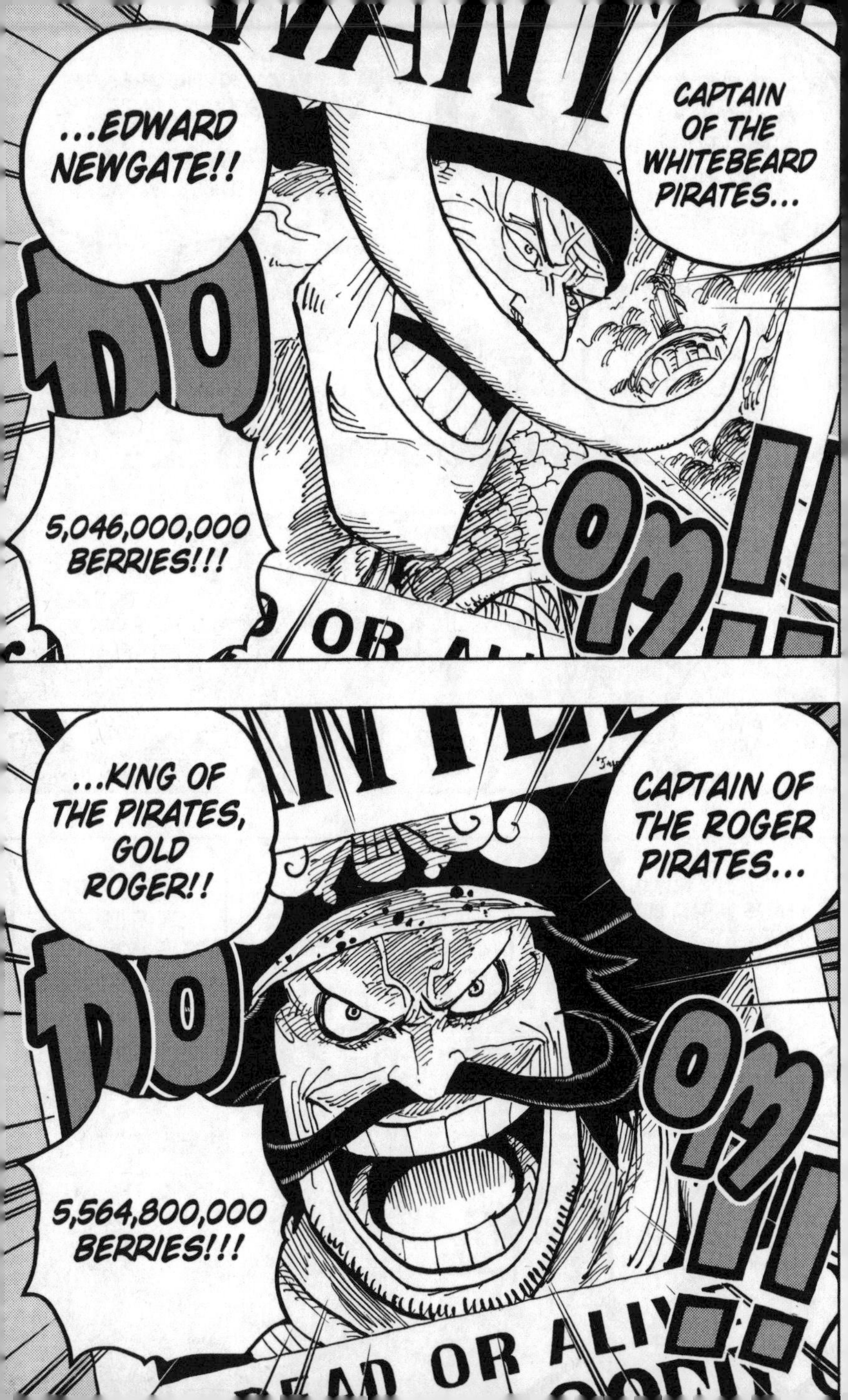
CAPTAIN OF THE WHITEBEARD PIRATES...
...EDWARD NEWGATE!!
DO
OM!!
5,046,000,000 BERRIES!!!
CAPTAIN OF THE ROGER PIRATES...
...KING OF THE PIRATES, GOLD ROGER!!
DO
OM!!
5,564,800,000 BERRIES!!!

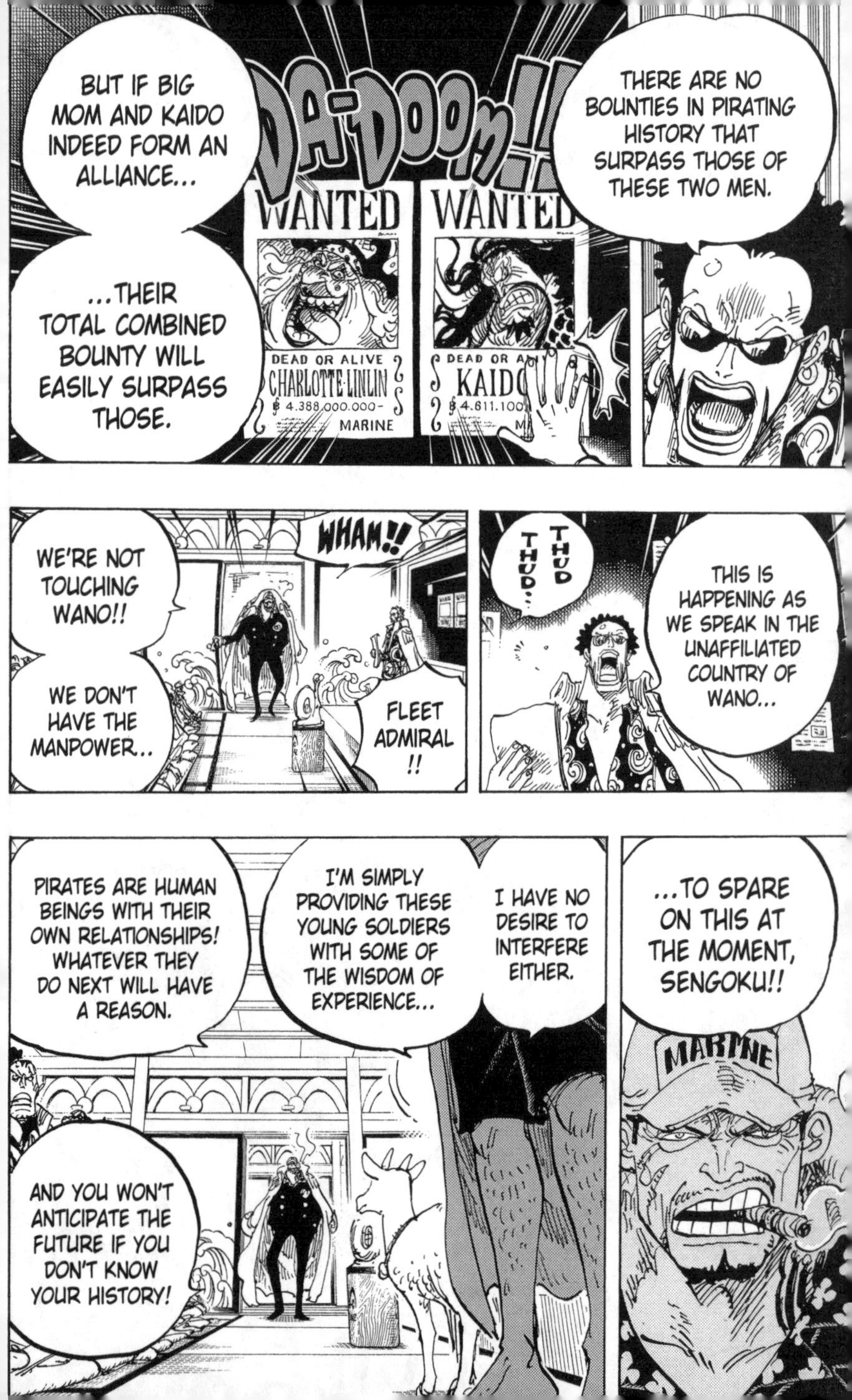
THERE ARE NO BOUNTIES IN PIRATING HISTORY THAT SURPASS THOSE OF THESE TWO MEN.
DA-DOOM!!
WANTED
DEAD OR ALIVE
CHARLOTTE LINLIN
฿4.388.000.000-
MARINE
WANTED
DEAD OR A
KAIDO
฿4.611.100
BUT IF BIG MOM AND KAIDO INDEED FORM AN ALLIANCE...
...THEIR TOTAL COMBINED BOUNTY WILL EASILY SURPASS THOSE.
THUD
THUD..
THIS IS HAPPENING AS WE SPEAK IN THE UNAFFILIATED COUNTRY OF WANO...
WHAM!!
FLEET ADMIRAL!!
WE'RE NOT TOUCHING WANO!!
WE DON'T HAVE THE MANPOWER..
...TO SPARE ON THIS AT THE MOMENT, SENGOKU!!
MARINE
I HAVE NO DESIRE TO INTERFERE EITHER.
I'M SIMPLY PROVIDING THESE YOUNG SOLDIERS WITH SOME OF THE WISDOM OF EXPERIENCE...
PIRATES ARE HUMAN BEINGS WITH THEIR OWN RELATIONSHIPS! WHATEVER THEY DO NEXT WILL HAVE A REASON.
AND YOU WON'T ANTICIPATE THE FUTURE IF YOU DON'T KNOW YOUR HISTORY!

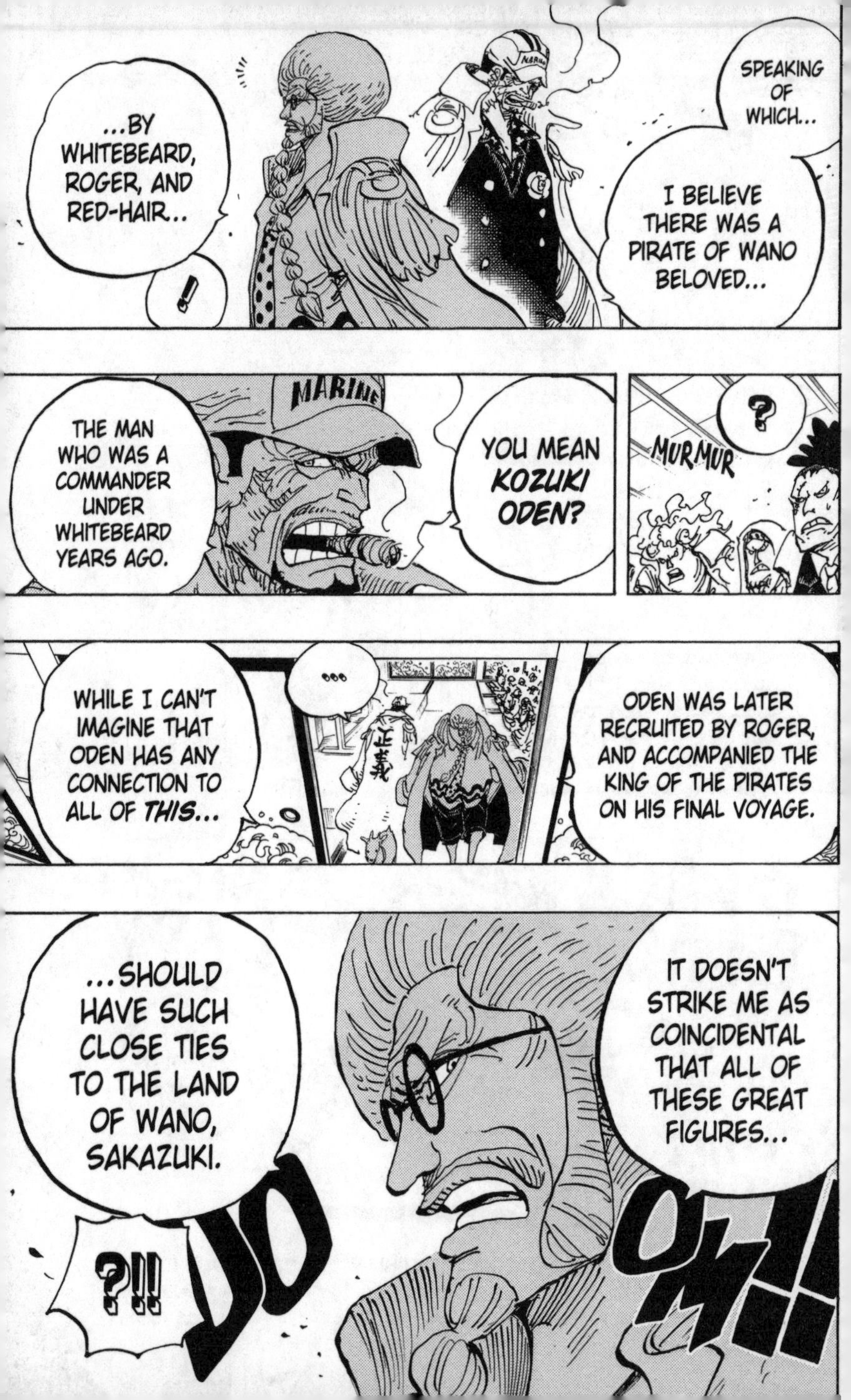
SPEAKING OF WHICH...
I BELIEVE THERE WAS A PIRATE OF WANO BELOVED...
...BY WHITEBEARD, ROGER, AND RED-HAIR...
!
?
MURMUR
YOU MEAN KOZUKI ODEN?
THE MAN WHO WAS A COMMANDER UNDER WHITEBEARD YEARS AGO.
ODEN WAS LATER RECRUITED BY ROGER, AND ACCOMPANIED THE KING OF THE PIRATES ON HIS FINAL VOYAGE.
...
WHILE I CAN'T IMAGINE THAT ODEN HAS ANY CONNECTION TO ALL OF THIS...
IT DOESN'T STRIKE ME AS COINCIDENTAL THAT ALL OF THESE GREAT FIGURES...
...SHOULD HAVE SUCH CLOSE TIES TO THE LAND OF WANO, SAKAZUKI.
DOOM!!
?!!

SBS Question Corner

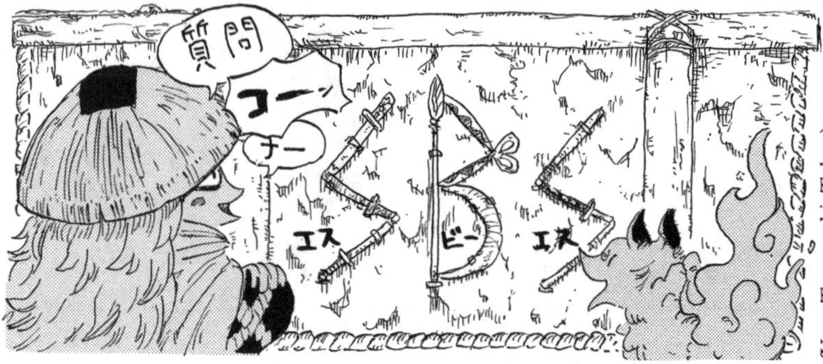
質問
コーー
ナー
エス
ビー
エス

(Yuto Teramachi, Tokyo)

Q: Oda Sensei! I would like to see anthropomorphized versions of Mihawk's black sword "Night" and his cross-shaped knife! The ones you've been drawing are gross! Boooo! So I'm asking you, please, make these weapons look just as cool as Mihawk is! You have to! Promise me!!

--Tokaguhi

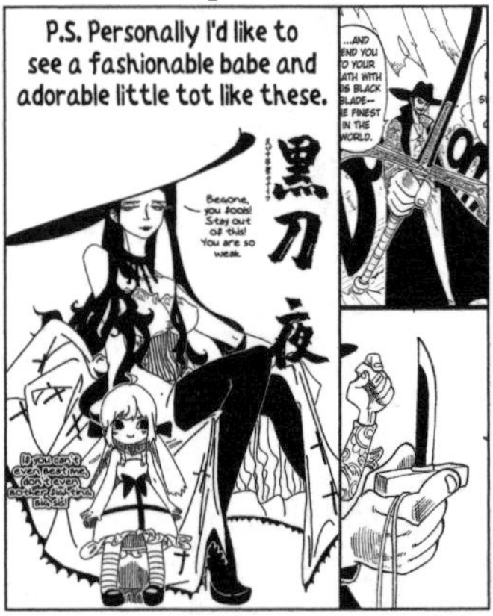
P.S. Personally I'd like to see a fashionable babe and adorable little tot like these.
黒刀
夜
Begone, you fools! Stay out of this! You are so weak.
If you can't even beat me, don't even bother big-time Big sis!

A: Oooh, very nice! Let's just go with that. But you described them so well, it's easy for me to envision. I like that they're women. Got it!!

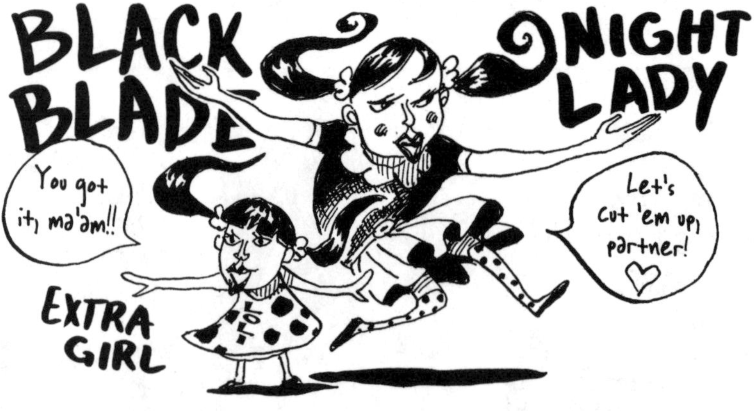
BLACK BLADE
NIGHT LADY
You got it, ma'am!!
Let's cut 'em up, partner! ♡
EXTRA GIRL
LOLI

I've successfully anthropomorphized them! Sorry to flex on you like that with my pro skills, I know that wasn't very mature of me! This will be their official design!

Chapter 958:

THE PROMISED PORT

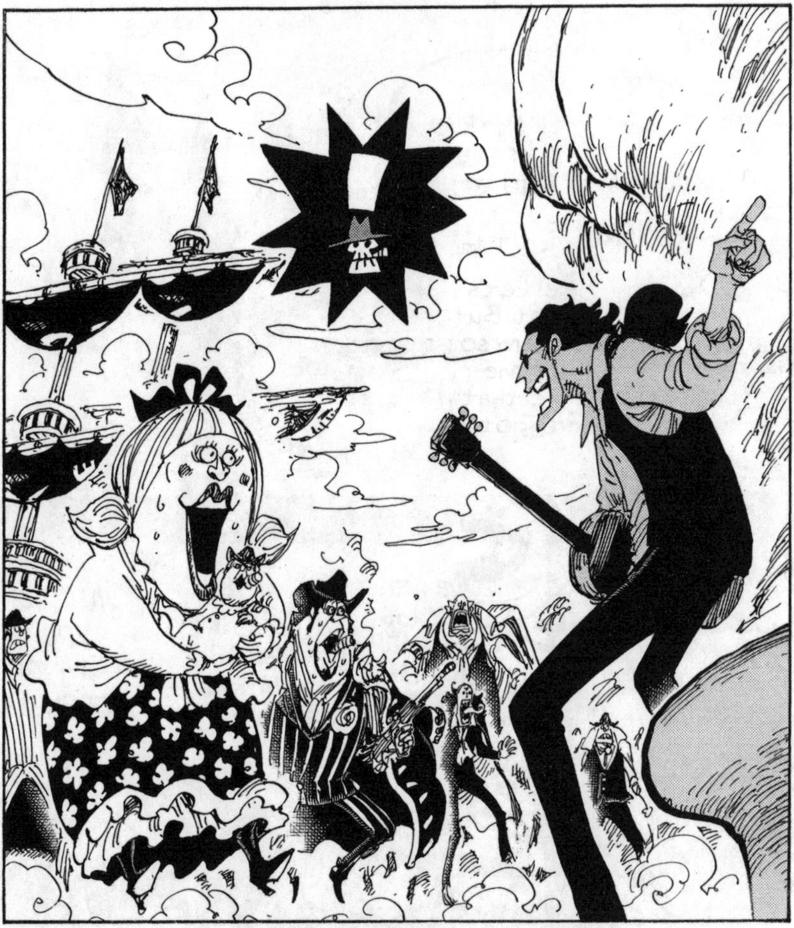

GANG BEGE'S OH MY FAMILY
VOL. 8: "YOU'RE SISTERS?! LOLA WENT TO DRESSROSA A FEW DAYS AGO"

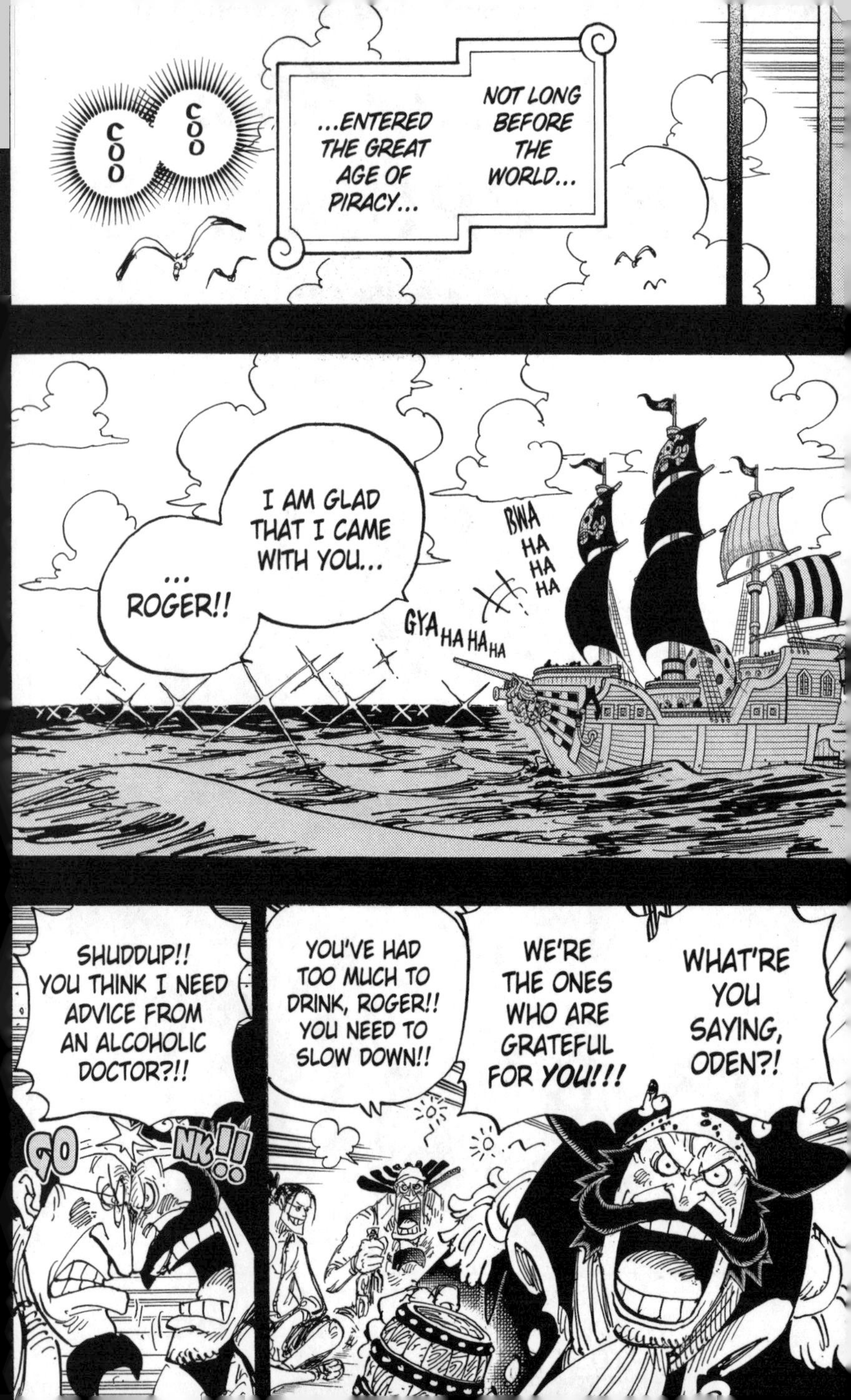
NOT LONG BEFORE THE WORLD...
...ENTERED THE GREAT AGE OF PIRACY...
COO
COO
BWA HA HA HA HA
GYA HA HA HA HA
I AM GLAD THAT I CAME WITH YOU... ...ROGER!!
WHAT'RE YOU SAYING, ODEN?!
WE'RE THE ONES WHO ARE GRATEFUL FOR YOU!!!
YOU'VE HAD TOO MUCH TO DRINK, ROGER!! YOU NEED TO SLOW DOWN!!
SHUDDUP!! YOU THINK I NEED ADVICE FROM AN ALCOHOLIC DOCTOR?!!
GONK!!

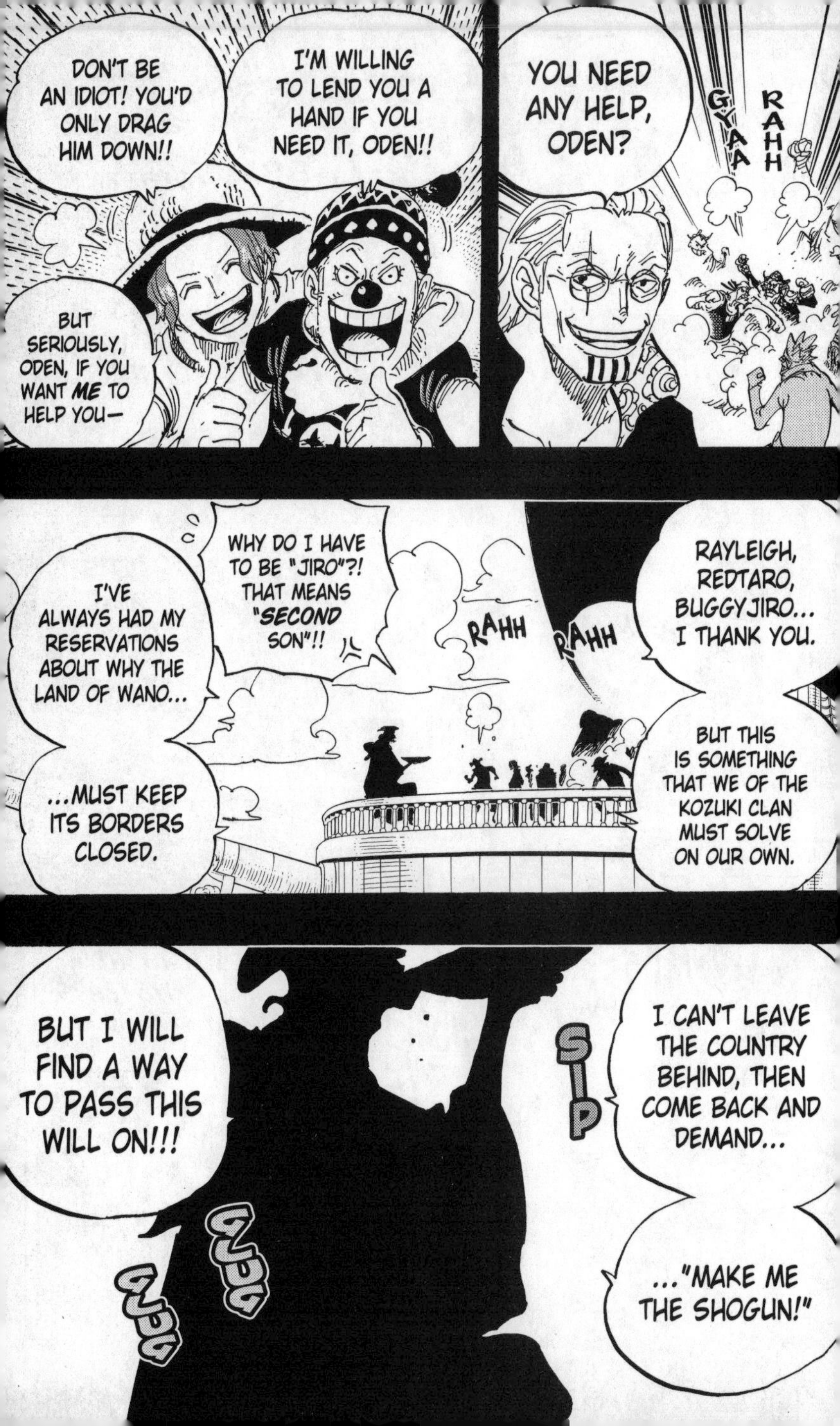
YOU NEED ANY HELP, ODEN?
GYAA
RAHH
I'M WILLING TO LEND YOU A HAND IF YOU NEED IT, ODEN!!
DON'T BE AN IDIOT! YOU'D ONLY DRAG HIM DOWN!!
BUT SERIOUSLY, ODEN, IF YOU WANT *ME* TO HELP YOU—
RAYLEIGH, REDTARO, BUGGYJIRO... I THANK YOU.
BUT THIS IS SOMETHING THAT WE OF THE KOZUKI CLAN MUST SOLVE ON OUR OWN.
RAHH
RAHH
WHY DO I HAVE TO BE "JIRO"?! THAT MEANS "*SECOND* SON"!!
I'VE ALWAYS HAD MY RESERVATIONS ABOUT WHY THE LAND OF WANO...
...MUST KEEP ITS BORDERS CLOSED.
I CAN'T LEAVE THE COUNTRY BEHIND, THEN COME BACK AND DEMAND...
..."MAKE ME THE SHOGUN!"
SIP
GULP
GULP
BUT I WILL FIND A WAY TO PASS THIS WILL ON!!!

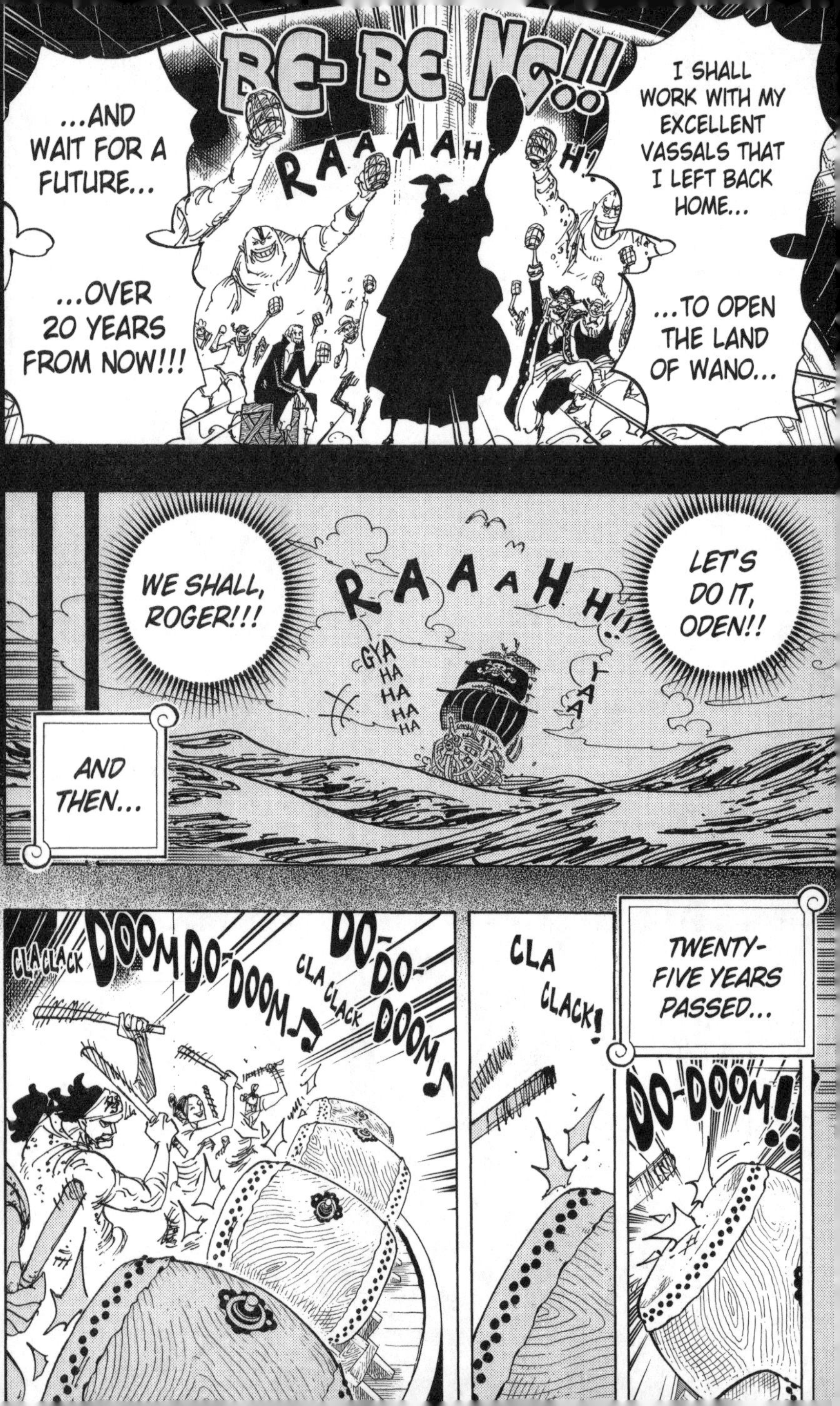
BE-BE NG!!
I SHALL WORK WITH MY EXCELLENT VASSALS THAT I LEFT BACK HOME...
...TO OPEN THE LAND OF WANO...
RAAAAAH
...AND WAIT FOR A FUTURE...
...OVER 20 YEARS FROM NOW!!!
LET'S DO IT, ODEN!!
RAAAAHH!!
WE SHALL, ROGER!!!
GYA HA HA HA HA
AND THEN...
TWENTY-FIVE YEARS PASSED...
CLA CLACK!
DO-DOOM!!
DO-DO-DOOM
CLA CLACK
DOOM DO-DOOM
CLACLACK

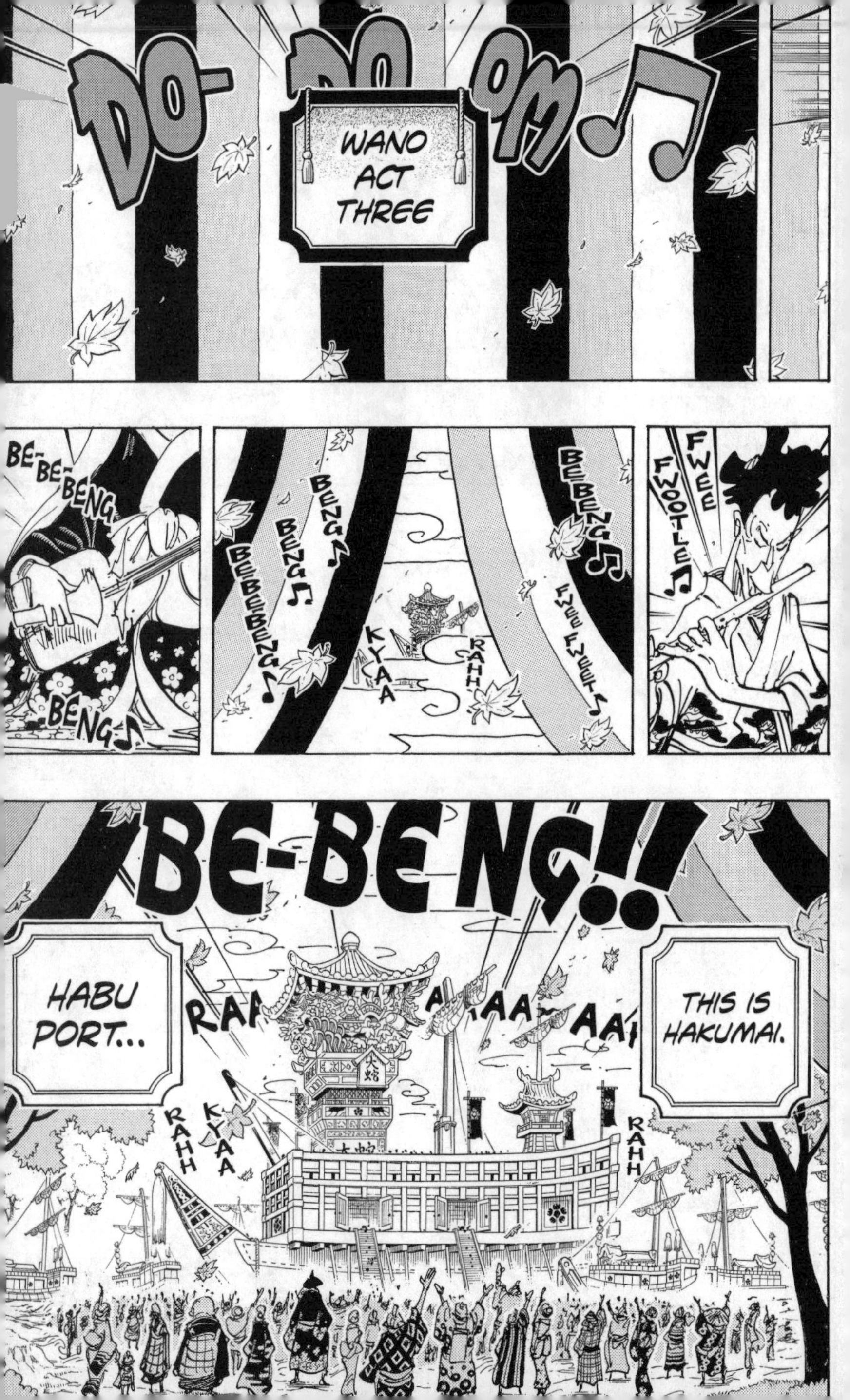
DO-DO-OM♪
WANO ACT THREE
FWEE
FWOOTLE♪
BE-BENG♪
FWEE FWEET♪
RAHH
KYAA
BENG♪
BENG♪
BEBEBENG♪
BE-BE-BENG
BENG♪
BE-BENG!!
THIS IS HAKUMAI.
RAHH
HABU PORT...
KYAA
RAHH

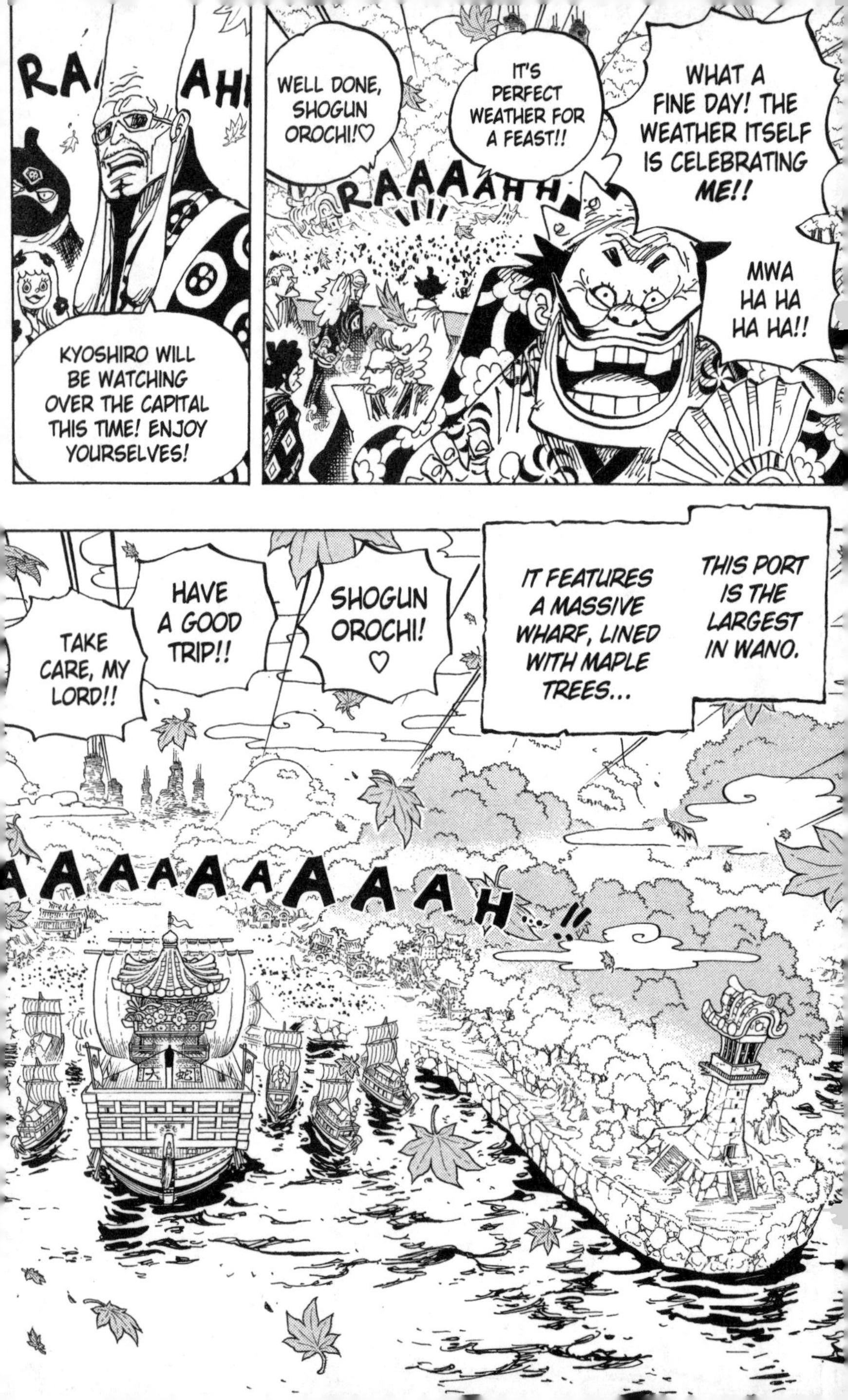
WHAT A FINE DAY! THE WEATHER ITSELF IS CELEBRATING ME!!
MWA HA HA HA HA!!
IT'S PERFECT WEATHER FOR A FEAST!!
WELL DONE, SHOGUN OROCHI!♡
RAAAAHH
RA AH
KYOSHIRO WILL BE WATCHING OVER THE CAPITAL THIS TIME! ENJOY YOURSELVES!
THIS PORT IS THE LARGEST IN WANO.
IT FEATURES A MASSIVE WHARF, LINED WITH MAPLE TREES...
SHOGUN OROCHI! ♡
HAVE A GOOD TRIP!!
TAKE CARE, MY LORD!!
AAAAAAAAAAH...!!

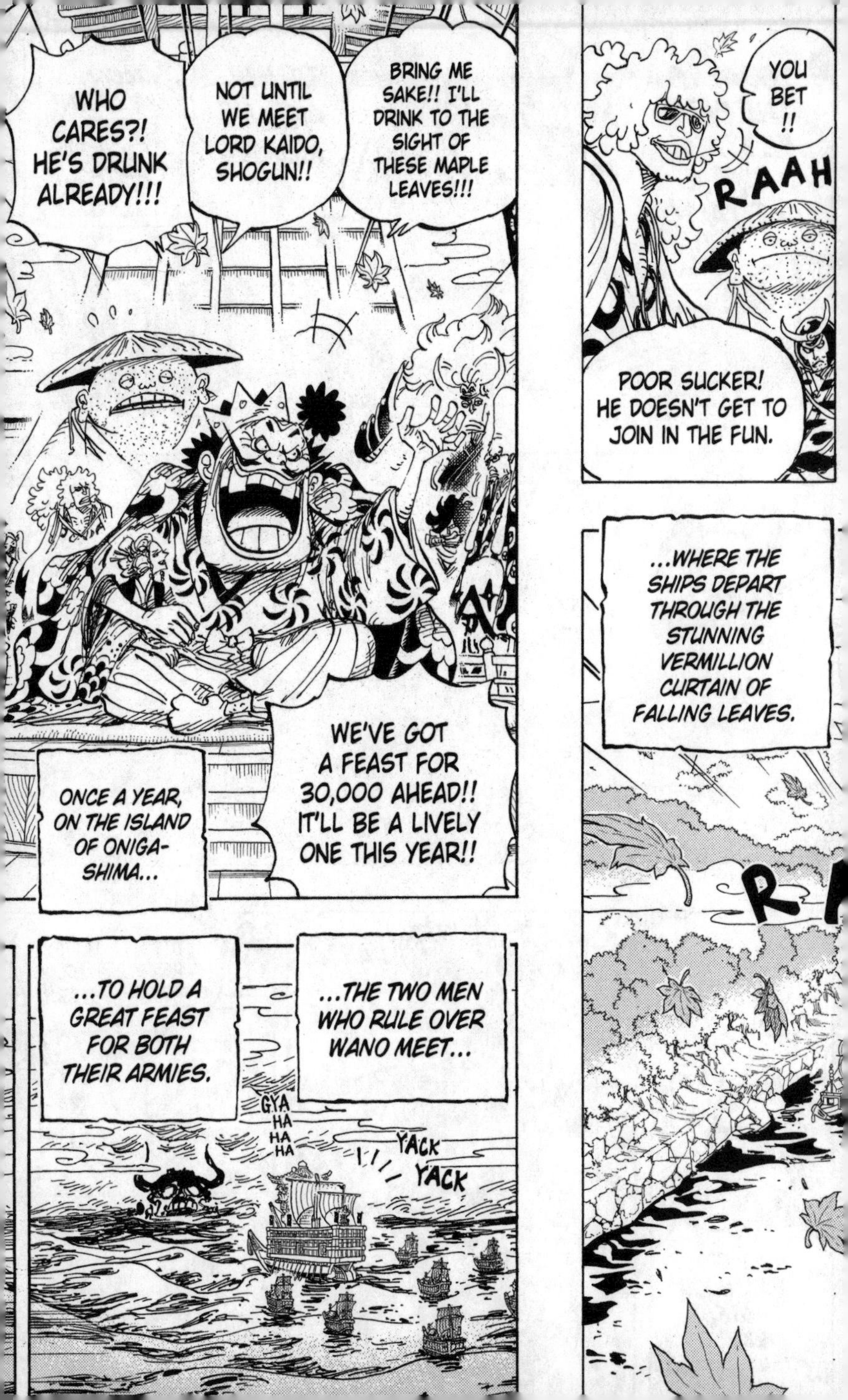
YOU BET!!
RAAH
POOR SUCKER! HE DOESN'T GET TO JOIN IN THE FUN.
...WHERE THE SHIPS DEPART THROUGH THE STUNNING VERMILLION CURTAIN OF FALLING LEAVES.
R
BRING ME SAKE!! I'LL DRINK TO THE SIGHT OF THESE MAPLE LEAVES!!!
NOT UNTIL WE MEET LORD KAIDO, SHOGUN!!
WHO CARES?! HE'S DRUNK ALREADY!!!
WE'VE GOT A FEAST FOR 30,000 AHEAD!! IT'LL BE A LIVELY ONE THIS YEAR!!
ONCE A YEAR, ON THE ISLAND OF ONIGA-SHIMA...
...THE TWO MEN WHO RULE OVER WANO MEET...
...TO HOLD A GREAT FEAST FOR BOTH THEIR ARMIES.
YACK YACK
GYA HA HA HA

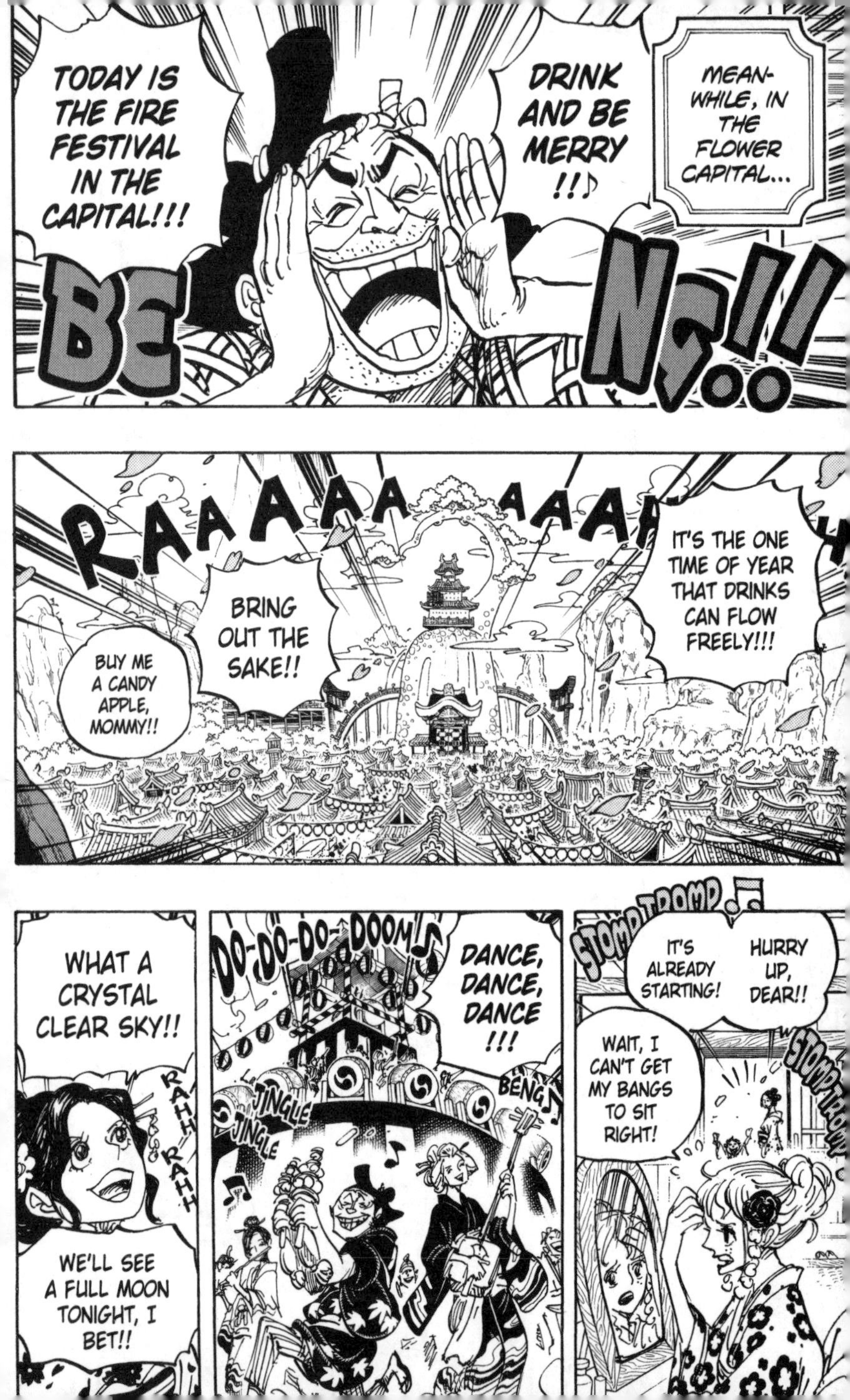
MEAN-WHILE, IN THE FLOWER CAPITAL...
DRINK AND BE MERRY!!♪
TODAY IS THE FIRE FESTIVAL IN THE CAPITAL!!!
BE
NG!!
RAAAAA AAAH
IT'S THE ONE TIME OF YEAR THAT DRINKS CAN FLOW FREELY!!!
BRING OUT THE SAKE!!
BUY ME A CANDY APPLE, MOMMY!!
STOMP TROMP
HURRY UP, DEAR!!
IT'S ALREADY STARTING!
STOMP TROMP
WAIT, I CAN'T GET MY BANGS TO SIT RIGHT!
DO-DO-DO-DOOM
DANCE, DANCE, DANCE!!!
BENG
JINGLE JINGLE
WHAT A CRYSTAL CLEAR SKY!!
RAHH RAHH
WE'LL SEE A FULL MOON TONIGHT, I BET!!

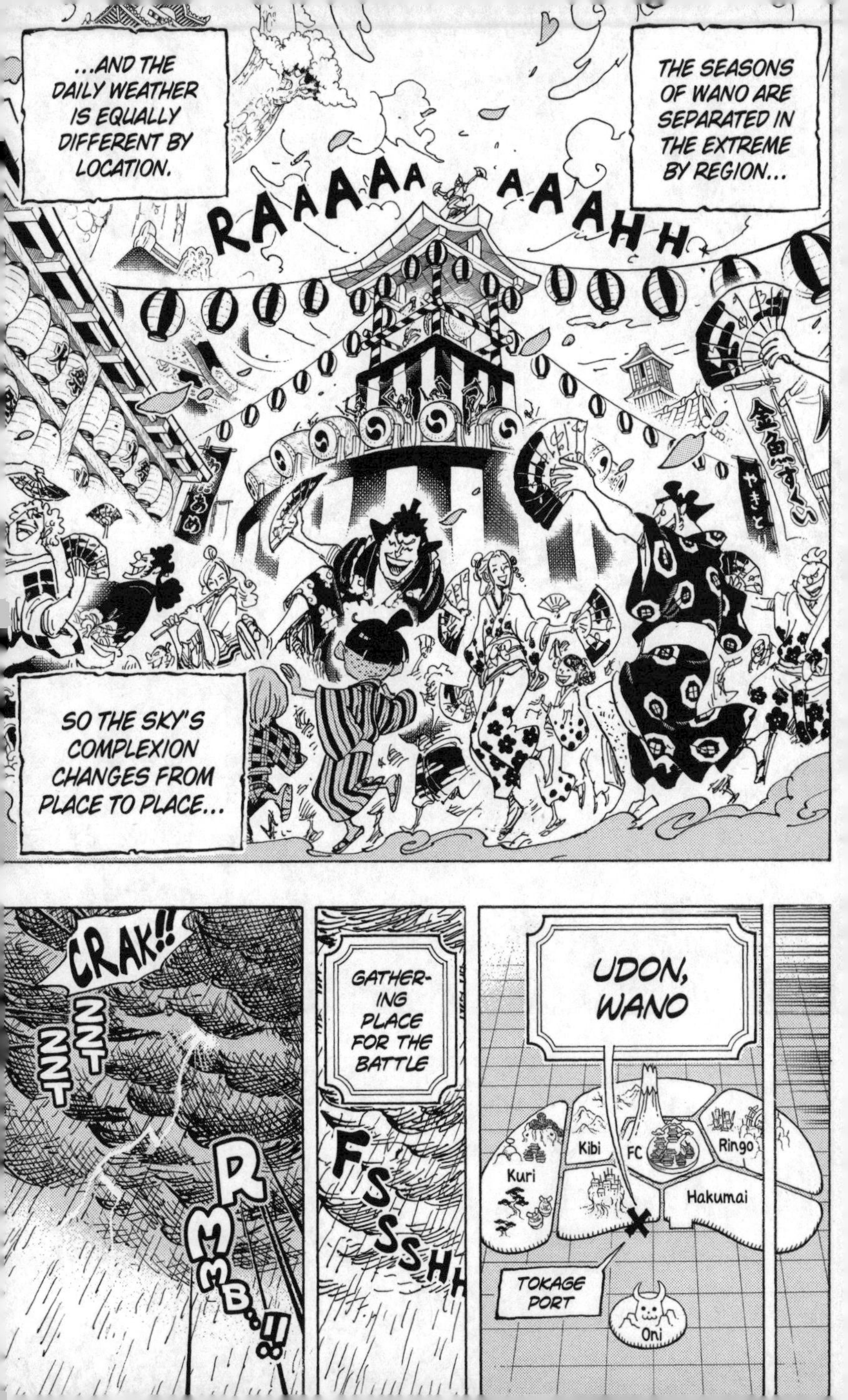
THE SEASONS OF WANO ARE SEPARATED IN THE EXTREME BY REGION...
...AND THE DAILY WEATHER IS EQUALLY DIFFERENT BY LOCATION.
RAAAAAA AAAHH
SO THE SKY'S COMPLEXION CHANGES FROM PLACE TO PLACE...
UDON, WANO
Kibi
FC
Ringo
Kuri
Hakumai
TOKAGE PORT
Oni
GATHER-ING PLACE FOR THE BATTLE
FSSSHH
CRAK!!
ZZT ZZT
RMMB..!!

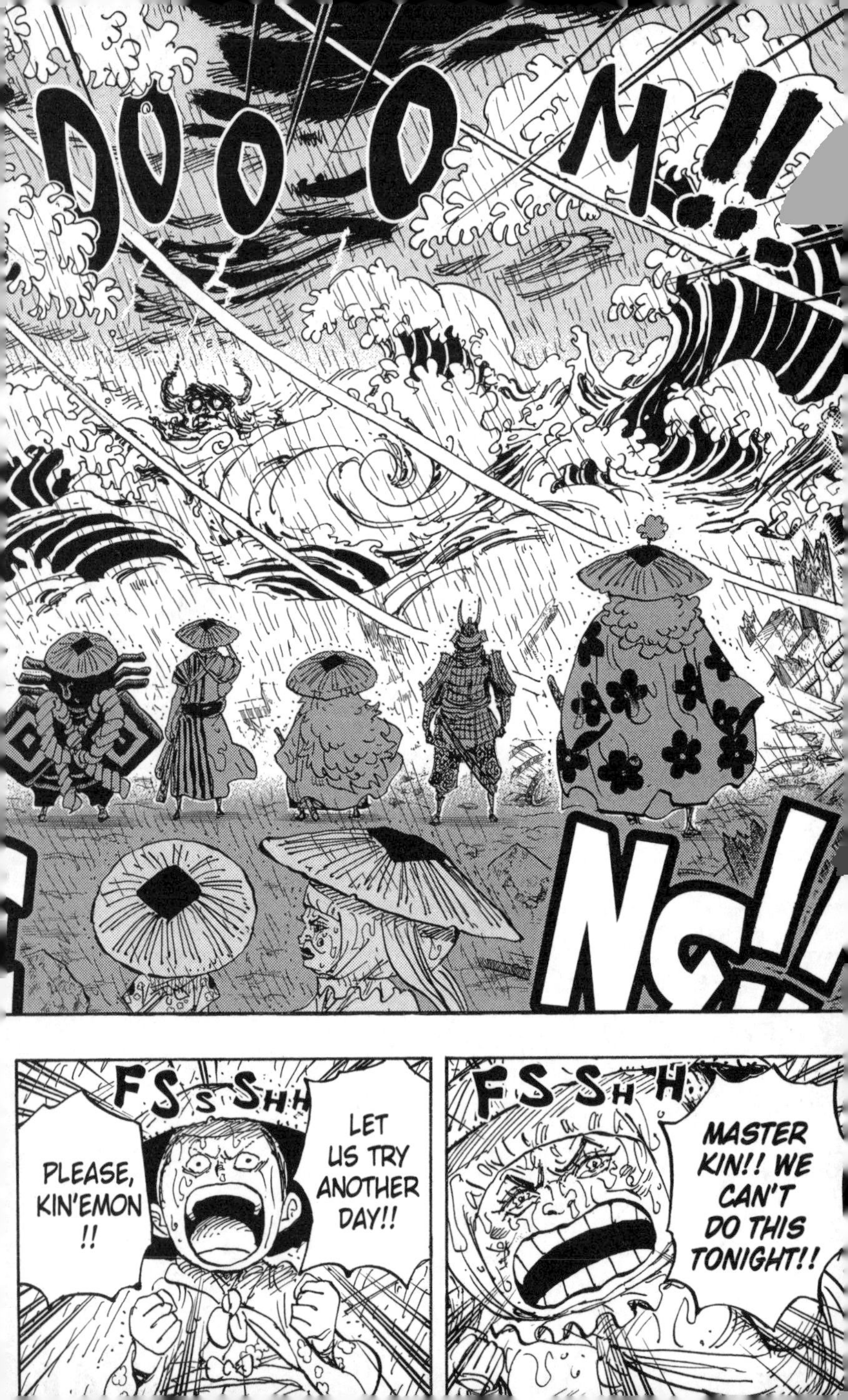
DOO-OM!!
FSSHH
MASTER KIN!! WE CAN'T DO THIS TONIGHT!!
FSSSHH
LET US TRY ANOTHER DAY!!
PLEASE, KIN'EMON!!

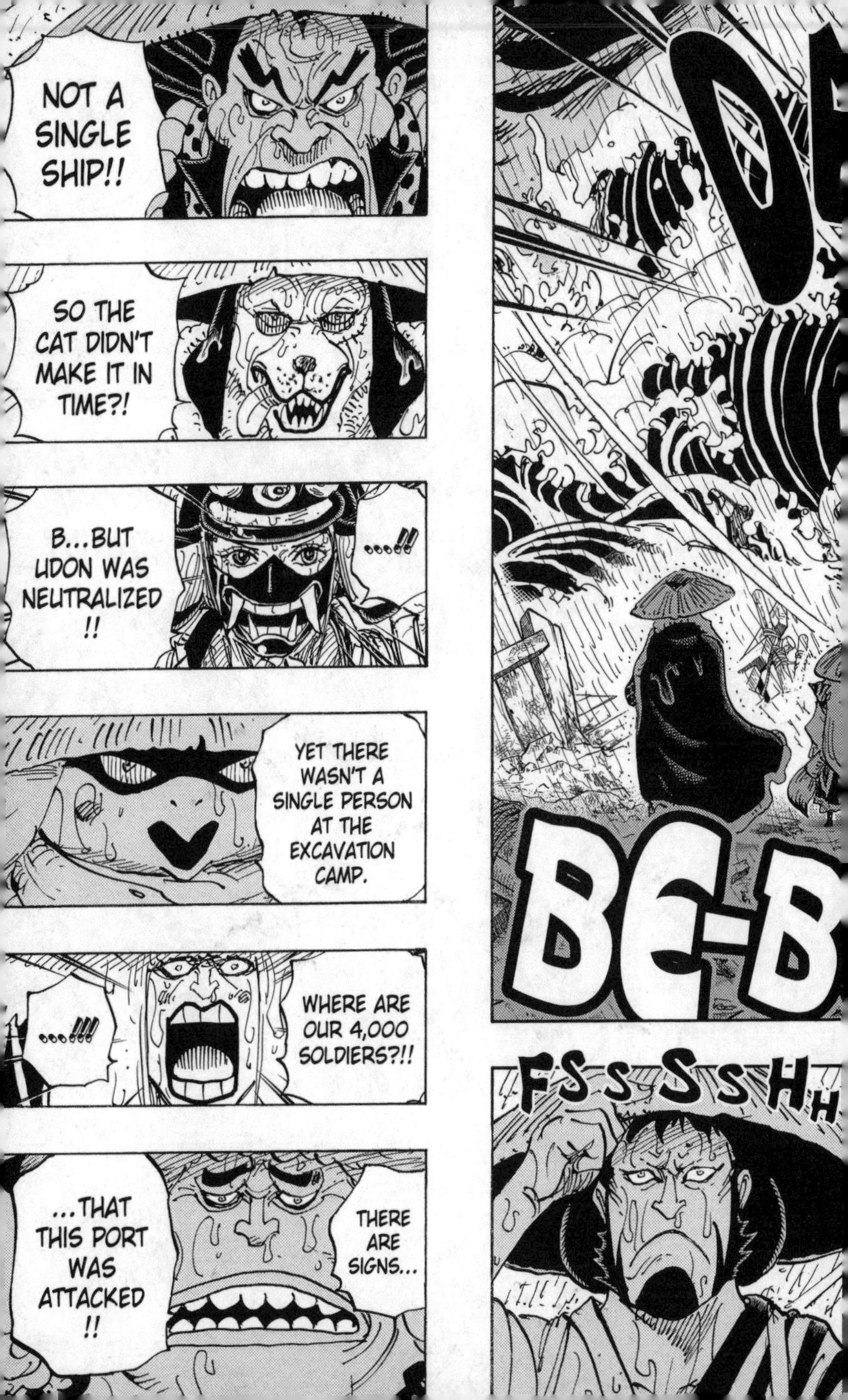
BC-B
FSSSSHH
NOT A SINGLE SHIP!!
SO THE CAT DIDN'T MAKE IT IN TIME?!
...!!
B...BUT UDON WAS NEUTRALIZED!!
YET THERE WASN'T A SINGLE PERSON AT THE EXCAVATION CAMP.
WHERE ARE OUR 4,000 SOLDIERS?!!
...!!!
THERE ARE SIGNS...
...THAT THIS PORT WAS ATTACKED!!

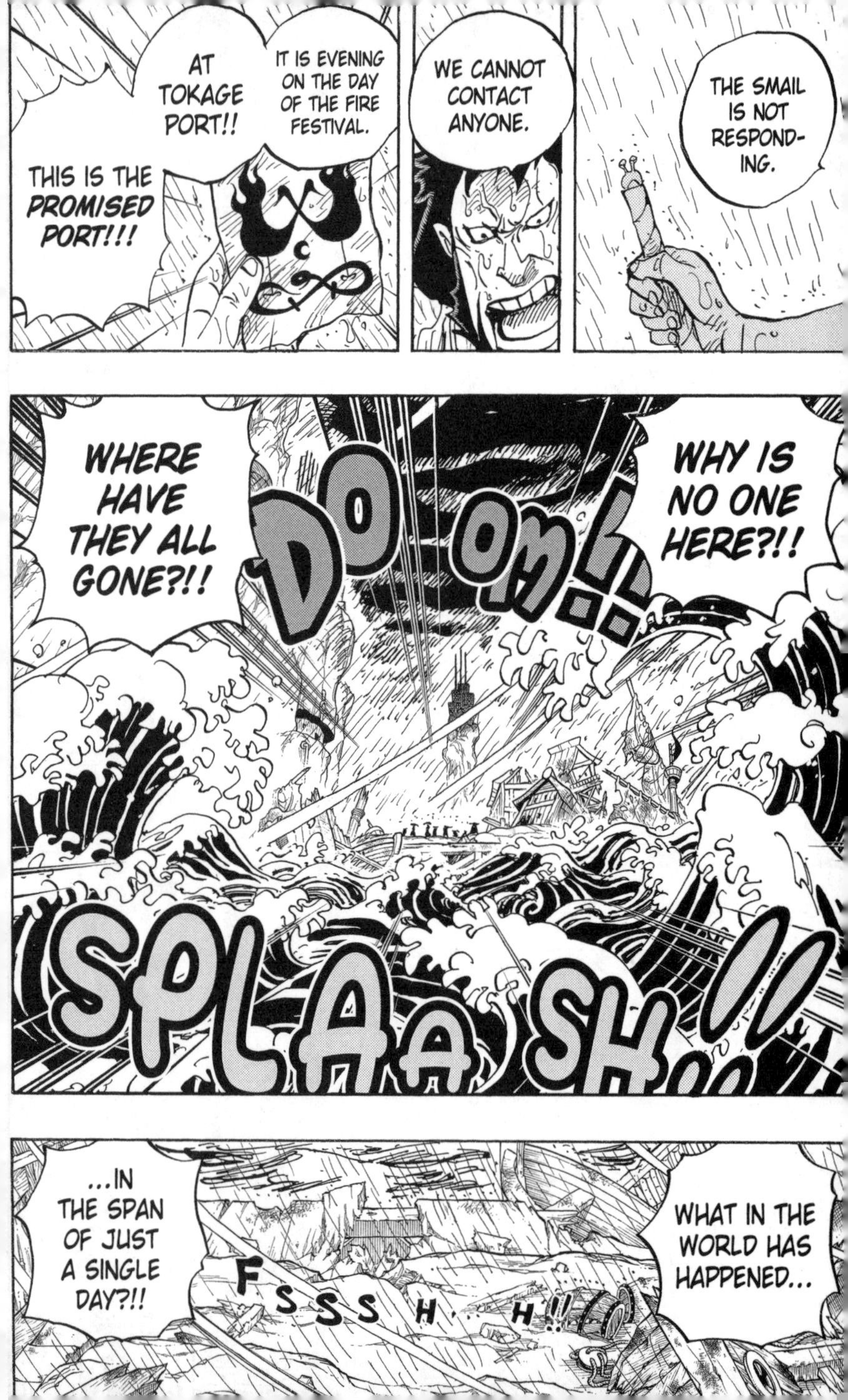
THE SMAIL IS NOT RESPONDING.
WE CANNOT CONTACT ANYONE.
IT IS EVENING ON THE DAY OF THE FIRE FESTIVAL.
AT TOKAGE PORT!!
THIS IS THE *PROMISED* PORT!!!
WHY IS NO ONE HERE?!!
DOOM!!
WHERE HAVE THEY ALL GONE?!!
SPLAASH!!
WHAT IN THE WORLD HAS HAPPENED...
FSSSHH!!
...IN THE SPAN OF JUST A SINGLE DAY?!!

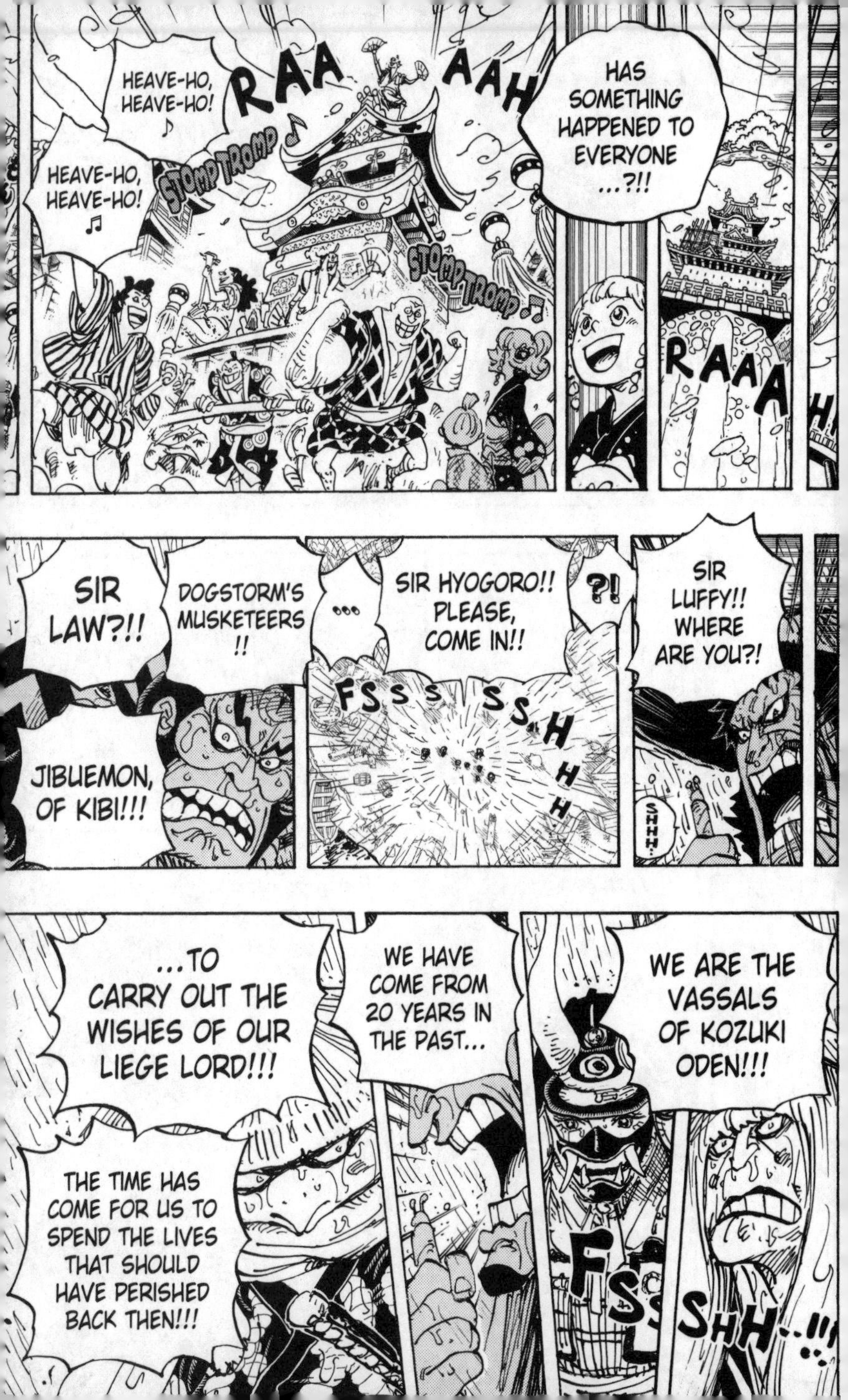
RAAAAH
HAS SOMETHING HAPPENED TO EVERYONE ...?!!
RAA AAH
HEAVE-HO, HEAVE-HO! ♪
HEAVE-HO, HEAVE-HO! ♫
STOMP TROMP ♪
STOMP TROMP ♫
SIR LUFFY!! WHERE ARE YOU?!
SHHH..
?!
SIR HYOGORO!! PLEASE, COME IN!!
...
FSSSSSHHHH
DOGSTORM'S MUSKETEERS !!
SIR LAW?!!
JIBUEMON, OF KIBI!!!
WE ARE THE VASSALS OF KOZUKI ODEN!!!
FSSSHH..!!!
WE HAVE COME FROM 20 YEARS IN THE PAST...
...TO CARRY OUT THE WISHES OF OUR LIEGE LORD!!!
THE TIME HAS COME FOR US TO SPEND THE LIVES THAT SHOULD HAVE PERISHED BACK THEN!!!

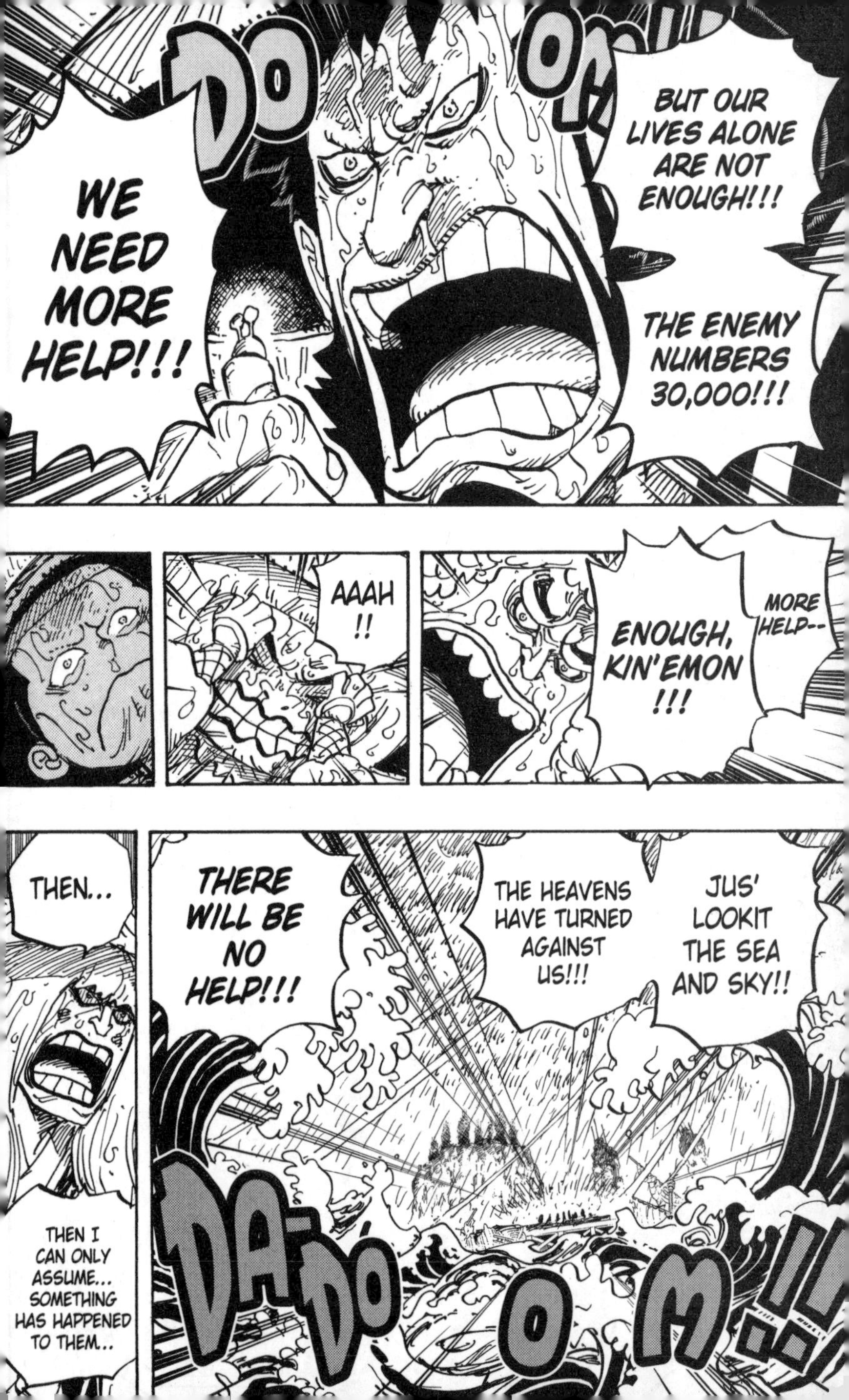
BUT OUR LIVES ALONE ARE NOT ENOUGH!!!
THE ENEMY NUMBERS 30,000!!!
WE NEED MORE HELP!!!
MORE HELP--
ENOUGH, KIN'EMON!!!
AAAH!!
JUS' LOOKIT THE SEA AND SKY!!
THE HEAVENS HAVE TURNED AGAINST US!!!
THERE WILL BE NO HELP!!!
DA-DOOM!!
THEN...
THEN I CAN ONLY ASSUME... SOMETHING HAS HAPPENED TO THEM...

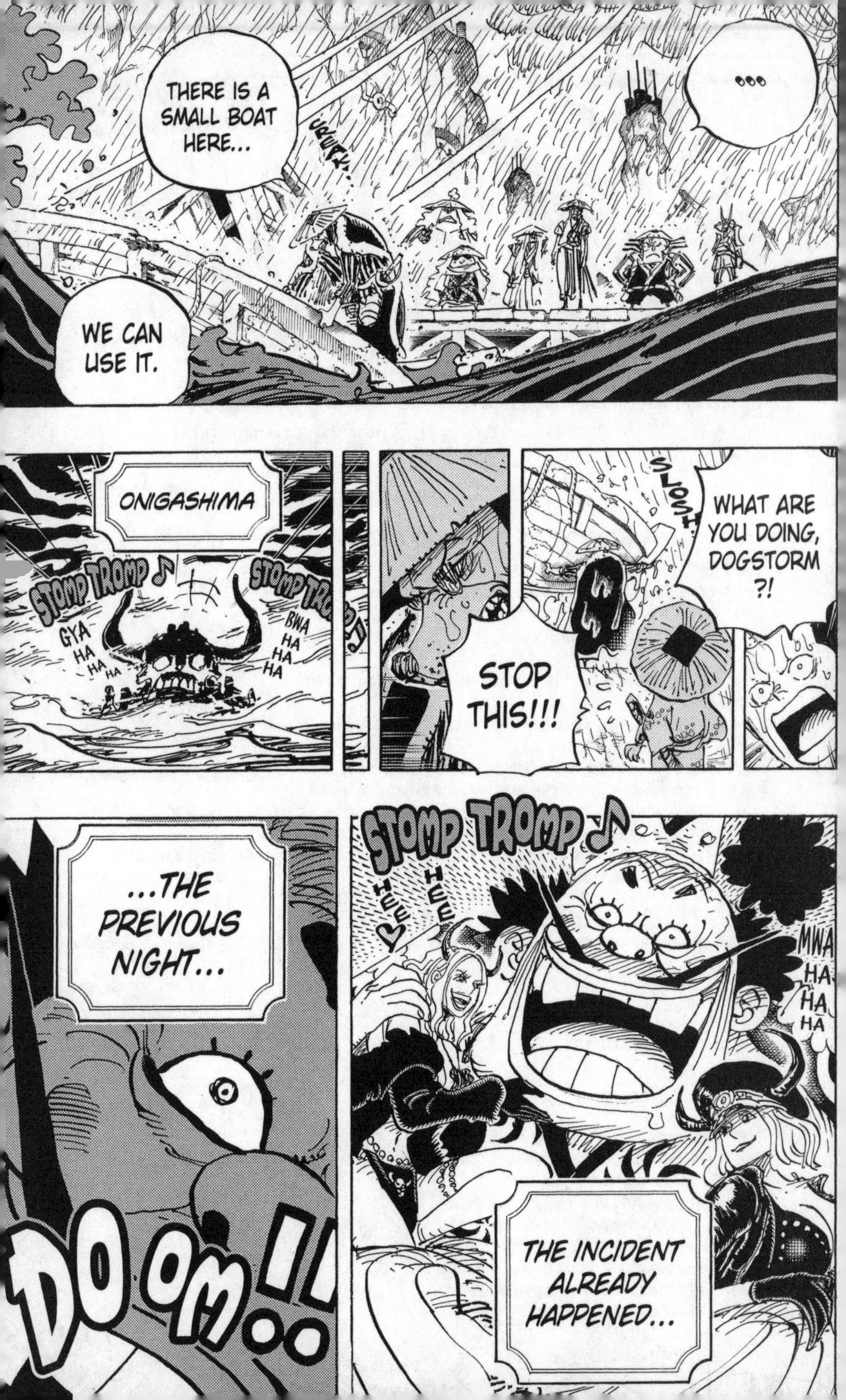
•••
THERE IS A SMALL BOAT HERE...
WE CAN USE IT.
SLOSH
WHAT ARE YOU DOING, DOGSTORM ?!
STOP THIS!!!
ONIGASHIMA
STOMP TROMP ♪
STOMP TROMP ♪
BWA HA HA HA HA
GYA HA HA HA
STOMP TROMP ♪
MWA HA HA HA
HEE HEE♥
THE INCIDENT ALREADY HAPPENED...
...THE PREVIOUS NIGHT...
DO OM..!!

SBS Question Corner

S
B
S

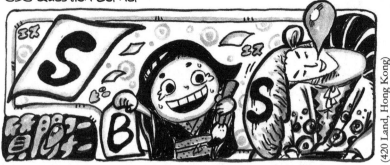

(420 Land, Hong Kong)

Q: Oda Sensei, I have been recognized by Guinness World Book for having the world's largest collection of One Piece merchandise, at **5,656** items!! Yippeeee!!! Buying merch for 18 years straight without taking a break wasn't a mistake after all.

--Sanadacchi

A: **What?! Guinness World Book?! Congra...!! What?! "Sanada"?!!**

MY

Why do I feel like I shouldn't be congratulating you...?! Is this a joke?! Or is this serious?! [Looking it up online] Well, it looks like it's true.
And how come I didn't know you're a Youtuber, Sanada?!
Listen up, people, you don't need to watch this pervert's Youtubes!
But I guess I have to admit that you really do love One Piece...despite being a pervert. And it's a real accomplishment to be the greatest in the world! So I'll be the better man and offer my sincere sentiments.
Despite being a pervert, congratulations! And despite being a pervert, thank you!

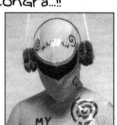

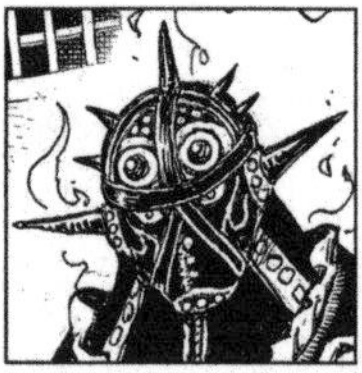

Q: You mentioned three races that can't be found in Totto Land. Is that giants, whatever King is…and me?

--Cora-Loving King

A: No.

Q: Tell us the name of the toad riding on Usopp's head, and how it got there.

--Match & Takeshi

RIBBIT
RAHH!

A: His name is Toad Boingnosuke. He was caught in a snake's sights when Usopp happened along, at which point he jumped atop Usopp's head. Usopp saw the snake, freaked out and ran away. Boingnosuke realized that he was safe atop of Usopp, so he's been there ever since.

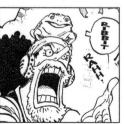

Chapter 959: SAMURAI

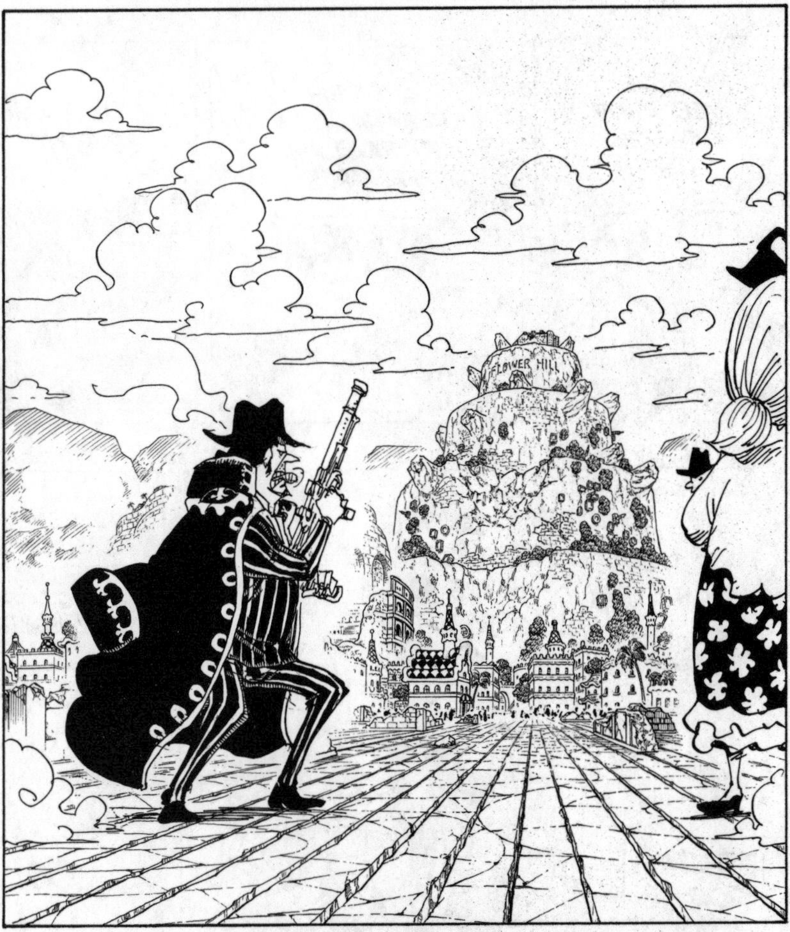

FLOWER HILL

GANG BEGE'S OH MY FAMILY
VOL. 9: "INSIDE THE COUNTRY! DRESSROSA, SCARRED BY BATTLE"

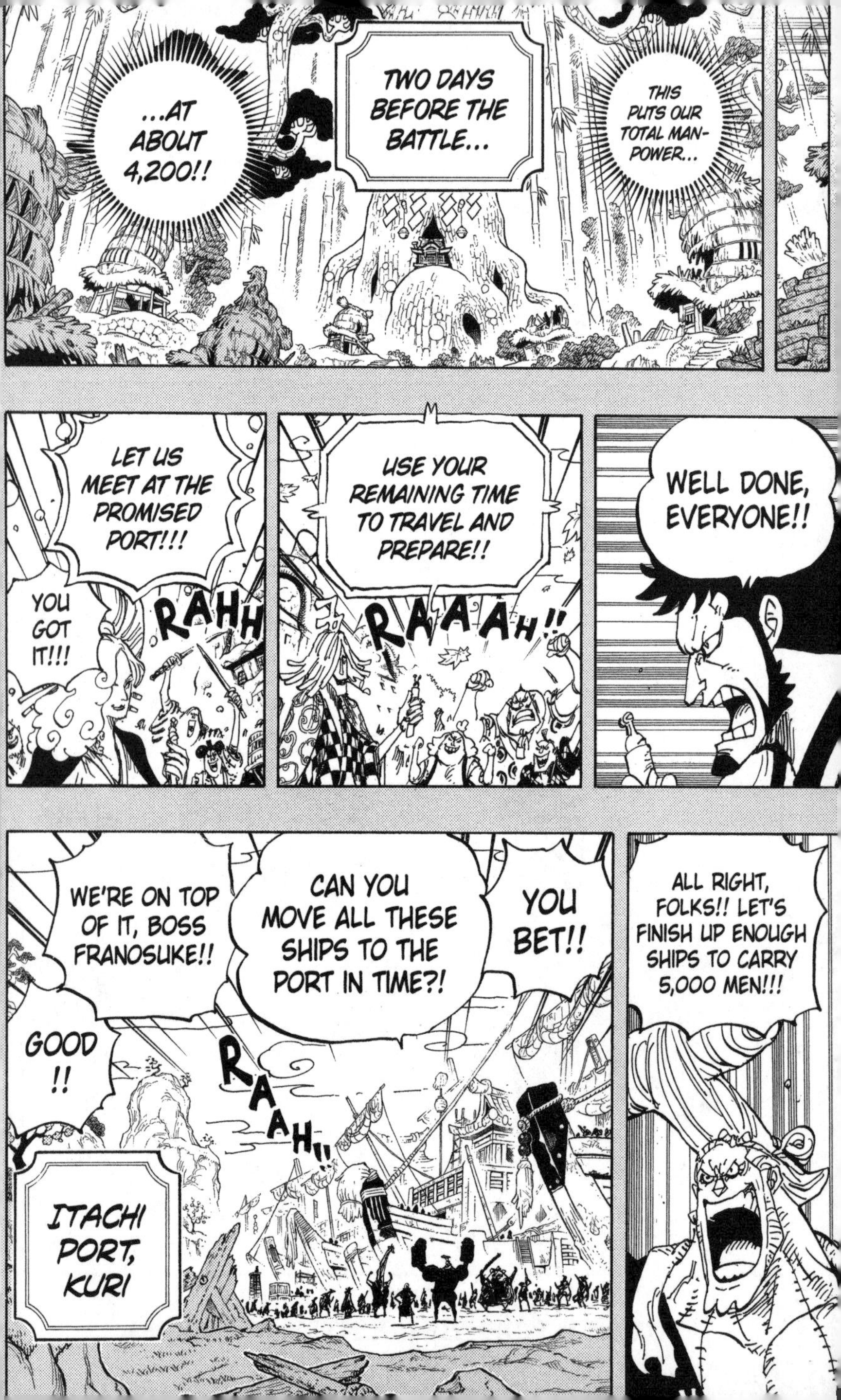

THIS PUTS OUR TOTAL MAN-POWER...
TWO DAYS BEFORE THE BATTLE...
...AT ABOUT 4,200!!
WELL DONE, EVERYONE!!
USE YOUR REMAINING TIME TO TRAVEL AND PREPARE!!
RAAAAH!!
LET US MEET AT THE PROMISED PORT!!!
RAHH
YOU GOT IT!!!
ALL RIGHT, FOLKS!! LET'S FINISH UP ENOUGH SHIPS TO CARRY 5,000 MEN!!!
CAN YOU MOVE ALL THESE SHIPS TO THE PORT IN TIME?!
YOU BET!!
WE'RE ON TOP OF IT, BOSS FRANOSUKE!!
GOOD!!
RAAAH!!
ITACHI PORT, KURI

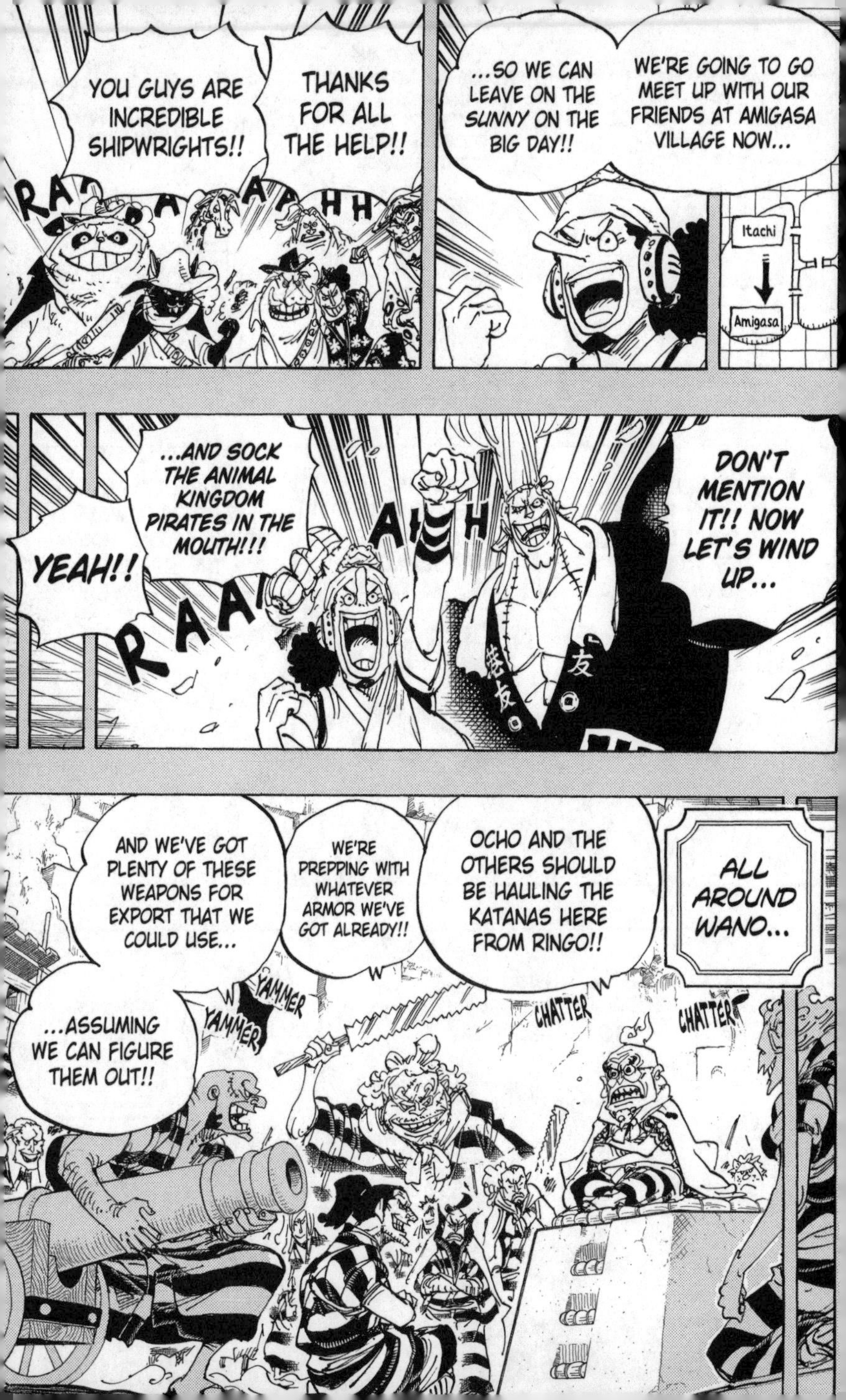
WE'RE GOING TO GO MEET UP WITH OUR FRIENDS AT AMIGASA VILLAGE NOW...
...SO WE CAN LEAVE ON THE SUNNY ON THE BIG DAY!!
Itachi
Amigasa
THANKS FOR ALL THE HELP!!
YOU GUYS ARE INCREDIBLE SHIPWRIGHTS!!
DON'T MENTION IT!! NOW LET'S WIND UP...
...AND SOCK THE ANIMAL KINGDOM PIRATES IN THE MOUTH!!!
YEAH!!
ALL AROUND WANO...
OCHO AND THE OTHERS SHOULD BE HAULING THE KATANAS HERE FROM RINGO!!
WE'RE PREPPING WITH WHATEVER ARMOR WE'VE GOT ALREADY!!
AND WE'VE GOT PLENTY OF THESE WEAPONS FOR EXPORT THAT WE COULD USE...
CHATTER
CHATTER
YAMMER
YAMMER
...ASSUMING WE CAN FIGURE THEM OUT!!

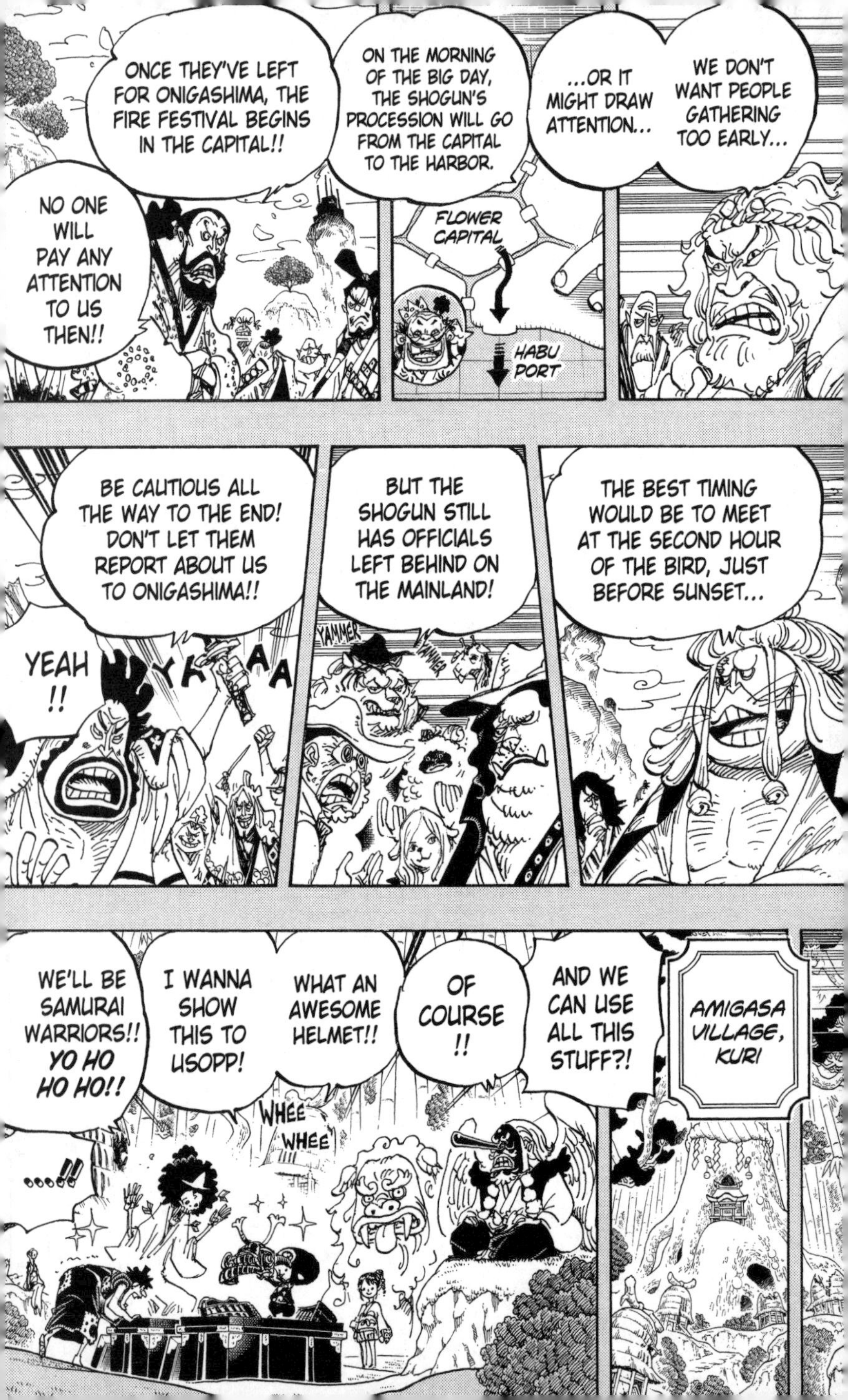
WE DON'T WANT PEOPLE GATHERING TOO EARLY...
...OR IT MIGHT DRAW ATTENTION...
ON THE MORNING OF THE BIG DAY, THE SHOGUN'S PROCESSION WILL GO FROM THE CAPITAL TO THE HARBOR.
FLOWER CAPITAL
HABU PORT
ONCE THEY'VE LEFT FOR ONIGASHIMA, THE FIRE FESTIVAL BEGINS IN THE CAPITAL!!
NO ONE WILL PAY ANY ATTENTION TO US THEN!!
THE BEST TIMING WOULD BE TO MEET AT THE SECOND HOUR OF THE BIRD, JUST BEFORE SUNSET...
BUT THE SHOGUN STILL HAS OFFICIALS LEFT BEHIND ON THE MAINLAND!
YAMMER
YAMMER
BE CAUTIOUS ALL THE WAY TO THE END! DON'T LET THEM REPORT ABOUT US TO ONIGASHIMA!!
YEAH !!
AMIGASA VILLAGE, KURI
AND WE CAN USE ALL THIS STUFF?!
OF COURSE !!
WHAT AN AWESOME HELMET!!
WHEE
WHEE
I WANNA SHOW THIS TO USOPP!
WE'LL BE SAMURAI WARRIORS!! YO HO HO HO!!
....!!

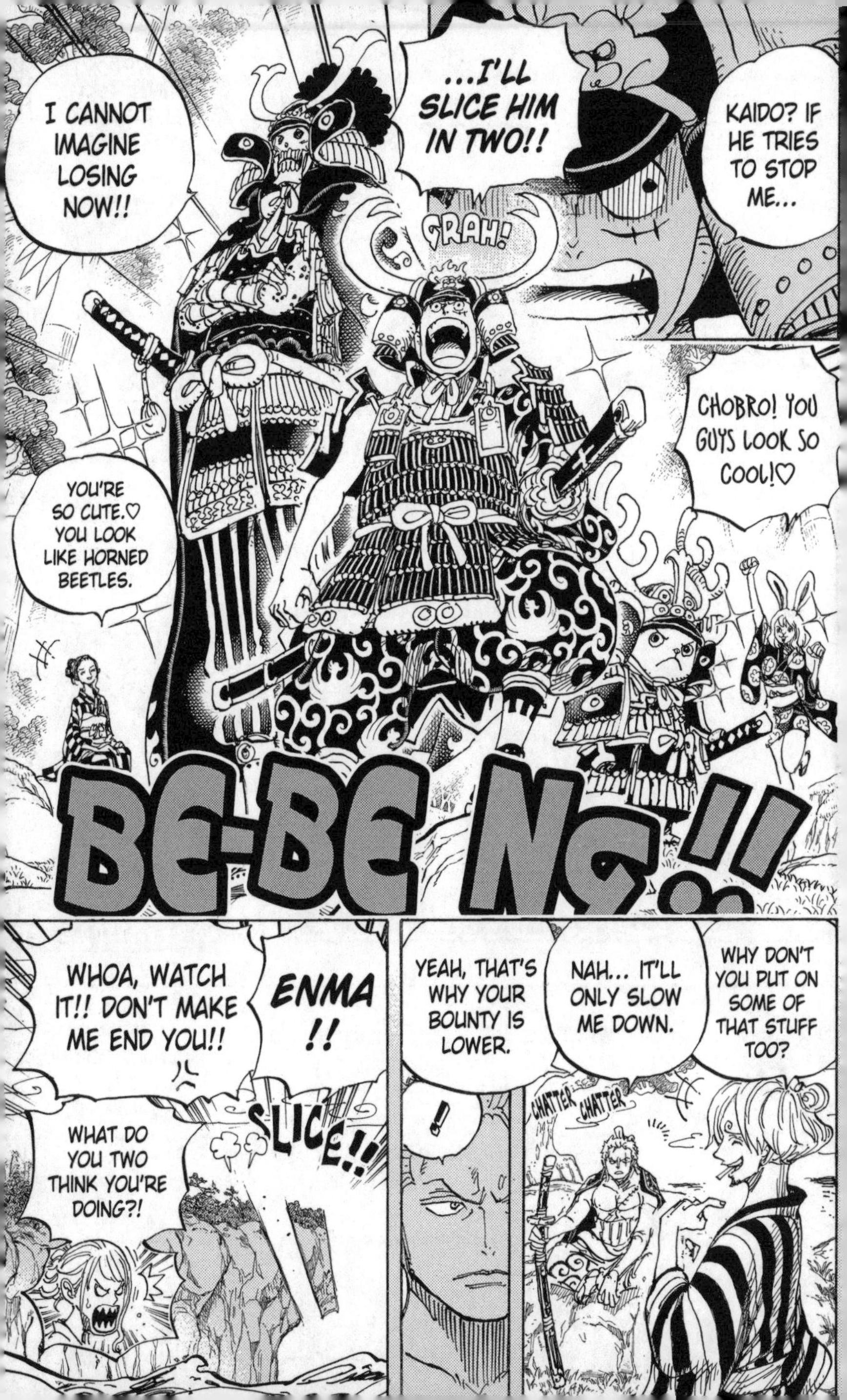
KAIDO? IF HE TRIES TO STOP ME...
...I'LL SLICE HIM IN TWO!!
GRAH!
I CANNOT IMAGINE LOSING NOW!!
CHOBRO! YOU GUYS LOOK SO COOL!♡
YOU'RE SO CUTE.♡ YOU LOOK LIKE HORNED BEETLES.
BE-BE NG!!
WHY DON'T YOU PUT ON SOME OF THAT STUFF TOO?
NAH... IT'LL ONLY SLOW ME DOWN.
CHATTER CHATTER
YEAH, THAT'S WHY YOUR BOUNTY IS LOWER.
!
ENMA!!
WHOA, WATCH IT!! DON'T MAKE ME END YOU!!
SLICE!!
WHAT DO YOU TWO THINK YOU'RE DOING?!

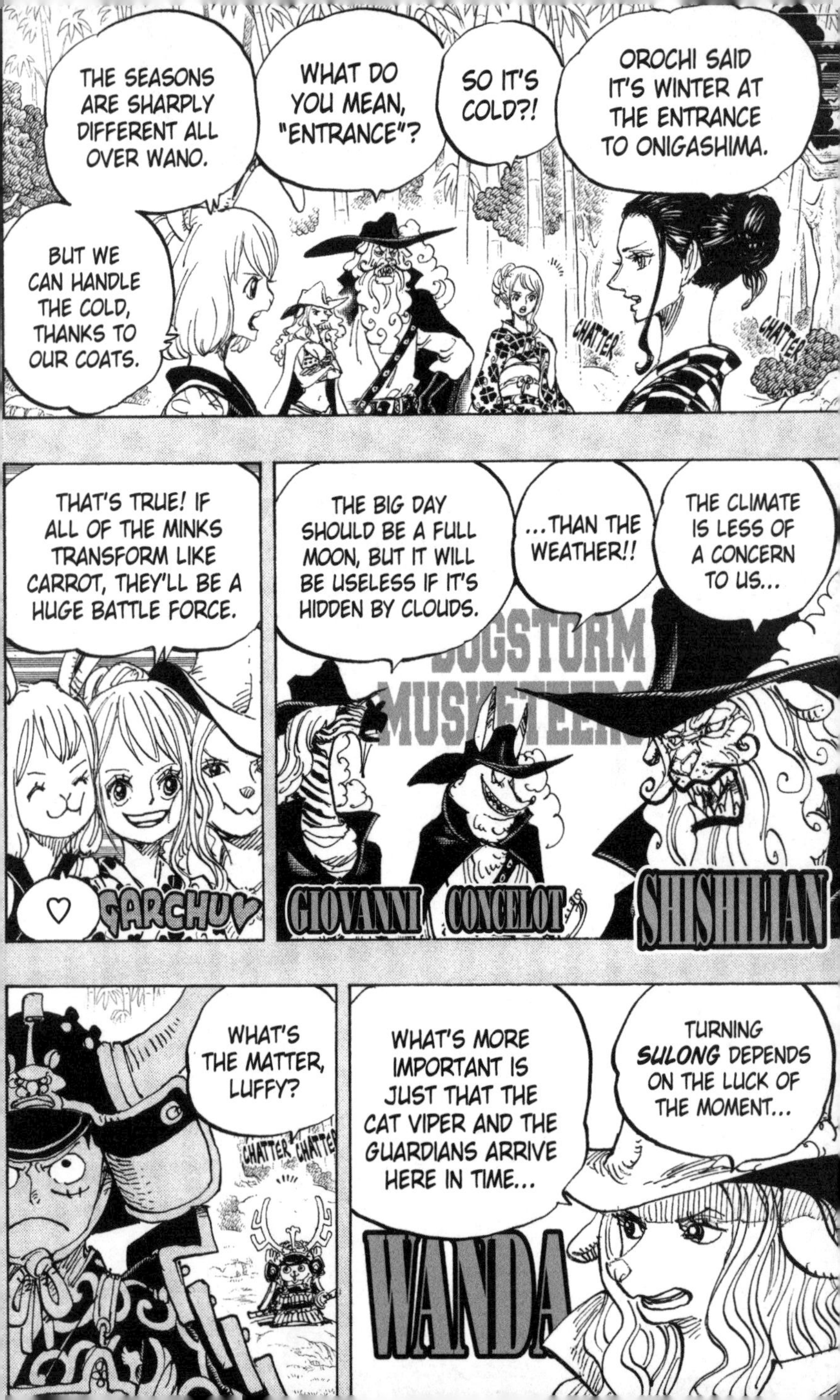
OROCHI SAID IT'S WINTER AT THE ENTRANCE TO ONIGASHIMA.
SO IT'S COLD?!
WHAT DO YOU MEAN, "ENTRANCE"?
THE SEASONS ARE SHARPLY DIFFERENT ALL OVER WANO.
BUT WE CAN HANDLE THE COLD, THANKS TO OUR COATS.
CHATTER
CHATTER
THE CLIMATE IS LESS OF A CONCERN TO US...
...THAN THE WEATHER!!
THE BIG DAY SHOULD BE A FULL MOON, BUT IT WILL BE USELESS IF IT'S HIDDEN BY CLOUDS.
DOGSTORM MUSKETEERS
SHISHILIAN
CONCELOT
GIOVANNI
THAT'S TRUE! IF ALL OF THE MINKS TRANSFORM LIKE CARROT, THEY'LL BE A HUGE BATTLE FORCE.
♡ GARCHU ♡
TURNING *SULONG* DEPENDS ON THE LUCK OF THE MOMENT...
WHAT'S MORE IMPORTANT IS JUST THAT THE CAT VIPER AND THE GUARDIANS ARRIVE HERE IN TIME...
WANDA
WHAT'S THE MATTER, LUFFY?
CHATTER CHATTER

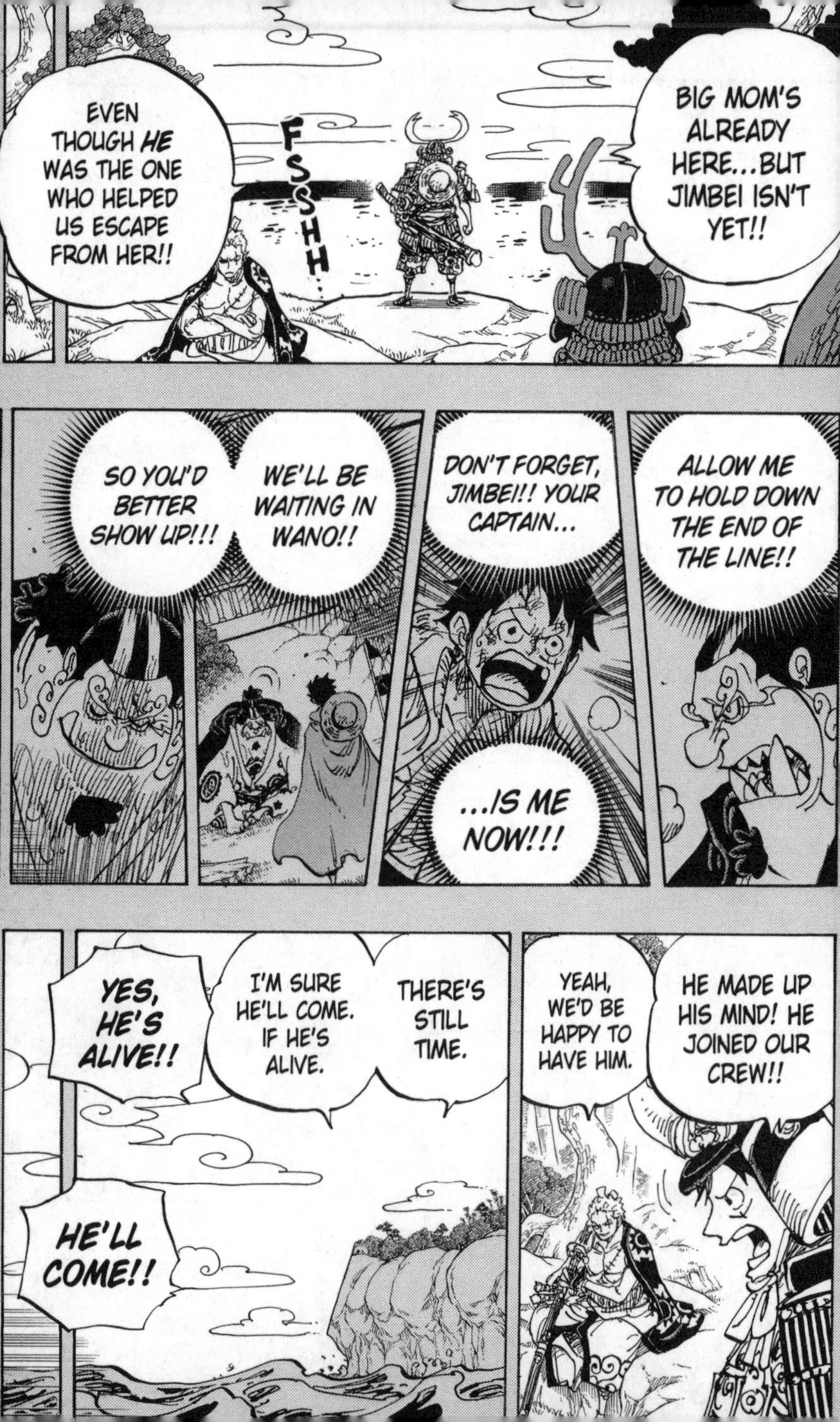
BIG MOM'S ALREADY HERE...BUT JIMBEI ISN'T YET!!
FSSHH
EVEN THOUGH HE WAS THE ONE WHO HELPED US ESCAPE FROM HER!!
ALLOW ME TO HOLD DOWN THE END OF THE LINE!!
DON'T FORGET, JIMBEI!! YOUR CAPTAIN...
...IS ME NOW!!!
WE'LL BE WAITING IN WANO!!
SO YOU'D BETTER SHOW UP!!!
HE MADE UP HIS MIND! HE JOINED OUR CREW!!
YEAH, WE'D BE HAPPY TO HAVE HIM.
THERE'S STILL TIME.
I'M SURE HE'LL COME. IF HE'S ALIVE.
YES, HE'S ALIVE!!
HE'LL COME!!

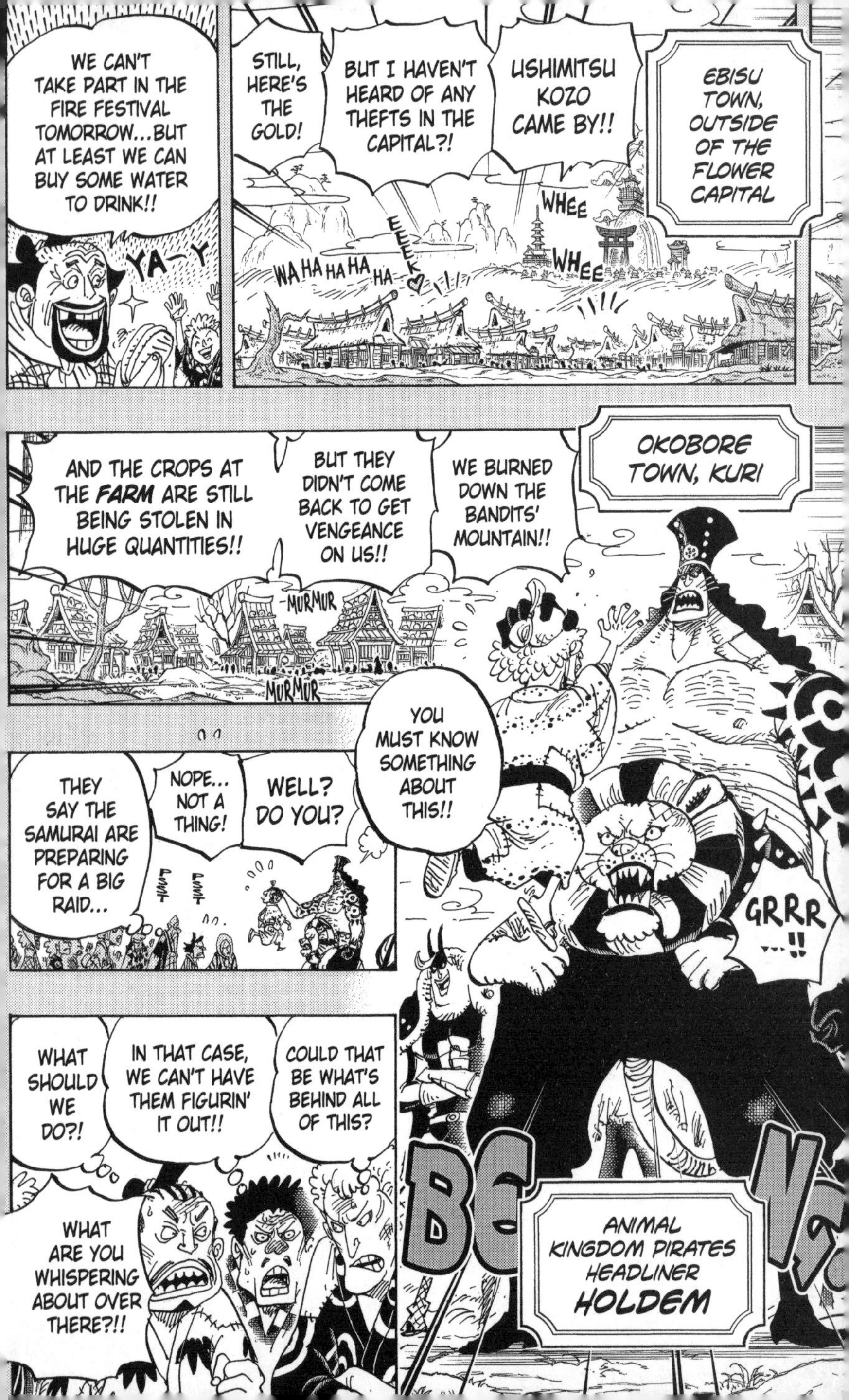
EBISU TOWN, OUTSIDE OF THE FLOWER CAPITAL
USHIMITSU KOZO CAME BY!!
BUT I HAVEN'T HEARD OF ANY THEFTS IN THE CAPITAL?!
STILL, HERE'S THE GOLD!
WHEE
WHEE
EEEK
WA HA HA HA HA HA
WE CAN'T TAKE PART IN THE FIRE FESTIVAL TOMORROW...BUT AT LEAST WE CAN BUY SOME WATER TO DRINK!!
YA-Y
OKOBORE TOWN, KURI
WE BURNED DOWN THE BANDITS' MOUNTAIN!!
BUT THEY DIDN'T COME BACK TO GET VENGEANCE ON US!!
AND THE CROPS AT THE FARM ARE STILL BEING STOLEN IN HUGE QUANTITIES!!
MURMUR
MURMUR
YOU MUST KNOW SOMETHING ABOUT THIS!!
GRRR...!!
ANIMAL KINGDOM PIRATES HEADLINER HOLDEM
WELL? DO YOU?
NOPE... NOT A THING!
THEY SAY THE SAMURAI ARE PREPARING FOR A BIG RAID...
PSST
PSST
COULD THAT BE WHAT'S BEHIND ALL OF THIS?
IN THAT CASE, WE CAN'T HAVE THEM FIGURIN' IT OUT!!
WHAT SHOULD WE DO?!
WHAT ARE YOU WHISPERING ABOUT OVER THERE?!!

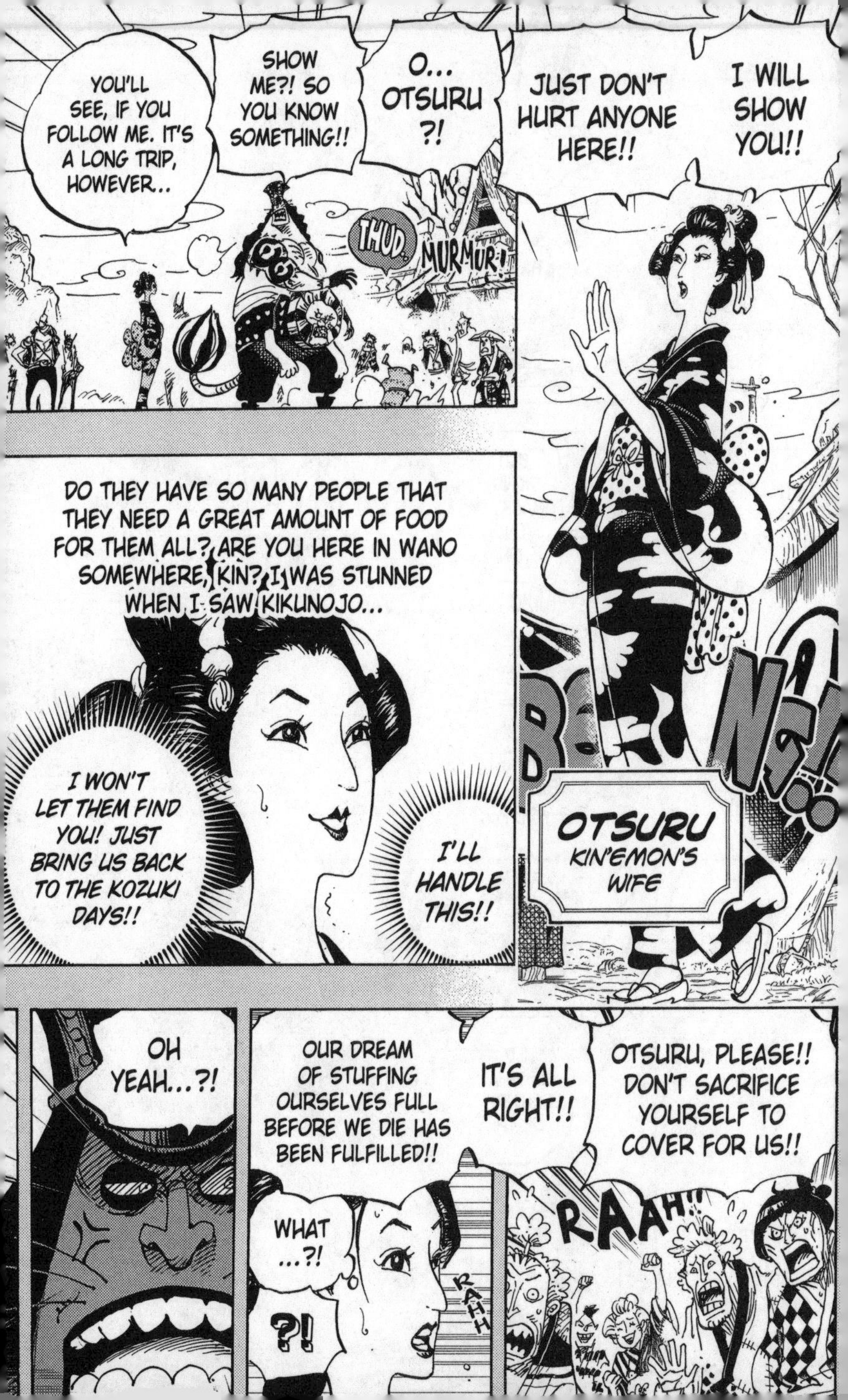
I WILL SHOW YOU!!
JUST DON'T HURT ANYONE HERE!!
BONG!!
OTSURU
KIN'EMON'S WIFE
O... OTSURU?!
SHOW ME?! SO YOU KNOW SOMETHING!!
THUD
MURMUR
YOU'LL SEE, IF YOU FOLLOW ME. IT'S A LONG TRIP, HOWEVER...
DO THEY HAVE SO MANY PEOPLE THAT THEY NEED A GREAT AMOUNT OF FOOD FOR THEM ALL? ARE YOU HERE IN WANO SOMEWHERE, KIN? I WAS STUNNED WHEN I SAW KIKUNOJO...
I'LL HANDLE THIS!!
I WON'T LET THEM FIND YOU! JUST BRING US BACK TO THE KOZUKI DAYS!!
OTSURU, PLEASE!! DON'T SACRIFICE YOURSELF TO COVER FOR US!!
RAAH!!
IT'S ALL RIGHT!!
OUR DREAM OF STUFFING OURSELVES FULL BEFORE WE DIE HAS BEEN FULFILLED!!
WHAT ...?!
RAHH
?!
OH YEAH...?!

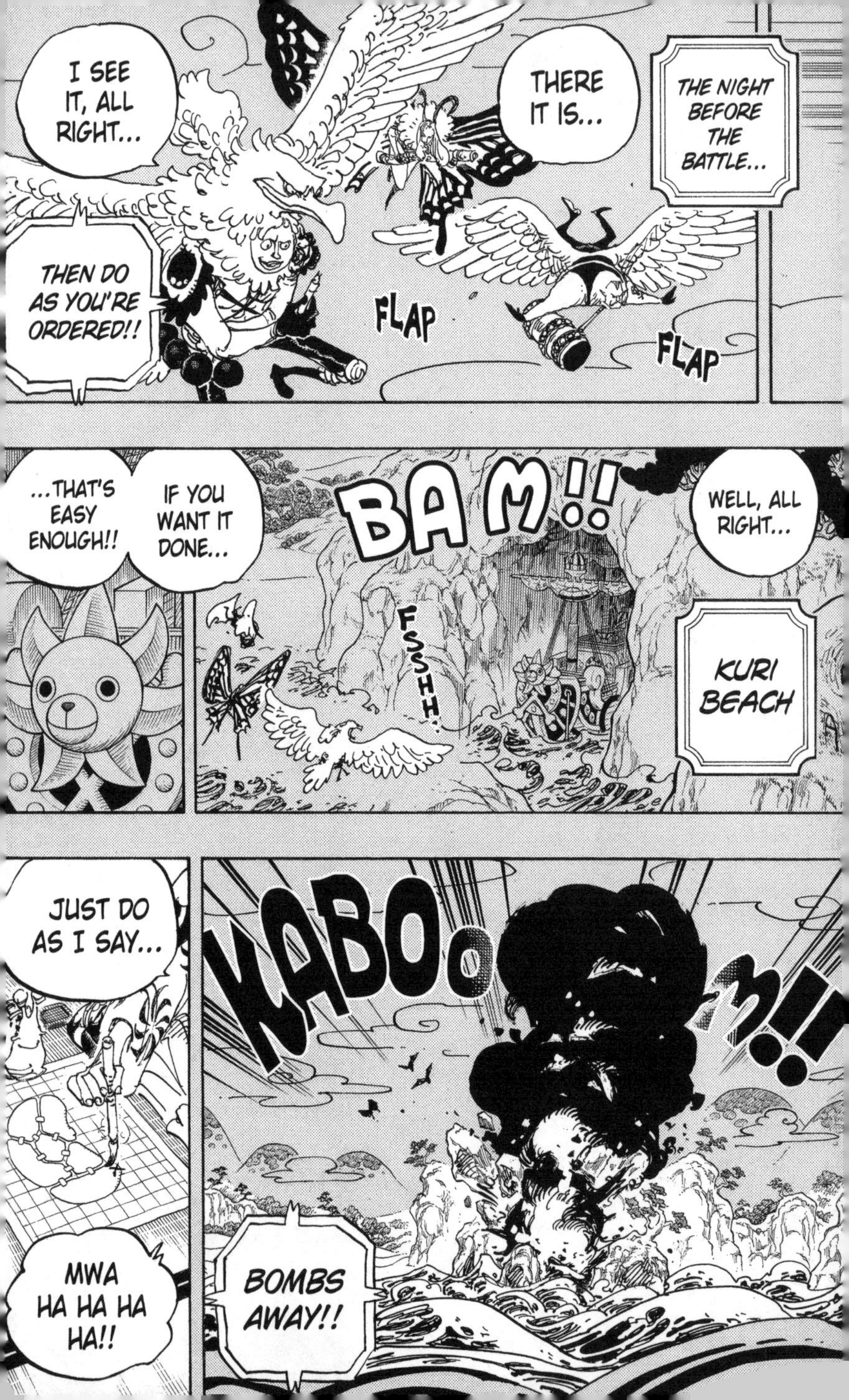
THE NIGHT BEFORE THE BATTLE...
THERE IT IS...
I SEE IT, ALL RIGHT...
FLAP
FLAP
THEN DO AS YOU'RE ORDERED!!
WELL, ALL RIGHT...
KURI BEACH
BAM!!
FSSHH
IF YOU WANT IT DONE...
...THAT'S EASY ENOUGH!!
KABOOM!!
BOMBS AWAY!!
JUST DO AS I SAY...
MWA HA HA HA HA!!

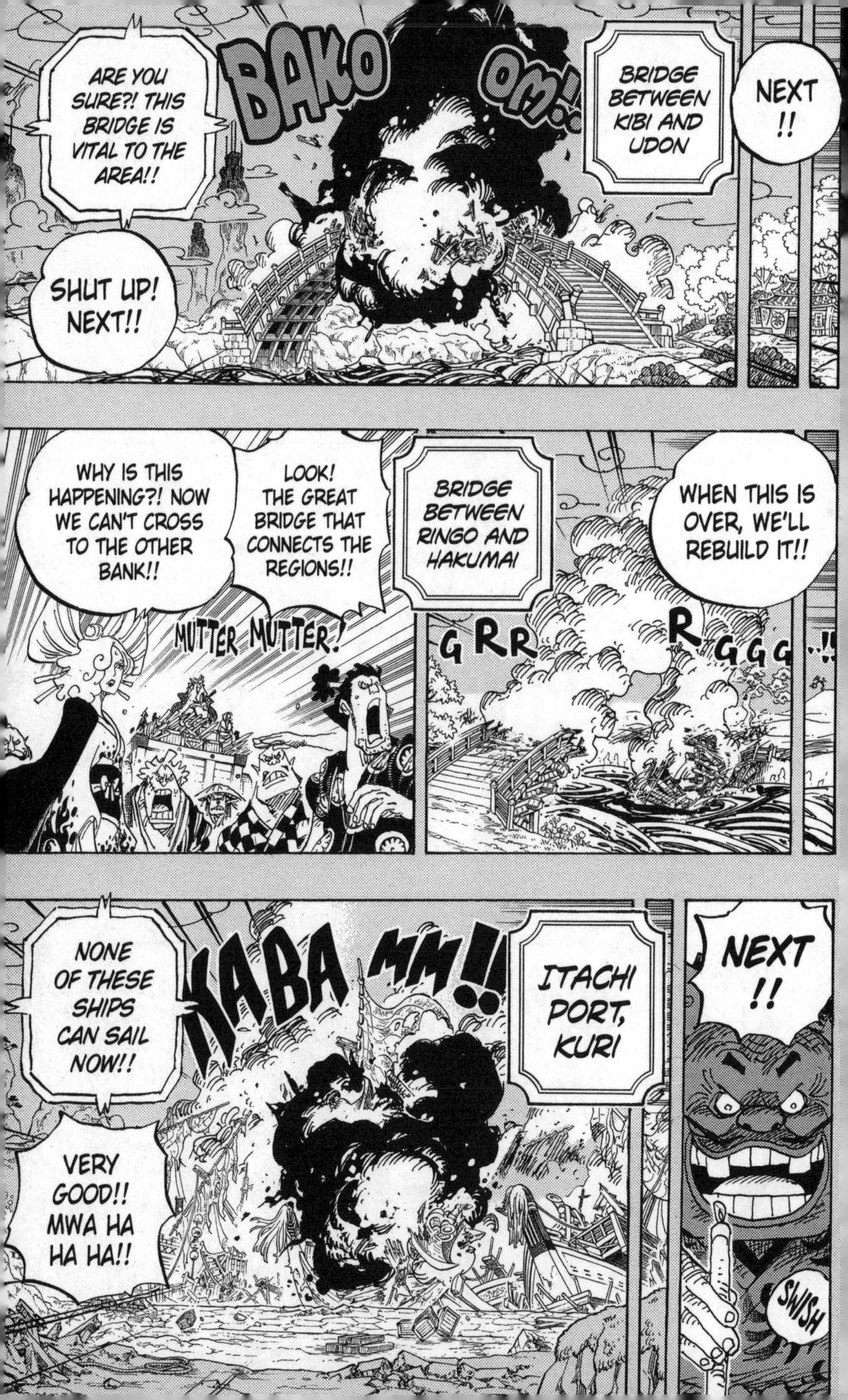
NEXT !!
BRIDGE BETWEEN KIBI AND UDON
BAKOOM!!
ARE YOU SURE?! THIS BRIDGE IS VITAL TO THE AREA!!
SHUT UP! NEXT!!
BRIDGE BETWEEN RINGO AND HAKUMAI
WHEN THIS IS OVER, WE'LL REBUILD IT!!
GRR R RGGG..!!
LOOK! THE GREAT BRIDGE THAT CONNECTS THE REGIONS!!
WHY IS THIS HAPPENING?! NOW WE CAN'T CROSS TO THE OTHER BANK!!
MUTTER MUTTER!
NEXT !!
SWISH
ITACHI PORT, KURI
KABAMM!!
NONE OF THESE SHIPS CAN SAIL NOW!!
VERY GOOD!! MWA HA HA HA!!

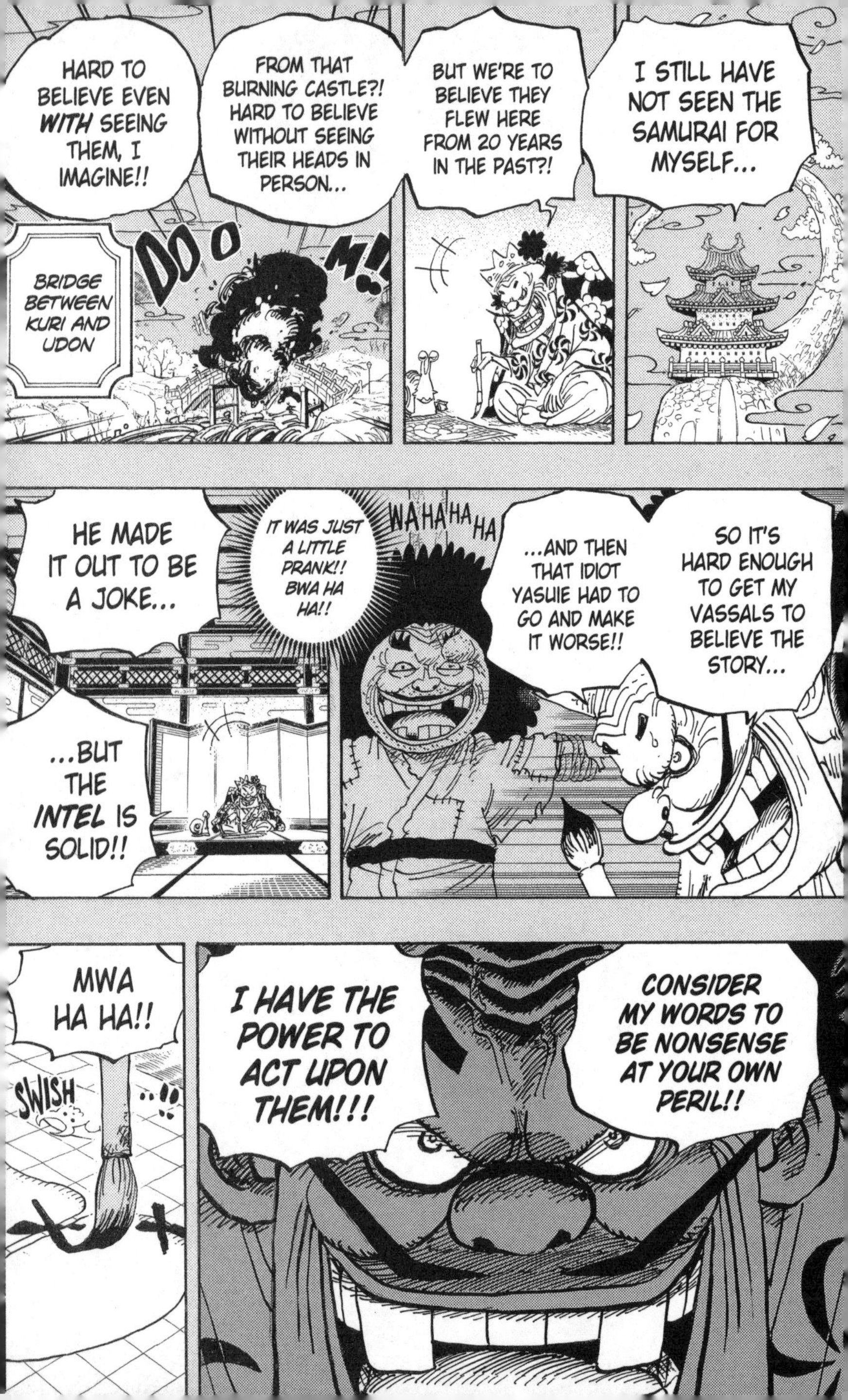
I STILL HAVE NOT SEEN THE SAMURAI FOR MYSELF...
BUT WE'RE TO BELIEVE THEY FLEW HERE FROM 20 YEARS IN THE PAST?!
FROM THAT BURNING CASTLE?! HARD TO BELIEVE WITHOUT SEEING THEIR HEADS IN PERSON...
HARD TO BELIEVE EVEN WITH SEEING THEM, I IMAGINE!!
DOOM!!
BRIDGE BETWEEN KURI AND UDON
SO IT'S HARD ENOUGH TO GET MY VASSALS TO BELIEVE THE STORY...
...AND THEN THAT IDIOT YASUIE HAD TO GO AND MAKE IT WORSE!!
WA HA HA HA
IT WAS JUST A LITTLE PRANK!! BWA HA HA!!
HE MADE IT OUT TO BE A JOKE...
...BUT THE INTEL IS SOLID!!
CONSIDER MY WORDS TO BE NONSENSE AT YOUR OWN PERIL!!
I HAVE THE POWER TO ACT UPON THEM!!!
MWA HA HA!!
SWISH
..!!

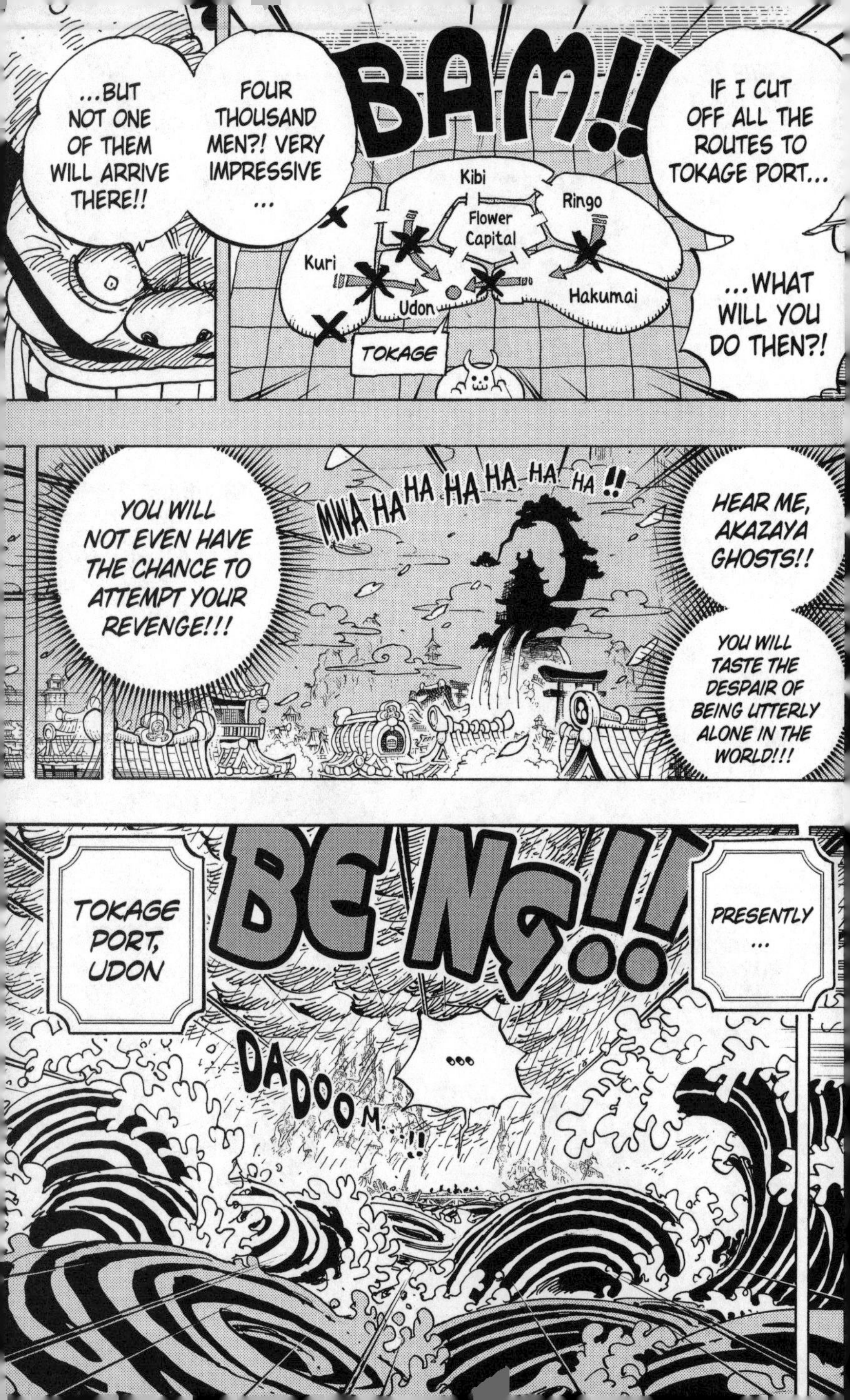
IF I CUT OFF ALL THE ROUTES TO TOKAGE PORT...
BAM!!
Kibi
Ringo
Flower Capital
Kuri
Hakumai
Udon
TOKAGE
...WHAT WILL YOU DO THEN?!
FOUR THOUSAND MEN?! VERY IMPRESSIVE ...
...BUT NOT ONE OF THEM WILL ARRIVE THERE!!
HEAR ME, AKAZAYA GHOSTS!!
YOU WILL TASTE THE DESPAIR OF BEING UTTERLY ALONE IN THE WORLD!!!
MWA HA HA HA HA HA HA!!
YOU WILL NOT EVEN HAVE THE CHANCE TO ATTEMPT YOUR REVENGE!!!
PRESENTLY ...
BENG!!
TOKAGE PORT, UDON
DADOOM..!!
...

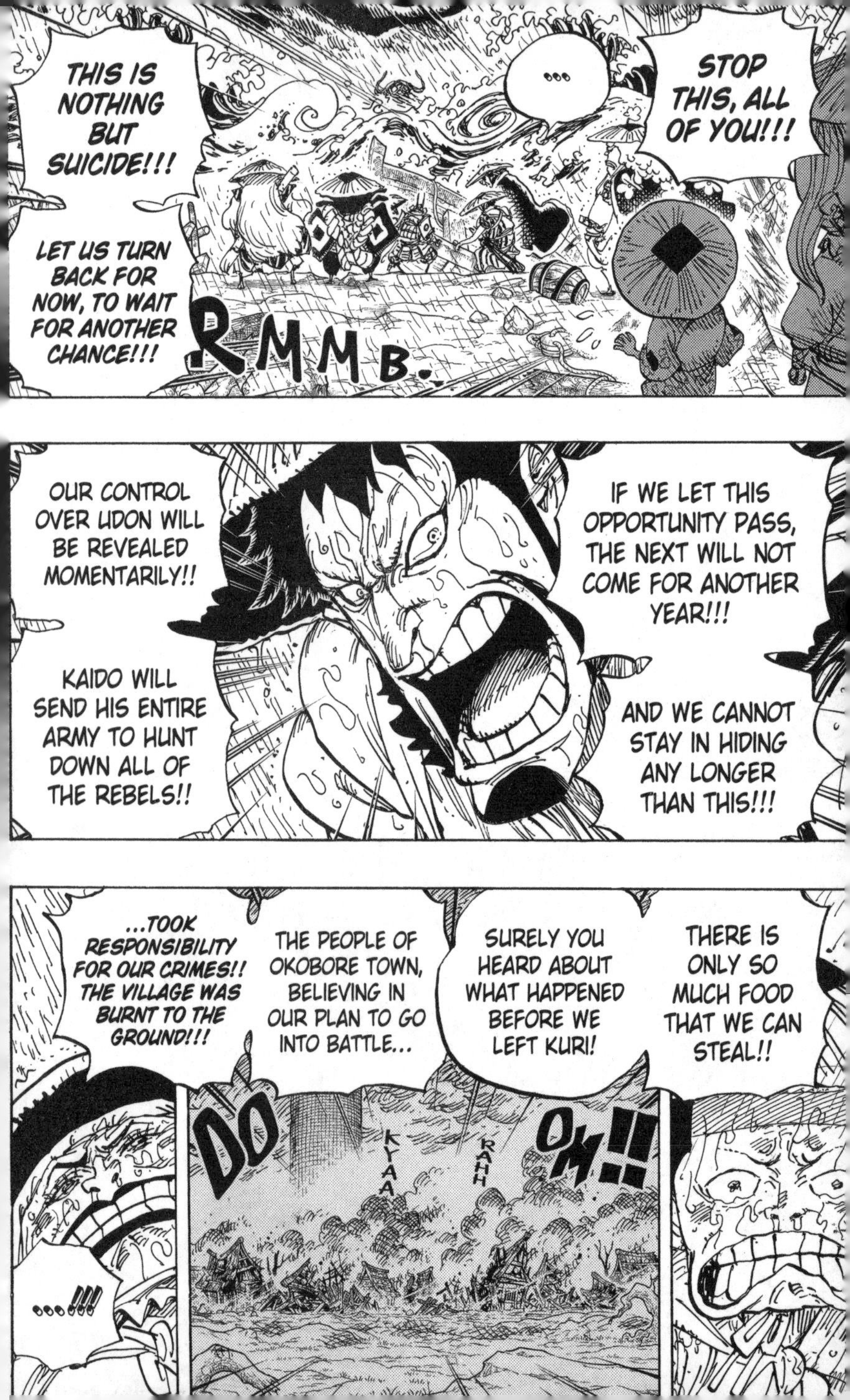
STOP THIS, ALL OF YOU!!!
...
THIS IS NOTHING BUT SUICIDE!!!
LET US TURN BACK FOR NOW, TO WAIT FOR ANOTHER CHANCE!!!
RMMB..
IF WE LET THIS OPPORTUNITY PASS, THE NEXT WILL NOT COME FOR ANOTHER YEAR!!!
AND WE CANNOT STAY IN HIDING ANY LONGER THAN THIS!!!
OUR CONTROL OVER UDON WILL BE REVEALED MOMENTARILY!!
KAIDO WILL SEND HIS ENTIRE ARMY TO HUNT DOWN ALL OF THE REBELS!!
THERE IS ONLY SO MUCH FOOD THAT WE CAN STEAL!!
SURELY YOU HEARD ABOUT WHAT HAPPENED BEFORE WE LEFT KURI!
THE PEOPLE OF OKOBORE TOWN, BELIEVING IN OUR PLAN TO GO INTO BATTLE...
...TOOK RESPONSIBILITY FOR OUR CRIMES!! THE VILLAGE WAS BURNT TO THE GROUND!!!
DOOM!!
RAHH
KYAAA
...!!!

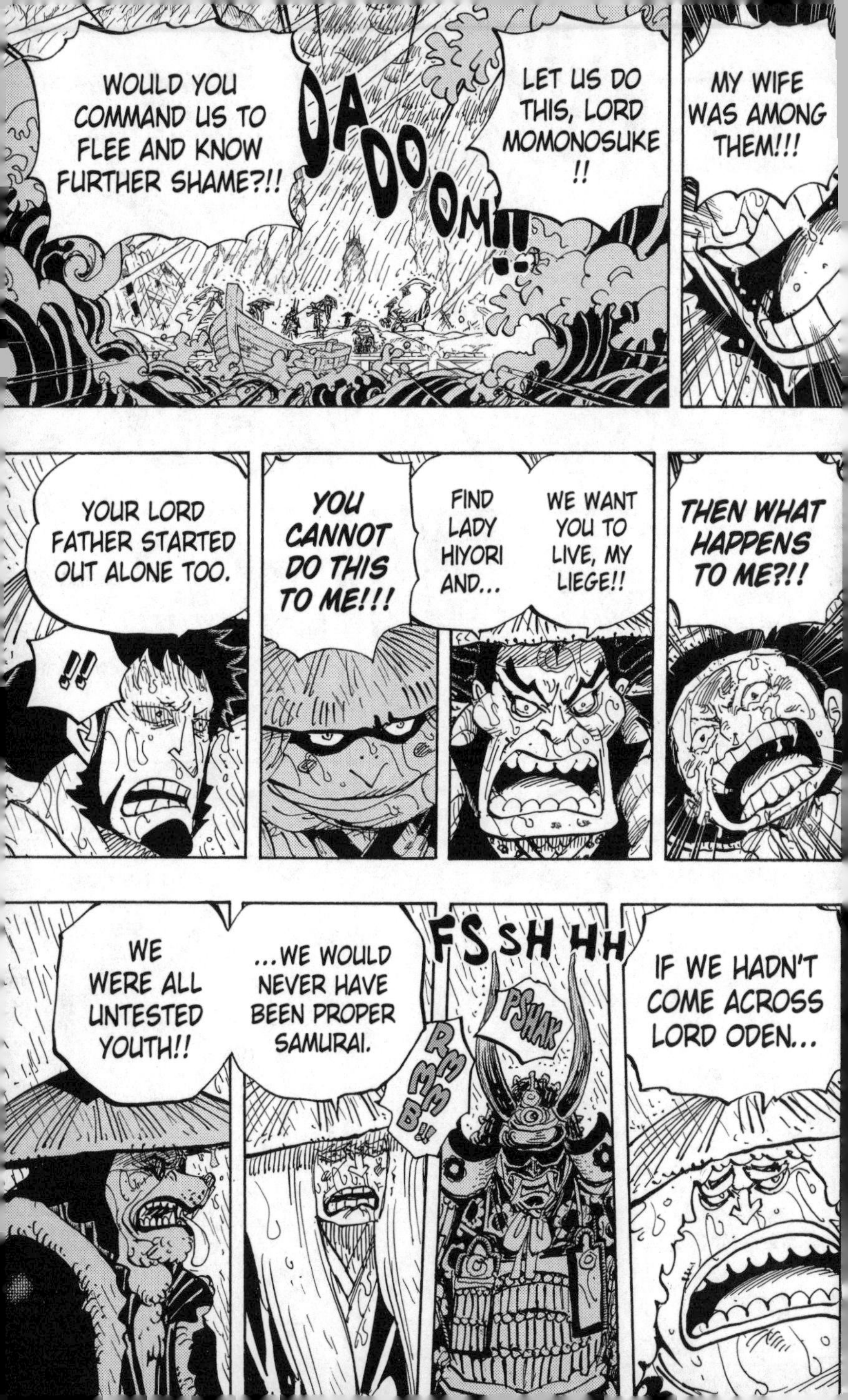
MY WIFE WAS AMONG THEM!!!
LET US DO THIS, LORD MOMONOSUKE !!
DADOOM!!
WOULD YOU COMMAND US TO FLEE AND KNOW FURTHER SHAME?!!
THEN WHAT HAPPENS TO ME?!!
WE WANT YOU TO LIVE, MY LIEGE!!
FIND LADY HIYORI AND...
YOU CANNOT DO THIS TO ME!!!
YOUR LORD FATHER STARTED OUT ALONE TOO.
!!
IF WE HADN'T COME ACROSS LORD ODEN...
FSSHHH
PSHAK
RMMMB!!
...WE WOULD NEVER HAVE BEEN PROPER SAMURAI.
WE WERE ALL UNTESTED YOUTH!!

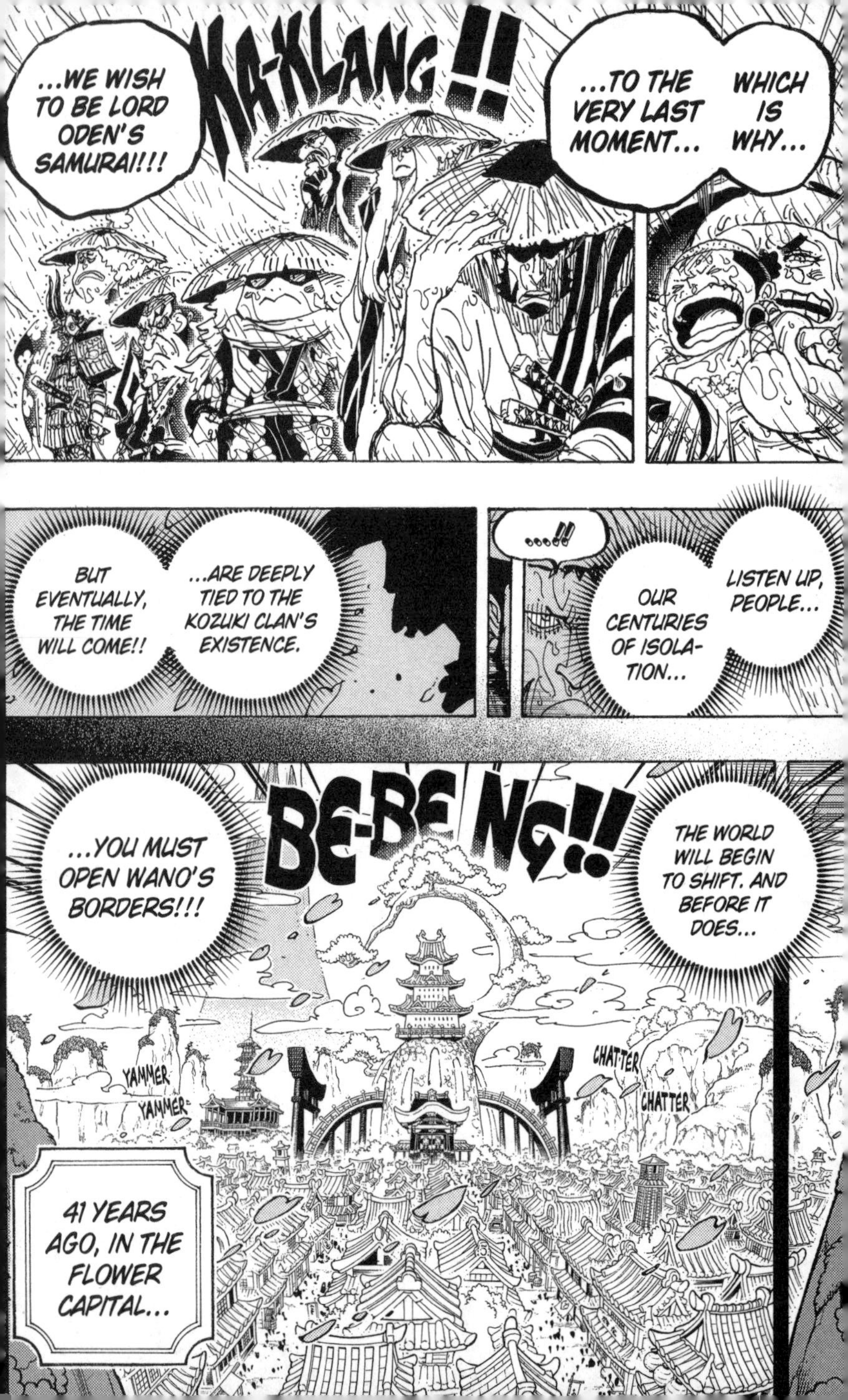
WHICH IS WHY...
...TO THE VERY LAST MOMENT...
...WE WISH TO BE LORD ODEN'S SAMURAI!!!
KA-KLANG!!
...!!
LISTEN UP, PEOPLE...
OUR CENTURIES OF ISOLATION...
...ARE DEEPLY TIED TO THE KOZUKI CLAN'S EXISTENCE.
BUT EVENTUALLY, THE TIME WILL COME!!
THE WORLD WILL BEGIN TO SHIFT. AND BEFORE IT DOES...
BE-BE NG!!
...YOU MUST OPEN WANO'S BORDERS!!!
CHAT-TER
CHATTER
YAMMER
YAMMER
41 YEARS AGO, IN THE FLOWER CAPITAL...

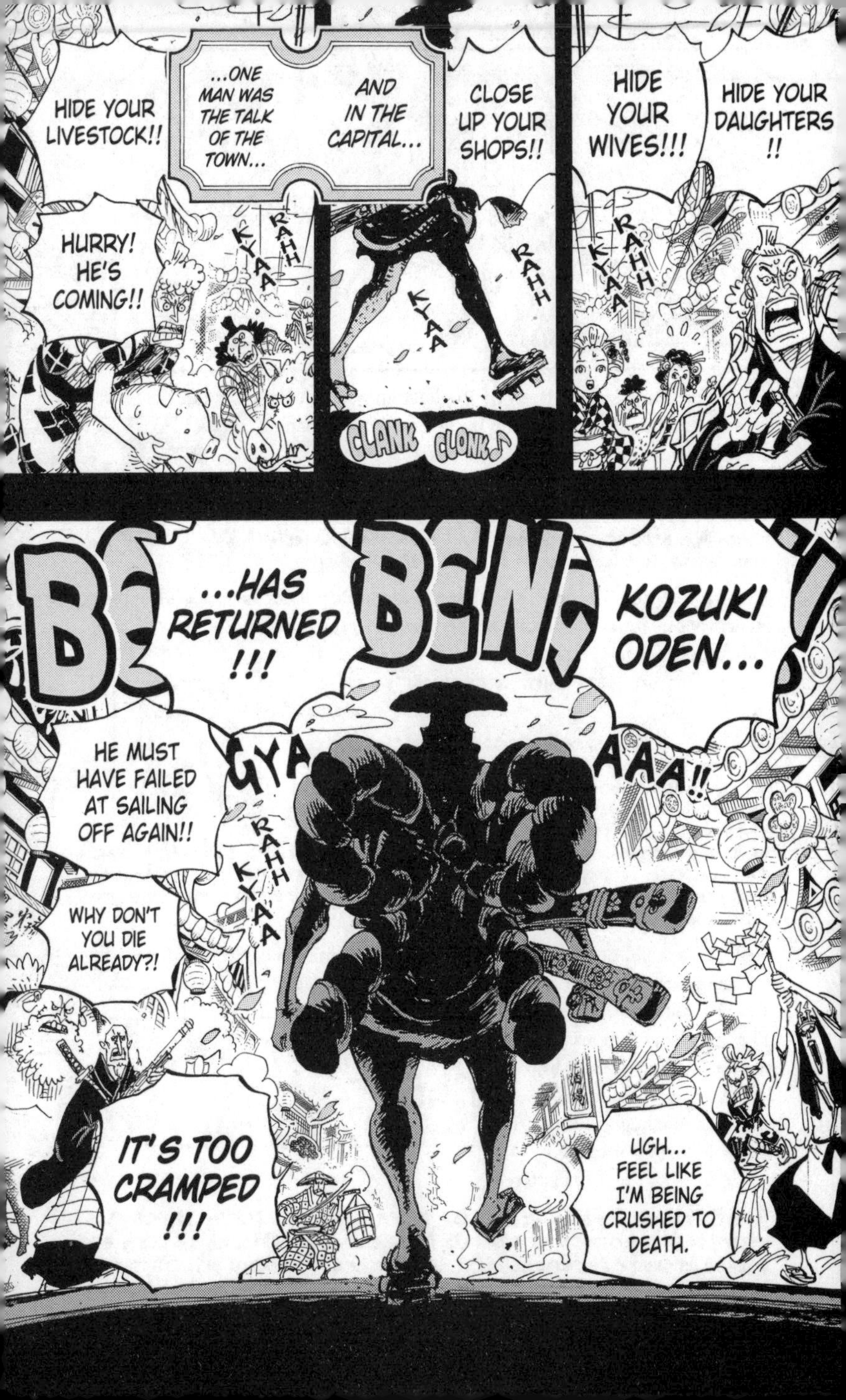

HIDE YOUR DAUGHTERS !!
HIDE YOUR WIVES!!!
RAHH
KYAA
CLOSE UP YOUR SHOPS!!
AND IN THE CAPITAL...
...ONE MAN WAS THE TALK OF THE TOWN...
RAHH
KYAA
CLANK
CLONK♪
HIDE YOUR LIVESTOCK!!
RAHH
KYAA
HURRY! HE'S COMING!!
BEN
BEN
KOZUKI ODEN...
...HAS RETURNED !!!
GYAAAA!!
HE MUST HAVE FAILED AT SAILING OFF AGAIN!!
RAHH
KYAA
WHY DON'T YOU DIE ALREADY?!
UGH... FEEL LIKE I'M BEING CRUSHED TO DEATH.
IT'S TOO CRAMPED !!!

SBS Question Corner

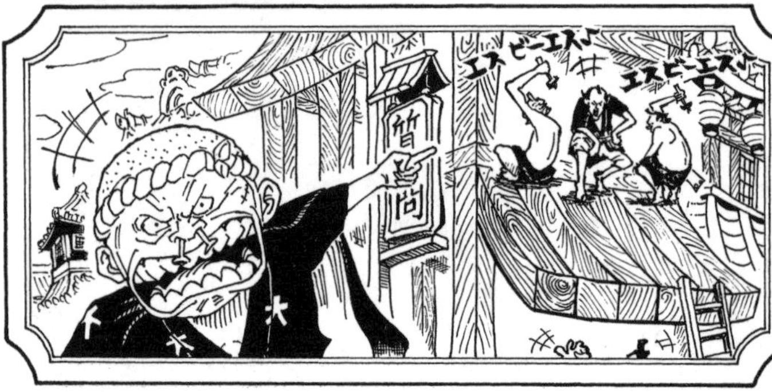
エスビーエス
エスビーエス

(Yuya, Gifu)

Q: I think that Captain Belo Betty of the Revolutionary Army's Eastern Forces is awesome and cool and beautiful! Is she based on Marianne, the figure from Delacroix's *Liberty Leading the People?*

--Yuito

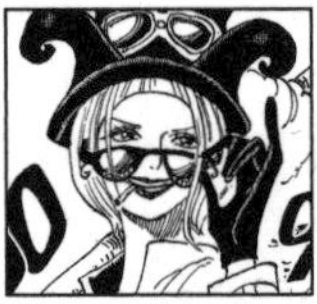

A: That's right. The painting where she's leading them like a tour bus guide! That was the image I was going for with Betty! She's very popular.

Q: This is a question for Odacchi!! How is it that transponder snails look like their owners? Sometimes they look like the person on the other end of the call, and sometimes they talk to people while looking like their owner! They are very mysterious creatures!

--Omame

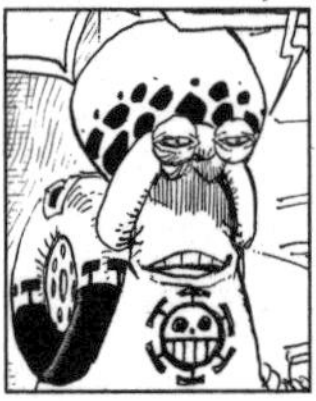

A: First of all, transponder snails have the ability to mimic the appearance of others. So they can disguise themselves with the features and looks of people who are close to them. When they're talking to someone else, they can pick up the expressions of the people they're talking to, but which one they choose, if any at all, is entirely up to the individual snail's mood. They're living things, not machines, so there are no hard rules on how they work.

Q: Hello, Odacchi! I noticed something about the people Franky tracks down while searching for the mansion plans in chapter 929. Kumagoro, Kobei, Kisegawa, Tokijiro, Rakuda... These are all names from famous *rakugo* stories! The line about Orochi having "tuna for sashimi" is also from a rakugo routine. You really do love your rakugo!

--The Eel Flatterer

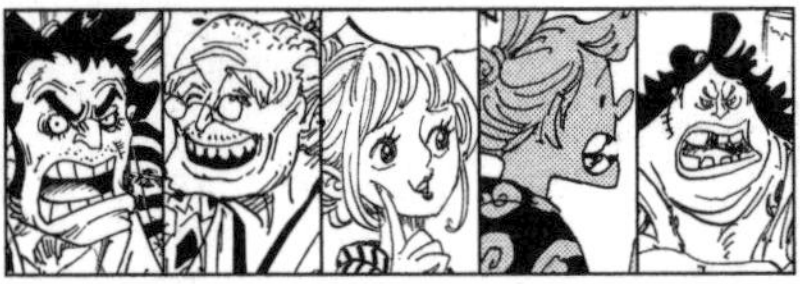

A: That's right! I'm a huge fan of the traditional form of comic storytelling known as rakugo. I've been stuffing this story arc full of little references! You don't need to know any of them, I'm just including them as Easter eggs for those in the know to recognize and enjoy!

Chapter 960:
INTRODUCING KOZUKI ODEN

GANG BEGE'S OH MY FAMILY
VOL. 10: "ON THE SEARCH!! FIND LOLA!!"

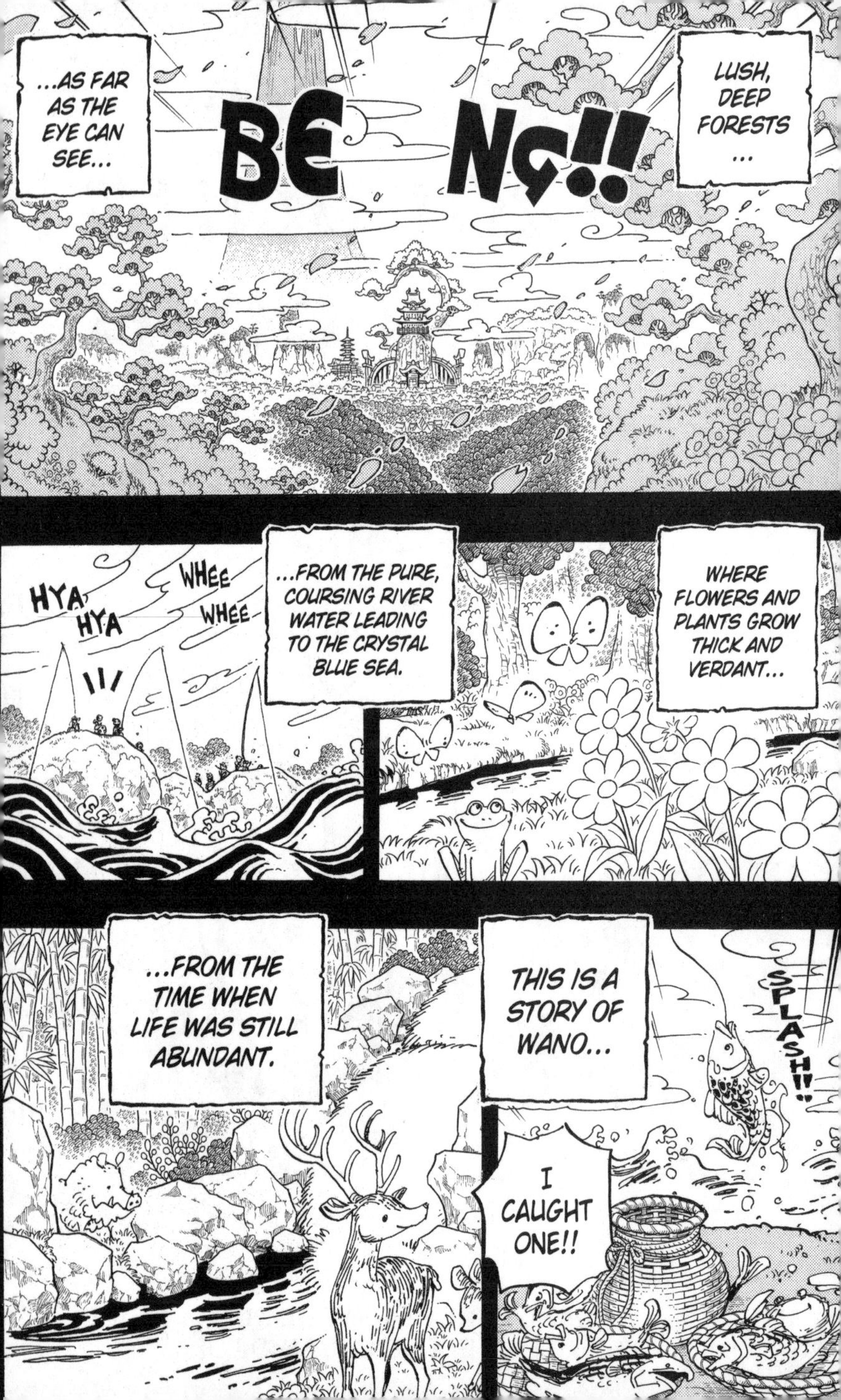
LUSH, DEEP FORESTS...
BENG!!
...AS FAR AS THE EYE CAN SEE...
WHERE FLOWERS AND PLANTS GROW THICK AND VERDANT...
...FROM THE PURE, COURSING RIVER WATER LEADING TO THE CRYSTAL BLUE SEA.
WHEE WHEE
HYA HYA
SPLASH!!
THIS IS A STORY OF WANO...
I CAUGHT ONE!!
...FROM THE TIME WHEN LIFE WAS STILL ABUNDANT.

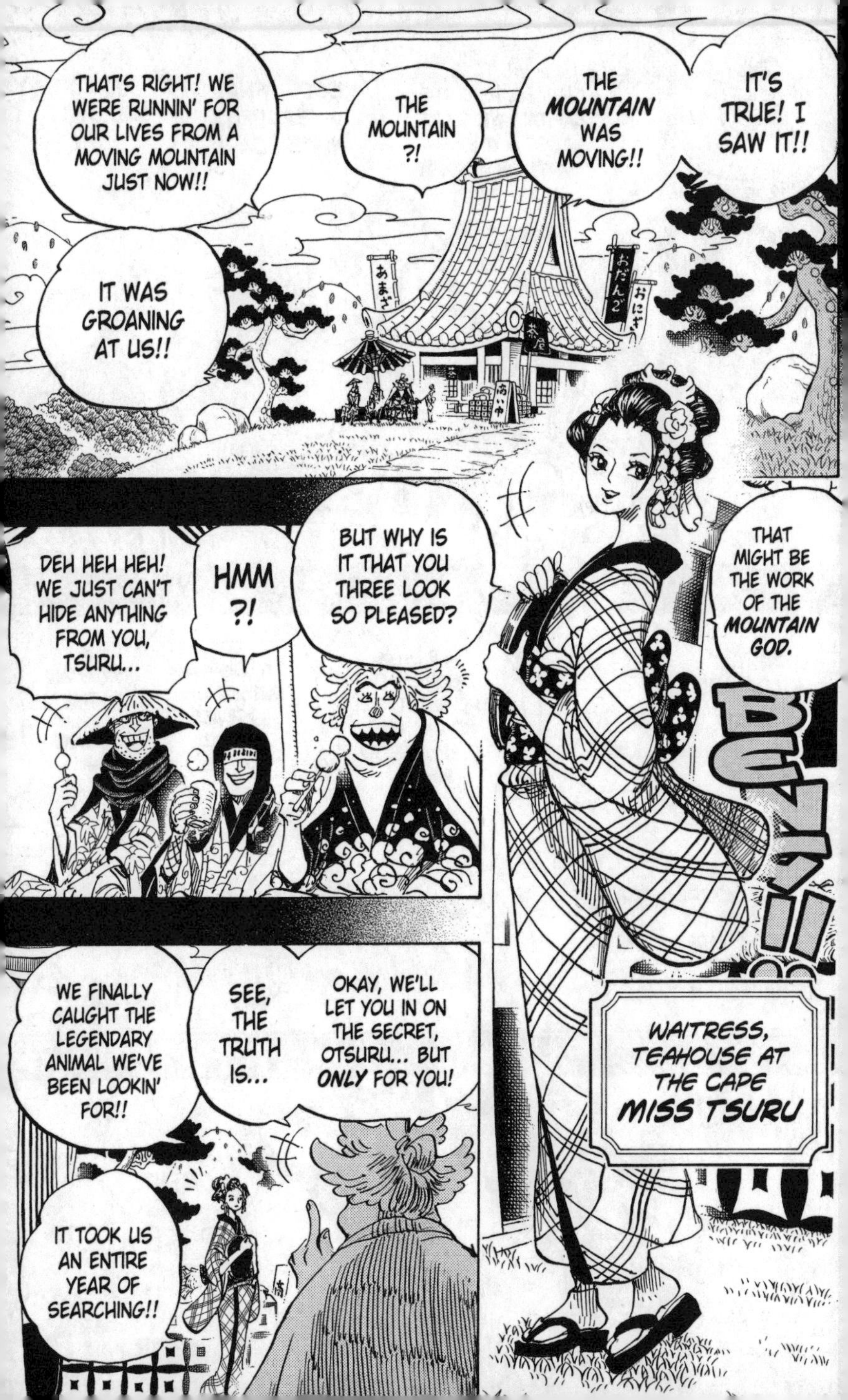
IT'S TRUE! I SAW IT!!
THE MOUNTAIN WAS MOVING!!
THE MOUNTAIN ?!
THAT'S RIGHT! WE WERE RUNNIN' FOR OUR LIVES FROM A MOVING MOUNTAIN JUST NOW!!
IT WAS GROANING AT US!!
あまざ
おだんご
おにぎ
茶屋
THAT MIGHT BE THE WORK OF THE MOUNTAIN GOD.
BUN!!
WAITRESS, TEAHOUSE AT THE CAPE MISS TSURU
BUT WHY IS IT THAT YOU THREE LOOK SO PLEASED?
HMM ?!
DEH HEH HEH! WE JUST CAN'T HIDE ANYTHING FROM YOU, TSURU...
OKAY, WE'LL LET YOU IN ON THE SECRET, OTSURU... BUT ONLY FOR YOU!
SEE, THE TRUTH IS...
WE FINALLY CAUGHT THE LEGENDARY ANIMAL WE'VE BEEN LOOKIN' FOR!!
IT TOOK US AN ENTIRE YEAR OF SEARCHING!!

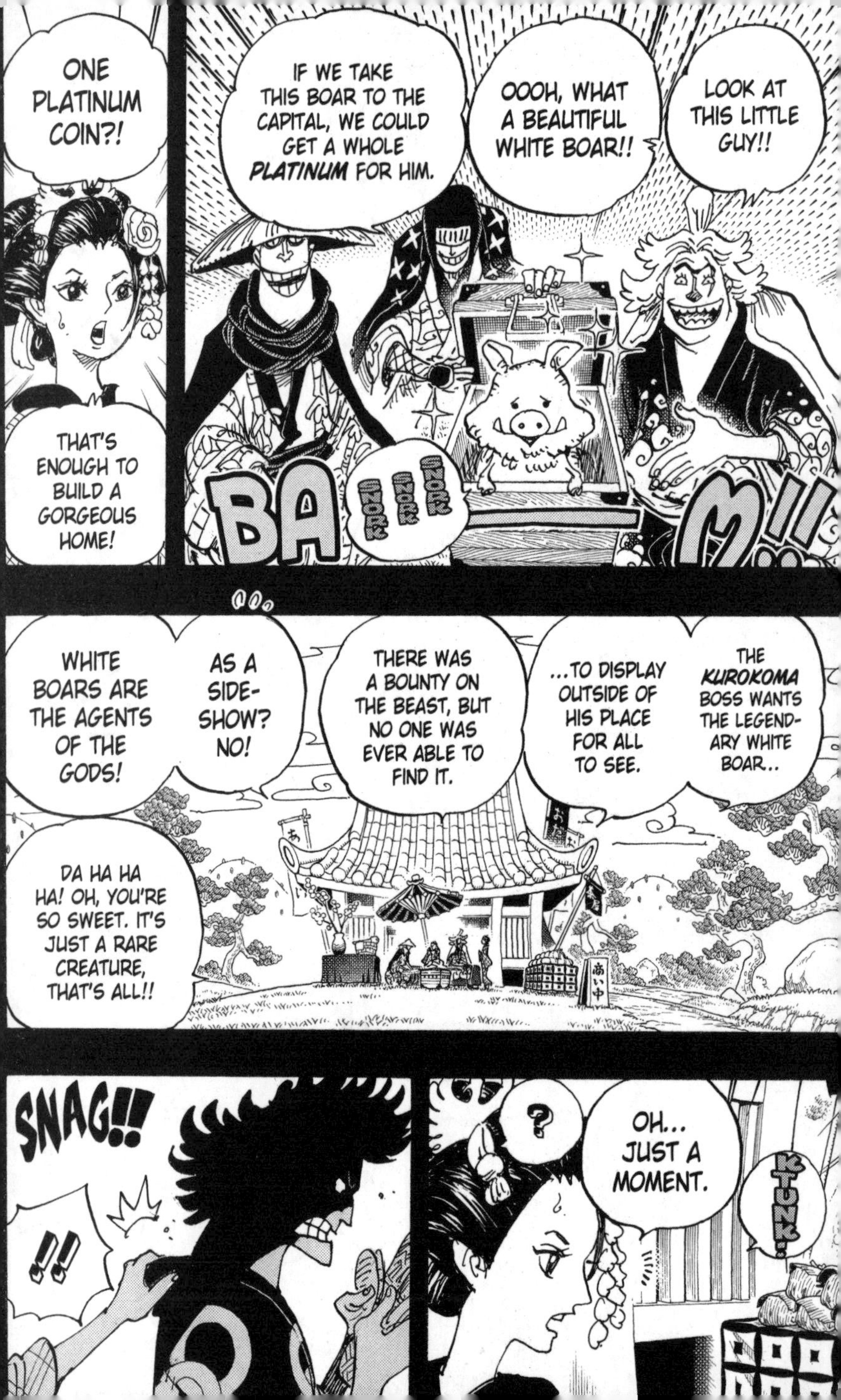

LOOK AT THIS LITTLE GUY!!
OOOH, WHAT A BEAUTIFUL WHITE BOAR!!
IF WE TAKE THIS BOAR TO THE CAPITAL, WE COULD GET A WHOLE PLATINUM FOR HIM.
BAM!!
SNORK SNORK SNORK
ONE PLATINUM COIN?!
THAT'S ENOUGH TO BUILD A GORGEOUS HOME!
THE KUROKOMA BOSS WANTS THE LEGENDARY WHITE BOAR..
...TO DISPLAY OUTSIDE OF HIS PLACE FOR ALL TO SEE.
THERE WAS A BOUNTY ON THE BEAST, BUT NO ONE WAS EVER ABLE TO FIND IT.
AS A SIDE-SHOW? NO!
WHITE BOARS ARE THE AGENTS OF THE GODS!
DA HA HA HA! OH, YOU'RE SO SWEET. IT'S JUST A RARE CREATURE, THAT'S ALL!!
?
OH... JUST A MOMENT.
KTUNK!
SNAG!!
!!

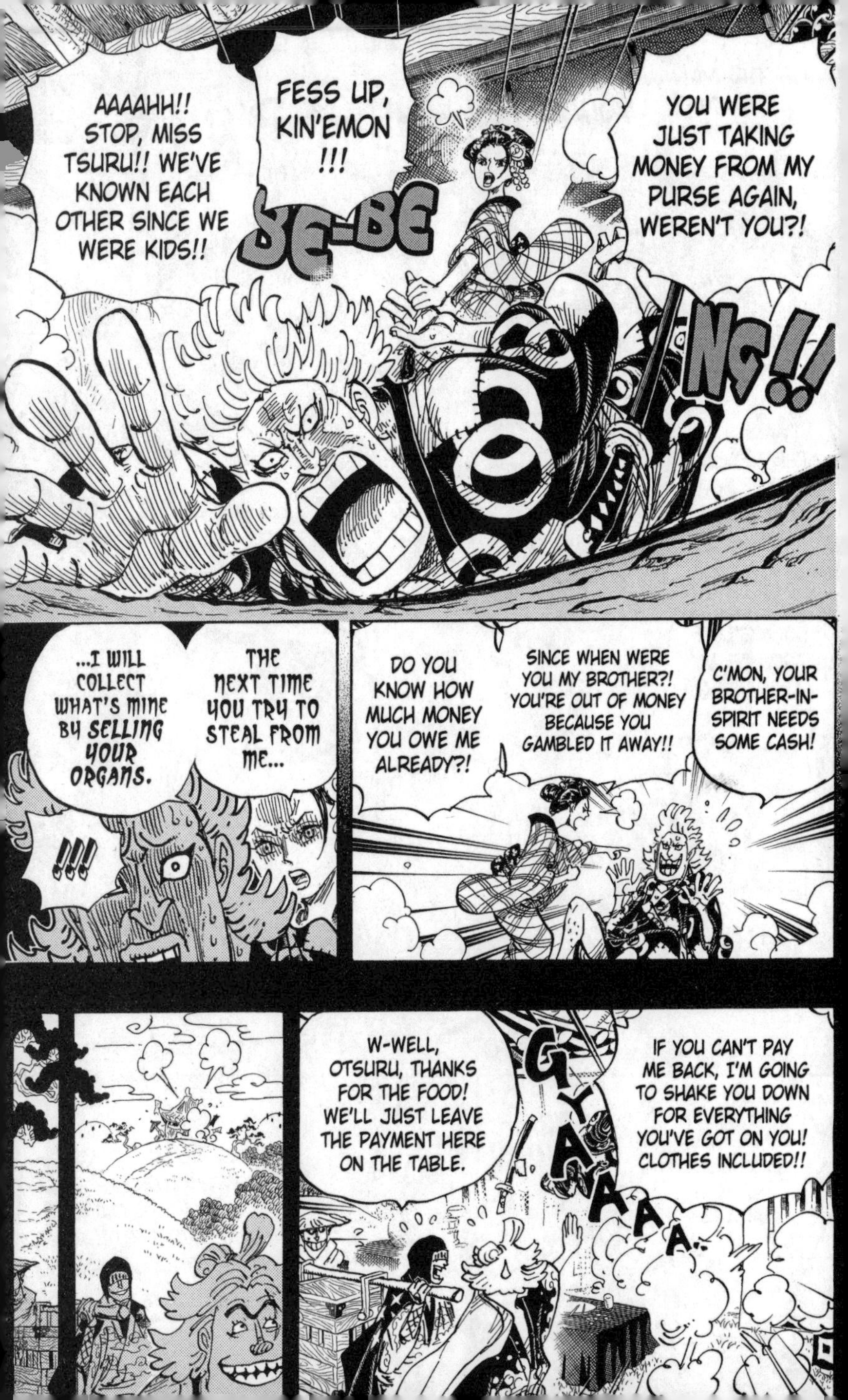
YOU WERE JUST TAKING MONEY FROM MY PURSE AGAIN, WEREN'T YOU?!
FESS UP, KIN'EMON!!!
AAAAHH!! STOP, MISS TSURU!! WE'VE KNOWN EACH OTHER SINCE WE WERE KIDS!!
BE-BE
NG!!
C'MON, YOUR BROTHER-IN-SPIRIT NEEDS SOME CASH!
SINCE WHEN WERE YOU MY BROTHER?! YOU'RE OUT OF MONEY BECAUSE YOU GAMBLED IT AWAY!!
DO YOU KNOW HOW MUCH MONEY YOU OWE ME ALREADY?!
THE NEXT TIME YOU TRY TO STEAL FROM ME...
...I WILL COLLECT WHAT'S MINE BY SELLING YOUR ORGANS.
!!!
IF YOU CAN'T PAY ME BACK, I'M GOING TO SHAKE YOU DOWN FOR EVERYTHING YOU'VE GOT ON YOU! CLOTHES INCLUDED!!
GYAAAAA
W-WELL, OTSURU, THANKS FOR THE FOOD! WE'LL JUST LEAVE THE PAYMENT HERE ON THE TABLE.

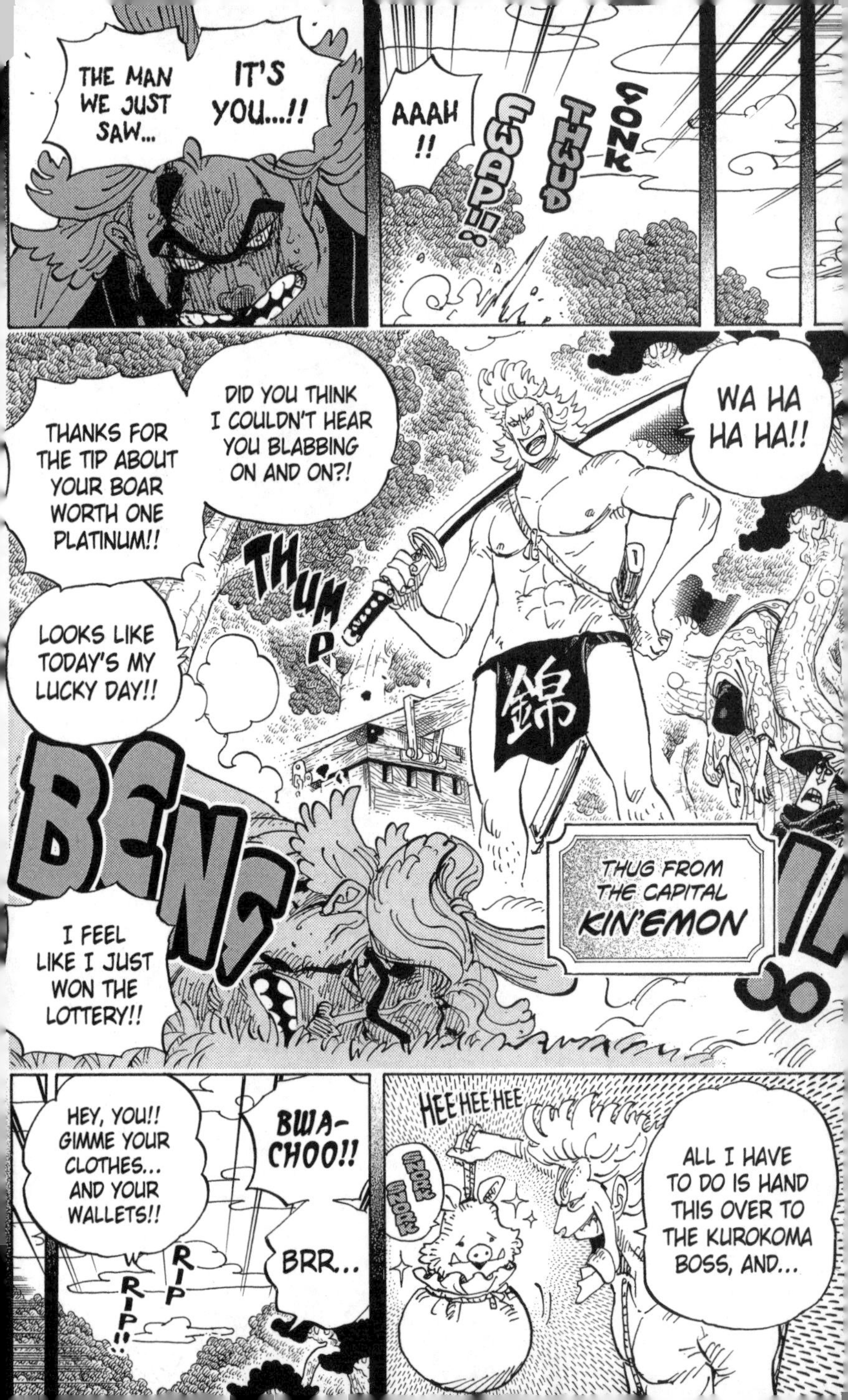
GONK
THWUD
FWAP!!
AAAH!!
IT'S YOU...!!
THE MAN WE JUST SAW...
WA HA HA HA!!
DID YOU THINK I COULDN'T HEAR YOU BLABBING ON AND ON?!
THANKS FOR THE TIP ABOUT YOUR BOAR WORTH ONE PLATINUM!!
THUMP
LOOKS LIKE TODAY'S MY LUCKY DAY!!
THUG FROM THE CAPITAL KIN'EMON
BENG
I FEEL LIKE I JUST WON THE LOTTERY!!
HEE HEE HEE
ALL I HAVE TO DO IS HAND THIS OVER TO THE KUROKOMA BOSS, AND...
BWA-CHOO!!
HEY, YOU!! GIMME YOUR CLOTHES... AND YOUR WALLETS!!
BRR...
RIP
RIP!!

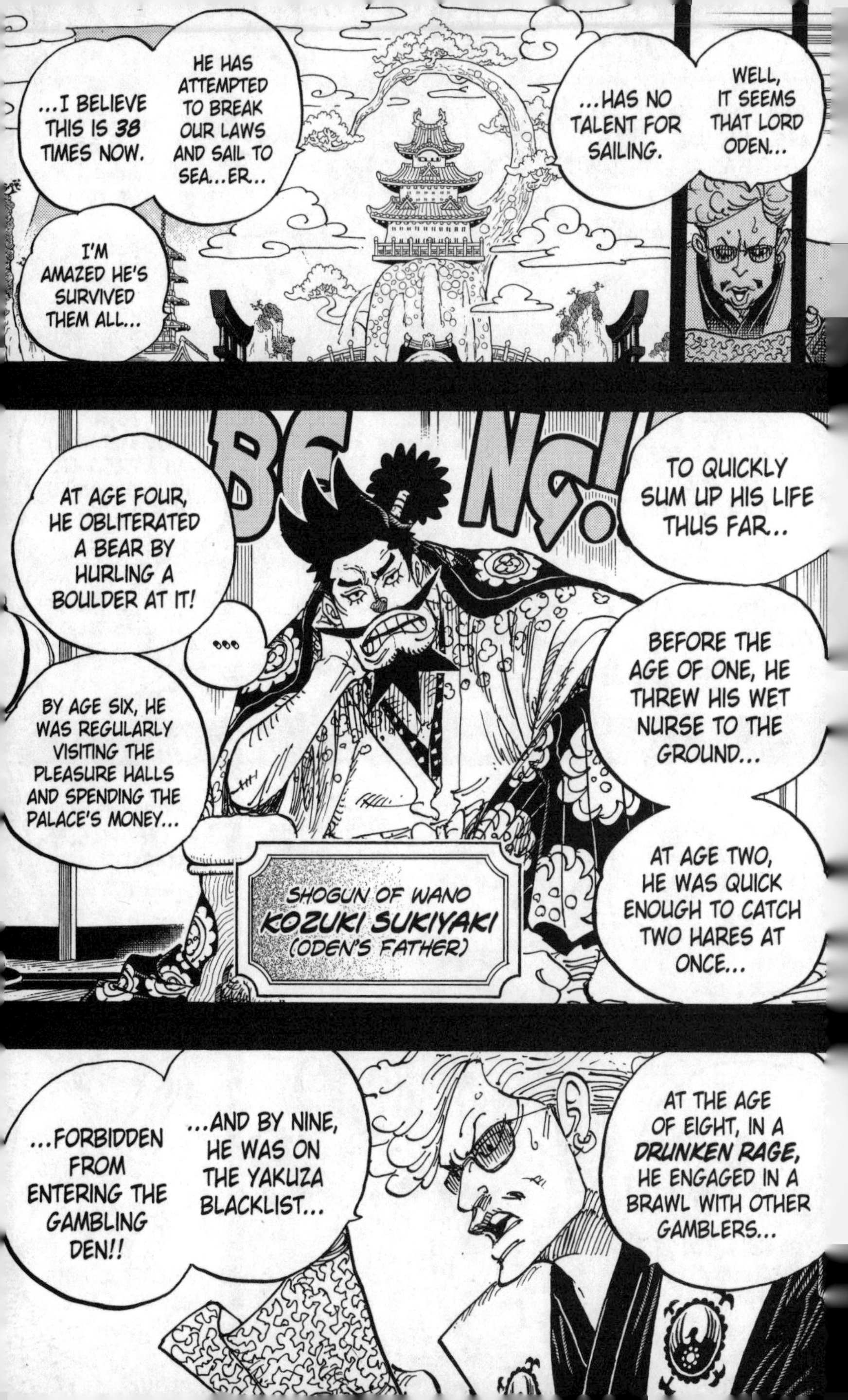
WELL, IT SEEMS THAT LORD ODEN...
...HAS NO TALENT FOR SAILING.
HE HAS ATTEMPTED TO BREAK OUR LAWS AND SAIL TO SEA...ER...
...I BELIEVE THIS IS 38 TIMES NOW.
I'M AMAZED HE'S SURVIVED THEM ALL...
TO QUICKLY SUM UP HIS LIFE THUS FAR...
BEFORE THE AGE OF ONE, HE THREW HIS WET NURSE TO THE GROUND...
AT AGE TWO, HE WAS QUICK ENOUGH TO CATCH TWO HARES AT ONCE...
AT AGE FOUR, HE OBLITERATED A BEAR BY HURLING A BOULDER AT IT!
...
BY AGE SIX, HE WAS REGULARLY VISITING THE PLEASURE HALLS AND SPENDING THE PALACE'S MONEY...
SHOGUN OF WANO
KOZUKI SUKIYAKI
(ODEN'S FATHER)
AT THE AGE OF EIGHT, IN A DRUNKEN RAGE, HE ENGAGED IN A BRAWL WITH OTHER GAMBLERS...
...AND BY NINE, HE WAS ON THE YAKUZA BLACKLIST...
...FORBIDDEN FROM ENTERING THE GAMBLING DEN!!

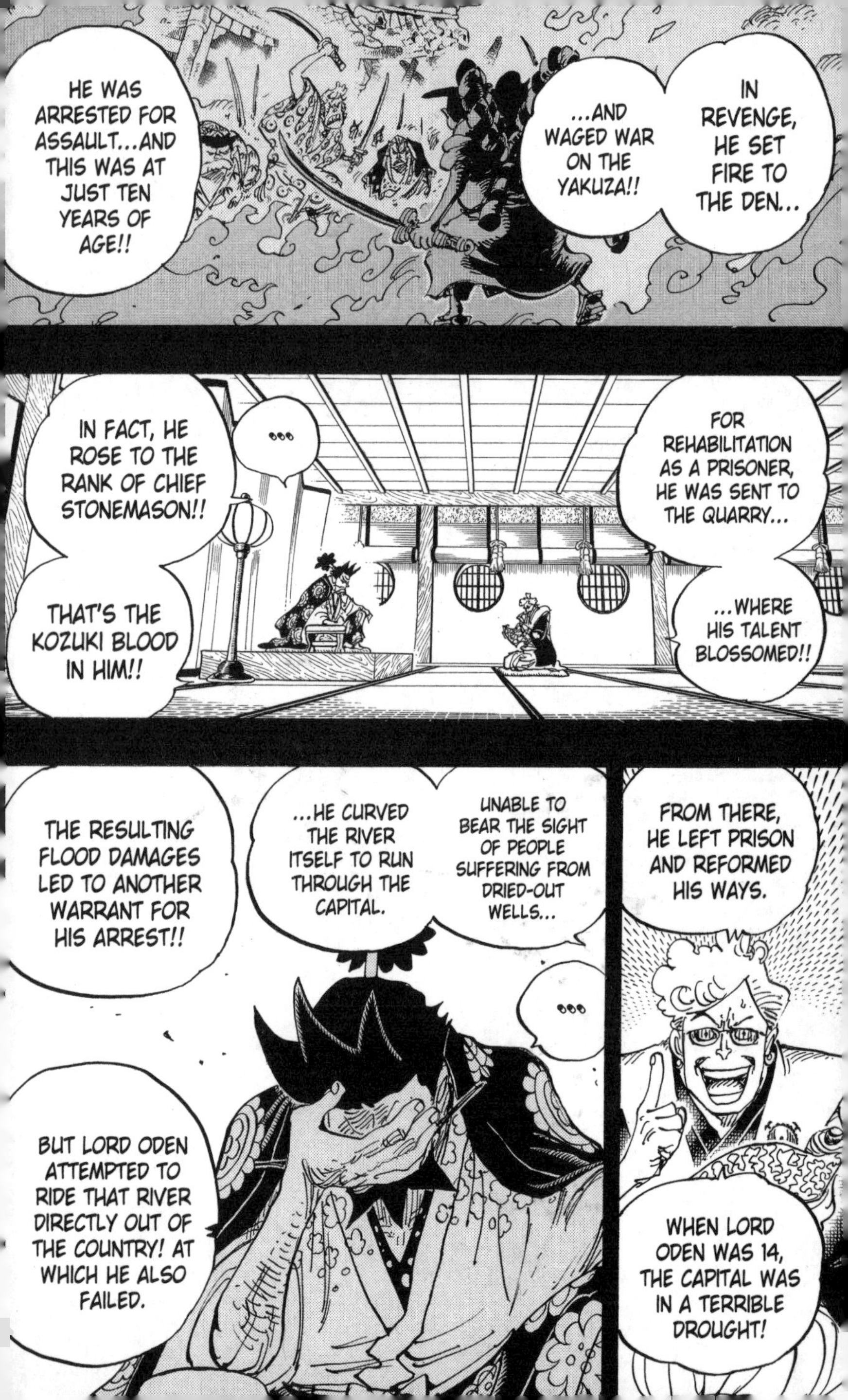
IN REVENGE, HE SET FIRE TO THE DEN...
...AND WAGED WAR ON THE YAKUZA!!
HE WAS ARRESTED FOR ASSAULT...AND THIS WAS AT JUST TEN YEARS OF AGE!!
FOR REHABILITATION AS A PRISONER, HE WAS SENT TO THE QUARRY...
...WHERE HIS TALENT BLOSSOMED!!
...
IN FACT, HE ROSE TO THE RANK OF CHIEF STONEMASON!!
THAT'S THE KOZUKI BLOOD IN HIM!!
FROM THERE, HE LEFT PRISON AND REFORMED HIS WAYS.
WHEN LORD ODEN WAS 14, THE CAPITAL WAS IN A TERRIBLE DROUGHT!
UNABLE TO BEAR THE SIGHT OF PEOPLE SUFFERING FROM DRIED-OUT WELLS...
...HE CURVED THE RIVER ITSELF TO RUN THROUGH THE CAPITAL.
THE RESULTING FLOOD DAMAGES LED TO ANOTHER WARRANT FOR HIS ARREST!!
...
BUT LORD ODEN ATTEMPTED TO RIDE THAT RIVER DIRECTLY OUT OF THE COUNTRY! AT WHICH HE ALSO FAILED.

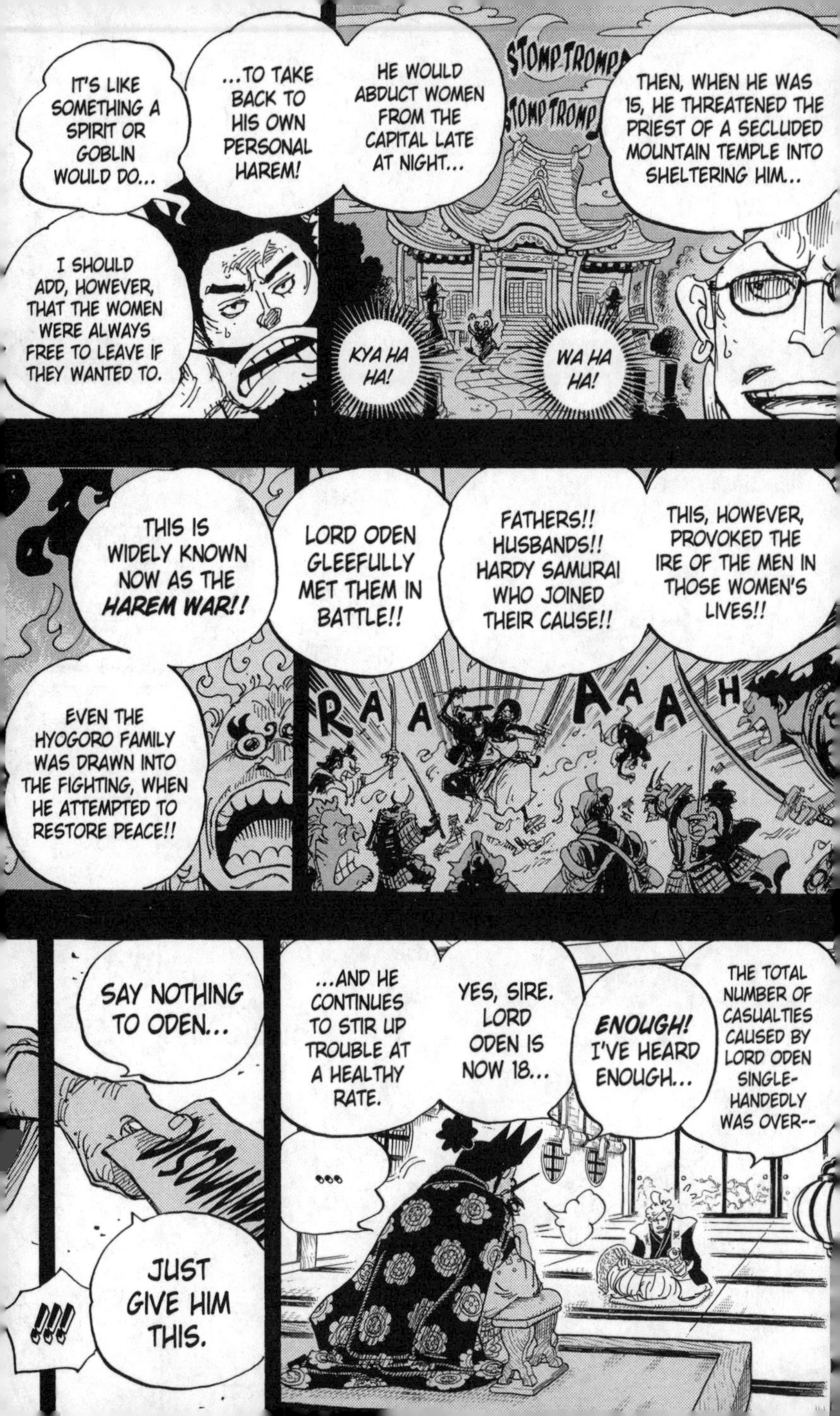
THEN, WHEN HE WAS 15, HE THREATENED THE PRIEST OF A SECLUDED MOUNTAIN TEMPLE INTO SHELTERING HIM...
STOMP TROMP
STOMP TROMP
HE WOULD ABDUCT WOMEN FROM THE CAPITAL LATE AT NIGHT...
WA HA HA!
KYA HA HA!
...TO TAKE BACK TO HIS OWN PERSONAL HAREM!
IT'S LIKE SOMETHING A SPIRIT OR GOBLIN WOULD DO...
I SHOULD ADD, HOWEVER, THAT THE WOMEN WERE ALWAYS FREE TO LEAVE IF THEY WANTED TO.
THIS, HOWEVER, PROVOKED THE IRE OF THE MEN IN THOSE WOMEN'S LIVES!!
FATHERS!! HUSBANDS!! HARDY SAMURAI WHO JOINED THEIR CAUSE!!
LORD ODEN GLEEFULLY MET THEM IN BATTLE!!
RAAAAAH
THIS IS WIDELY KNOWN NOW AS THE HAREM WAR!!
EVEN THE HYOGORO FAMILY WAS DRAWN INTO THE FIGHTING, WHEN HE ATTEMPTED TO RESTORE PEACE!!
THE TOTAL NUMBER OF CASUALTIES CAUSED BY LORD ODEN SINGLE-HANDEDLY WAS OVER--
ENOUGH! I'VE HEARD ENOUGH...
YES, SIRE. LORD ODEN IS NOW 18...
...AND HE CONTINUES TO STIR UP TROUBLE AT A HEALTHY RATE.
...
SAY NOTHING TO ODEN...
!!!
JUST GIVE HIM THIS.

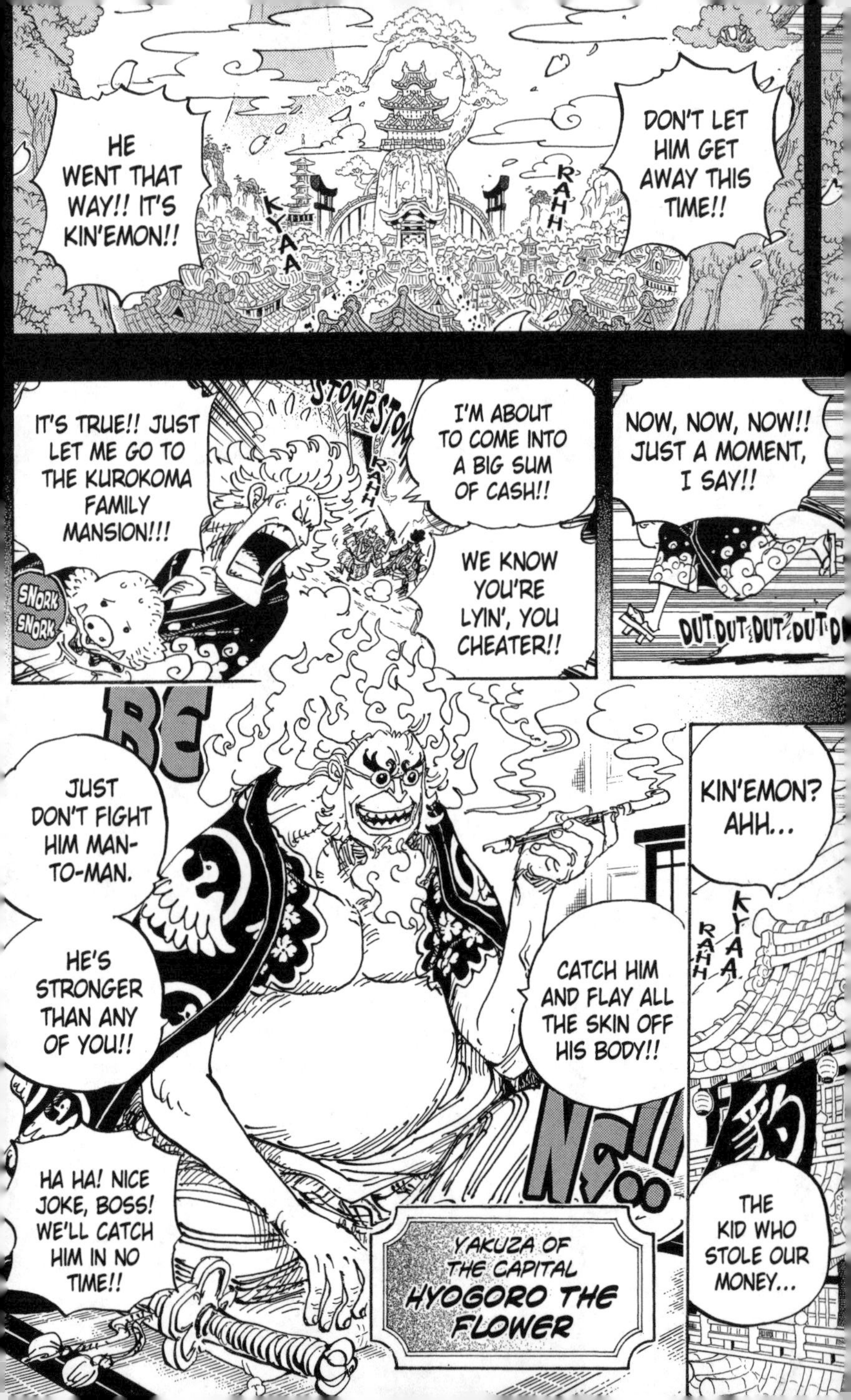
DON'T LET HIM GET AWAY THIS TIME!!
RAHH
KYAA
HE WENT THAT WAY!! IT'S KIN'EMON!!
NOW, NOW, NOW!! JUST A MOMENT, I SAY!!
DUT DUT DUT DUT
I'M ABOUT TO COME INTO A BIG SUM OF CASH!!
STOMP
RAHH
IT'S TRUE!! JUST LET ME GO TO THE KUROKOMA FAMILY MANSION!!!
WE KNOW YOU'RE LYIN', YOU CHEATER!!
SNORK SNORK
KIN'EMON? AHH...
KYAA
RAHH
THE KID WHO STOLE OUR MONEY...
CATCH HIM AND FLAY ALL THE SKIN OFF HIS BODY!!
JUST DON'T FIGHT HIM MAN-TO-MAN.
HE'S STRONGER THAN ANY OF YOU!!
HA HA! NICE JOKE, BOSS! WE'LL CATCH HIM IN NO TIME!!
YAKUZA OF THE CAPITAL
HYOGORO THE FLOWER

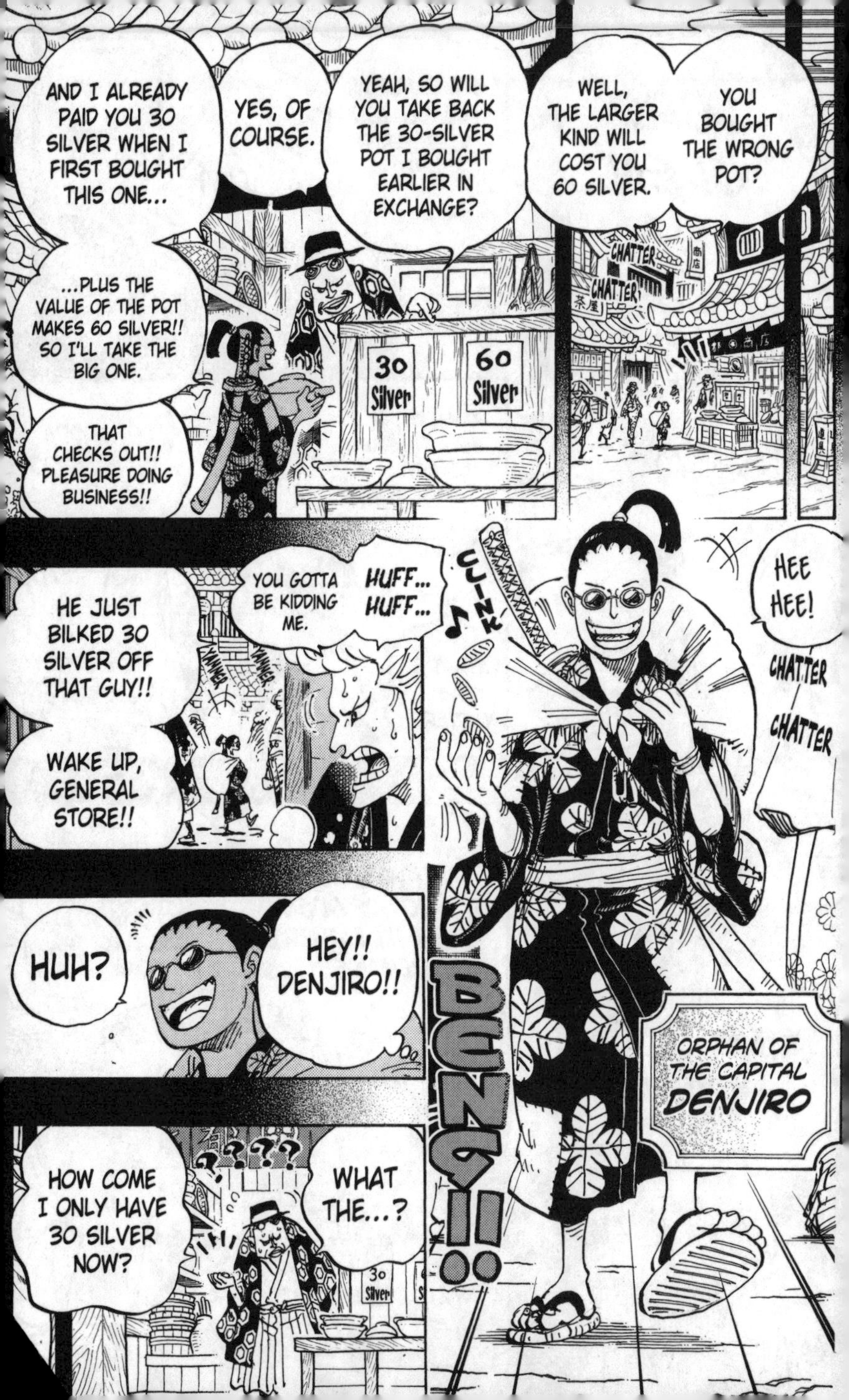
YOU BOUGHT THE WRONG POT?
WELL, THE LARGER KIND WILL COST YOU 60 SILVER.
CHATTER
CHATTER
YEAH, SO WILL YOU TAKE BACK THE 30-SILVER POT I BOUGHT EARLIER IN EXCHANGE?
YES, OF COURSE.
AND I ALREADY PAID YOU 30 SILVER WHEN I FIRST BOUGHT THIS ONE...
60 Silver
30 Silver
...PLUS THE VALUE OF THE POT MAKES 60 SILVER!! SO I'LL TAKE THE BIG ONE.
THAT CHECKS OUT!! PLEASURE DOING BUSINESS!!
HEE HEE!
CLINK
CHATTER
CHATTER
BENG!!
ORPHAN OF THE CAPITAL DENJIRO
HUFF... HUFF...
YOU GOTTA BE KIDDING ME.
YAMMER
YAMMER
HE JUST BILKED 30 SILVER OFF THAT GUY!!
WAKE UP, GENERAL STORE!!
HEY!! DENJIRO!!
HUH?
WHAT THE...?
HOW COME I ONLY HAVE 30 SILVER NOW?
30 Silver

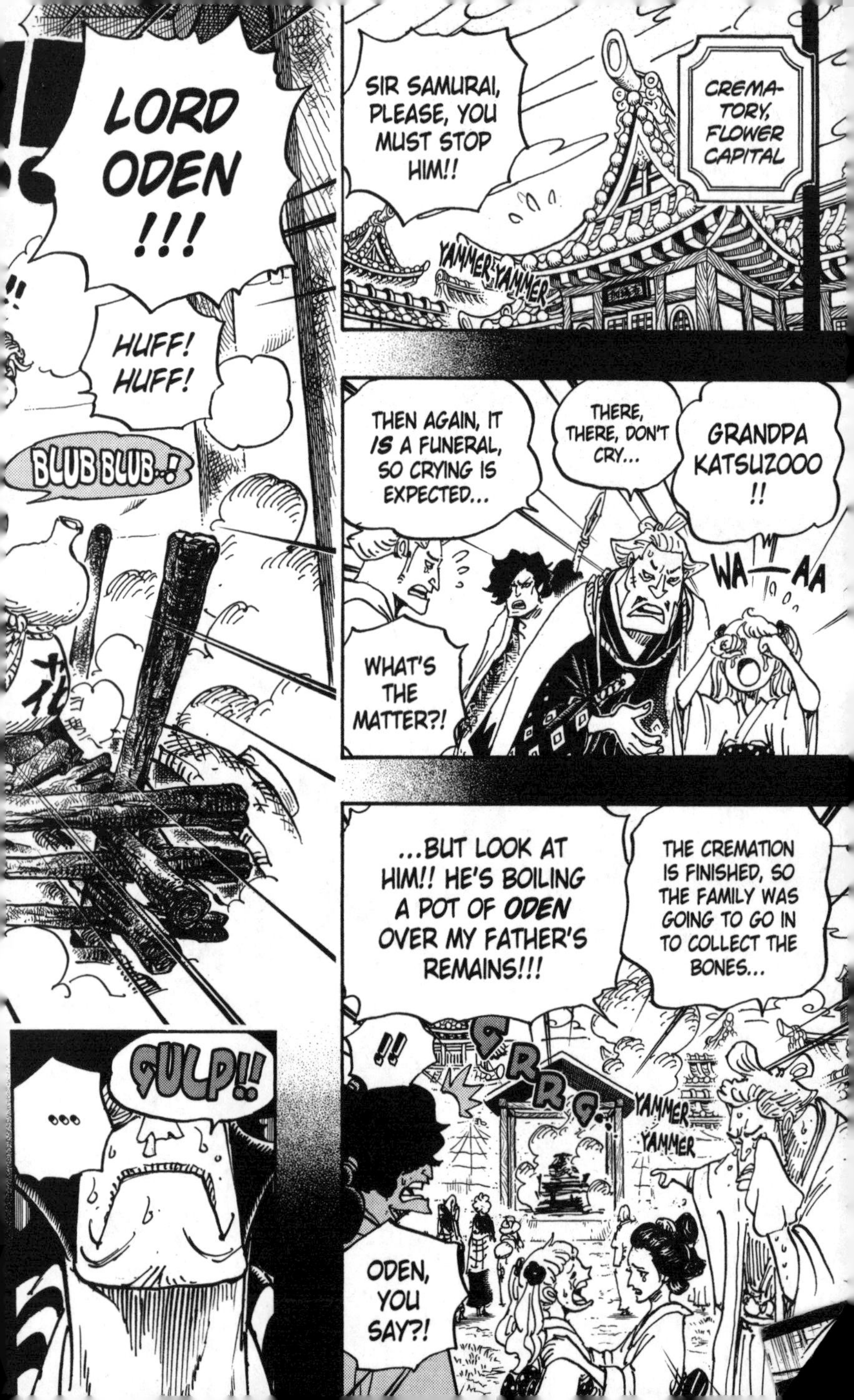
CREMATORY, FLOWER CAPITAL
SIR SAMURAI, PLEASE, YOU MUST STOP HIM!!
YAMMER YAMMER
GRANDPA KATSUZOOO!!
WA—AA
THERE, THERE, DON'T CRY...
THEN AGAIN, IT IS A FUNERAL, SO CRYING IS EXPECTED...
WHAT'S THE MATTER?!
THE CREMATION IS FINISHED, SO THE FAMILY WAS GOING TO GO IN TO COLLECT THE BONES...
...BUT LOOK AT HIM!! HE'S BOILING A POT OF ODEN OVER MY FATHER'S REMAINS!!!
!!
GRRRG..!
YAMMER YAMMER
ODEN, YOU SAY?!
LORD ODEN!!!
HUFF! HUFF!
BLUB BLUB..!
GULP!!
...

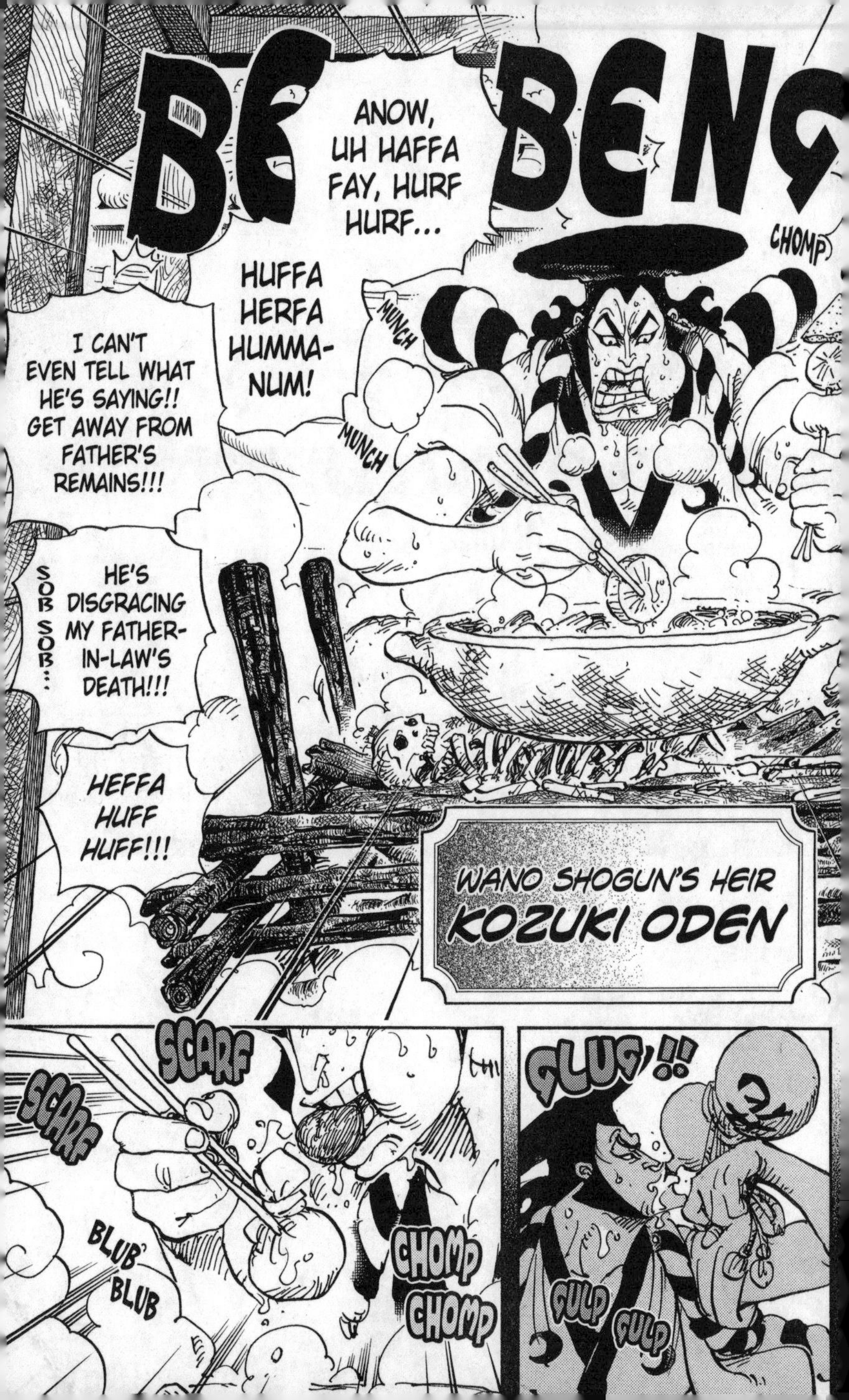

BENG
CHOMP
BE
ANOW, UH HAFFA FAY, HURF HURF...
HUFFA HERFA HUMMA-NUM!
MUNCH
MUNCH
I CAN'T EVEN TELL WHAT HE'S SAYING!! GET AWAY FROM FATHER'S REMAINS!!!
HE'S DISGRACING MY FATHER-IN-LAW'S DEATH!!!
SOB SOB...
HEFFA HUFF HUFF!!!
WANO SHOGUN'S HEIR
KOZUKI ODEN
GLUG!!
GULP GULP
SCARF
SCARF
CHOMP CHOMP
BLUB BLUB

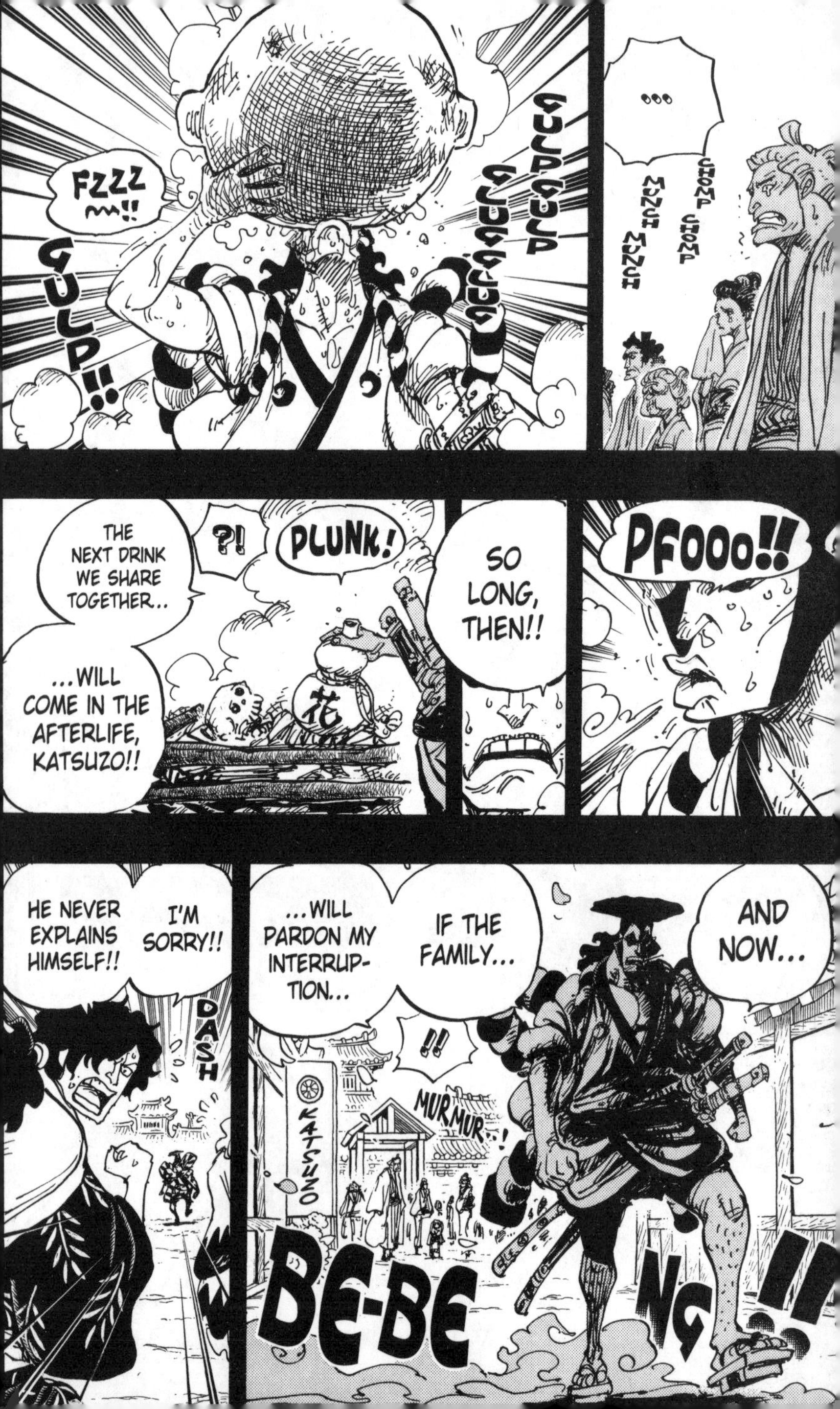
...
CHOMP CHOMP
MUNCH MUNCH
GULP GULP
GLUG GLUG
FZZZ~!!
GULP!!
PFOOO!!
SO LONG, THEN!!
?!
PLUNK!
THE NEXT DRINK WE SHARE TOGETHER..
...WILL COME IN THE AFTERLIFE, KATSUZO!!
AND NOW...
IF THE FAMILY...
...WILL PARDON MY INTERRUP-TION...
!!
MURMUR..!
KATSUZO
BE-BENG!!
I'M SORRY!!
HE NEVER EXPLAINS HIMSELF!!
DASH

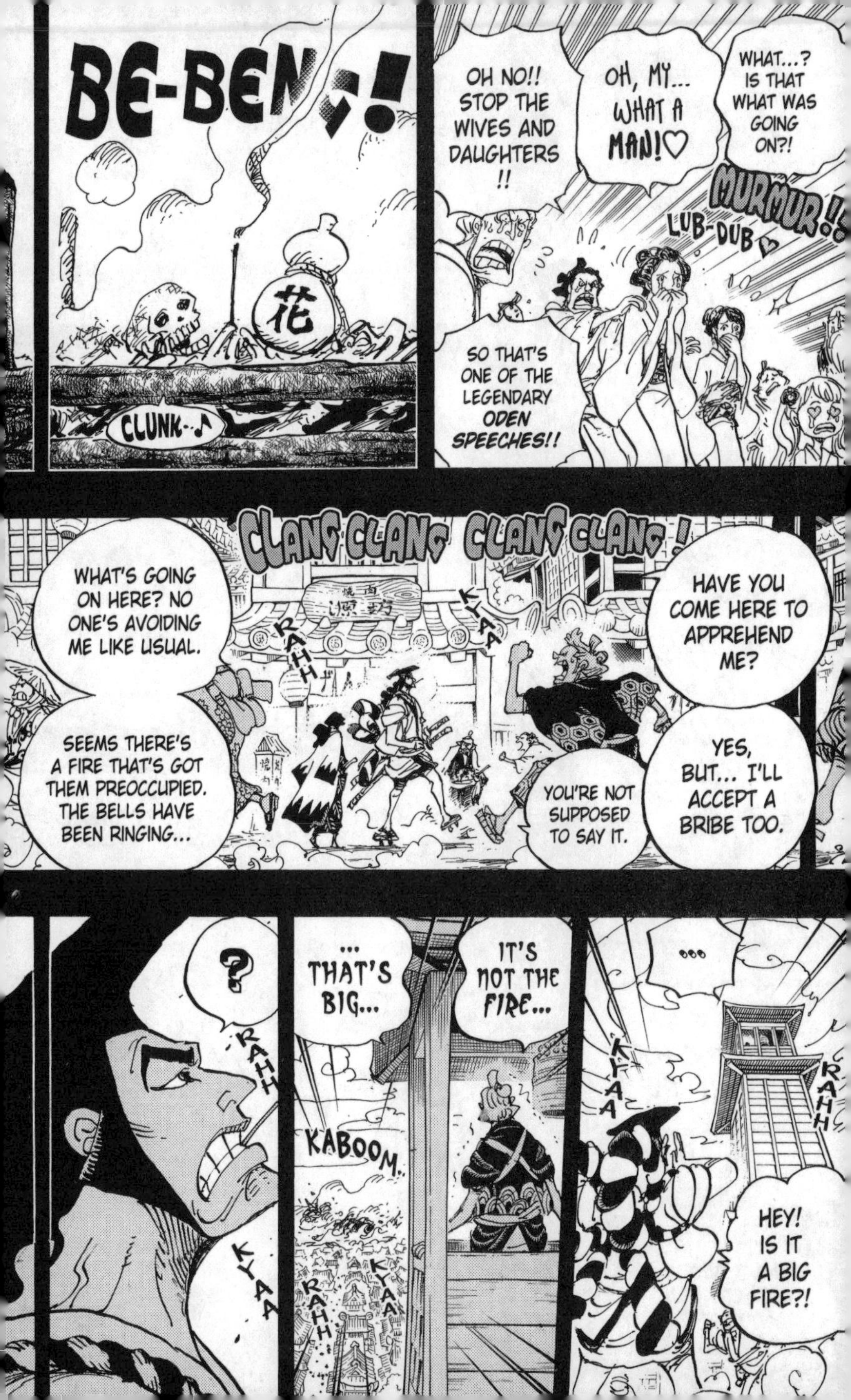
WHAT...? IS THAT WHAT WAS GOING ON?!
OH, MY... WHAT A MAN!♡
MURMUR!!
LUB-DUB♡
OH NO!! STOP THE WIVES AND DAUGHTERS!!
SO THAT'S ONE OF THE LEGENDARY ODEN SPEECHES!!
BE-BEN!!
CLUNK..♪
CLANG CLANG CLANG CLANG!
HAVE YOU COME HERE TO APPREHEND ME?
KYAA
YES, BUT... I'LL ACCEPT A BRIBE TOO.
YOU'RE NOT SUPPOSED TO SAY IT.
RAHH
WHAT'S GOING ON HERE? NO ONE'S AVOIDING ME LIKE USUAL.
SEEMS THERE'S A FIRE THAT'S GOT THEM PREOCCUPIED. THE BELLS HAVE BEEN RINGING...
...
RAHH
KYAA
HEY! IS IT A BIG FIRE?!
IT'S NOT THE FIRE...
... THAT'S BIG...
KABOOM..
KYAA
RAHH
?
RAHH
KYAA

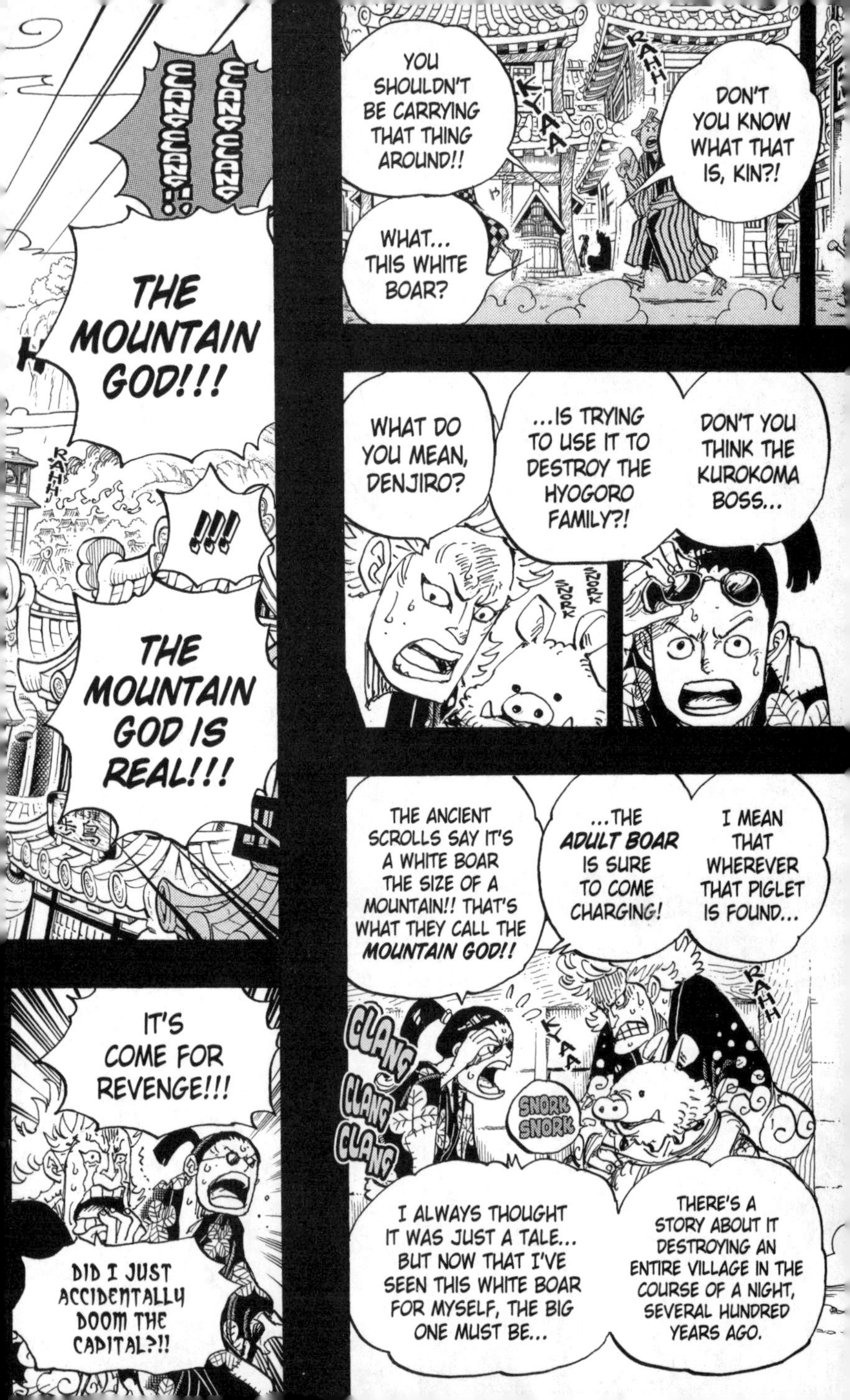
RAHH
DON'T YOU KNOW WHAT THAT IS, KIN?!
KYAA
YOU SHOULDN'T BE CARRYING THAT THING AROUND!!
WHAT... THIS WHITE BOAR?
DON'T YOU THINK THE KUROKOMA BOSS...
...IS TRYING TO USE IT TO DESTROY THE HYOGORO FAMILY?!
WHAT DO YOU MEAN, DENJIRO?
SNORK SNORK
I MEAN THAT WHEREVER THAT PIGLET IS FOUND...
...THE ADULT BOAR IS SURE TO COME CHARGING!
THE ANCIENT SCROLLS SAY IT'S A WHITE BOAR THE SIZE OF A MOUNTAIN!! THAT'S WHAT THEY CALL THE MOUNTAIN GOD!!
RAHH
KYAA
SNORK SNORK
CLANG CLANG CLANG
THERE'S A STORY ABOUT IT DESTROYING AN ENTIRE VILLAGE IN THE COURSE OF A NIGHT, SEVERAL HUNDRED YEARS AGO.
I ALWAYS THOUGHT IT WAS JUST A TALE... BUT NOW THAT I'VE SEEN THIS WHITE BOAR FOR MYSELF, THE BIG ONE MUST BE...
CLANGCLANG CLANGCLANG!!
THE MOUNTAIN GOD!!!
RAHH
!!!
THE MOUNTAIN GOD IS REAL!!!
IT'S JUST COME FOR REVENGE!!!
DID I JUST ACCIDENTALLY DOOM THE CAPITAL?!!

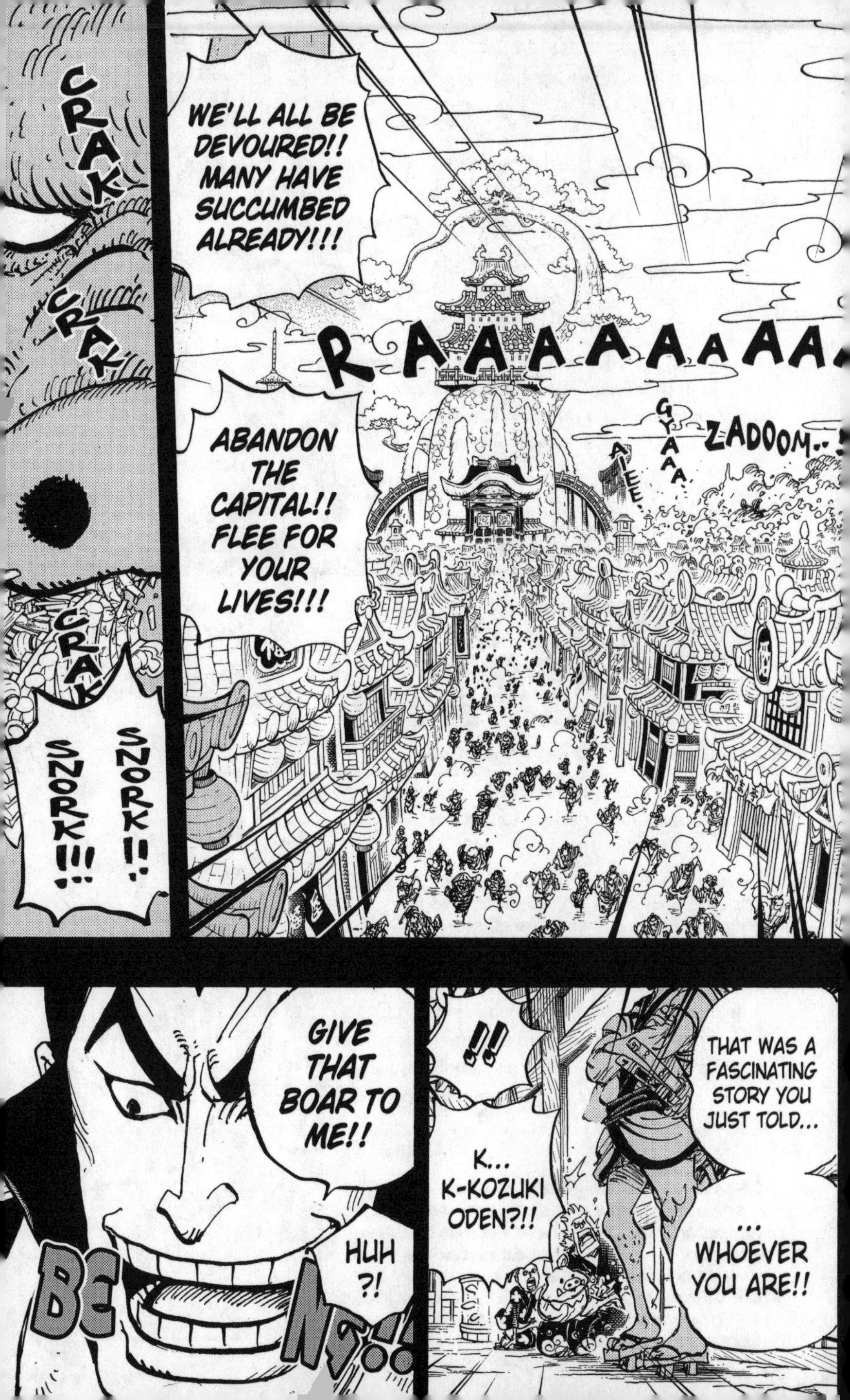
RAAAAAAAA...
ZADOOM..
GYAAA
AIEEE..
WE'LL ALL BE DEVOURED!! MANY HAVE SUCCUMBED ALREADY!!!
ABANDON THE CAPITAL!! FLEE FOR YOUR LIVES!!!
CRAK
CRAK
CRAK
SNORK!!
SNORK!!!
THAT WAS A FASCINATING STORY YOU JUST TOLD...
!!
K... K-KOZUKI ODEN?!!
... WHOEVER YOU ARE!!
GIVE THAT BOAR TO ME!!
HUH ?!
BENG!!

質問コーナー

(Age 10, Kanagawa)

Q: Have you ever used one of those apps that makes your face look younger? I don't care about your face, I just want to see what my favorite characters (Mihawk, Crocodile, Doflamingo) would look like if they used those apps.

--Purple Panda

A: What do you mean, you don't care about my face? C'mon, don't be shy now... Anyway, I love those newfangled apps.

Hee hee hee.
Ku ha ha ha.
For fun.

Hmm. Who would want these kids?

Q: Odacchi! Why don't Kid and Killer just use the butt-breathing technique to survive?

--420 Land

GLUB GLUB

A: Good point! Then they wouldn't drown!! Hey... you know that the Kid Pirates have a lot of fans, right?! Watch your back!!

Q: Hi there, Odacchi! I've been wondering something. I've noticed that when you write characters talking tough and slurring their vowels in Japanese, you use katakana symbols instead of the usual hiragana. Is this just something you do for the fun of it?

--Kanamaru

AKIRA
OTOMO KATSUHIRO
1
KODANSHA

©MASH·ROOM/KODANSHA

A: Oh, this one's easy! See, there's this manga called *Akira*. It's a world-famous classic and has a legendary animated film version. The author used katakana that way too, and it left a big impression on me when I read it in middle school. It looks a bit more striking that way, and it's way cool, if you ask me!!

Chapter 961:
THE MOUNTAIN GOD INCIDENT

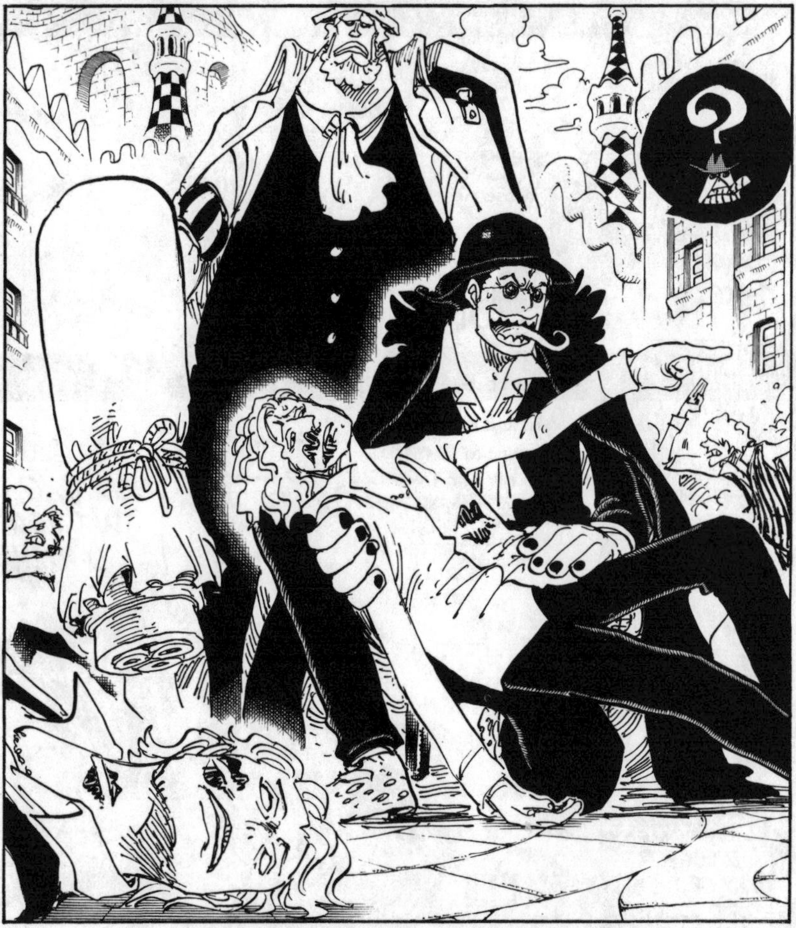
?

GANG BEGE'S OH MY FAMILY
VOL. 11: "THESE GUYS HAVE SUFFERED DAMAGE OF SOME KIND"

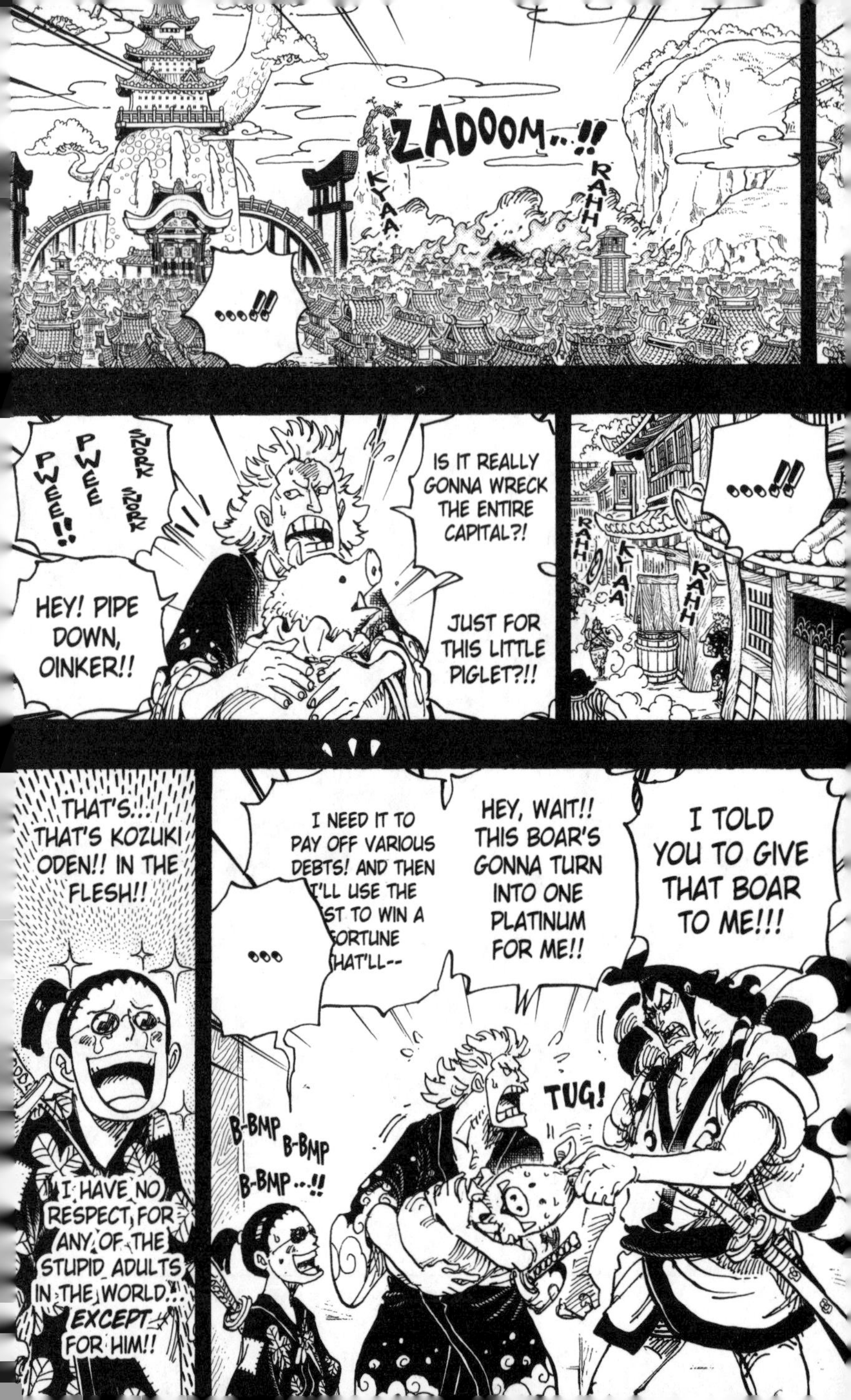

ZADOOM..!!
KYAA
RAHH
...!!
...!!
RAHH
KYAA
RAHH
IS IT REALLY GONNA WRECK THE ENTIRE CAPITAL?!
JUST FOR THIS LITTLE PIGLET?!!
SNORK SNORK
PWEE PWEE!!
HEY! PIPE DOWN, OINKER!!
I TOLD YOU TO GIVE THAT BOAR TO ME!!!
HEY, WAIT!! THIS BOAR'S GONNA TURN INTO ONE PLATINUM FOR ME!!
I NEED IT TO PAY OFF VARIOUS DEBTS! AND THEN I'LL USE THE ST TO WIN A ORTUNE HAT'LL--
...
TUG!
B-BMP B-BMP B-BMP..!!
THAT'S... THAT'S KOZUKI ODEN!! IN THE FLESH!!
I HAVE NO RESPECT FOR ANY OF THE STUPID ADULTS IN THE WORLD... EXCEPT FOR HIM!!

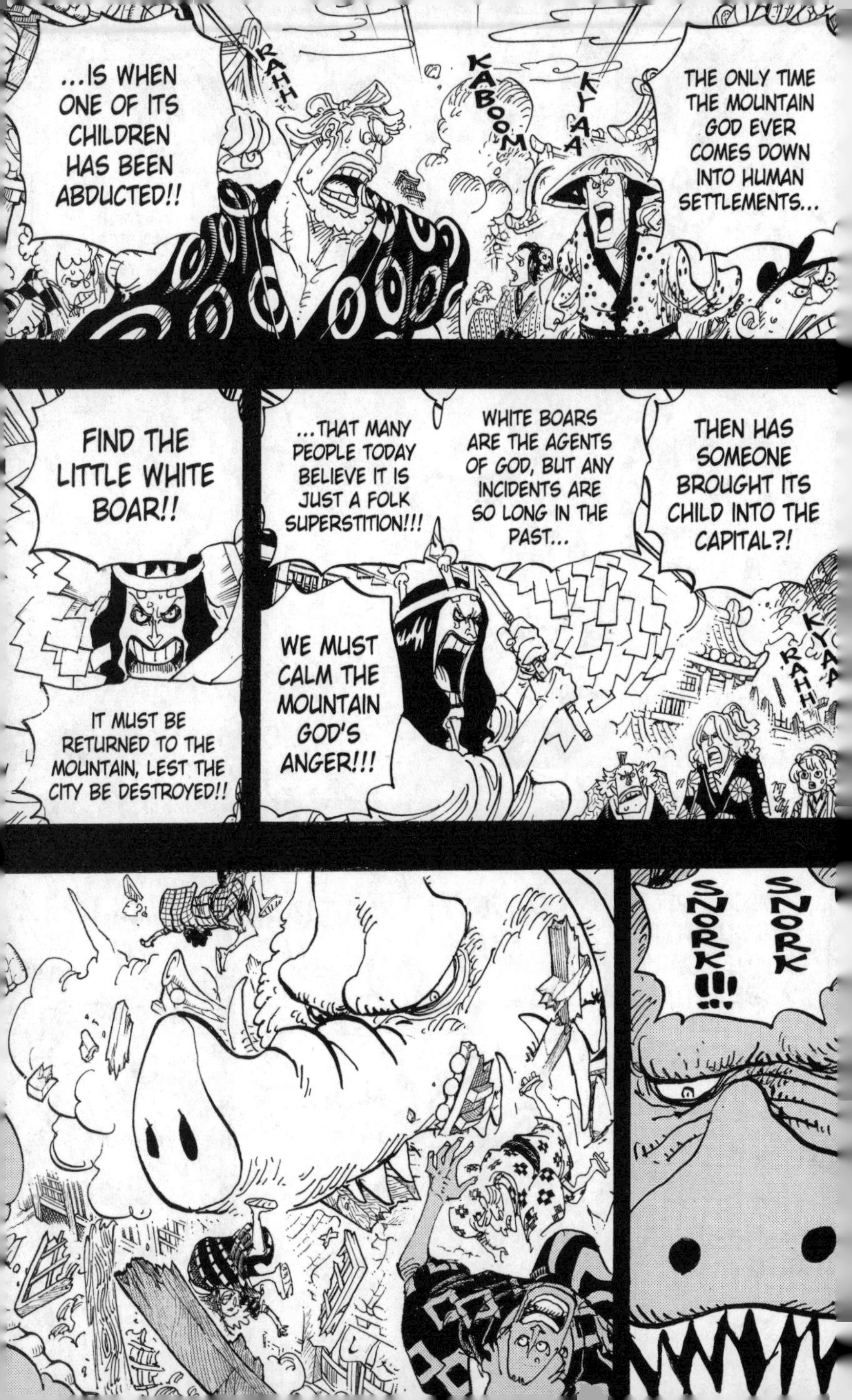
THE ONLY TIME THE MOUNTAIN GOD EVER COMES DOWN INTO HUMAN SETTLEMENTS...
KYAA
KABOOM
RAHH
...IS WHEN ONE OF ITS CHILDREN HAS BEEN ABDUCTED!!
THEN HAS SOMEONE BROUGHT ITS CHILD INTO THE CAPITAL?!
WHITE BOARS ARE THE AGENTS OF GOD, BUT ANY INCIDENTS ARE SO LONG IN THE PAST...
...THAT MANY PEOPLE TODAY BELIEVE IT IS JUST A FOLK SUPERSTITION!!!
KYAA
RAHH
WE MUST CALM THE MOUNTAIN GOD'S ANGER!!!
FIND THE LITTLE WHITE BOAR!!
IT MUST BE RETURNED TO THE MOUNTAIN, LEST THE CITY BE DESTROYED!!
SNORK
SNORK!!!

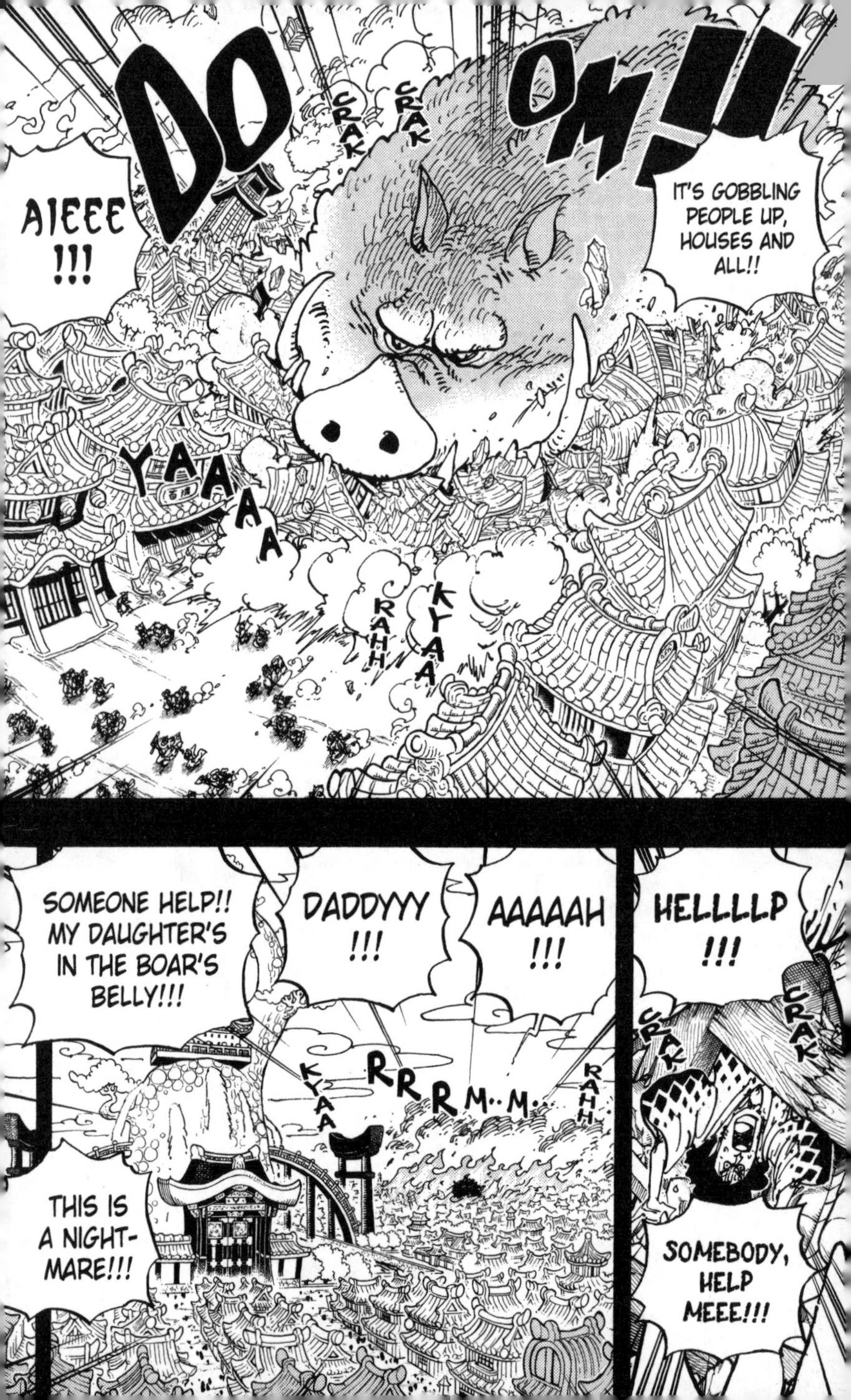
DOOM!!!
IT'S GOBBLING PEOPLE UP, HOUSES AND ALL!!
CRAK
CRAK
AIEEE!!!
YAAAAA
KYAAA
RAHH
HELLLLP!!!
CRAK
CRAK
SOMEBODY, HELP MEEE!!!
AAAAAH!!!
DADDYYY!!!
SOMEONE HELP!! MY DAUGHTER'S IN THE BOAR'S BELLY!!!
RAHH
RRRM..M..
KYAA
THIS IS A NIGHT-MARE!!!

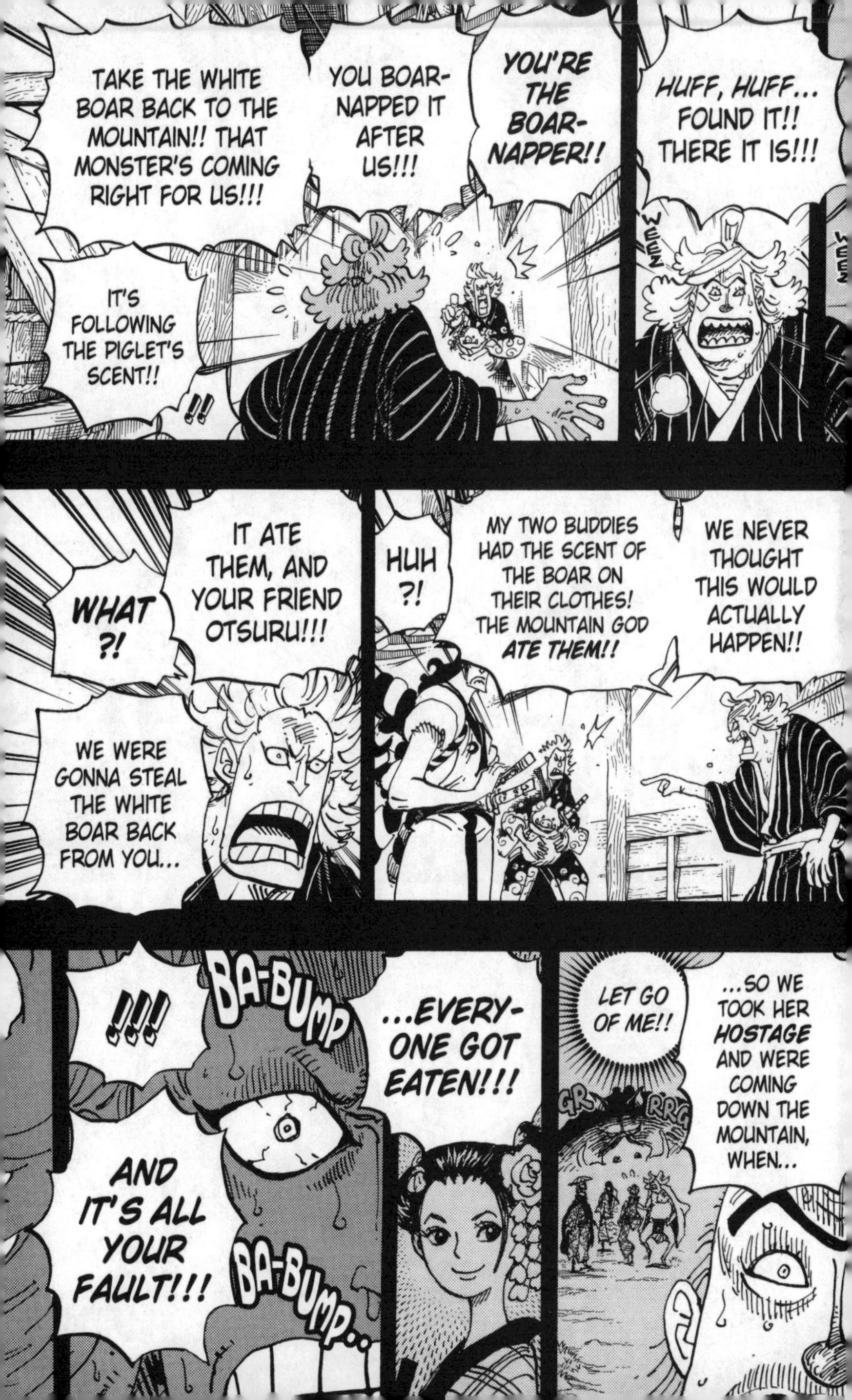
HUFF, HUFF... FOUND IT!! THERE IT IS!!!
WEEZ
WEEZ
YOU'RE THE BOAR-NAPPER!!
YOU BOAR-NAPPED IT AFTER US!!!
TAKE THE WHITE BOAR BACK TO THE MOUNTAIN!! THAT MONSTER'S COMING RIGHT FOR US!!!
IT'S FOLLOWING THE PIGLET'S SCENT!!
!!
WE NEVER THOUGHT THIS WOULD ACTUALLY HAPPEN!!
MY TWO BUDDIES HAD THE SCENT OF THE BOAR ON THEIR CLOTHES! THE MOUNTAIN GOD ATE THEM!!
HUH ?!
IT ATE THEM, AND YOUR FRIEND OTSURU!!!
WHAT ?!
WE WERE GONNA STEAL THE WHITE BOAR BACK FROM YOU...
...SO WE TOOK HER HOSTAGE AND WERE COMING DOWN THE MOUNTAIN, WHEN...
LET GO OF ME!!
GR
RRG
...EVERY-ONE GOT EATEN!!!
BA-BUMP
!!!
AND IT'S ALL YOUR FAULT!!!
BA-BUMP...

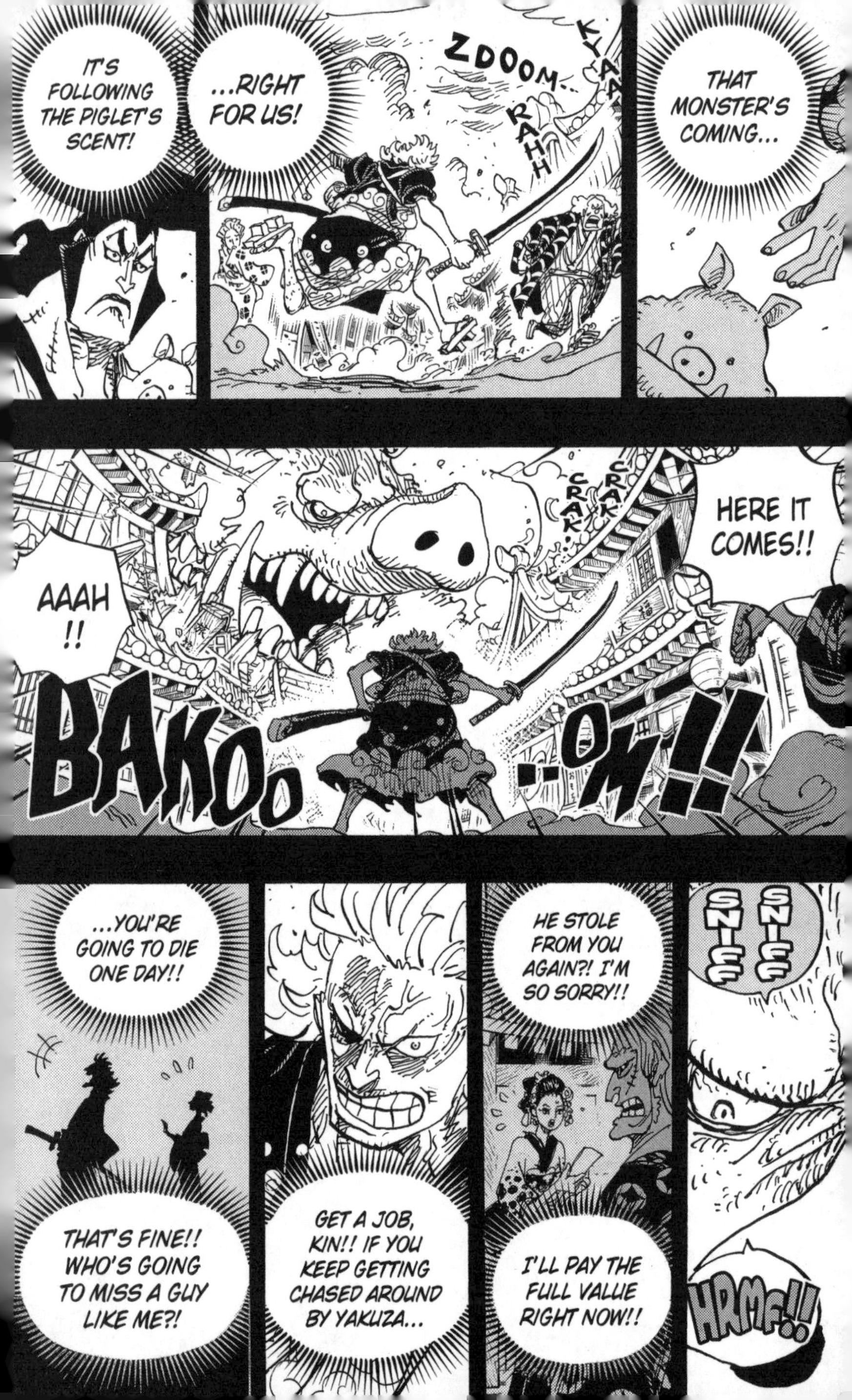
THAT MONSTER'S COMING...
...RIGHT FOR US!
ZDOOM...
KYAA
RAHHH
IT'S FOLLOWING THE PIGLET'S SCENT!
HERE IT COMES!!
CRAK
CRAK
AAAH!!
BAKOOOM!!
SNIFF SNIFF
HRMF!!
HE STOLE FROM YOU AGAIN?! I'M SO SORRY!!
I'LL PAY THE FULL VALUE RIGHT NOW!!
GET A JOB, KIN!! IF YOU KEEP GETTING CHASED AROUND BY YAKUZA...
...YOU'RE GOING TO DIE ONE DAY!!
THAT'S FINE!! WHO'S GOING TO MISS A GUY LIKE ME?!

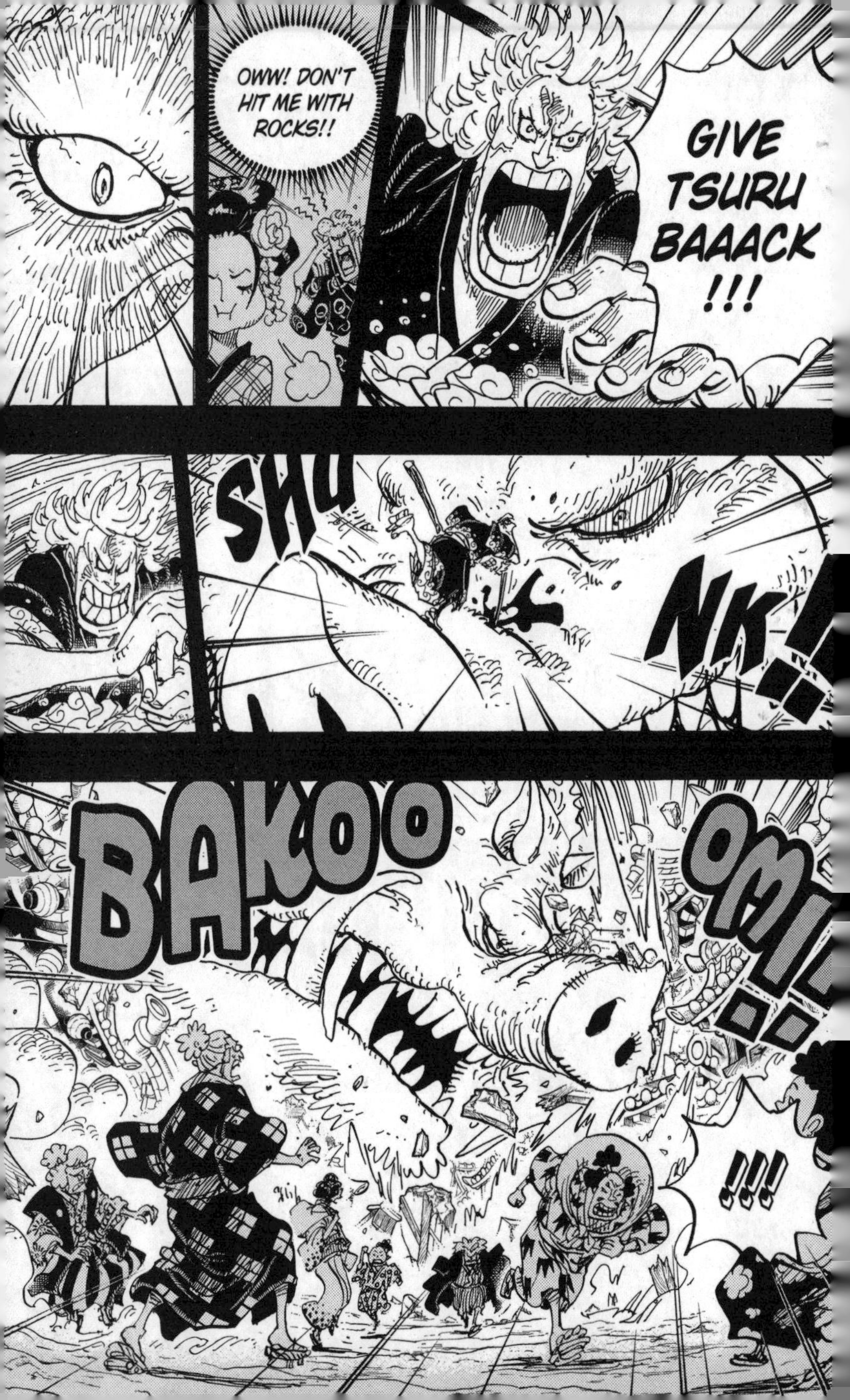
GIVE TSURU BAAACK!!!
OWW! DON'T HIT ME WITH ROCKS!!
SHUNK!!
BAKOOOM!!
!!!

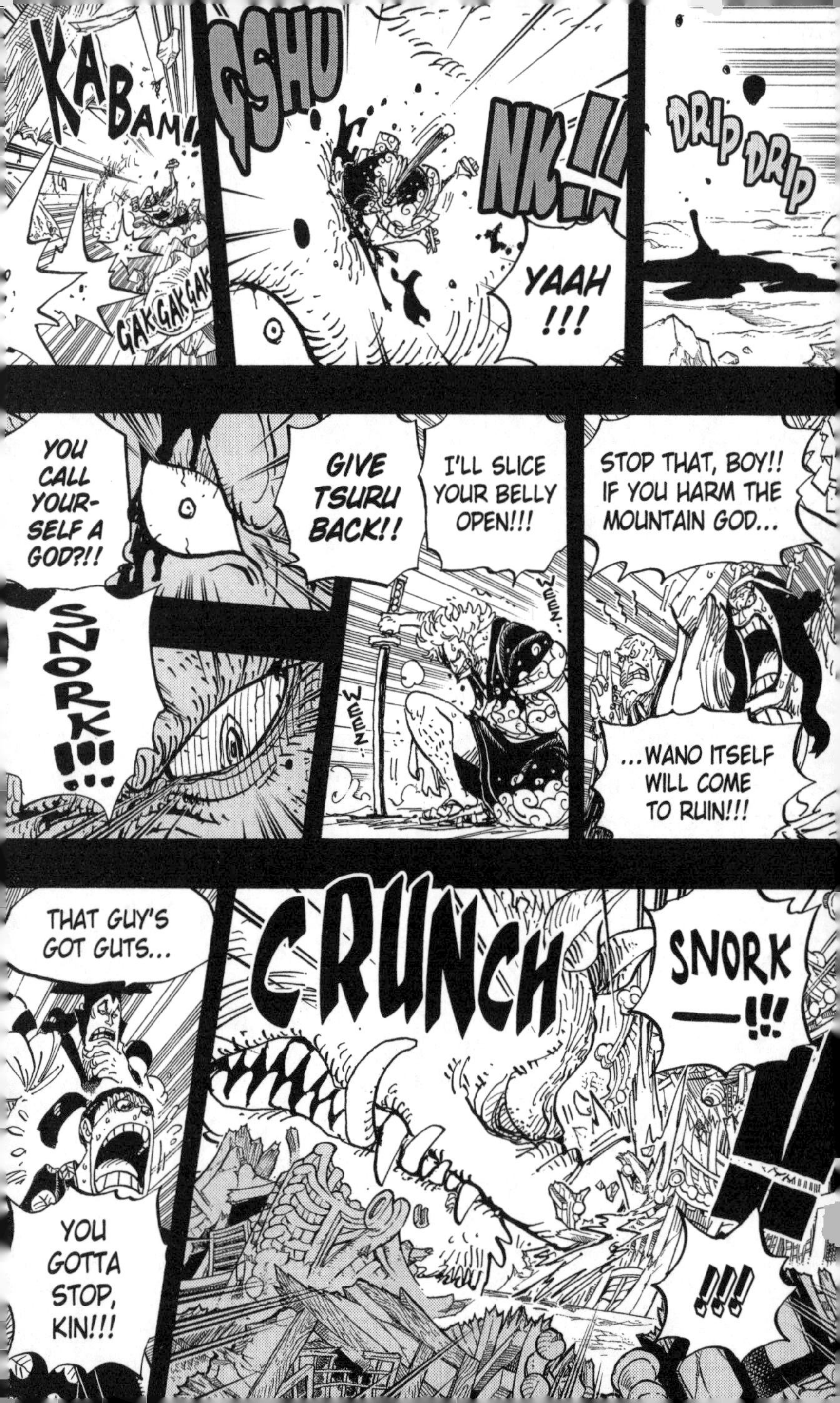
DRIP DRIP
GSHU
NK..!!
YAAH !!!
KABAM!!
GAK GAK GAK
STOP THAT, BOY!! IF YOU HARM THE MOUNTAIN GOD...
...WANO ITSELF WILL COME TO RUIN!!!
I'LL SLICE YOUR BELLY OPEN!!!
GIVE TSURU BACK!!
WEEN...
WEEN...
YOU CALL YOURSELF A GOD?!!
SNORK!!!
SNORK——!!!
CRUNCH
!!!
THAT GUY'S GOT GUTS...
YOU GOTTA STOP, KIN!!!

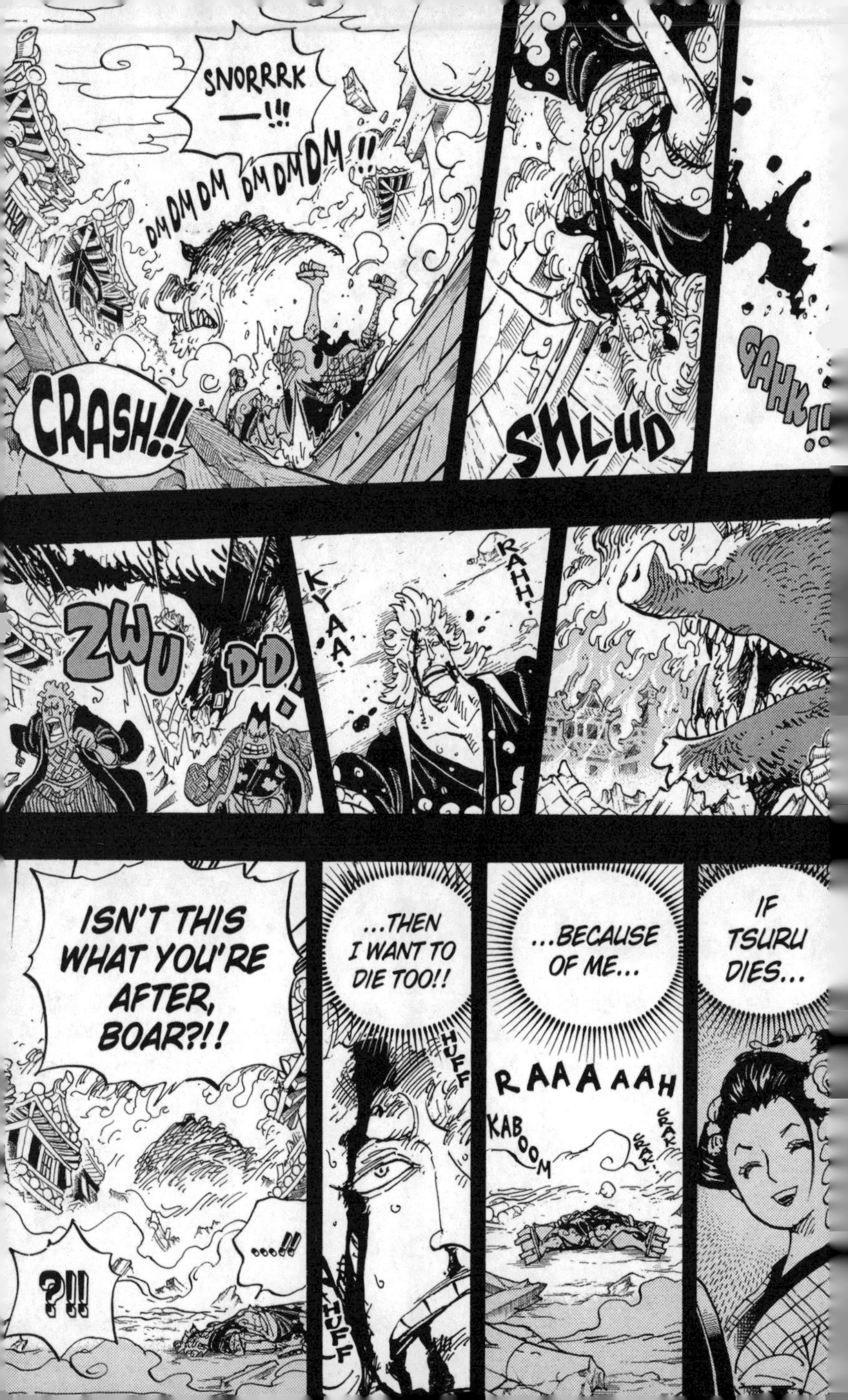
GAHK!!
SHLUD
SNORRRK—!!!
DM DM DM DM DM DM DM!!
CRASH!!
RAHH!
KYAA!
ZWU
DD!
IF TSURU DIES...
...BECAUSE OF ME...
RAAAAAH
CRAK CRAK...
KABOOM
...THEN I WANT TO DIE TOO!!
HUFF
HUFF
ISN'T THIS WHAT YOU'RE AFTER, BOAR?!!
...!!
?!!

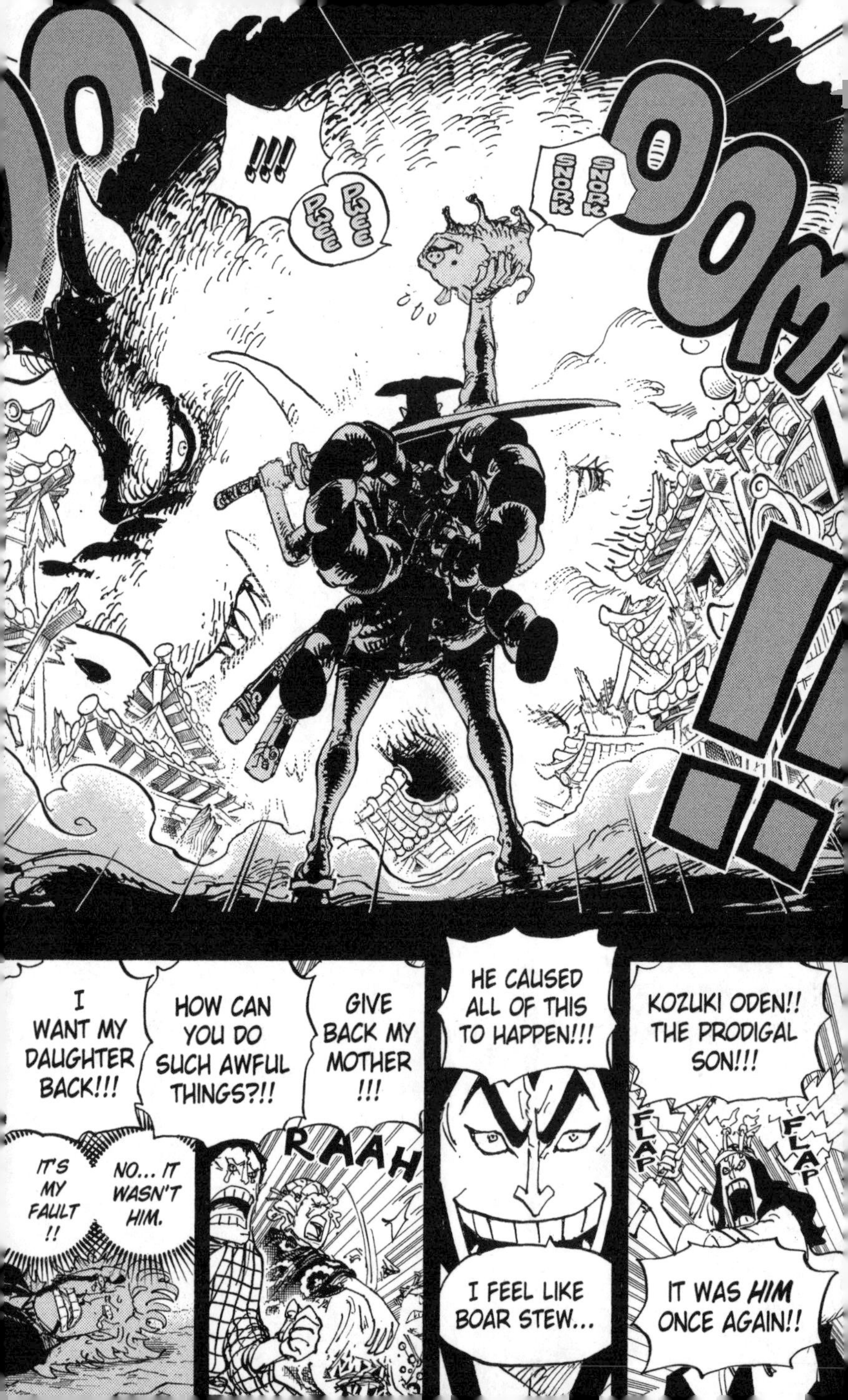
OOOM!!
SNORK SNORK
PWEE PWEE
!!!
OO
KOZUKI ODEN!! THE PRODIGAL SON!!!
FLAP
FLAP
IT WAS HIM ONCE AGAIN!!
HE CAUSED ALL OF THIS TO HAPPEN!!!
I FEEL LIKE BOAR STEW...
GIVE BACK MY MOTHER!!!
HOW CAN YOU DO SUCH AWFUL THINGS?!!
I WANT MY DAUGHTER BACK!!!
RAAH
NO... IT WASN'T HIM.
IT'S MY FAULT!!

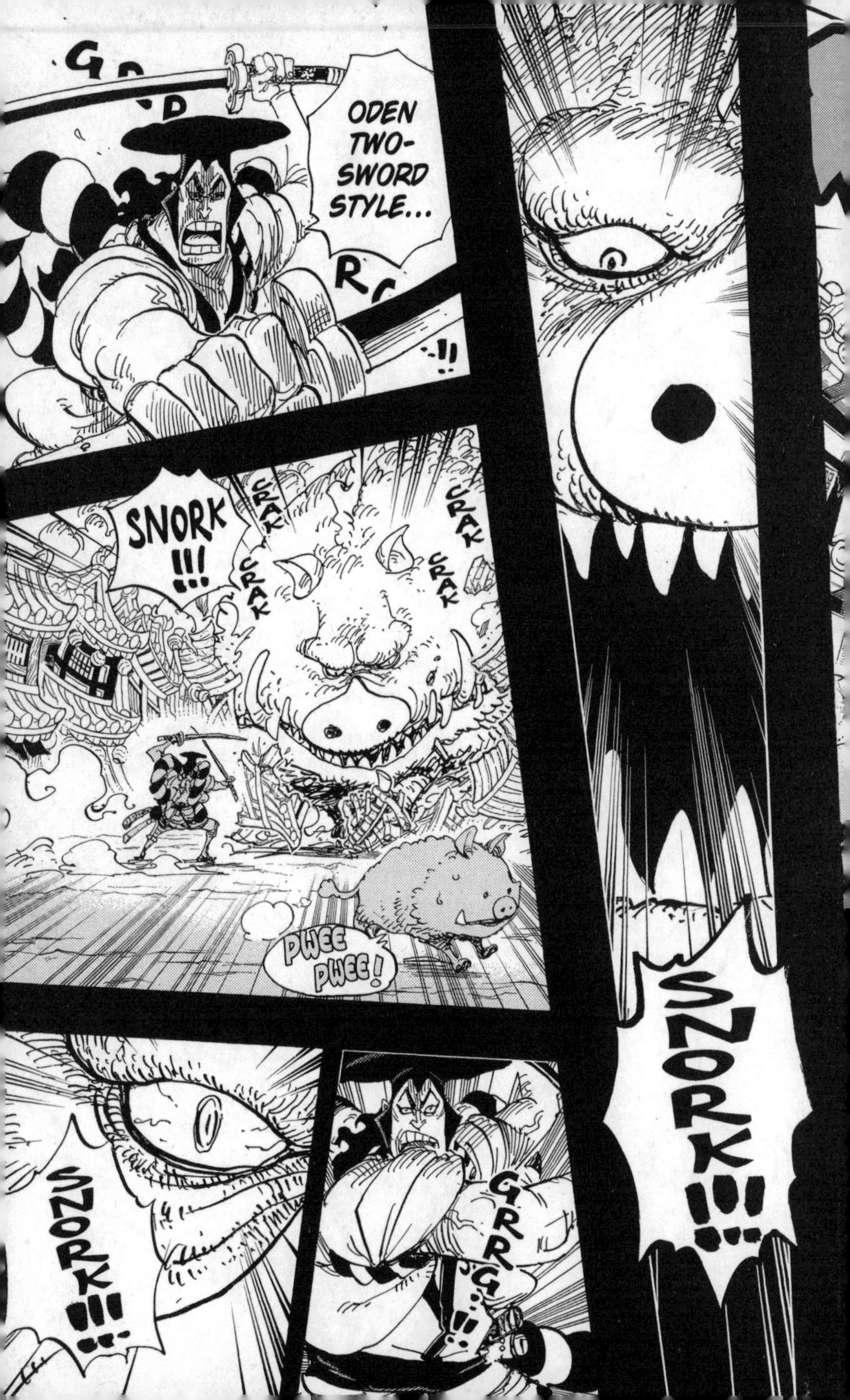

SNORK!!!
ODEN TWO-SWORD STYLE...
!!
SNORK!!!
CRAK CRAK
CRAK CRAK
PWEE PWEE!
GRRRG!!
SNORK!!!

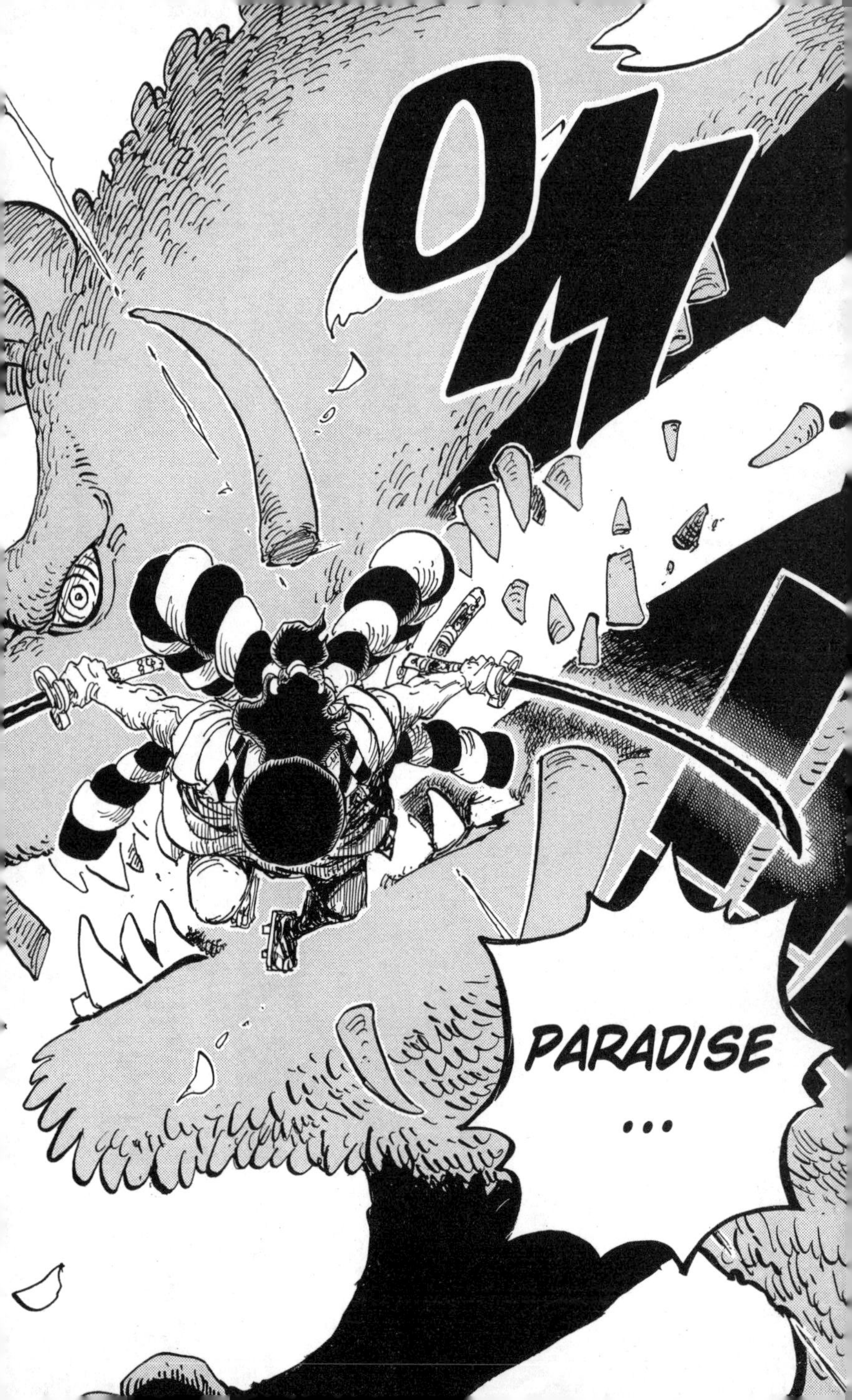
OM
PARADISE ...

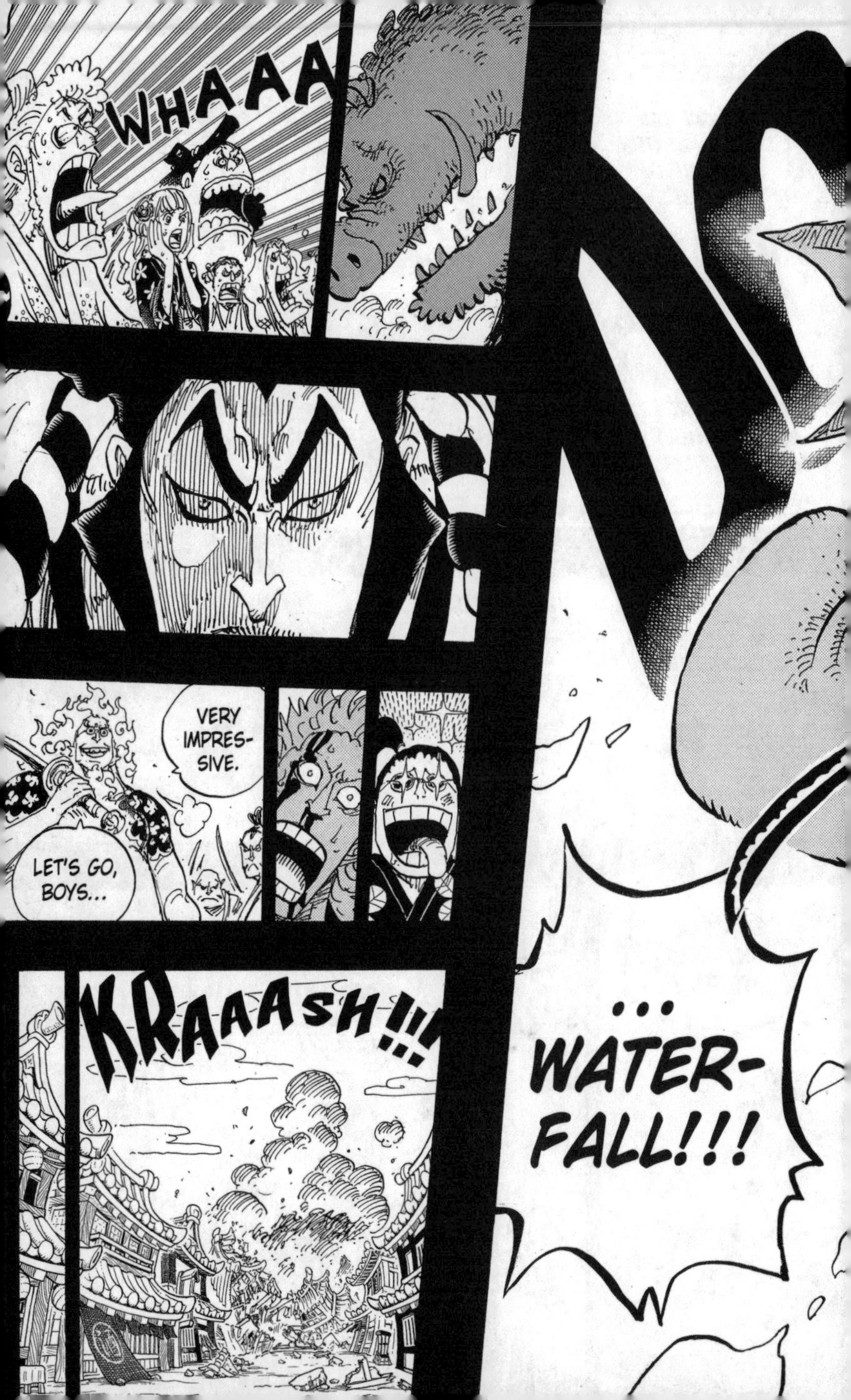
...WATER-FALL!!!
WHAAA
VERY IMPRES-SIVE.
LET'S GO, BOYS...
KRAAASH!!!

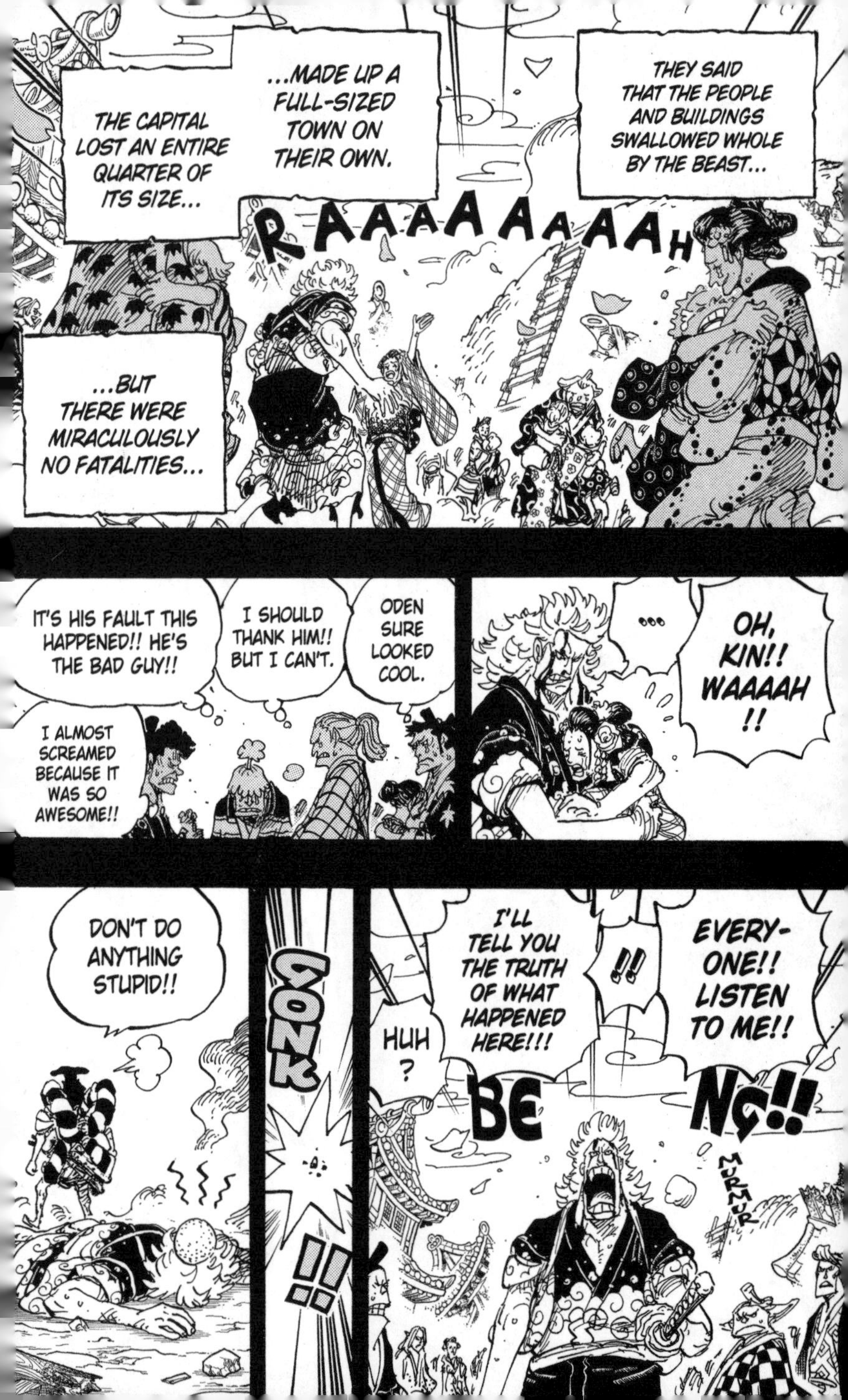
THEY SAID THAT THE PEOPLE AND BUILDINGS SWALLOWED WHOLE BY THE BEAST...
...MADE UP A FULL-SIZED TOWN ON THEIR OWN.
THE CAPITAL LOST AN ENTIRE QUARTER OF ITS SIZE...
RAAAAAAAAH
...BUT THERE WERE MIRACULOUSLY NO FATALITIES...
...
OH, KIN!! WAAAAH!!
ODEN SURE LOOKED COOL.
I SHOULD THANK HIM!! BUT I CAN'T.
IT'S HIS FAULT THIS HAPPENED!! HE'S THE BAD GUY!!
I ALMOST SCREAMED BECAUSE IT WAS SO AWESOME!!
EVERY-ONE!! LISTEN TO ME!!
!!
I'LL TELL YOU THE TRUTH OF WHAT HAPPENED HERE!!!
HUH?
BENG!!
MURMUR
GONK
!!
DON'T DO ANYTHING STUPID!!

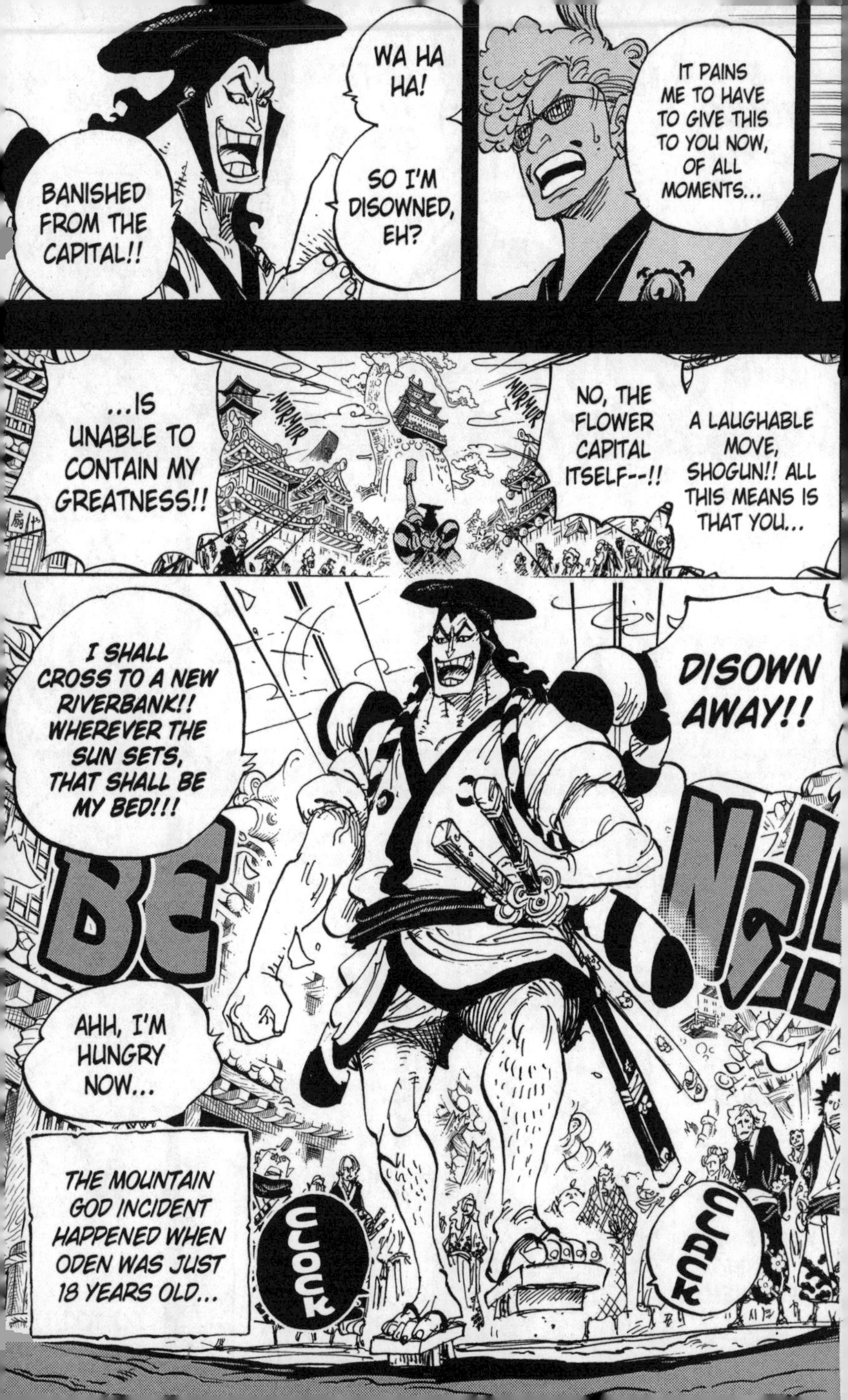
IT PAINS ME TO HAVE TO GIVE THIS TO YOU NOW, OF ALL MOMENTS...
WA HA HA!
SO I'M DISOWNED, EH?
BANISHED FROM THE CAPITAL!!
A LAUGHABLE MOVE, SHOGUN!! ALL THIS MEANS IS THAT YOU...
NO, THE FLOWER CAPITAL ITSELF--!!
MURMUR
MURMUR
...IS UNABLE TO CONTAIN MY GREATNESS!!
DISOWN AWAY!!
I SHALL CROSS TO A NEW RIVERBANK!! WHEREVER THE SUN SETS, THAT SHALL BE MY BED!!!
BE
N!!
AHH, I'M HUNGRY NOW...
CLACK
CLOCK
THE MOUNTAIN GOD INCIDENT HAPPENED WHEN ODEN WAS JUST 18 YEARS OLD...

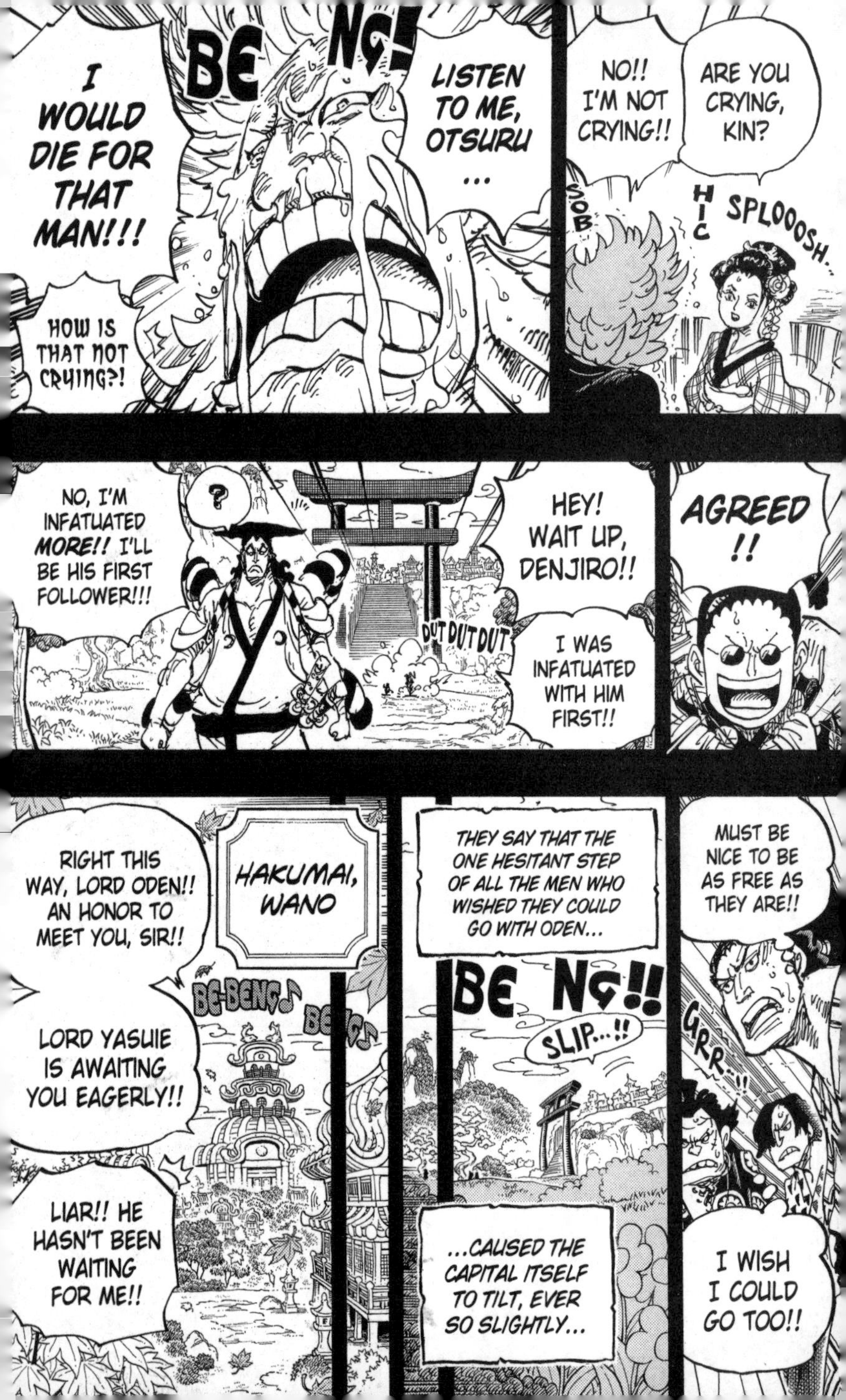
ARE YOU CRYING, KIN?
NO!! I'M NOT CRYING!!
SOB
HIC
SPLOOOSH...
LISTEN TO ME, OTSURU...
BE NG!
I WOULD DIE FOR THAT MAN!!!
HOW IS THAT NOT CRYING?!
AGREED!!
HEY! WAIT UP, DENJIRO!!
I WAS INFATUATED WITH HIM FIRST!!
DUT DUT DUT
?
NO, I'M INFATUATED MORE!! I'LL BE HIS FIRST FOLLOWER!!!
MUST BE NICE TO BE AS FREE AS THEY ARE!!
GRR...!!
I WISH I COULD GO TOO!!
THEY SAY THAT THE ONE HESITANT STEP OF ALL THE MEN WHO WISHED THEY COULD GO WITH ODEN...
BE NG!!
SLIP...!!
...CAUSED THE CAPITAL ITSELF TO TILT, EVER SO SLIGHTLY...
HAKUMAI, WANO
RIGHT THIS WAY, LORD ODEN!! AN HONOR TO MEET YOU, SIR!!
BE-BENG♪
BENG♪
LORD YASUIE IS AWAITING YOU EAGERLY!!
LIAR!! HE HASN'T BEEN WAITING FOR ME!!

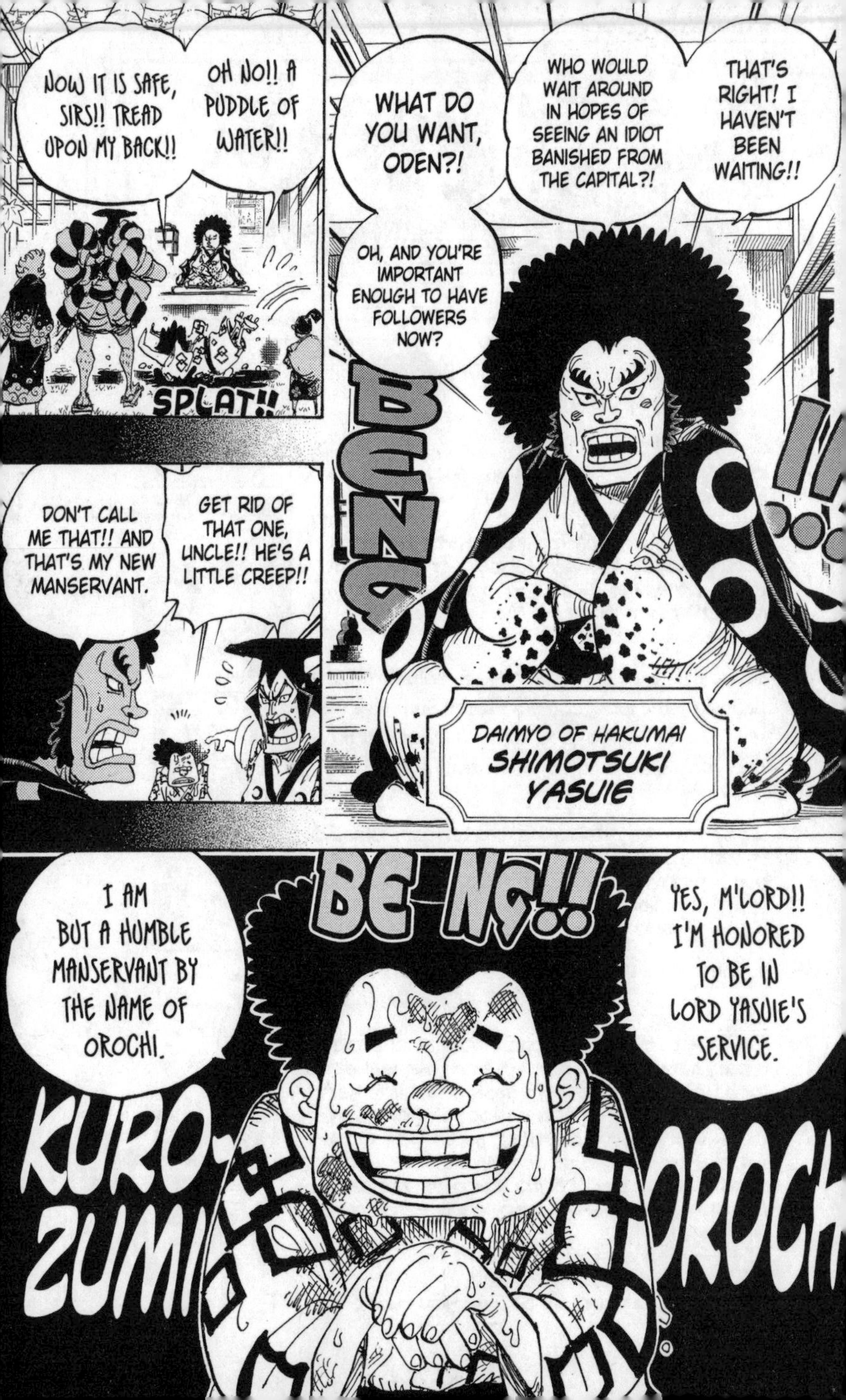
THAT'S RIGHT! I HAVEN'T BEEN WAITING!!
WHO WOULD WAIT AROUND IN HOPES OF SEEING AN IDIOT BANISHED FROM THE CAPITAL?!
WHAT DO YOU WANT, ODEN?!
OH, AND YOU'RE IMPORTANT ENOUGH TO HAVE FOLLOWERS NOW?
BENG
DAIMYO OF HAKUMAI SHIMOTSUKI YASUIE
OH NO!! A PUDDLE OF WATER!!
NOW IT IS SAFE, SIRS!! TREAD UPON MY BACK!!
SPLAT!!
GET RID OF THAT ONE, UNCLE!! HE'S A LITTLE CREEP!!
DON'T CALL ME THAT!! AND THAT'S MY NEW MANSERVANT.
YES, M'LORD!! I'M HONORED TO BE IN LORD YASUIE'S SERVICE.
BE NG!!
I AM BUT A HUMBLE MANSERVANT BY THE NAME OF OROCHI.
KURO-ZUMI
OROCH

SBS Question Corner

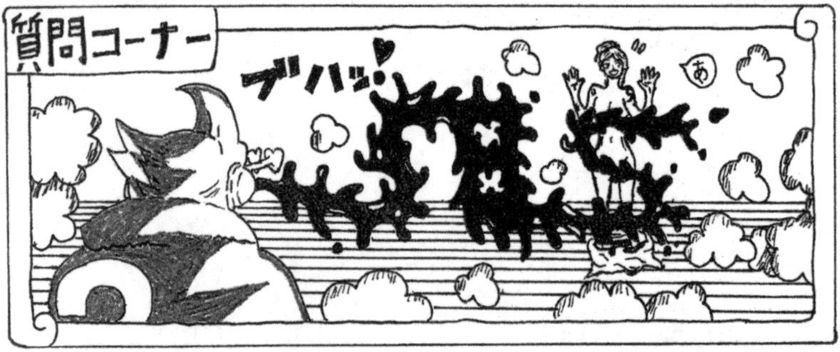
質問コーナー
ブハッ!
あ

(Yuta Kida, Tokyo)

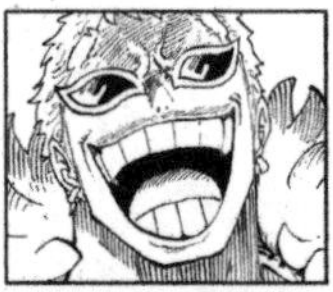

Q: Am I the only one who thinks Doflamingo kind of looks like Spider-Man?

--Ebi

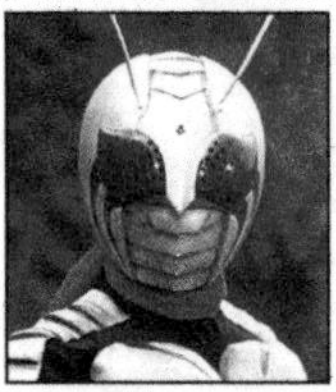

© Ishinomori Pro - Toei

A: Interesting. But if you ask me, that character only got popular in Japan recently. No, the shape of his eyes is more likely based on something that was very popular when I was in kindergarten, and which I drew all the time: a show called Kamen Rider Super-1. Man, I loved how those eyes look!!

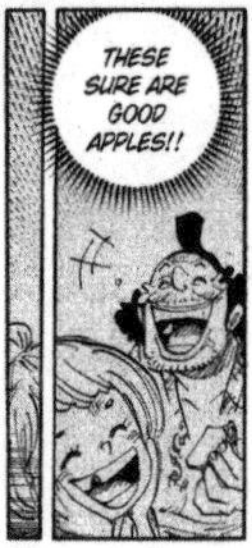
THESE SURE ARE GOOD APPLES!!

Q: In the flashback of chapter 943 in volume 94, the people of the leftover town eat the Smile fruits and say "These sure are good apples!" Does that mean they actually taste good, unlike real Devil Fruits?

--Miketora

A: They say the real ones taste terrible. So it would seem that Smile fruits just taste like a normal fruit. I suppose you could say that this fact is what led to the tragedy of Ebisu Town.

Q: I want to pull on Nami's kimono sash.

--Captain Nobuo

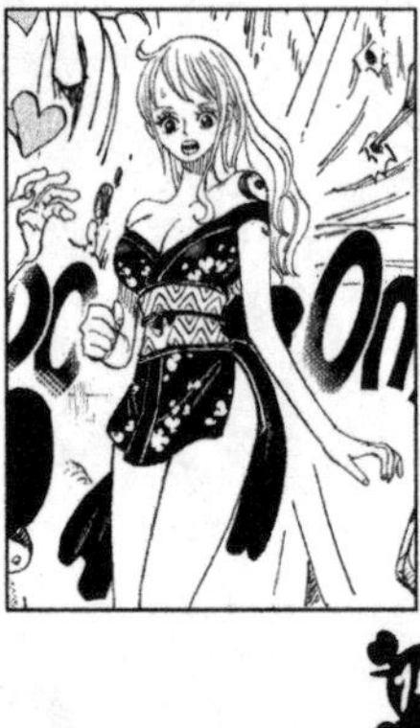

A: Oh, I get it! That trope from all the old-timey samurai movies, where the lecherous lord unravels the lady's sash and spins her around until it all comes loose! Honestly, I really wanted to do that, but I just couldn't work it into the story. I'm so sorry for that!! I've got more to learn about being a mangaka who makes people's dreams come true!!
Oh!! Er...I mean...that wasn't me! That's what Sanada said!! Not me!!!
That's all for the SBS! See you next volume!!

Chapter 962:

DAIMYO AND VASSALS

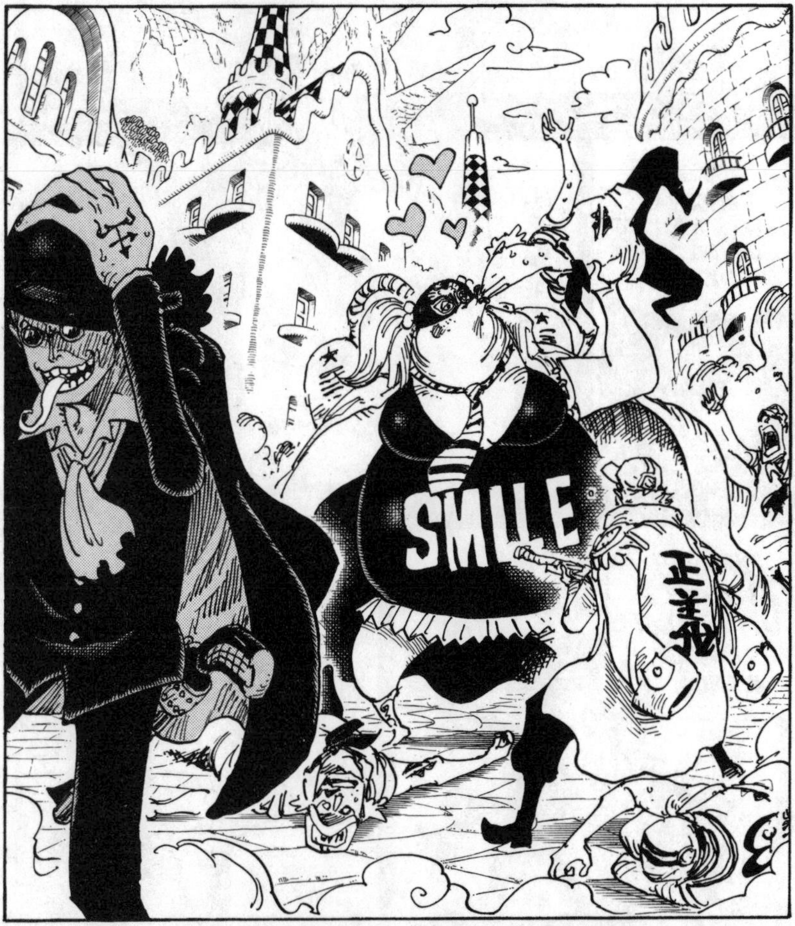
SMILE
正義

GANG BEGE'S OH MY FAMILY
VOL. 12: "FOUND THE NAVY CHASING A DRUNKEN VACUUM KISSAHOLIC"

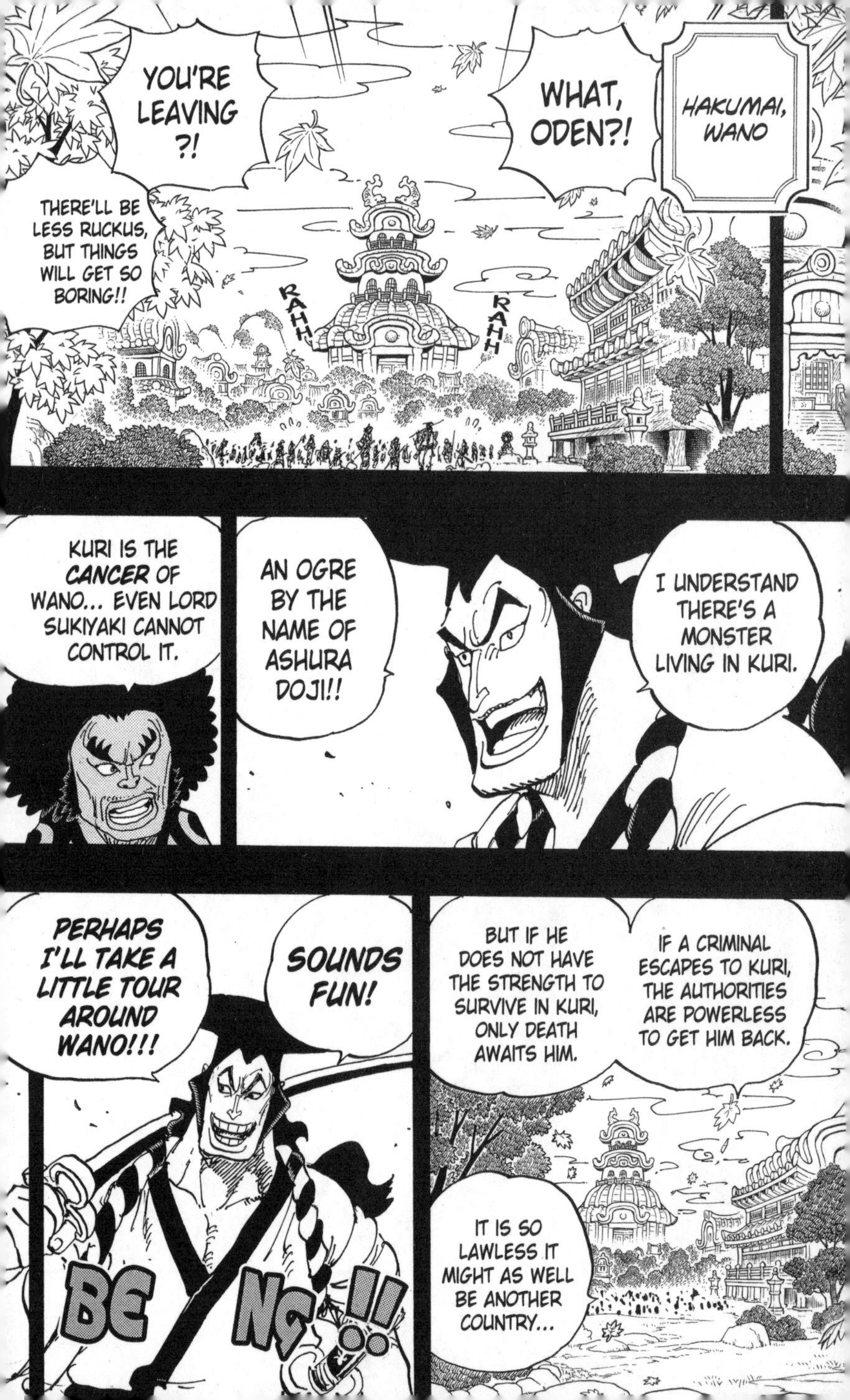
HAKUMAI, WANO
WHAT, ODEN?!
YOU'RE LEAVING?!
THERE'LL BE LESS RUCKUS, BUT THINGS WILL GET SO BORING!!
RAHH
RAHH
I UNDERSTAND THERE'S A MONSTER LIVING IN KURI.
AN OGRE BY THE NAME OF ASHURA DOJI!!
KURI IS THE CANCER OF WANO... EVEN LORD SUKIYAKI CANNOT CONTROL IT.
IF A CRIMINAL ESCAPES TO KURI, THE AUTHORITIES ARE POWERLESS TO GET HIM BACK.
BUT IF HE DOES NOT HAVE THE STRENGTH TO SURVIVE IN KURI, ONLY DEATH AWAITS HIM.
IT IS SO LAWLESS IT MIGHT AS WELL BE ANOTHER COUNTRY...
SOUNDS FUN!
PERHAPS I'LL TAKE A LITTLE TOUR AROUND WANO!!!
BENG!!

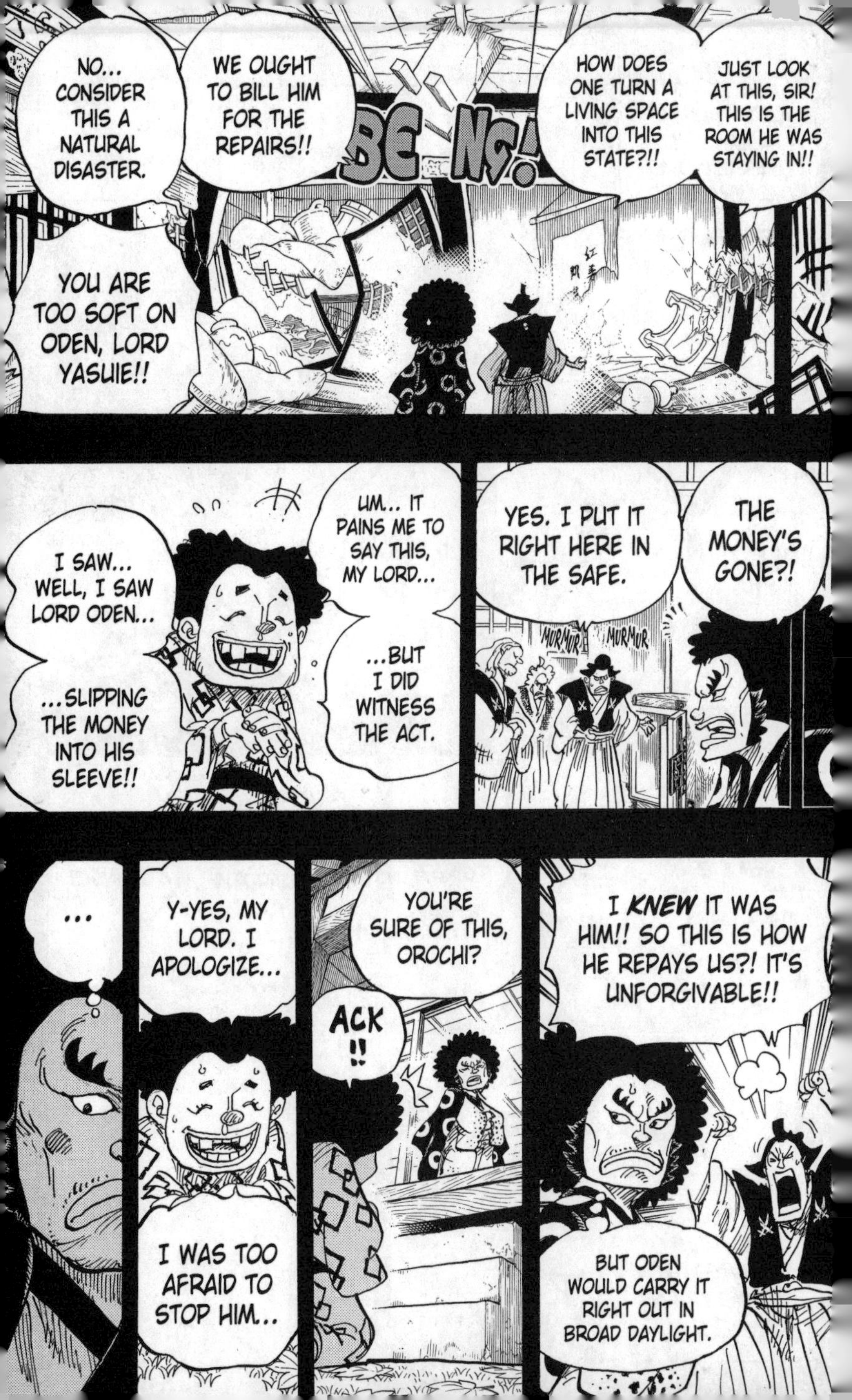
JUST LOOK AT THIS, SIR! THIS IS THE ROOM HE WAS STAYING IN!!
HOW DOES ONE TURN A LIVING SPACE INTO THIS STATE?!!
WE OUGHT TO BILL HIM FOR THE REPAIRS!!
NO... CONSIDER THIS A NATURAL DISASTER.
YOU ARE TOO SOFT ON ODEN, LORD YASUIE!!
THE MONEY'S GONE?!
YES. I PUT IT RIGHT HERE IN THE SAFE.
MURMUR
MURMUR
UM... IT PAINS ME TO SAY THIS, MY LORD...
...BUT I DID WITNESS THE ACT.
I SAW... WELL, I SAW LORD ODEN...
...SLIPPING THE MONEY INTO HIS SLEEVE!!
I *KNEW* IT WAS HIM!! SO THIS IS HOW HE REPAYS US?! IT'S UNFORGIVABLE!!
BUT ODEN WOULD CARRY IT RIGHT OUT IN BROAD DAYLIGHT.
YOU'RE SURE OF THIS, OROCHI?
ACK !!
Y-YES, MY LORD. I APOLOGIZE...
I WAS TOO AFRAID TO STOP HIM...
...

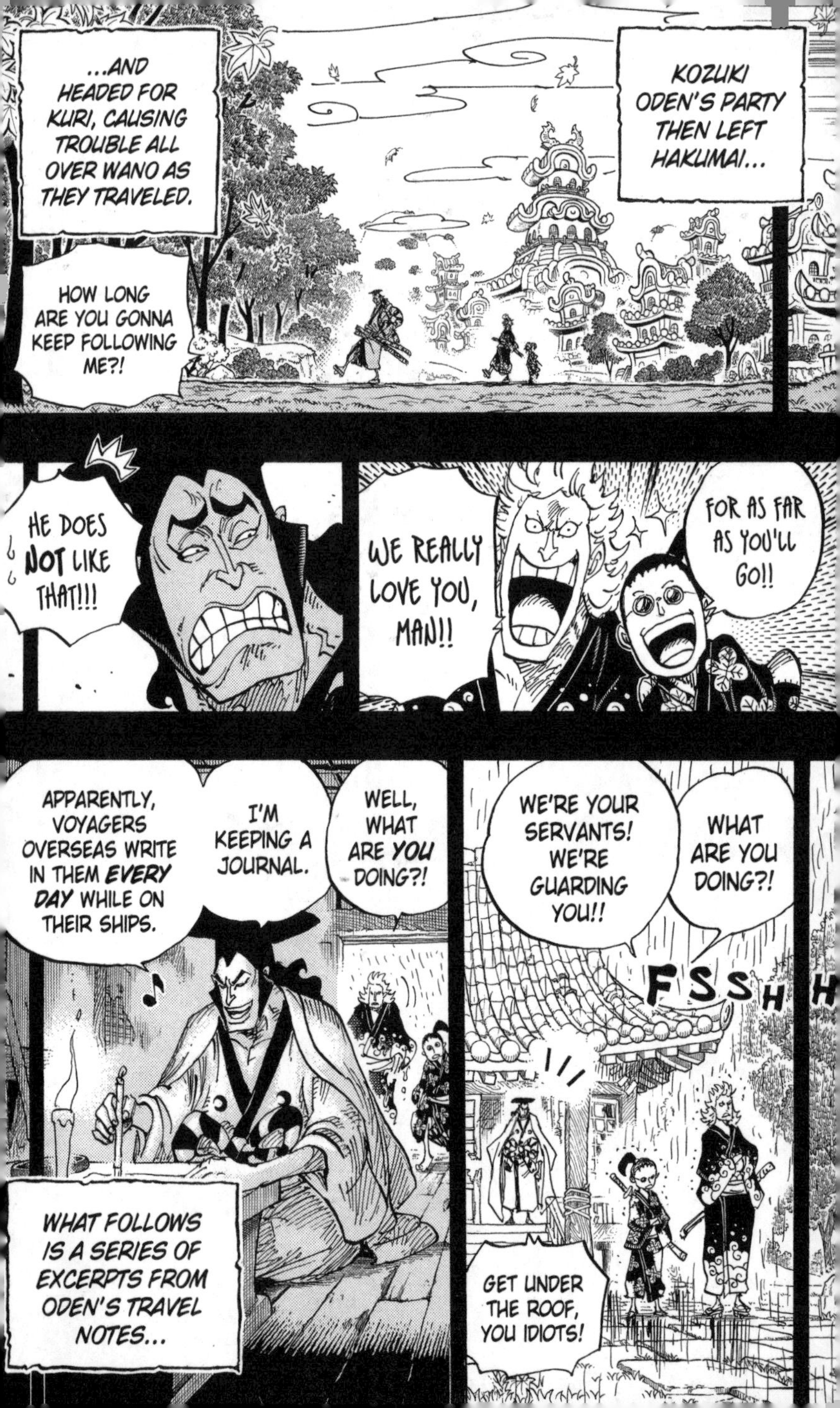
KOZUKI ODEN'S PARTY THEN LEFT HAKUMAI...
...AND HEADED FOR KURI, CAUSING TROUBLE ALL OVER WANO AS THEY TRAVELED.
HOW LONG ARE YOU GONNA KEEP FOLLOWING ME?!
FOR AS FAR AS YOU'LL GO!!
WE REALLY LOVE YOU, MAN!!
HE DOES NOT LIKE THAT!!!
WHAT ARE YOU DOING?!
WE'RE YOUR SERVANTS! WE'RE GUARDING YOU!!
FSSHH
GET UNDER THE ROOF, YOU IDIOTS!
WELL, WHAT ARE YOU DOING?!
I'M KEEPING A JOURNAL.
APPARENTLY, VOYAGERS OVERSEAS WRITE IN THEM EVERY DAY WHILE ON THEIR SHIPS.
WHAT FOLLOWS IS A SERIES OF EXCERPTS FROM ODEN'S TRAVEL NOTES...

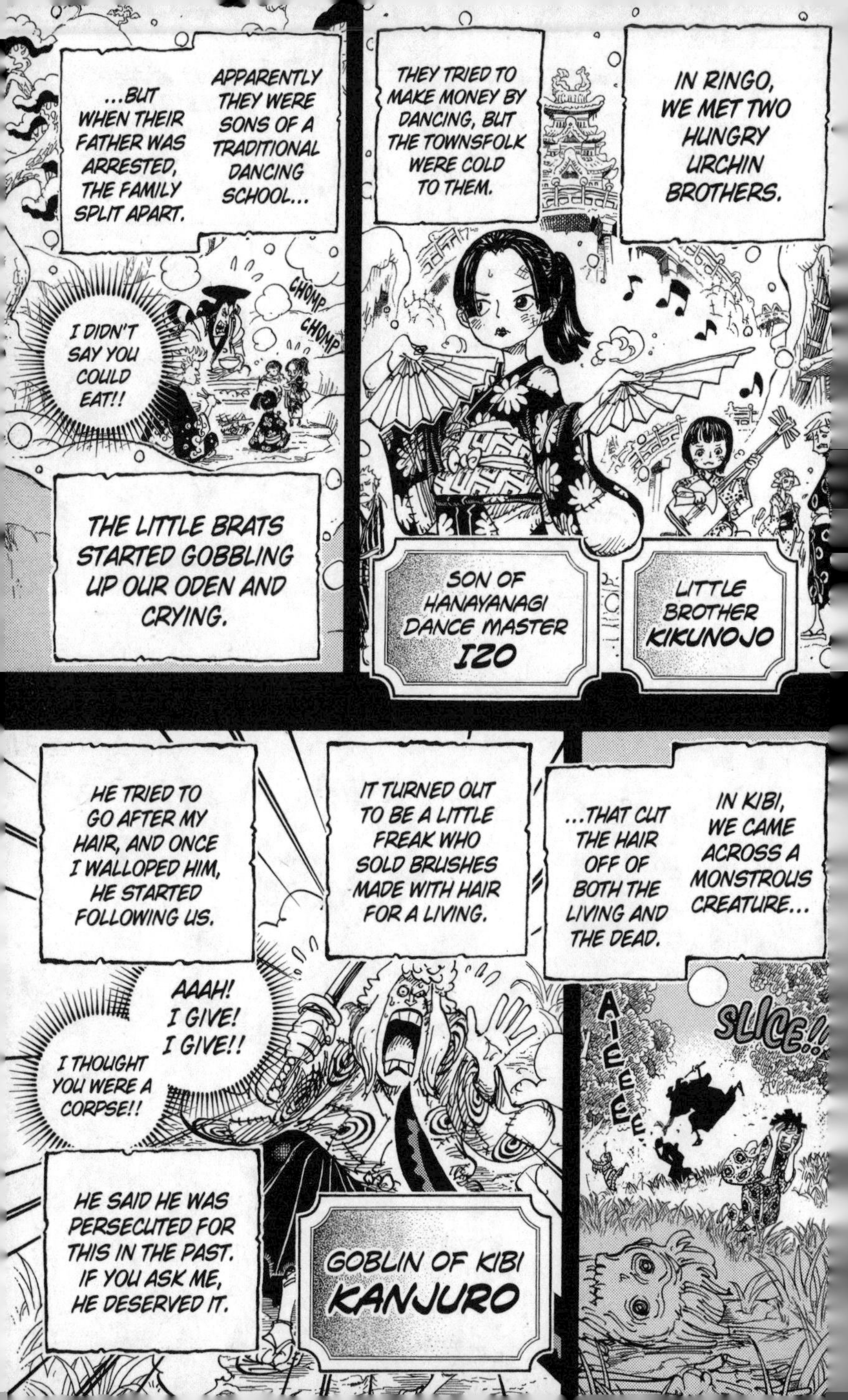
IN RINGO, WE MET TWO HUNGRY URCHIN BROTHERS.
THEY TRIED TO MAKE MONEY BY DANCING, BUT THE TOWNSFOLK WERE COLD TO THEM.
LITTLE BROTHER KIKUNOJO
SON OF HANAYANAGI DANCE MASTER IZO
APPARENTLY THEY WERE SONS OF A TRADITIONAL DANCING SCHOOL...
...BUT WHEN THEIR FATHER WAS ARRESTED, THE FAMILY SPLIT APART.
CHOMP
CHOMP
I DIDN'T SAY YOU COULD EAT!!
THE LITTLE BRATS STARTED GOBBLING UP OUR ODEN AND CRYING.
IN KIBI, WE CAME ACROSS A MONSTROUS CREATURE...
...THAT CUT THE HAIR OFF OF BOTH THE LIVING AND THE DEAD.
SLICE!!
AIEEEE
IT TURNED OUT TO BE A LITTLE FREAK WHO SOLD BRUSHES MADE WITH HAIR FOR A LIVING.
HE TRIED TO GO AFTER MY HAIR, AND ONCE I WALLOPED HIM, HE STARTED FOLLOWING US.
AAAH! I GIVE! I GIVE!!
I THOUGHT YOU WERE A CORPSE!!
GOBLIN OF KIBI KANJURO
HE SAID HE WAS PERSECUTED FOR THIS IN THE PAST. IF YOU ASK ME, HE DESERVED IT.

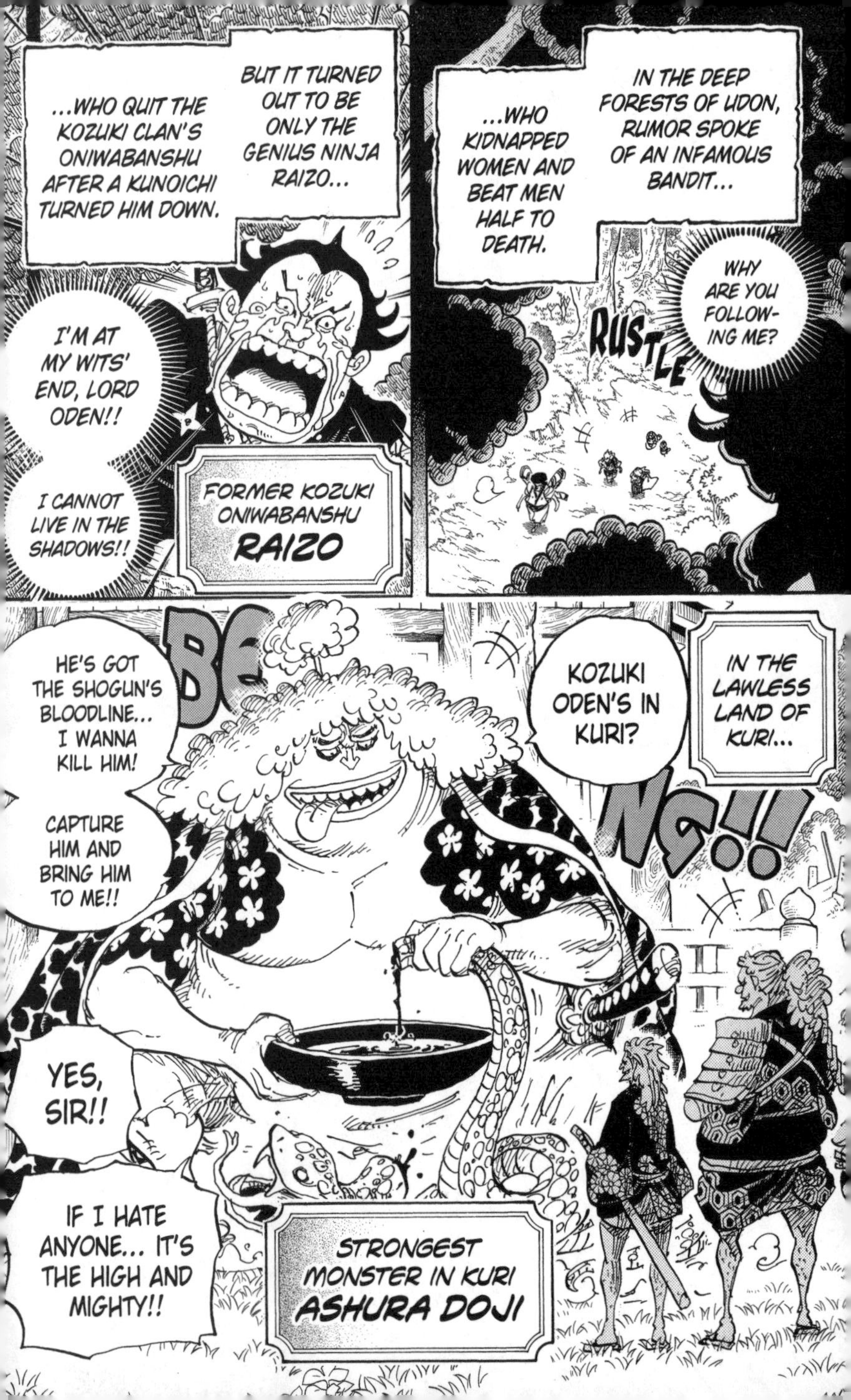
IN THE DEEP FORESTS OF UDON, RUMOR SPOKE OF AN INFAMOUS BANDIT...
...WHO KIDNAPPED WOMEN AND BEAT MEN HALF TO DEATH.
RUSTLE
WHY ARE YOU FOLLOWING ME?
BUT IT TURNED OUT TO BE ONLY THE GENIUS NINJA RAIZO...
...WHO QUIT THE KOZUKI CLAN'S ONIWABANSHU AFTER A KUNOICHI TURNED HIM DOWN.
I'M AT MY WITS' END, LORD ODEN!!
I CANNOT LIVE IN THE SHADOWS!!
FORMER KOZUKI ONIWABANSHU RAIZO
IN THE LAWLESS LAND OF KURI...
KOZUKI ODEN'S IN KURI?
BENG!!
HE'S GOT THE SHOGUN'S BLOODLINE... I WANNA KILL HIM!
CAPTURE HIM AND BRING HIM TO ME!!
YES, SIR!!
STRONGEST MONSTER IN KURI ASHURA DOJI
IF I HATE ANYONE... IT'S THE HIGH AND MIGHTY!!

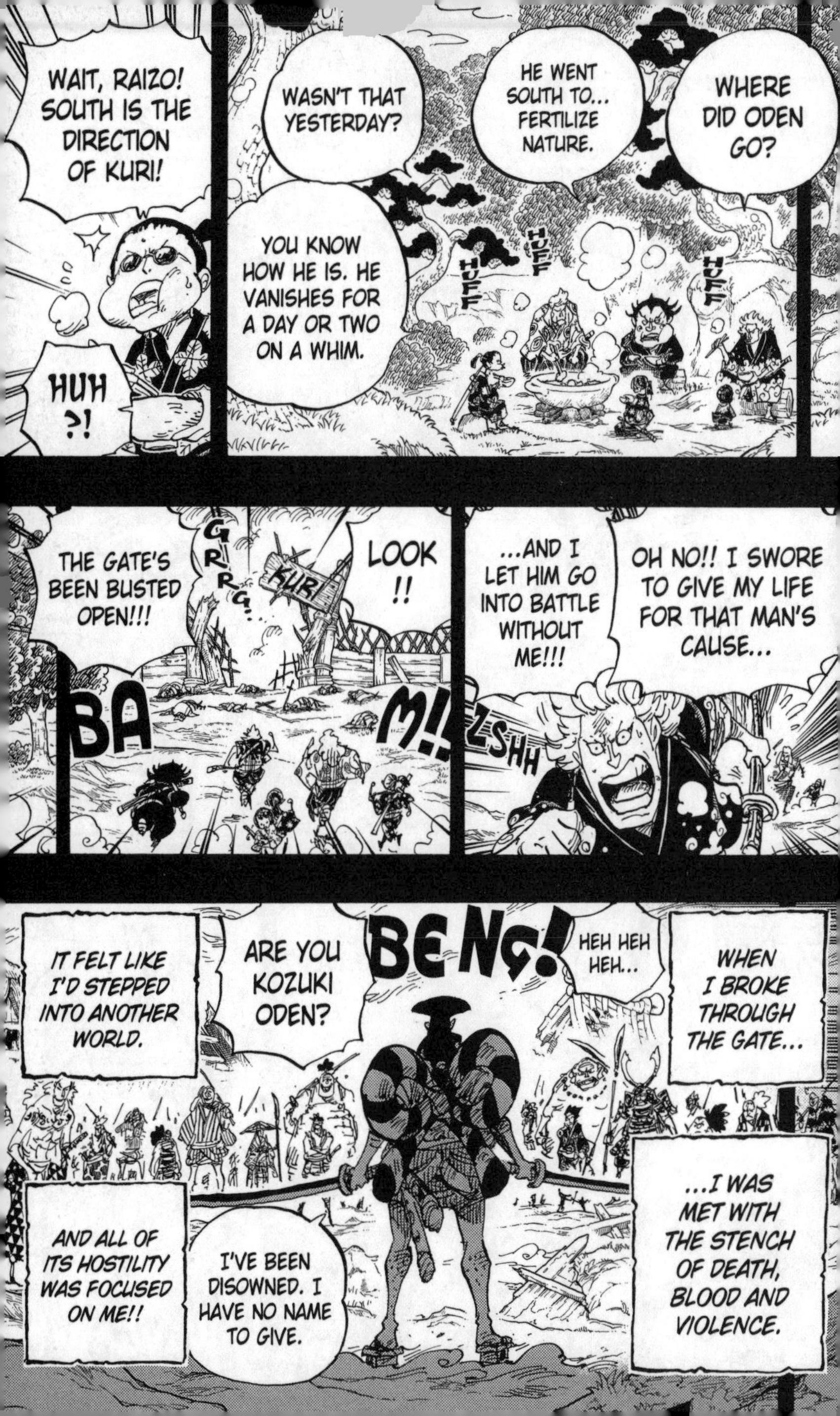
WHERE DID ODEN GO?
HE WENT SOUTH TO... FERTILIZE NATURE.
WASN'T THAT YESTERDAY?
YOU KNOW HOW HE IS. HE VANISHES FOR A DAY OR TWO ON A WHIM.
HUFF
HUFF
HUFF
WAIT, RAIZO! SOUTH IS THE DIRECTION OF KURI!
HUH ?!
OH NO!! I SWORE TO GIVE MY LIFE FOR THAT MAN'S CAUSE...
...AND I LET HIM GO INTO BATTLE WITHOUT ME!!!
ZSHH
LOOK !!
KURI
GRRRG...
THE GATE'S BEEN BUSTED OPEN!!!
BAM!!
WHEN I BROKE THROUGH THE GATE...
...I WAS MET WITH THE STENCH OF DEATH, BLOOD AND VIOLENCE.
HEH HEH HEH...
BENG!
ARE YOU KOZUKI ODEN?
IT FELT LIKE I'D STEPPED INTO ANOTHER WORLD.
I'VE BEEN DISOWNED. I HAVE NO NAME TO GIVE.
AND ALL OF ITS HOSTILITY WAS FOCUSED ON ME!!

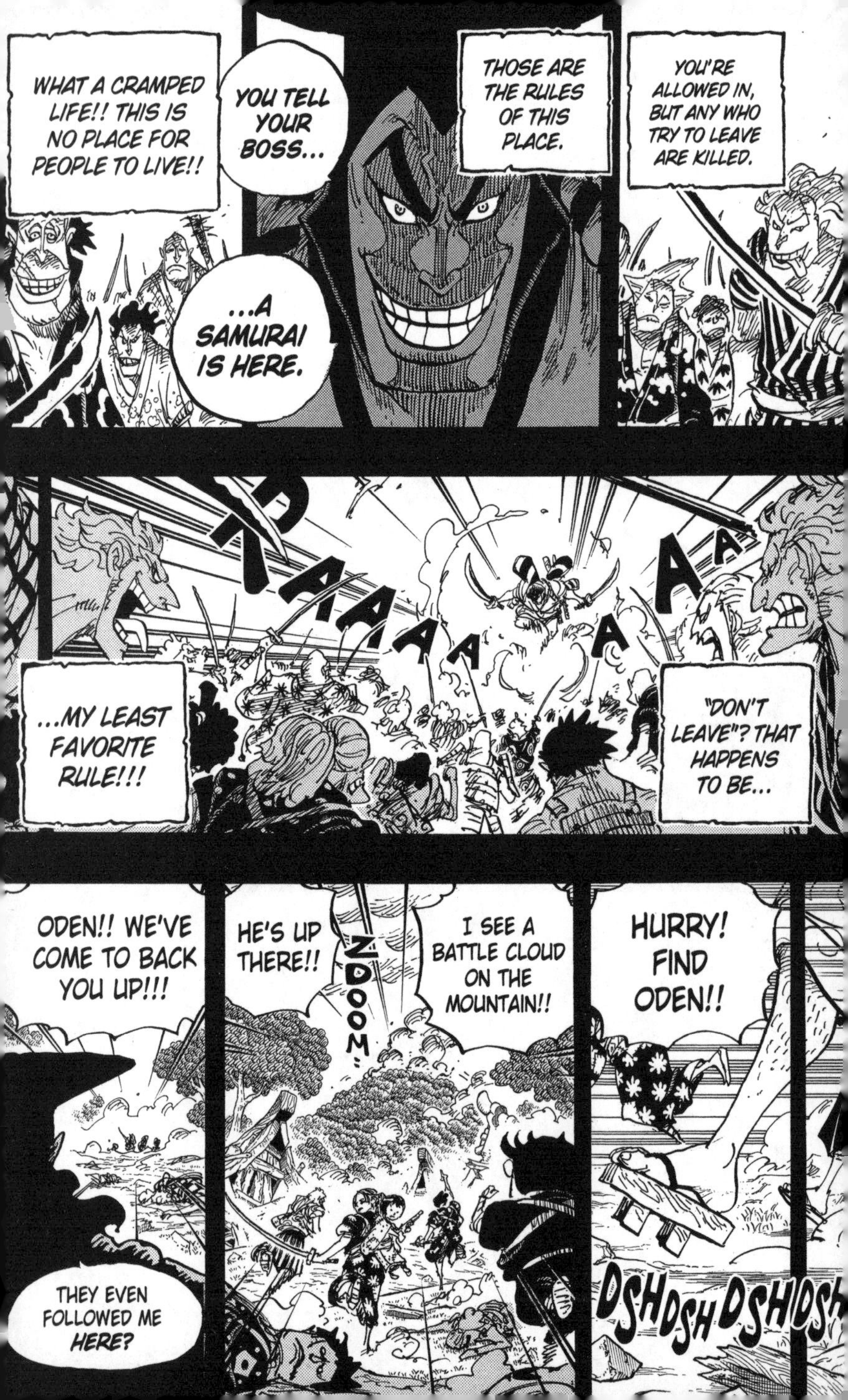
YOU'RE ALLOWED IN, BUT ANY WHO TRY TO LEAVE ARE KILLED.
THOSE ARE THE RULES OF THIS PLACE.
YOU TELL YOUR BOSS...
...A SAMURAI IS HERE.
WHAT A CRAMPED LIFE!! THIS IS NO PLACE FOR PEOPLE TO LIVE!!
"DON'T LEAVE"? THAT HAPPENS TO BE...
RAAAAAAAA
...MY LEAST FAVORITE RULE!!!
HURRY! FIND ODEN!!
DSHDSH DSHDSH
I SEE A BATTLE CLOUD ON THE MOUNTAIN!!
ZDOOM!
HE'S UP THERE!!
ODEN!! WE'VE COME TO BACK YOU UP!!!
THEY EVEN FOLLOWED ME HERE?

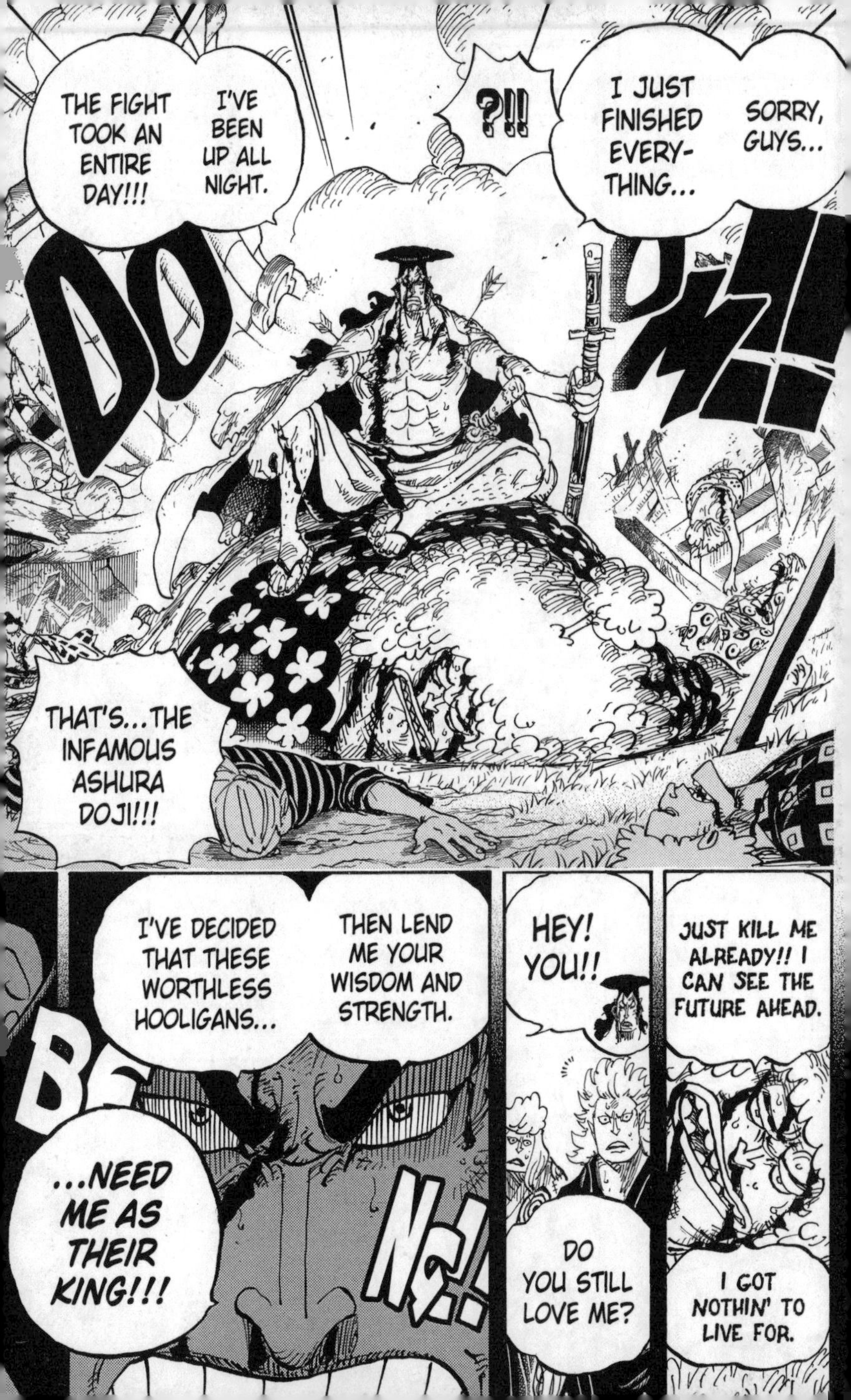
SORRY, GUYS...
I JUST FINISHED EVERY-THING...
?!!
I'VE BEEN UP ALL NIGHT.
THE FIGHT TOOK AN ENTIRE DAY!!!
DON!!
THAT'S...THE INFAMOUS ASHURA DOJI!!!
JUST KILL ME ALREADY!! I CAN SEE THE FUTURE AHEAD.
I GOT NOTHIN' TO LIVE FOR.
HEY! YOU!!
DO YOU STILL LOVE ME?
THEN LEND ME YOUR WISDOM AND STRENGTH.
I'VE DECIDED THAT THESE WORTHLESS HOOLIGANS...
...NEED ME AS THEIR KING!!!

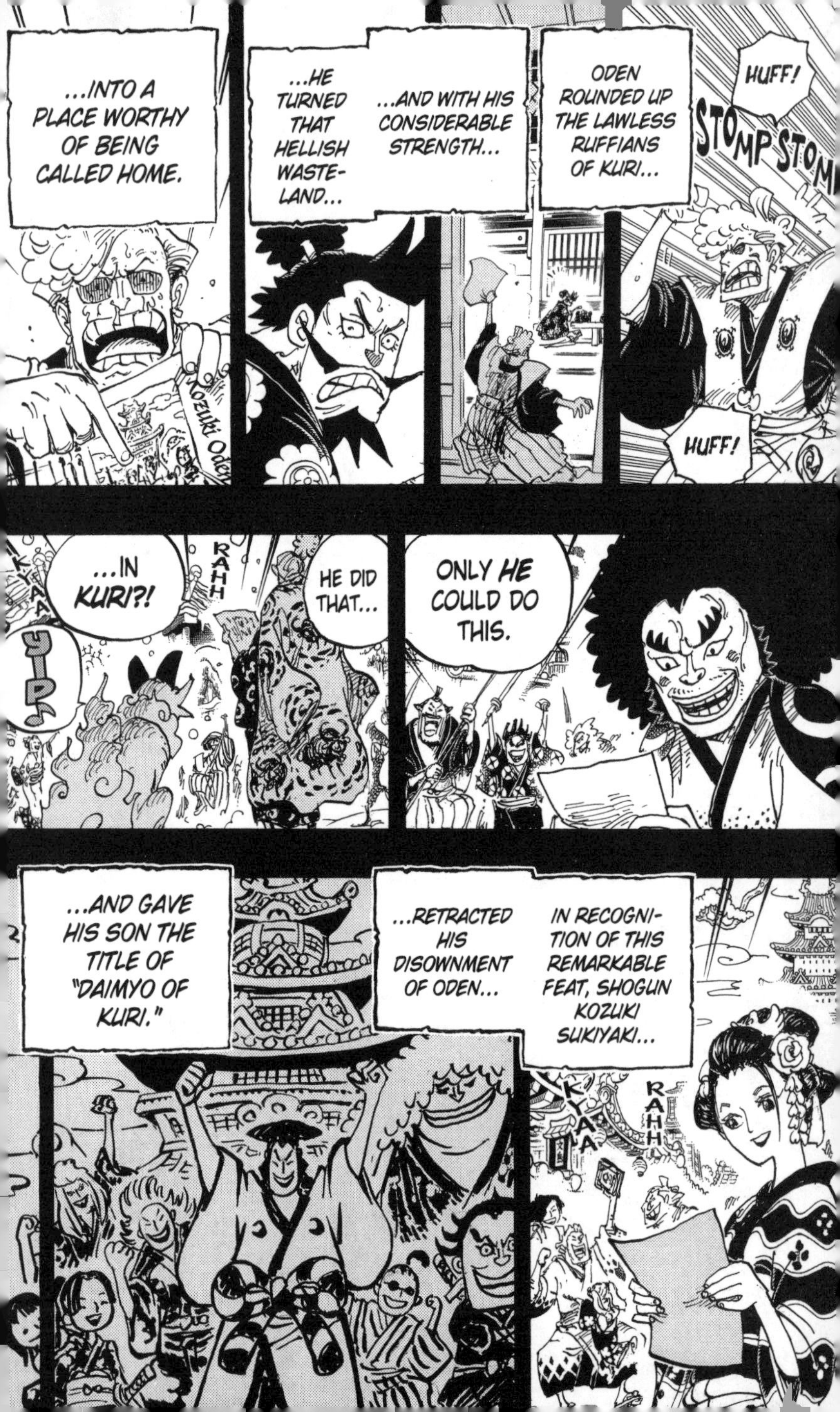
HUFF!
STOMP STOMP
ODEN ROUNDED UP THE LAWLESS RUFFIANS OF KURI...
HUFF!
...AND WITH HIS CONSIDERABLE STRENGTH...
...HE TURNED THAT HELLISH WASTE-LAND...
...INTO A PLACE WORTHY OF BEING CALLED HOME.
Kozuki Oden
ONLY HE COULD DO THIS.
HE DID THAT...
RAHH
...IN KURI?!
KYAA
YIP♪
IN RECOGNI-TION OF THIS REMARKABLE FEAT, SHOGUN KOZUKI SUKIYAKI...
...RETRACTED HIS DISOWNMENT OF ODEN...
RAHH
KYAA
...AND GAVE HIS SON THE TITLE OF "DAIMYO OF KURI."

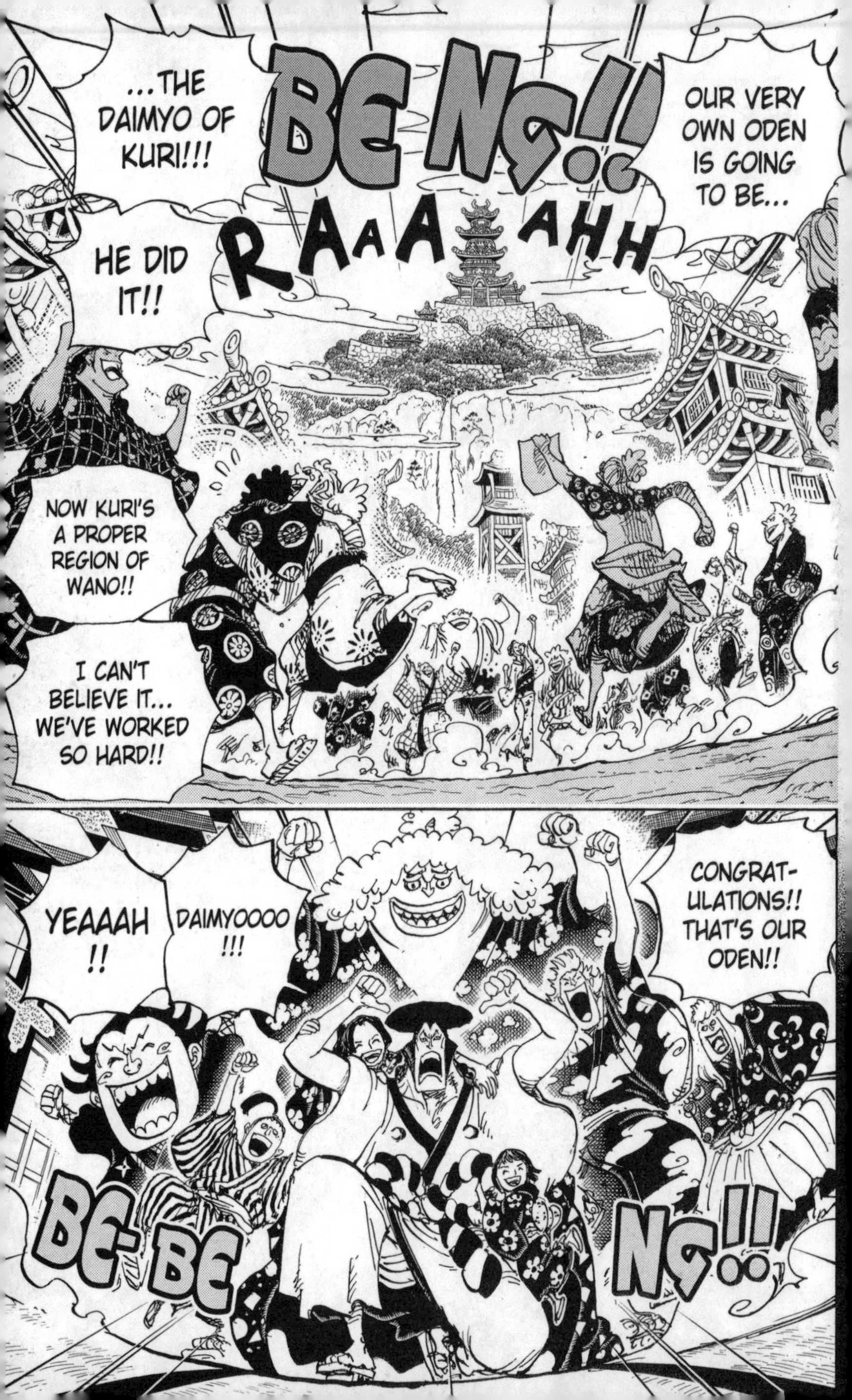
OUR VERY OWN ODEN IS GOING TO BE...
...THE DAIMYO OF KURI!!!
BE NG!!
RAAAAHH
HE DID IT!!
NOW KURI'S A PROPER REGION OF WANO!!
I CAN'T BELIEVE IT... WE'VE WORKED SO HARD!!
CONGRAT-ULATIONS!! THAT'S OUR ODEN!!
DAIMYOOOO !!!
YEAAAH !!
BE-BE NG!!

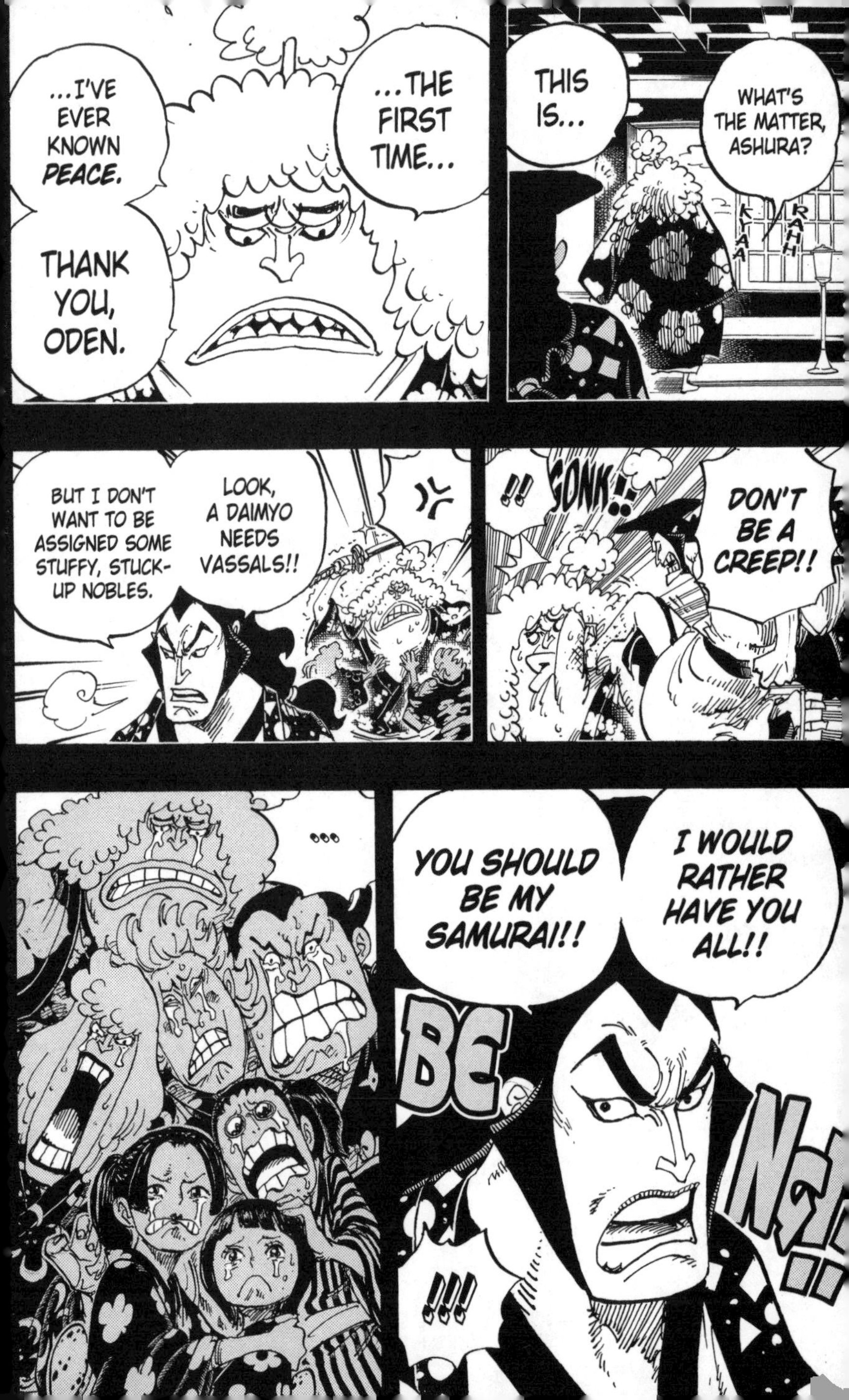
WHAT'S THE MATTER, ASHURA?
THIS IS...
KYAA
RAHH
...THE FIRST TIME...
...I'VE EVER KNOWN PEACE.
THANK YOU, ODEN.
!!
SONK!!
DON'T BE A CREEP!!
LOOK, A DAIMYO NEEDS VASSALS!!
BUT I DON'T WANT TO BE ASSIGNED SOME STUFFY, STUCK-UP NOBLES.
I WOULD RATHER HAVE YOU ALL!!
YOU SHOULD BE MY SAMURAI!!
BE
NG
!!!
...

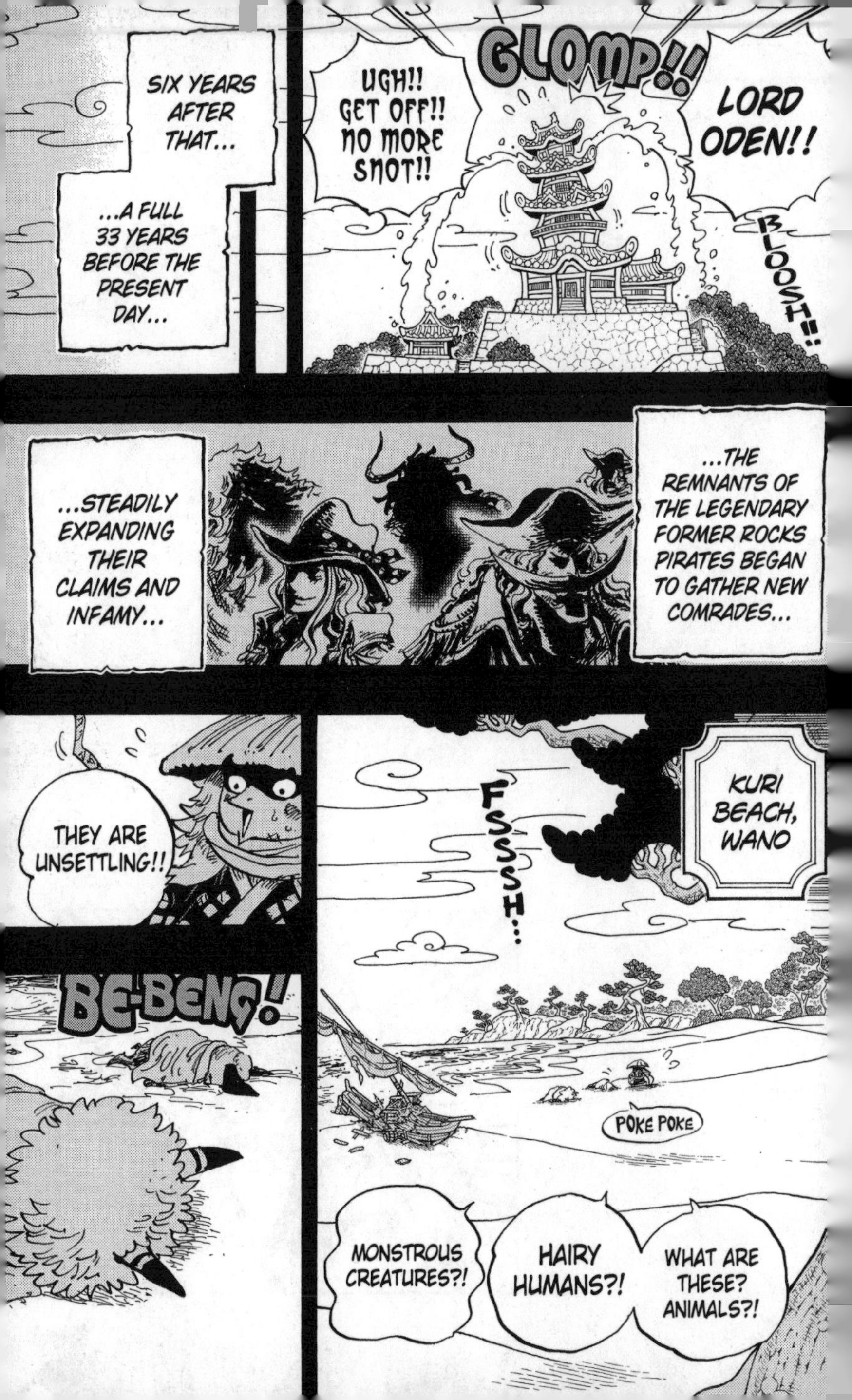
GLOMP!!
LORD ODEN!!
UGH!! GET OFF!! NO MORE SNOT!!
BLOOSH!!
SIX YEARS AFTER THAT...
...A FULL 33 YEARS BEFORE THE PRESENT DAY...
...THE REMNANTS OF THE LEGENDARY FORMER ROCKS PIRATES BEGAN TO GATHER NEW COMRADES...
...STEADILY EXPANDING THEIR CLAIMS AND INFAMY...
KURI BEACH, WANO
FSSSH...
POKE POKE
WHAT ARE THESE? ANIMALS?!
HAIRY HUMANS?!
MONSTROUS CREATURES?!
THEY ARE UNSETTLING!!
BE-BENG!

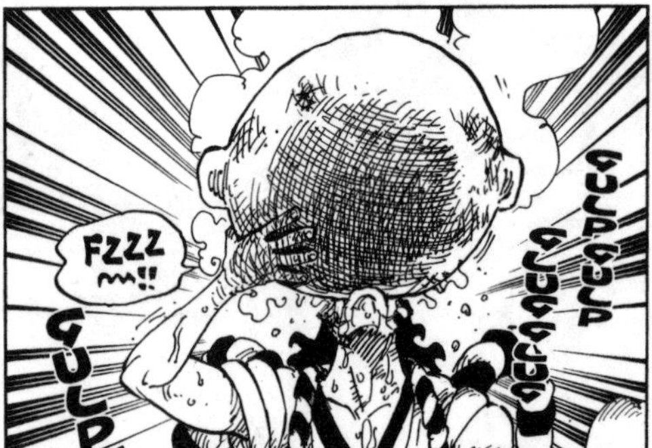
GULP GULP
GULGGULG
FZZZ
mm!!
GULP!!

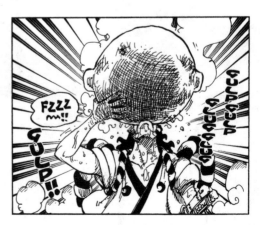

Chapter 963:
BECOMING SAMURAI

**GANG BEGE'S OH MY FAMILY
VOL. 13: "THE GERM PIRATES ATTACK
COUNTRIES WITHOUT A KING"**

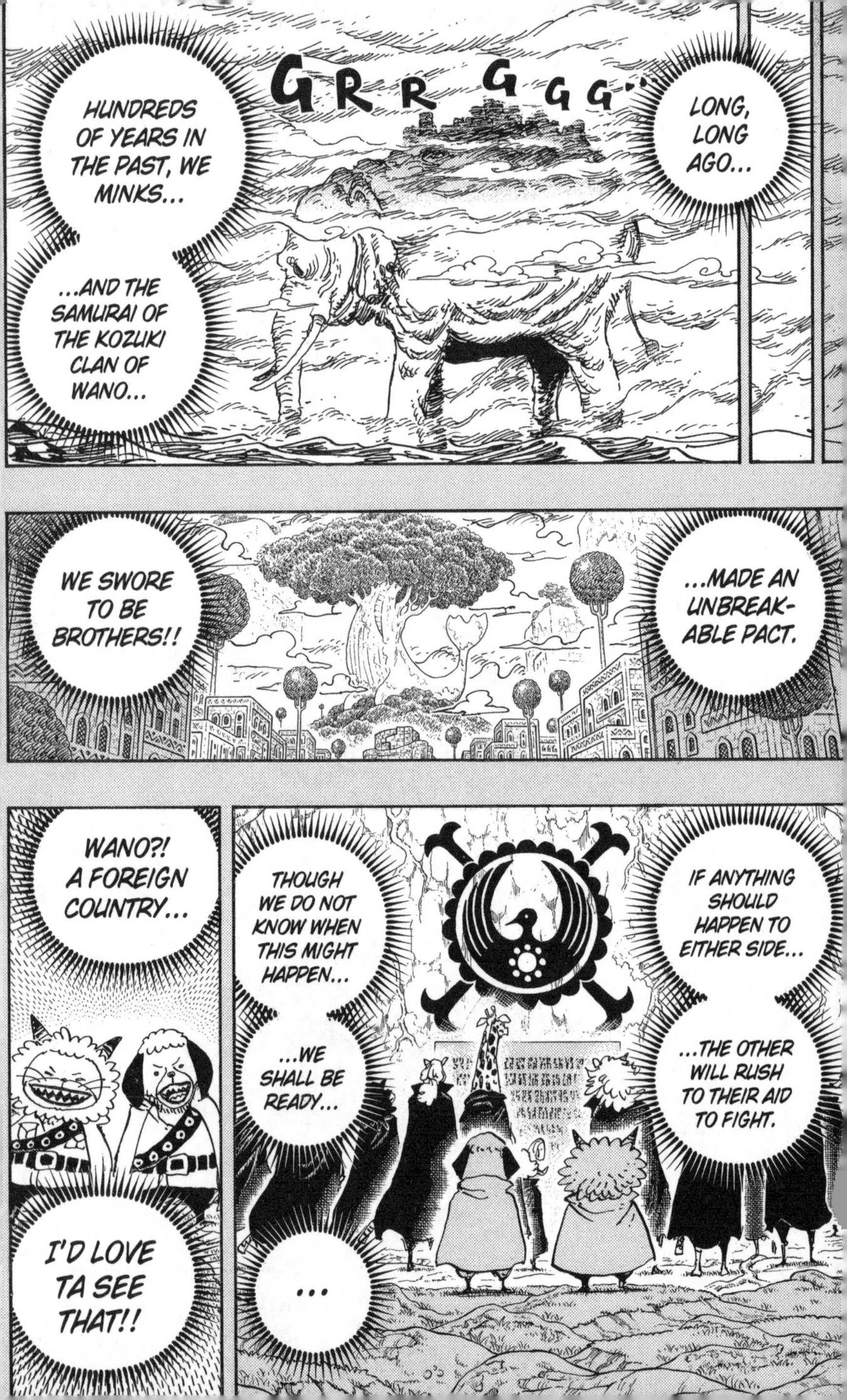
LONG, LONG AGO...
GRR GGG...
HUNDREDS OF YEARS IN THE PAST, WE MINKS...
...AND THE SAMURAI OF THE KOZUKI CLAN OF WANO...
...MADE AN UNBREAKABLE PACT.
WE SWORE TO BE BROTHERS!!
IF ANYTHING SHOULD HAPPEN TO EITHER SIDE...
...THE OTHER WILL RUSH TO THEIR AID TO FIGHT.
THOUGH WE DO NOT KNOW WHEN THIS MIGHT HAPPEN...
...WE SHALL BE READY...
...
WANO?! A FOREIGN COUNTRY...
I'D LOVE TA SEE THAT!!

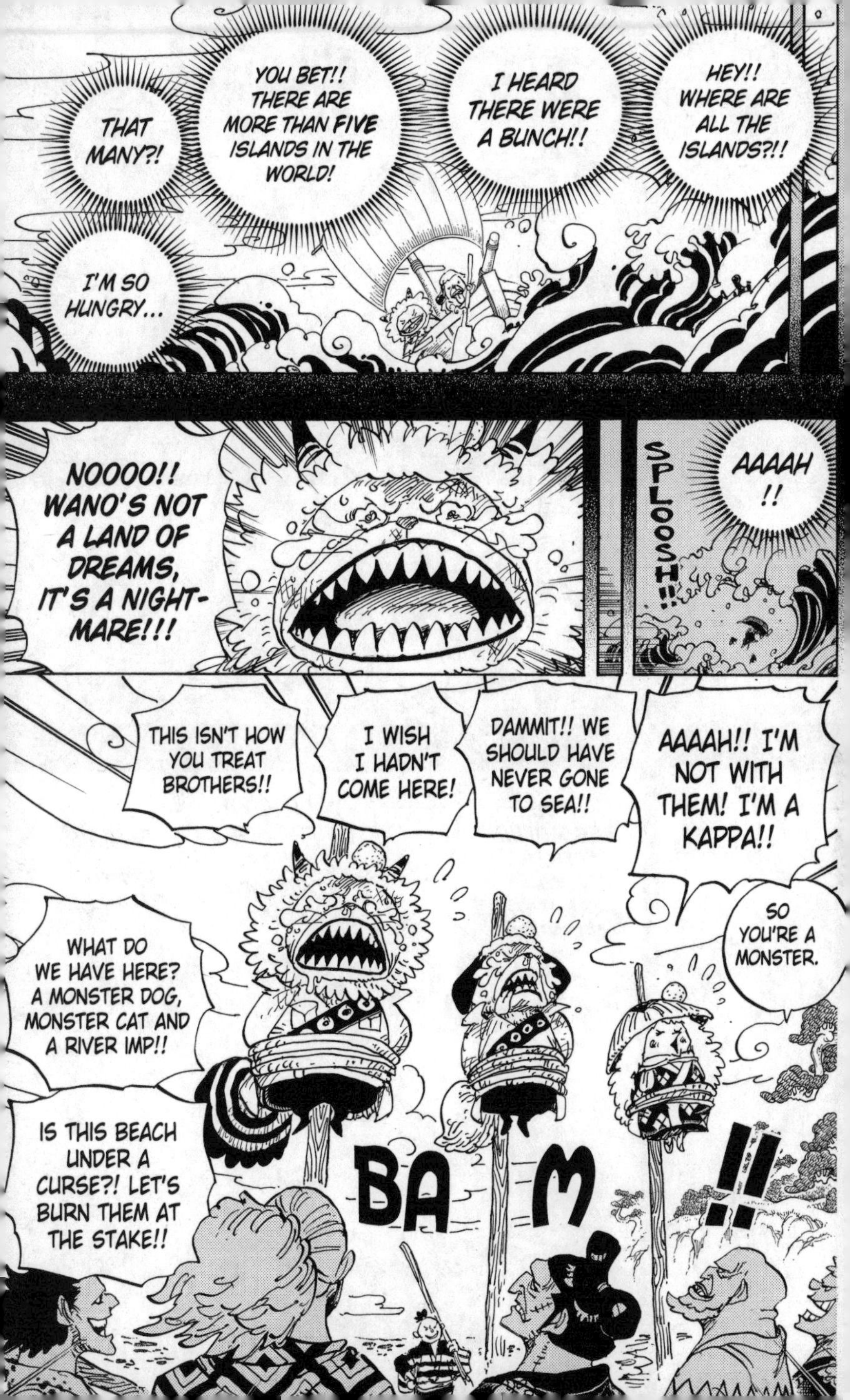
HEY!! WHERE ARE ALL THE ISLANDS?!!
I HEARD THERE WERE A BUNCH!!
YOU BET!! THERE ARE MORE THAN FIVE ISLANDS IN THE WORLD!
THAT MANY?!
I'M SO HUNGRY...
SPLOOSH!!
AAAAH!!
NOOOO!! WANO'S NOT A LAND OF DREAMS, IT'S A NIGHT-MARE!!!
AAAAH!! I'M NOT WITH THEM! I'M A KAPPA!!
DAMMIT!! WE SHOULD HAVE NEVER GONE TO SEA!!
I WISH I HADN'T COME HERE!
THIS ISN'T HOW YOU TREAT BROTHERS!!
SO YOU'RE A MONSTER.
WHAT DO WE HAVE HERE? A MONSTER DOG, MONSTER CAT AND A RIVER IMP!!
BAM!!
IS THIS BEACH UNDER A CURSE?! LET'S BURN THEM AT THE STAKE!!

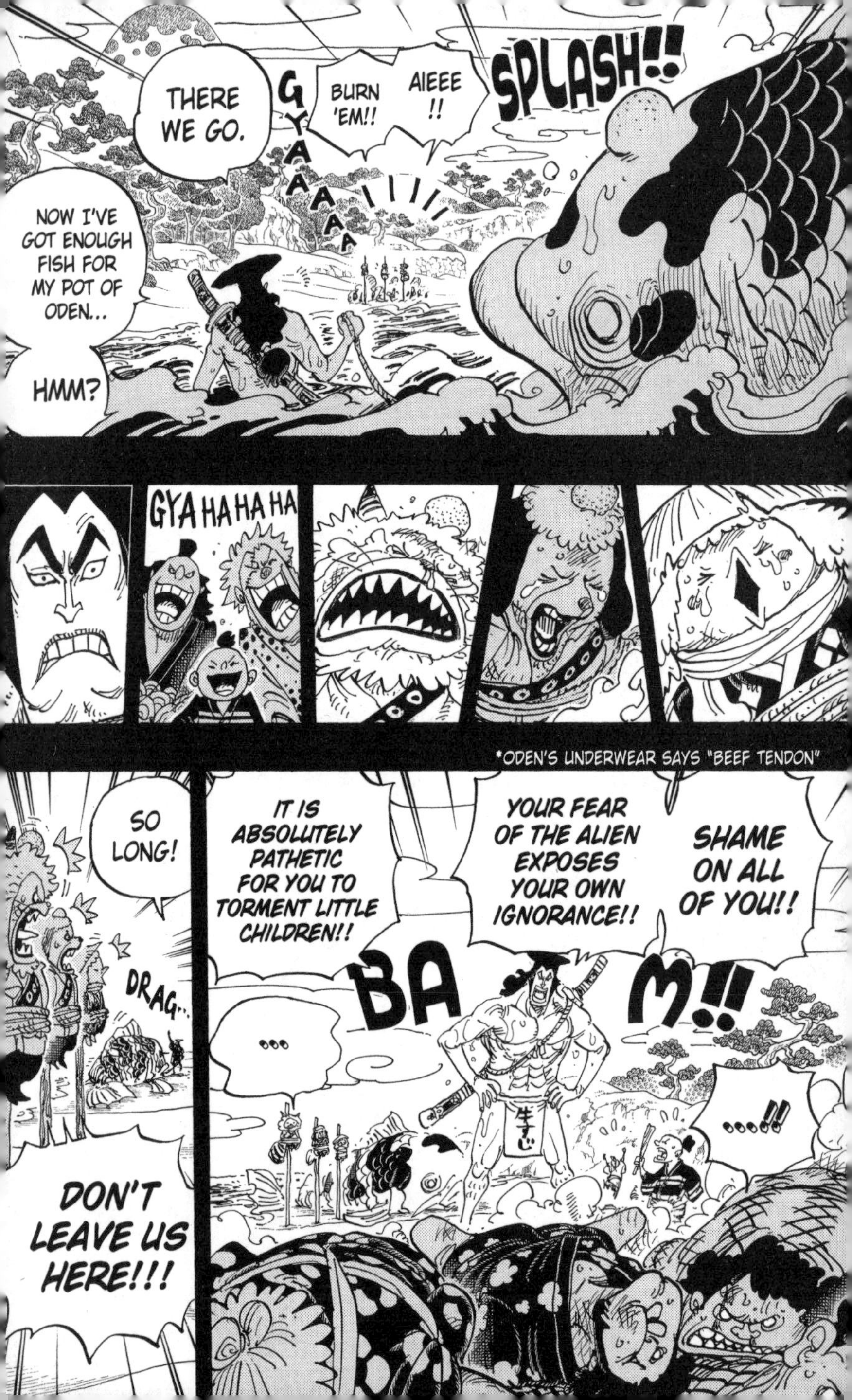
SPLASH!!
AIEEE!!
BURN 'EM!!
GYAAAAA
THERE WE GO.
NOW I'VE GOT ENOUGH FISH FOR MY POT OF ODEN...
HMM?
GYA HA HA HA
SHAME ON ALL OF YOU!!
YOUR FEAR OF THE ALIEN EXPOSES YOUR OWN IGNORANCE!!
IT IS ABSOLUTELY PATHETIC FOR YOU TO TORMENT LITTLE CHILDREN!!
BAM!!
...!!
...
SO LONG!
DRAG...
DON'T LEAVE US HERE!!!

*ODEN'S UNDERWEAR SAYS "BEEF TENDON"

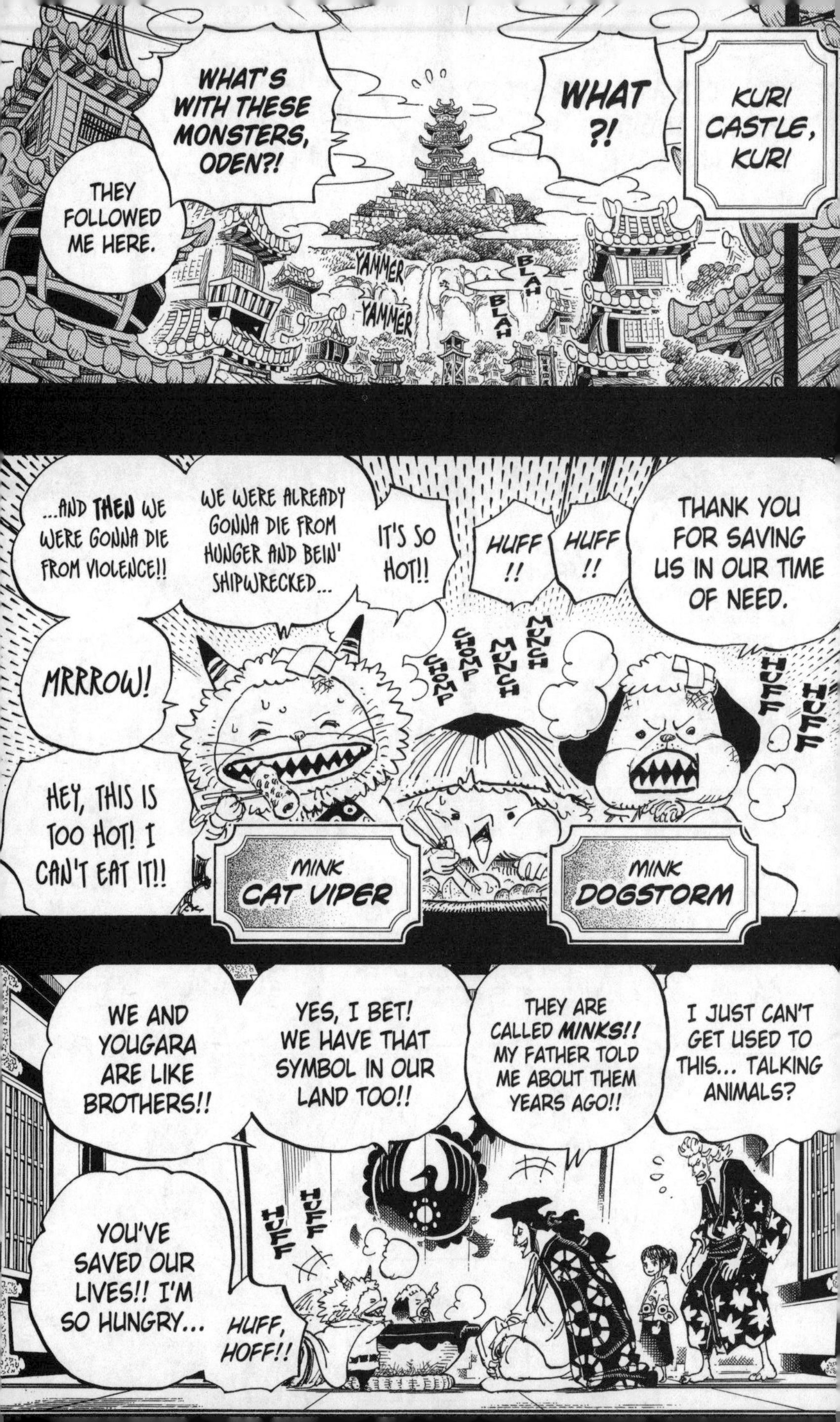
KURI CASTLE, KURI
WHAT ?!
WHAT'S WITH THESE MONSTERS, ODEN?!
THEY FOLLOWED ME HERE.
BLAH BLAH
YAMMER YAMMER
THANK YOU FOR SAVING US IN OUR TIME OF NEED.
HUFF !!
HUFF !!
IT'S SO HOT!!
WE WERE ALREADY GONNA DIE FROM HUNGER AND BEIN' SHIPWRECKED...
...AND THEN WE WERE GONNA DIE FROM VIOLENCE!!
HUFF HUFF
MUNCH MUNCH
CHOMP CHOMP
MRRROW!
HEY, THIS IS TOO HOT! I CAN'T EAT IT!!
MINK DOGSTORM
MINK CAT VIPER
I JUST CAN'T GET USED TO THIS... TALKING ANIMALS?
THEY ARE CALLED MINKS!! MY FATHER TOLD ME ABOUT THEM YEARS AGO!!
YES, I BET! WE HAVE THAT SYMBOL IN OUR LAND TOO!!
WE AND YOUGARA ARE LIKE BROTHERS!!
HUFF HUFF
YOU'VE SAVED OUR LIVES!! I'M SO HUNGRY...
HUFF, HOFF!!

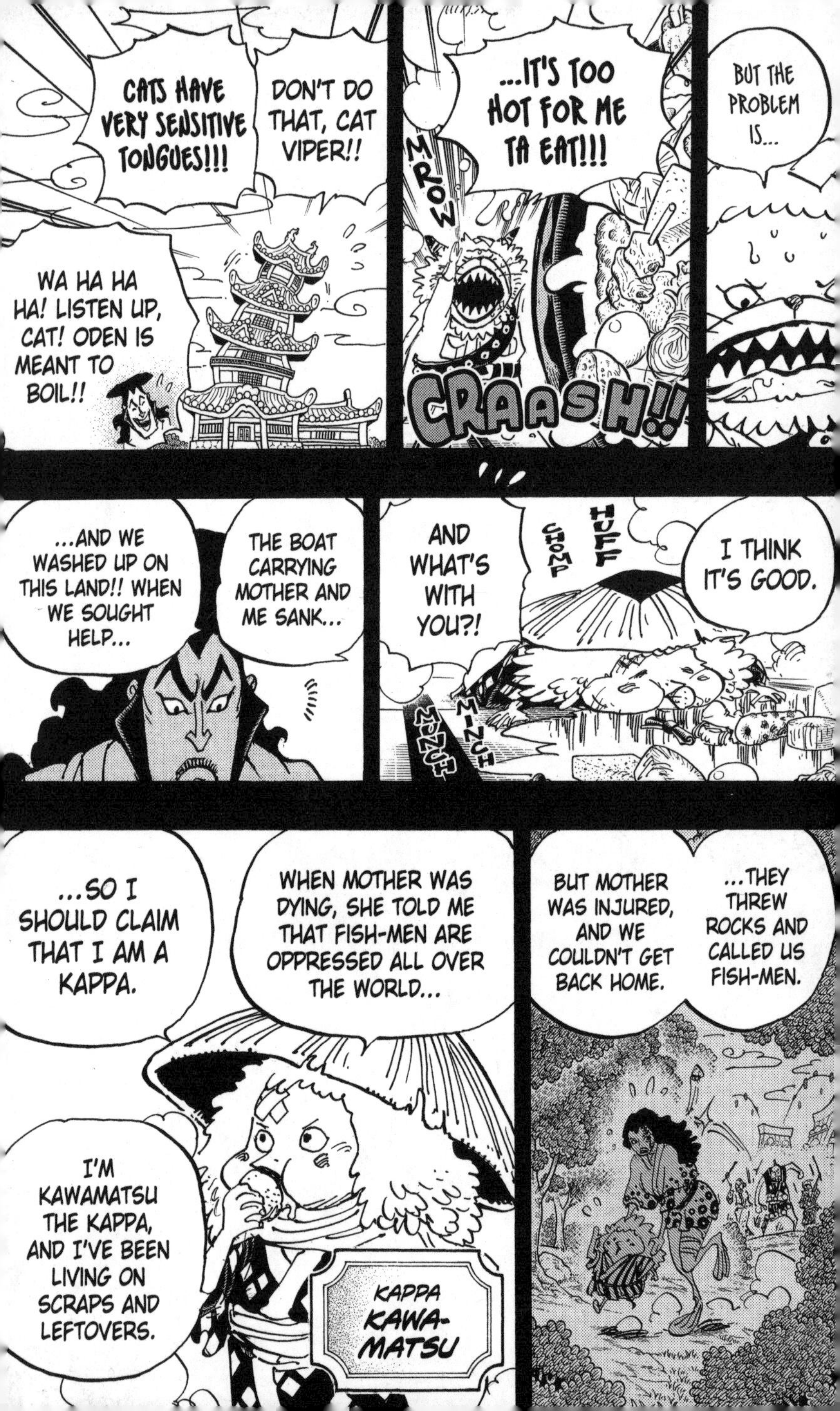
BUT THE PROBLEM IS...
...IT'S TOO HOT FOR ME TA EAT!!!
MROW
CRAASH!!
DON'T DO THAT, CAT VIPER!!
CATS HAVE VERY SENSITIVE TONGUES!!!
WA HA HA HA! LISTEN UP, CAT! ODEN IS MEANT TO BOIL!!
I THINK IT'S GOOD.
HUFF
CHOMP
AND WHAT'S WITH YOU?!
MINCH
MUNCH
THE BOAT CARRYING MOTHER AND ME SANK...
...AND WE WASHED UP ON THIS LAND!! WHEN WE SOUGHT HELP...
...THEY THREW ROCKS AND CALLED US FISH-MEN.
BUT MOTHER WAS INJURED, AND WE COULDN'T GET BACK HOME.
WHEN MOTHER WAS DYING, SHE TOLD ME THAT FISH-MEN ARE OPPRESSED ALL OVER THE WORLD...
...SO I SHOULD CLAIM THAT I AM A KAPPA.
I'M KAWAMATSU THE KAPPA, AND I'VE BEEN LIVING ON SCRAPS AND LEFTOVERS.
KAPPA KAWA-MATSU

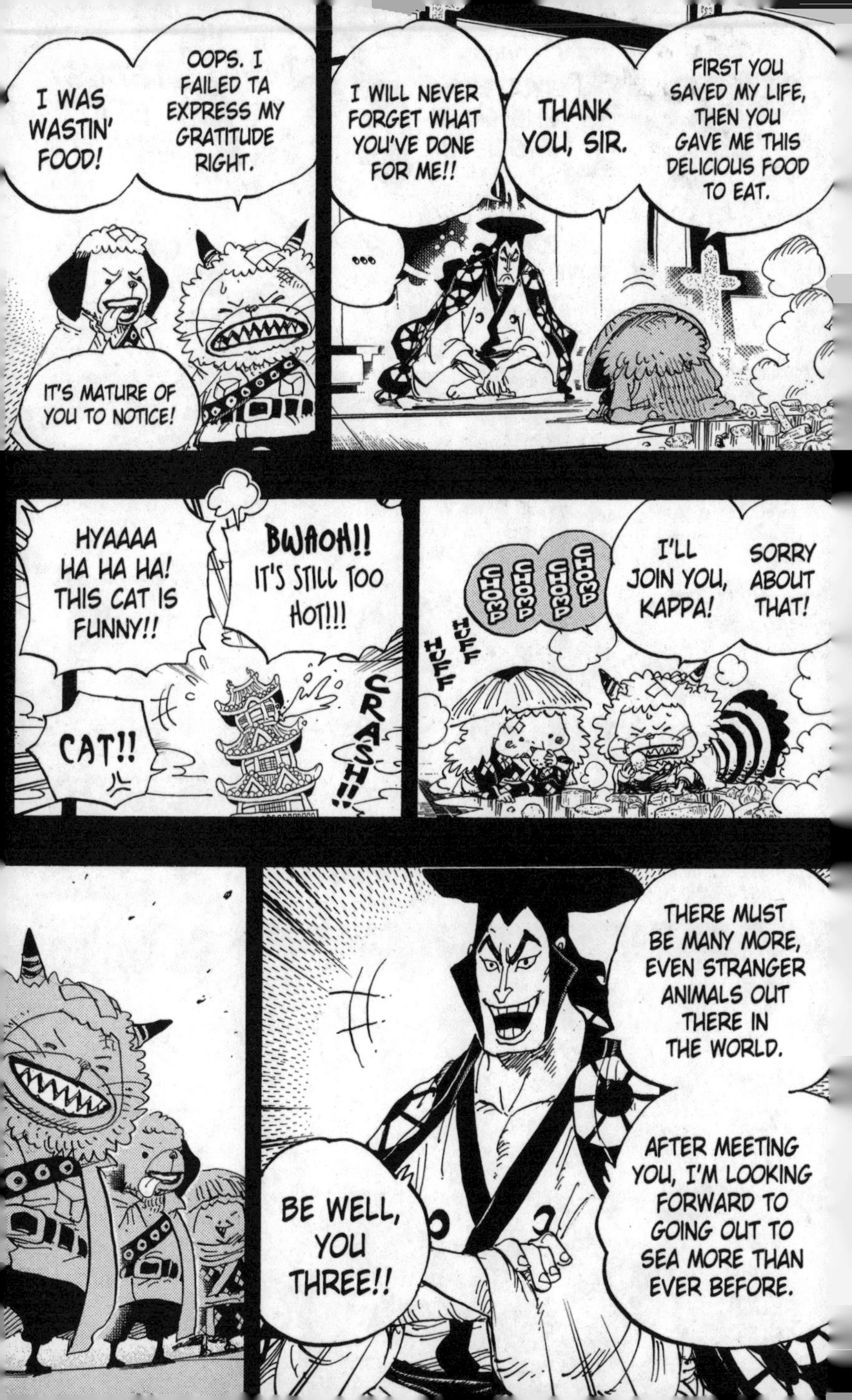
FIRST YOU SAVED MY LIFE, THEN YOU GAVE ME THIS DELICIOUS FOOD TO EAT.
THANK YOU, SIR.
I WILL NEVER FORGET WHAT YOU'VE DONE FOR ME!!
...
OOPS. I FAILED TA EXPRESS MY GRATITUDE RIGHT.
I WAS WASTIN' FOOD!
IT'S MATURE OF YOU TO NOTICE!
SORRY ABOUT THAT!
I'LL JOIN YOU, KAPPA!
CHOMP CHOMP CHOMP CHOMP
HUFF HUFF
BWAOH!! IT'S STILL TOO HOT!!!
CRASH!!
HYAAAA HA HA HA! THIS CAT IS FUNNY!!
CAT!!
THERE MUST BE MANY MORE, EVEN STRANGER ANIMALS OUT THERE IN THE WORLD.
AFTER MEETING YOU, I'M LOOKING FORWARD TO GOING OUT TO SEA MORE THAN EVER BEFORE.
BE WELL, YOU THREE!!

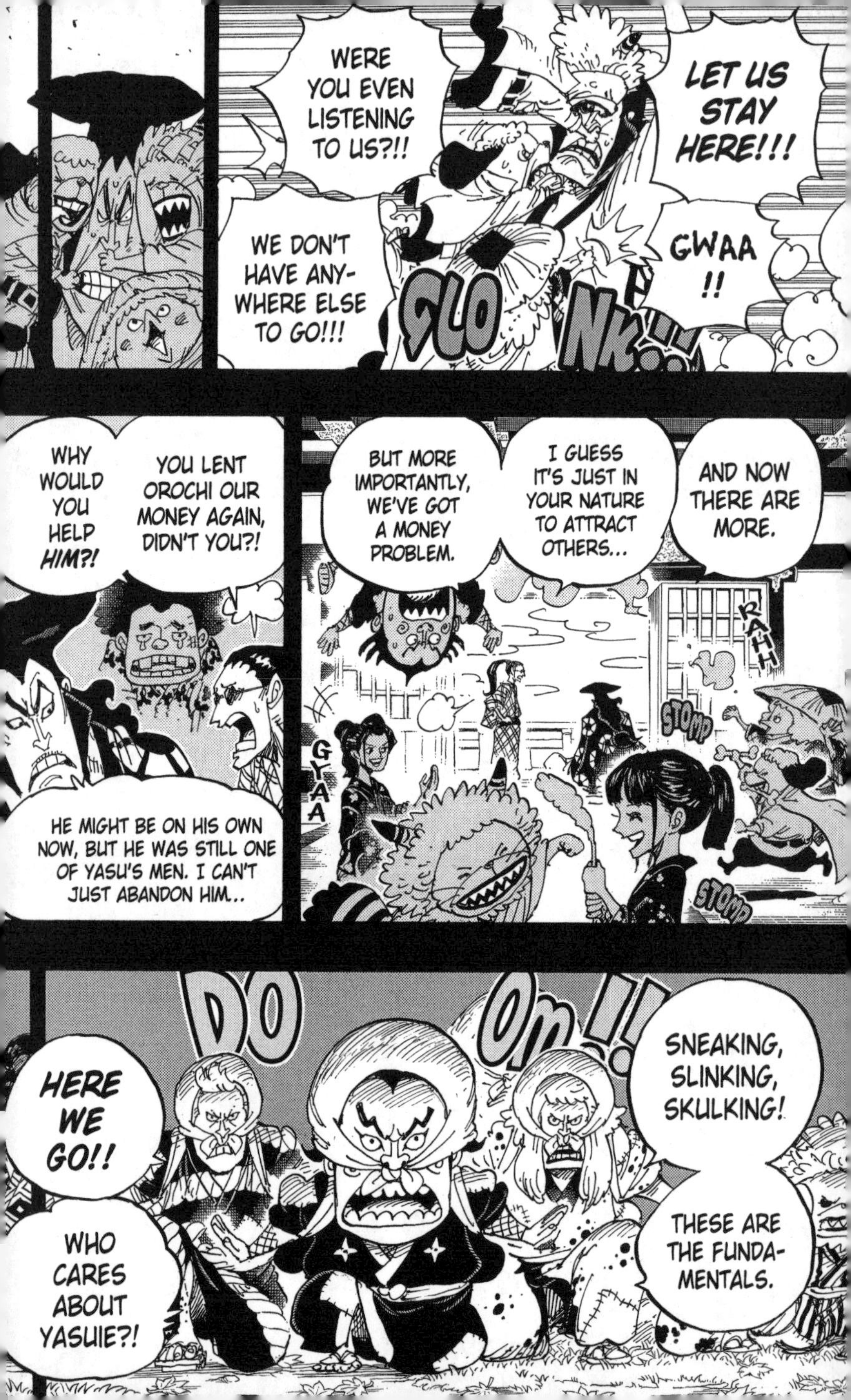
LET US STAY HERE!!!
WERE YOU EVEN LISTENING TO US?!!
GWAA !!
WE DON'T HAVE ANY-WHERE ELSE TO GO!!!
GLONK!!
AND NOW THERE ARE MORE.
I GUESS IT'S JUST IN YOUR NATURE TO ATTRACT OTHERS...
BUT MORE IMPORTANTLY, WE'VE GOT A MONEY PROBLEM.
RAHH
STOMP
GYAA
STOMP
YOU LENT OROCHI OUR MONEY AGAIN, DIDN'T YOU?!
WHY WOULD YOU HELP *HIM?!*
HE MIGHT BE ON HIS OWN NOW, BUT HE WAS STILL ONE OF YASU'S MEN. I CAN'T JUST ABANDON HIM...
DOOM!!
SNEAKING, SLINKING, SKULKING!
HERE WE GO!!
THESE ARE THE FUNDA-MENTALS.
WHO CARES ABOUT YASUIE?!

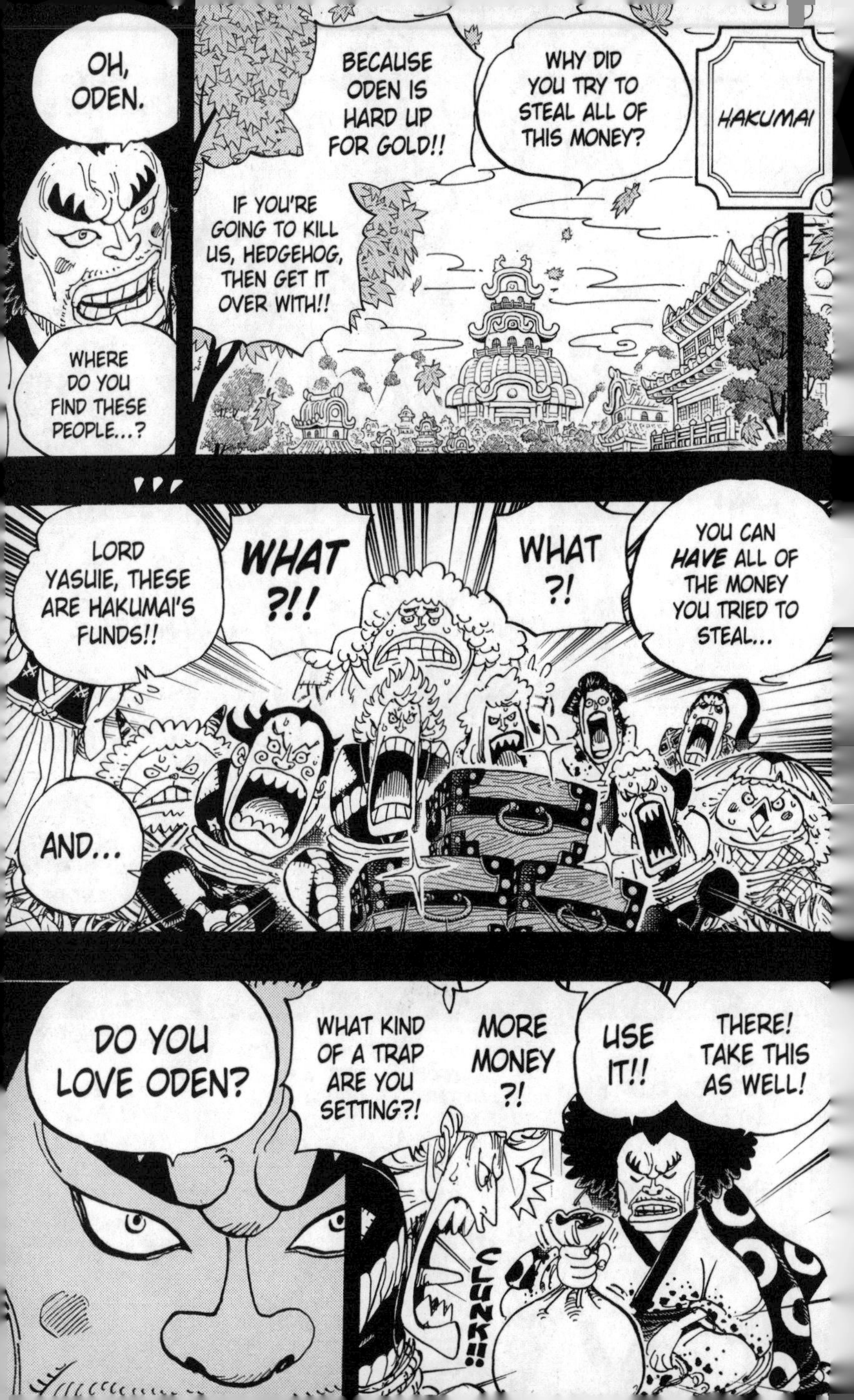
HAKUMAI
WHY DID YOU TRY TO STEAL ALL OF THIS MONEY?
BECAUSE ODEN IS HARD UP FOR GOLD!!
IF YOU'RE GOING TO KILL US, HEDGEHOG, THEN GET IT OVER WITH!!
OH, ODEN.
WHERE DO YOU FIND THESE PEOPLE...?
YOU CAN *HAVE* ALL OF THE MONEY YOU TRIED TO STEAL...
WHAT ?!
WHAT ?!!
LORD YASUIE, THESE ARE HAKUMAI'S FUNDS!!
AND...
THERE! TAKE THIS AS WELL!
USE IT!!
MORE MONEY ?!
WHAT KIND OF A TRAP ARE YOU SETTING?!
CLUNK!!
DO YOU LOVE ODEN?

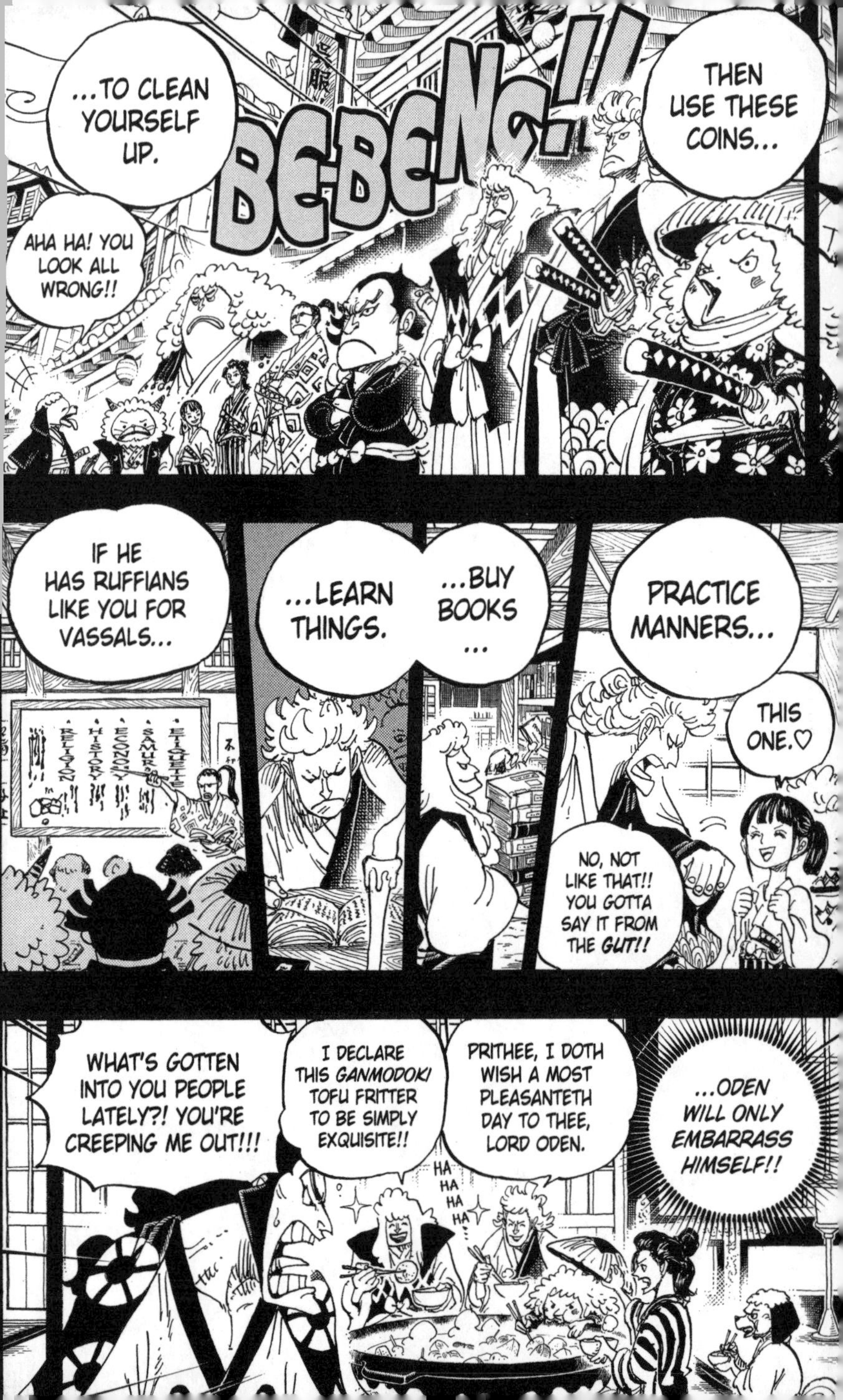
THEN USE THESE COINS...
BE-BENG!!
...TO CLEAN YOURSELF UP.
AHA HA! YOU LOOK ALL WRONG!!
PRACTICE MANNERS...
THIS ONE.♡
NO, NOT LIKE THAT!! YOU GOTTA SAY IT FROM THE *GUT*!!
...BUY BOOKS ...
...LEARN THINGS.
IF HE HAS RUFFIANS LIKE YOU FOR VASSALS...
ETIQUETTE
ECONOMY
HISTORY
RELIGION
...ODEN WILL ONLY EMBARRASS HIMSELF!!
PRITHEE, I DOTH WISH A MOST PLEASANTETH DAY TO THEE, LORD ODEN.
I DECLARE THIS *GANMODOKI* TOFU FRITTER TO BE SIMPLY EXQUISITE!!
HA HA HA HA
WHAT'S GOTTEN INTO YOU PEOPLE LATELY?! YOU'RE CREEPING ME OUT!!!

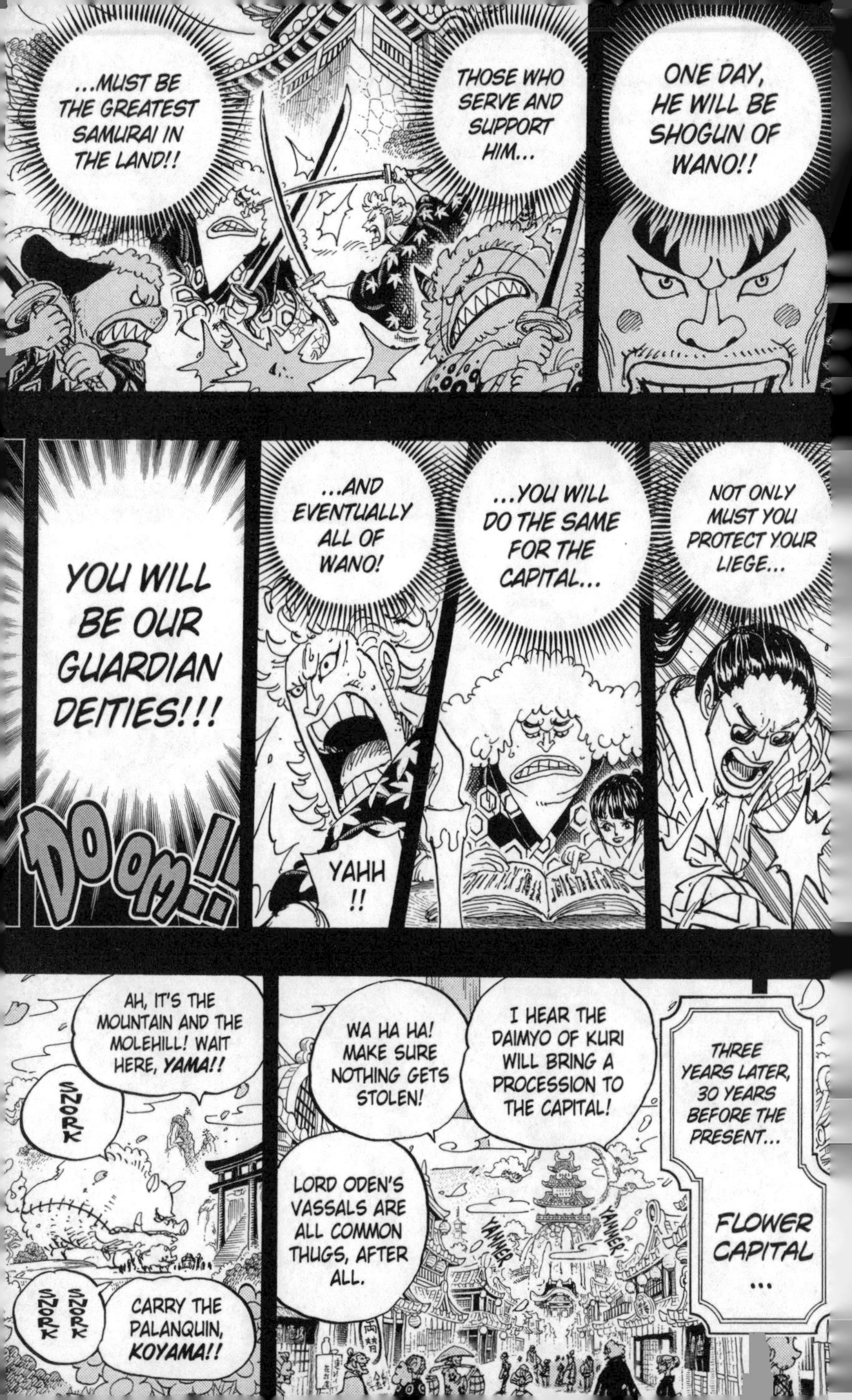
ONE DAY, HE WILL BE SHOGUN OF WANO!!
THOSE WHO SERVE AND SUPPORT HIM...
...MUST BE THE GREATEST SAMURAI IN THE LAND!!
NOT ONLY MUST YOU PROTECT YOUR LIEGE...
...YOU WILL DO THE SAME FOR THE CAPITAL...
...AND EVENTUALLY ALL OF WANO!
YAHH !!
YOU WILL BE OUR GUARDIAN DEITIES!!!
DOOM!!
THREE YEARS LATER, 30 YEARS BEFORE THE PRESENT...
FLOWER CAPITAL
...
I HEAR THE DAIMYO OF KURI WILL BRING A PROCESSION TO THE CAPITAL!
WA HA HA! MAKE SURE NOTHING GETS STOLEN!
YAMMER
YAMMER
LORD ODEN'S VASSALS ARE ALL COMMON THUGS, AFTER ALL.
AH, IT'S THE MOUNTAIN AND THE MOLEHILL! WAIT HERE, YAMA!!
SNORK
SNORK SNORK
CARRY THE PALANQUIN, KOYAMA!!

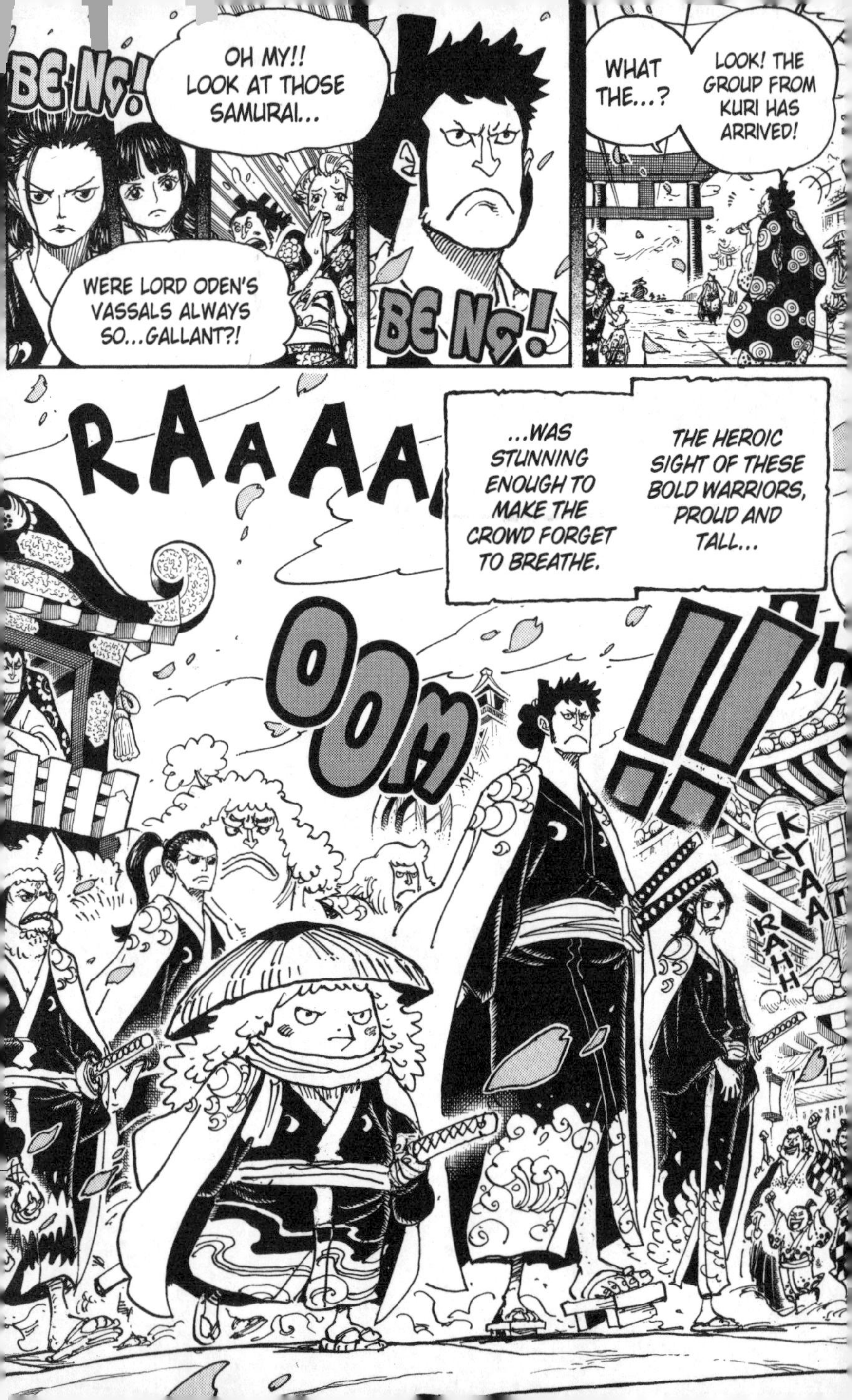

LOOK! THE GROUP FROM KURI HAS ARRIVED!
WHAT THE...?
BE NG!
BE NG!
OH MY!! LOOK AT THOSE SAMURAI...
WERE LORD ODEN'S VASSALS ALWAYS SO...GALLANT?!
THE HEROIC SIGHT OF THESE BOLD WARRIORS, PROUD AND TALL...
...WAS STUNNING ENOUGH TO MAKE THE CROWD FORGET TO BREATHE.
RAAAA
KYAAA
RAHH

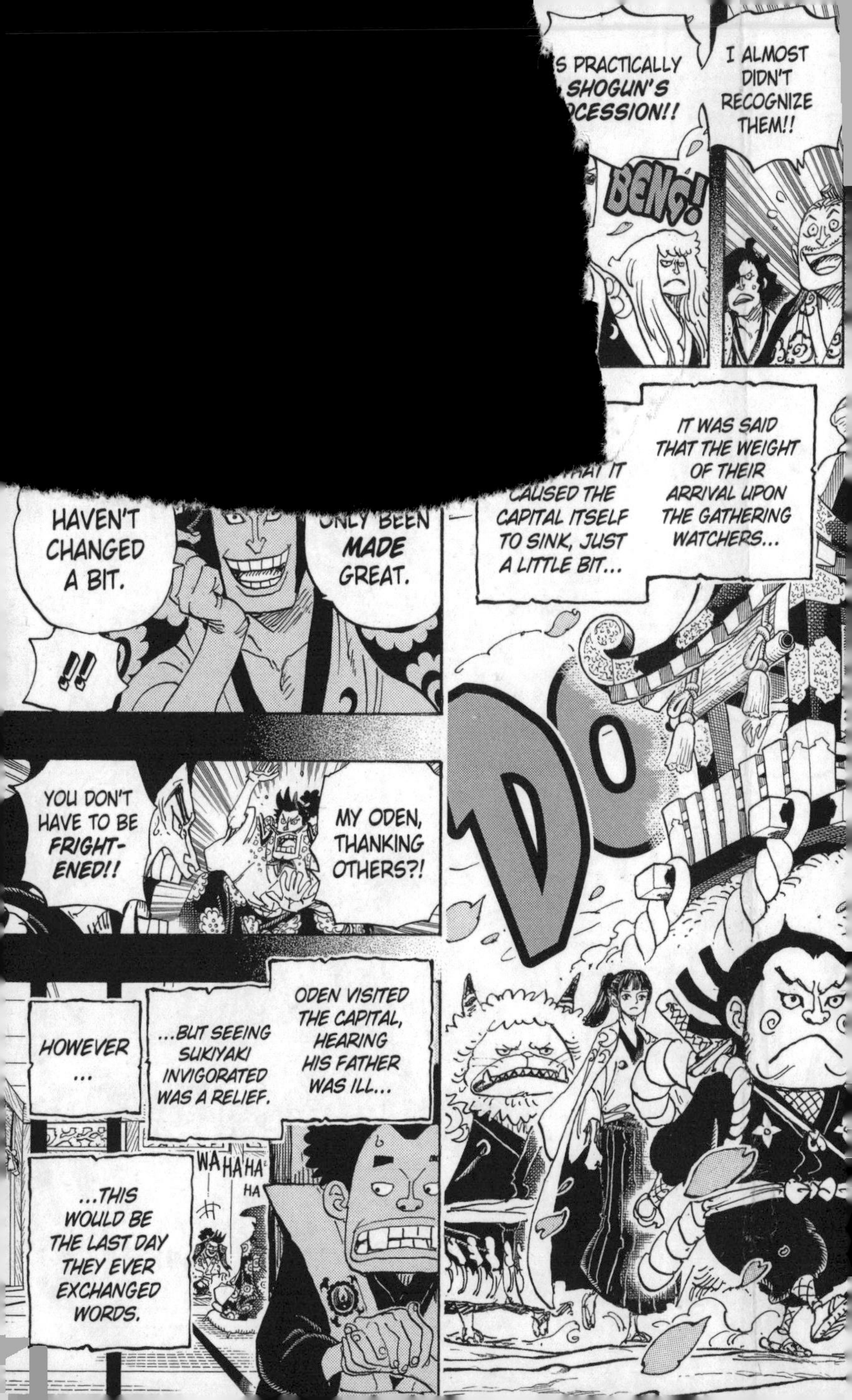
I ALMOST DIDN'T RECOGNIZE THEM!!
S PRACTICALLY SHOGUN'S OCESSION!!
BENG!!
IT WAS SAID THAT THE WEIGHT OF THEIR ARRIVAL UPON THE GATHERING WATCHERS...
THAT IT CAUSED THE CAPITAL ITSELF TO SINK, JUST A LITTLE BIT...
DO
ONLY BEEN MADE GREAT.
HAVEN'T CHANGED A BIT.
!!
MY ODEN, THANKING OTHERS?!
YOU DON'T HAVE TO BE FRIGHT-ENED!!
ODEN VISITED THE CAPITAL, HEARING HIS FATHER WAS ILL...
...BUT SEEING SUKIYAKI INVIGORATED WAS A RELIEF.
HOWEVER...
WA HA HA HA HA
...THIS WOULD BE THE LAST DAY THEY EVER EXCHANGED WORDS.

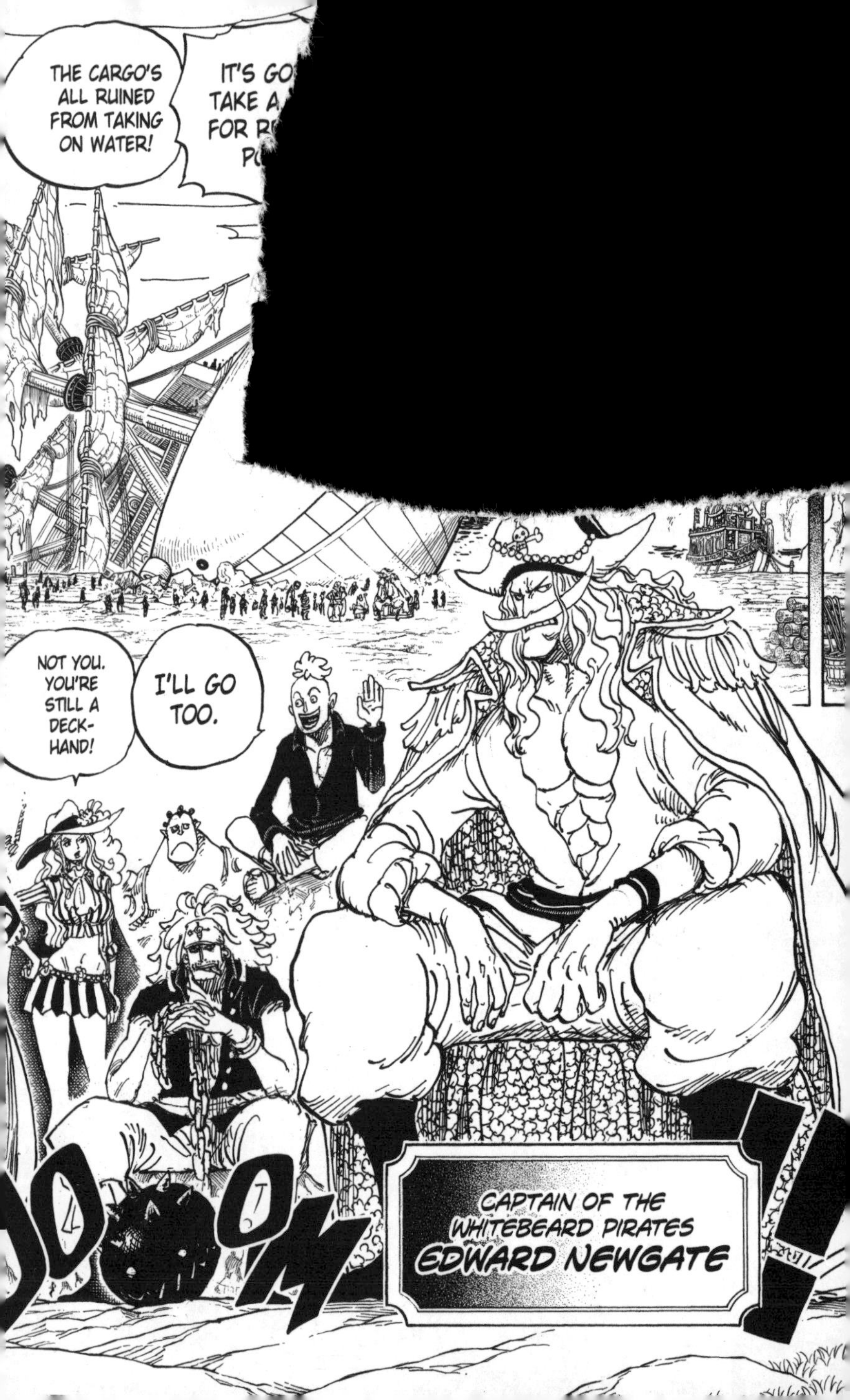
IT'S GO TAKE A FOR R PO [redacted]
THE CARGO'S ALL RUINED FROM TAKING ON WATER!
I'LL GO TOO.
NOT YOU. YOU'RE STILL A DECK-HAND!
CAPTAIN OF THE WHITEBEARD PIRATES EDWARD NEWGATE
DOOM!

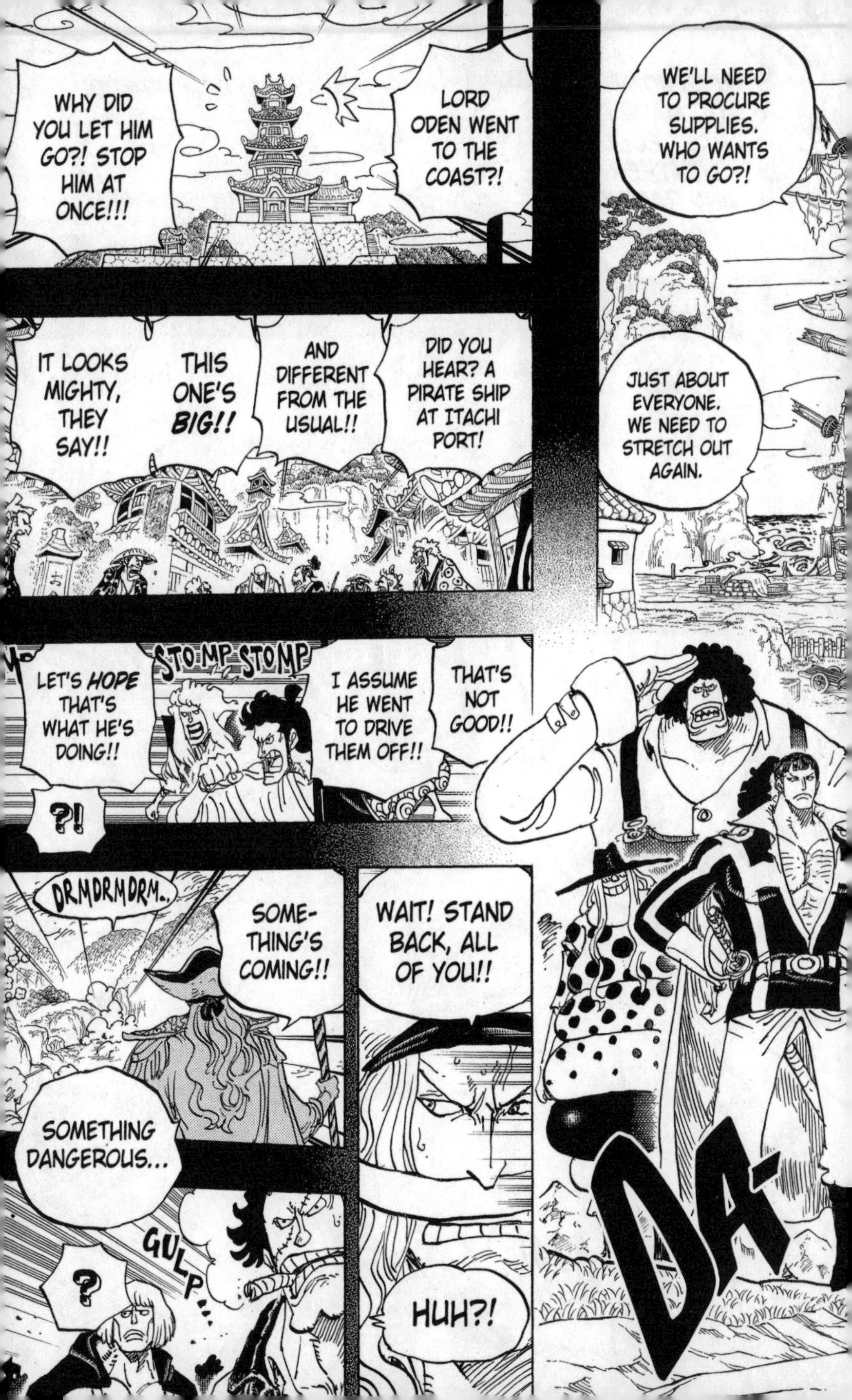
WE'LL NEED TO PROCURE SUPPLIES. WHO WANTS TO GO?!
JUST ABOUT EVERYONE. WE NEED TO STRETCH OUT AGAIN.
LORD ODEN WENT TO THE COAST?!
WHY DID YOU LET HIM GO?! STOP HIM AT ONCE!!!
DID YOU HEAR? A PIRATE SHIP AT ITACHI PORT!
AND DIFFERENT FROM THE USUAL!!
THIS ONE'S *BIG!!*
IT LOOKS MIGHTY, THEY SAY!!
THAT'S NOT GOOD!!
I ASSUME HE WENT TO DRIVE THEM OFF!!
STOMP STOMP
LET'S *HOPE* THAT'S WHAT HE'S DOING!!
?!
WAIT! STAND BACK, ALL OF YOU!!
HUH?!
DRMDRMDRM..
SOME-THING'S COMING!!
SOMETHING DANGEROUS...
GULP...
?
DA-

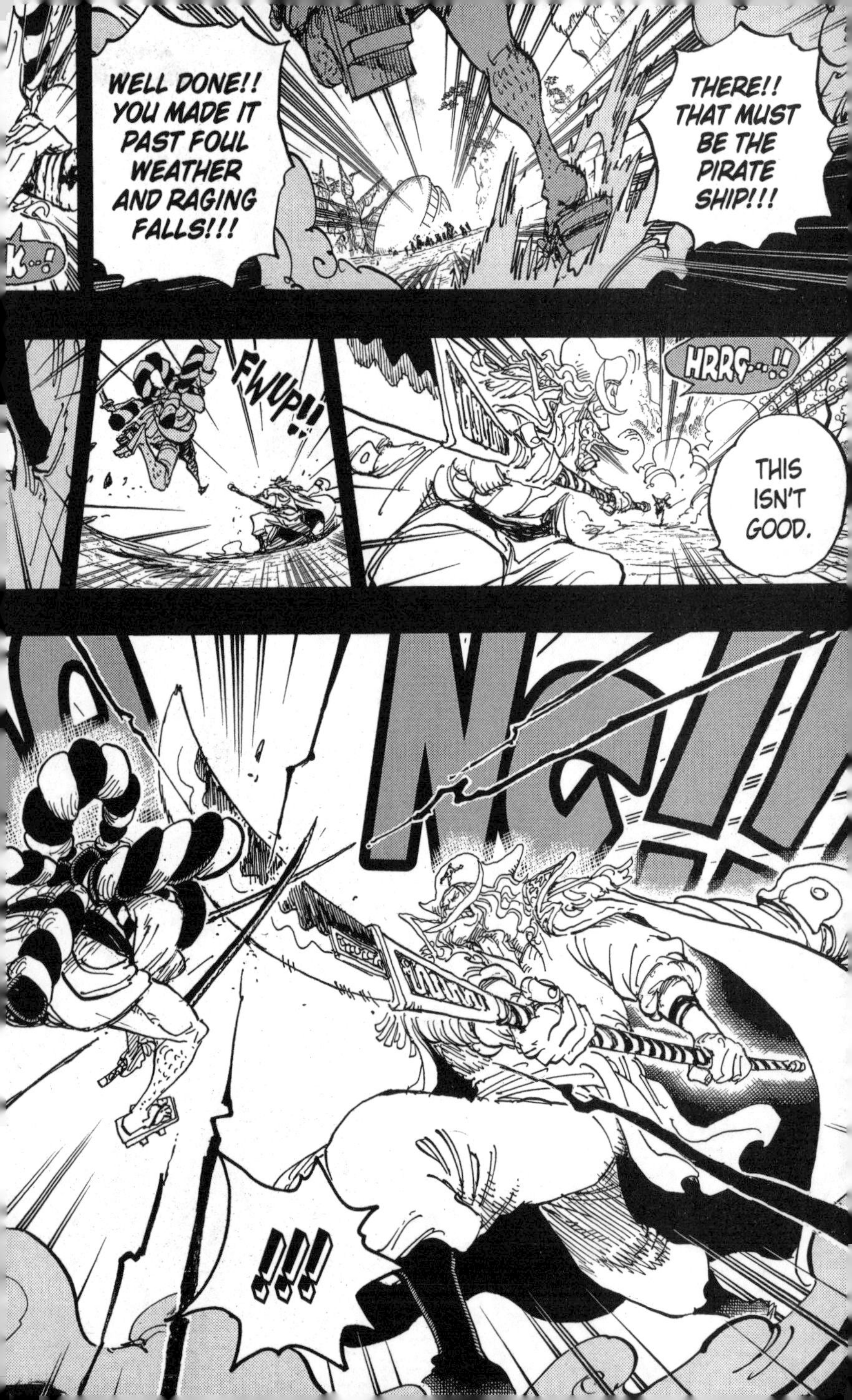

THERE!! THAT MUST BE THE PIRATE SHIP!!!
WELL DONE!! YOU MADE IT PAST FOUL WEATHER AND RAGING FALLS!!!
HRRG...!!
THIS ISN'T GOOD.
FWUP!!
!!!

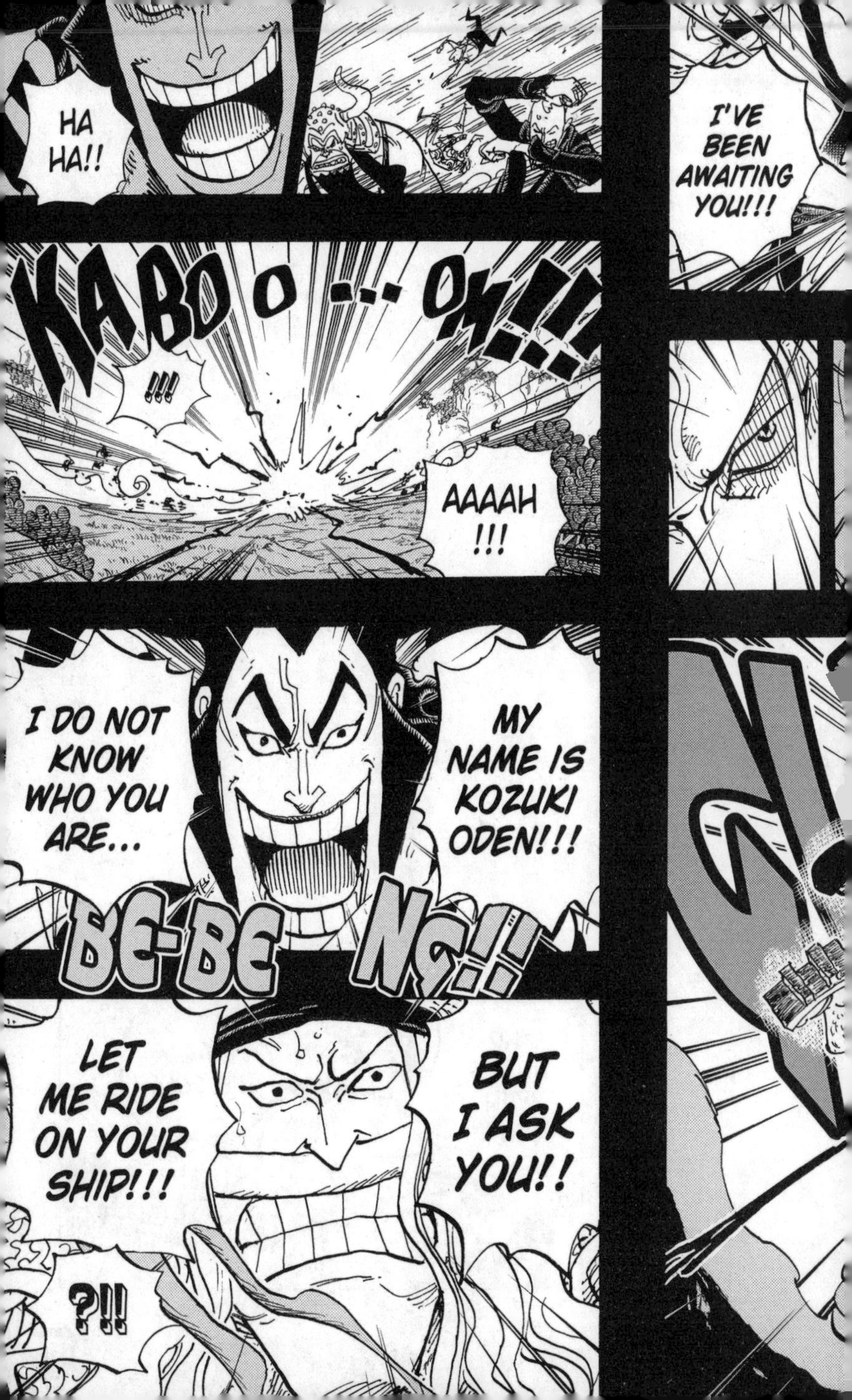
I'VE BEEN AWAITING YOU!!!
HA HA!!
KABOO...OM!!!
AAAAH !!!
!!!
MY NAME IS KOZUKI ODEN!!!
I DO NOT KNOW WHO YOU ARE...
BE-BENG!!
BUT I ASK YOU!!
LET ME RIDE ON YOUR SHIP!!!
?!!

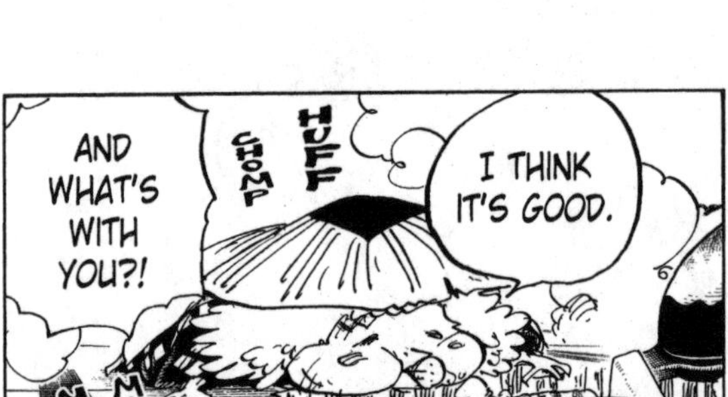
I THINK IT'S GOOD.
HUFF
CHOMP
AND WHAT'S WITH YOU?!
MUNCH
MUNCH

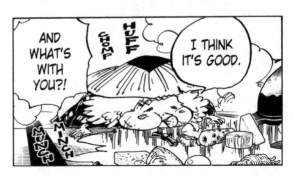

Chapter 964:
ODEN'S ADVENTURE

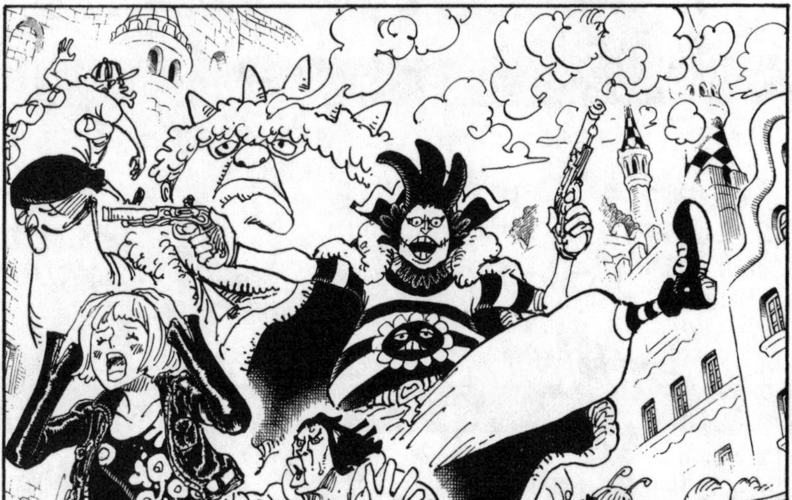
KISSSEN

GANG BEGE'S OH MY FAMILY
VOL. 14: "WE'RE GONNA SHOOT YOU
WITH KISS-KISS COOTIES TOO!!"

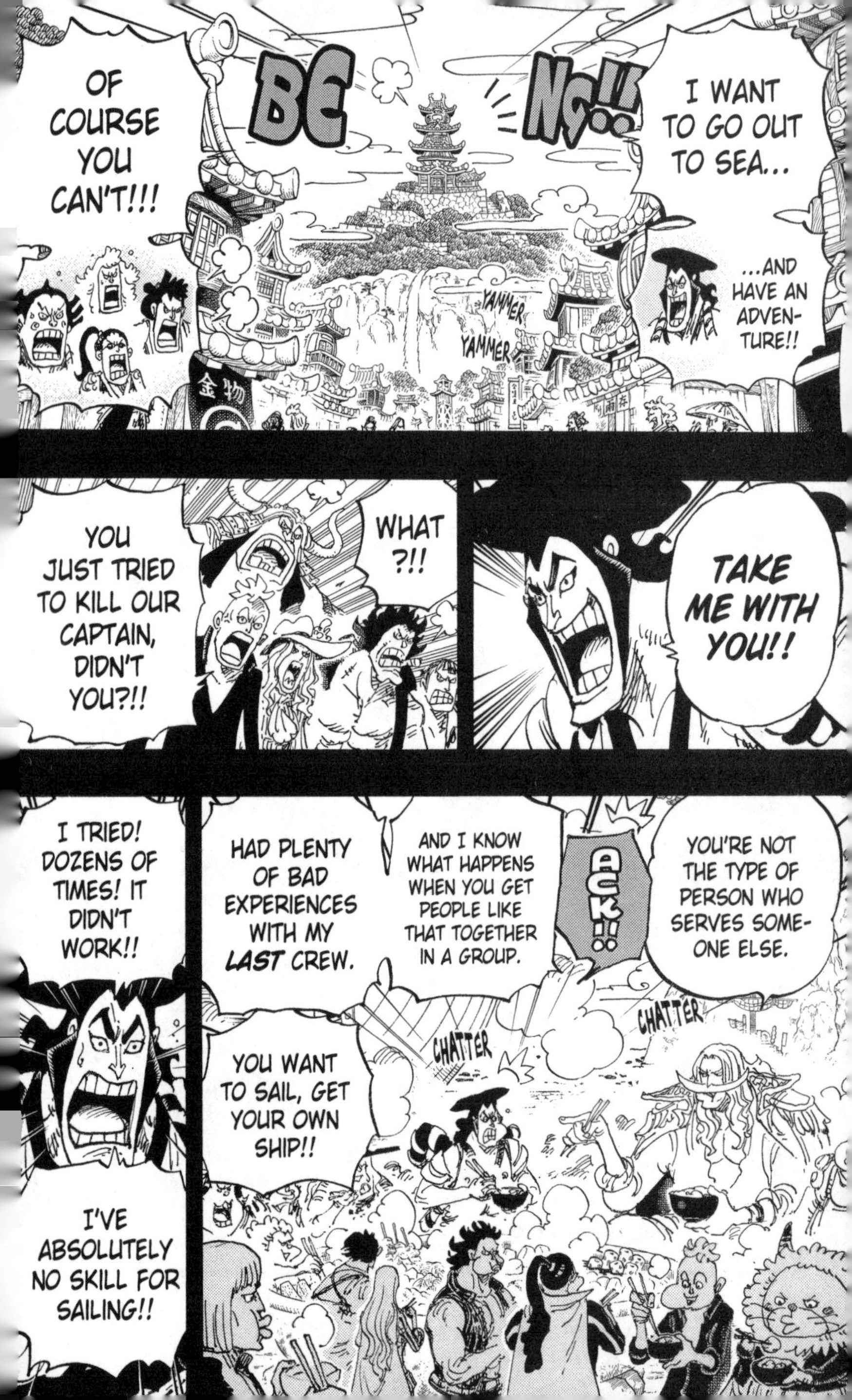
I WANT TO GO OUT TO SEA...
...AND HAVE AN ADVENTURE!!
BE NG!!
YAMMER
YAMMER
OF COURSE YOU CAN'T!!!
金物
TAKE ME WITH YOU!!
WHAT?!!
YOU JUST TRIED TO KILL OUR CAPTAIN, DIDN'T YOU?!!
YOU'RE NOT THE TYPE OF PERSON WHO SERVES SOMEONE ELSE.
ACK!!
AND I KNOW WHAT HAPPENS WHEN YOU GET PEOPLE LIKE THAT TOGETHER IN A GROUP.
HAD PLENTY OF BAD EXPERIENCES WITH MY *LAST* CREW.
CHATTER
CHATTER
YOU WANT TO SAIL, GET YOUR OWN SHIP!!
I TRIED! DOZENS OF TIMES! IT DIDN'T WORK!!
I'VE ABSOLUTELY NO SKILL FOR SAILING!!

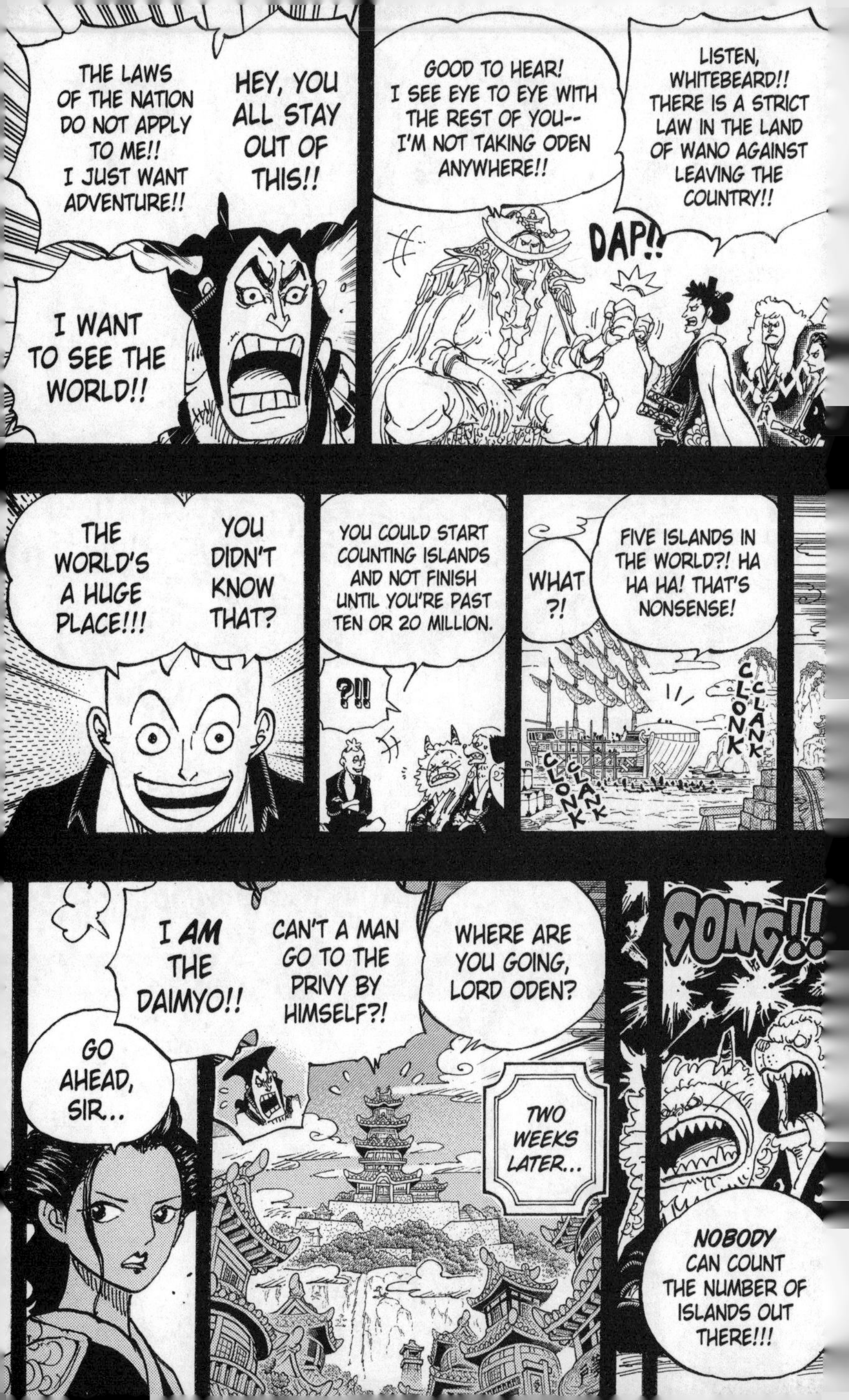
LISTEN, WHITEBEARD!! THERE IS A STRICT LAW IN THE LAND OF WANO AGAINST LEAVING THE COUNTRY!!
GOOD TO HEAR! I SEE EYE TO EYE WITH THE REST OF YOU-- I'M NOT TAKING ODEN ANYWHERE!!
DAP!!
HEY, YOU ALL STAY OUT OF THIS!!
THE LAWS OF THE NATION DO NOT APPLY TO ME!! I JUST WANT ADVENTURE!!
I WANT TO SEE THE WORLD!!
FIVE ISLANDS IN THE WORLD?! HA HA HA! THAT'S NONSENSE!
WHAT ?!
CLANK CLONK
CLANK CLONK
YOU COULD START COUNTING ISLANDS AND NOT FINISH UNTIL YOU'RE PAST TEN OR 20 MILLION.
?!!
YOU DIDN'T KNOW THAT?
THE WORLD'S A HUGE PLACE!!!
GONG!!
NOBODY CAN COUNT THE NUMBER OF ISLANDS OUT THERE!!!
WHERE ARE YOU GOING, LORD ODEN?
TWO WEEKS LATER...
CAN'T A MAN GO TO THE PRIVY BY HIMSELF?!
I AM THE DAIMYO!!
GO AHEAD, SIR...

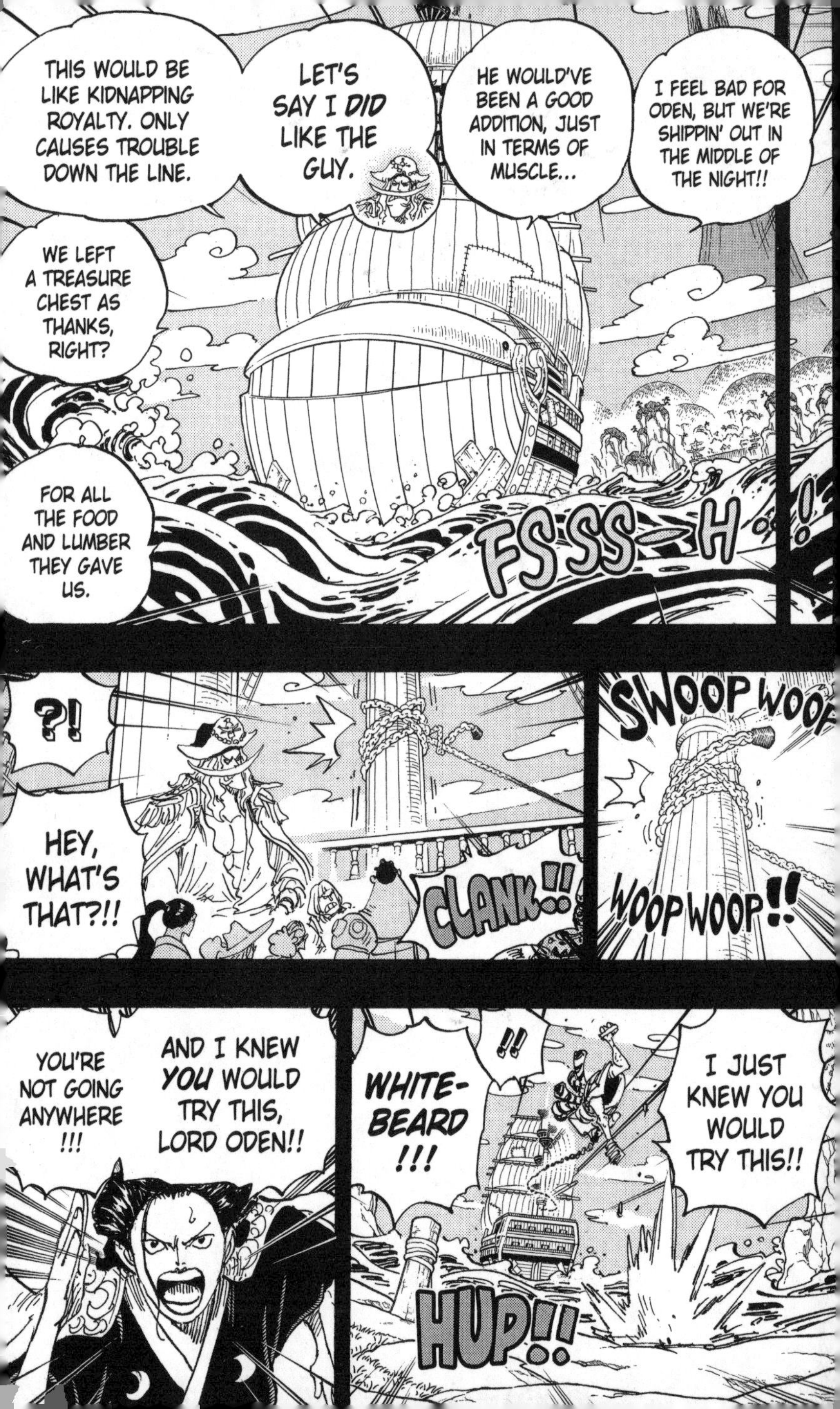
I FEEL BAD FOR ODEN, BUT WE'RE SHIPPIN' OUT IN THE MIDDLE OF THE NIGHT!!
HE WOULD'VE BEEN A GOOD ADDITION, JUST IN TERMS OF MUSCLE...
LET'S SAY I DID LIKE THE GUY.
THIS WOULD BE LIKE KIDNAPPING ROYALTY. ONLY CAUSES TROUBLE DOWN THE LINE.
WE LEFT A TREASURE CHEST AS THANKS, RIGHT?
FOR ALL THE FOOD AND LUMBER THEY GAVE US.
FSSS—H!
SWOOP WOOF
WOOP WOOP!!
?!
CLANK!!
HEY, WHAT'S THAT?!!
I JUST KNEW YOU WOULD TRY THIS!!
!!
WHITE-BEARD!!!
HUP!!
AND I KNEW YOU WOULD TRY THIS, LORD ODEN!!
YOU'RE NOT GOING ANYWHERE!!!

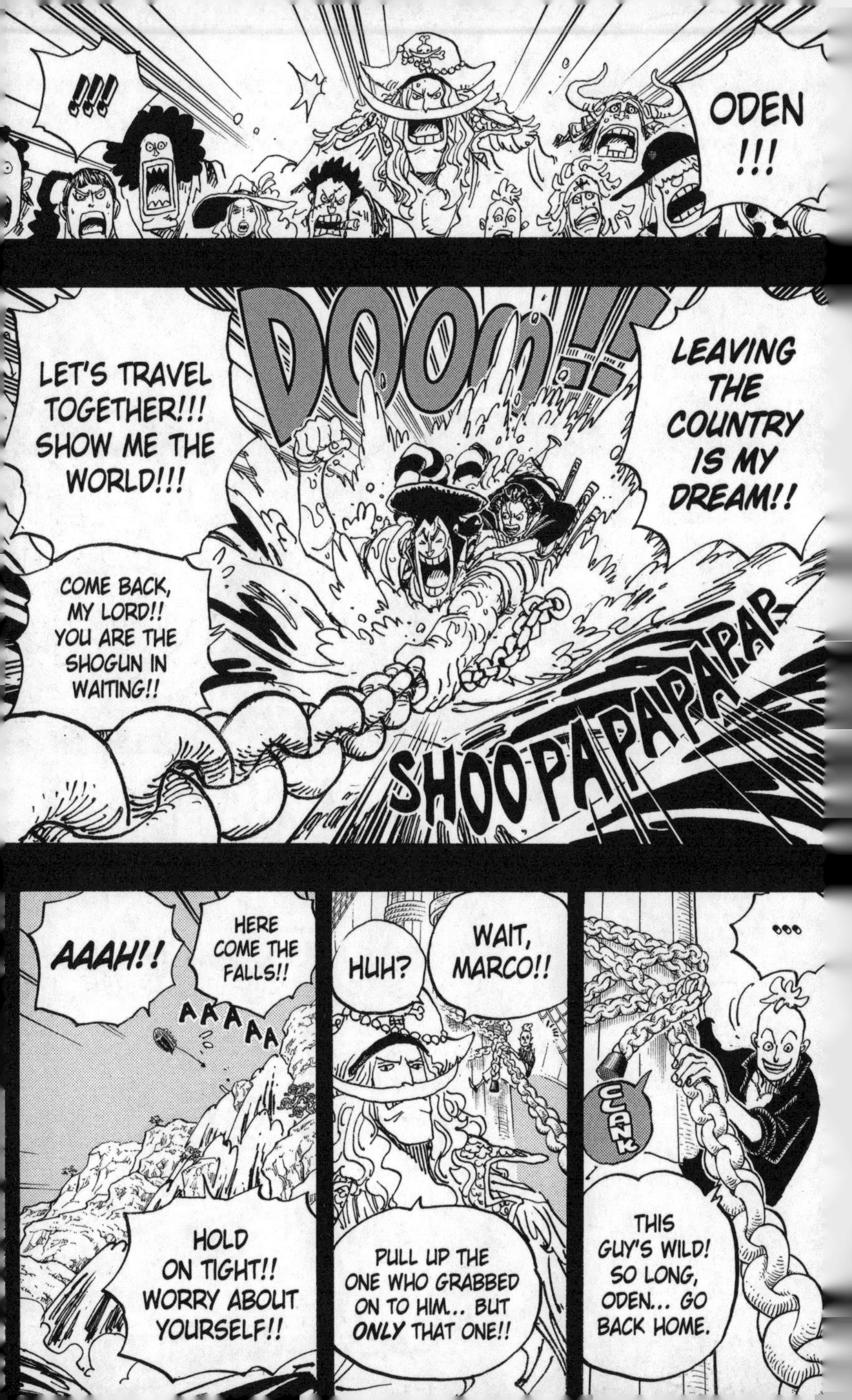
ODEN !!!
!!!
LEAVING THE COUNTRY IS MY DREAM!!
DOOOM!!
LET'S TRAVEL TOGETHER!!! SHOW ME THE WORLD!!!
COME BACK, MY LORD!! YOU ARE THE SHOGUN IN WAITING!!
SHOOPAPAPAPAP
...
CLANK
THIS GUY'S WILD! SO LONG, ODEN... GO BACK HOME.
WAIT, MARCO!!
HUH?
PULL UP THE ONE WHO GRABBED ON TO HIM... BUT *ONLY* THAT ONE!!
HERE COME THE FALLS!!
AAAH!!
AAAAA
HOLD ON TIGHT!! WORRY ABOUT YOURSELF!!

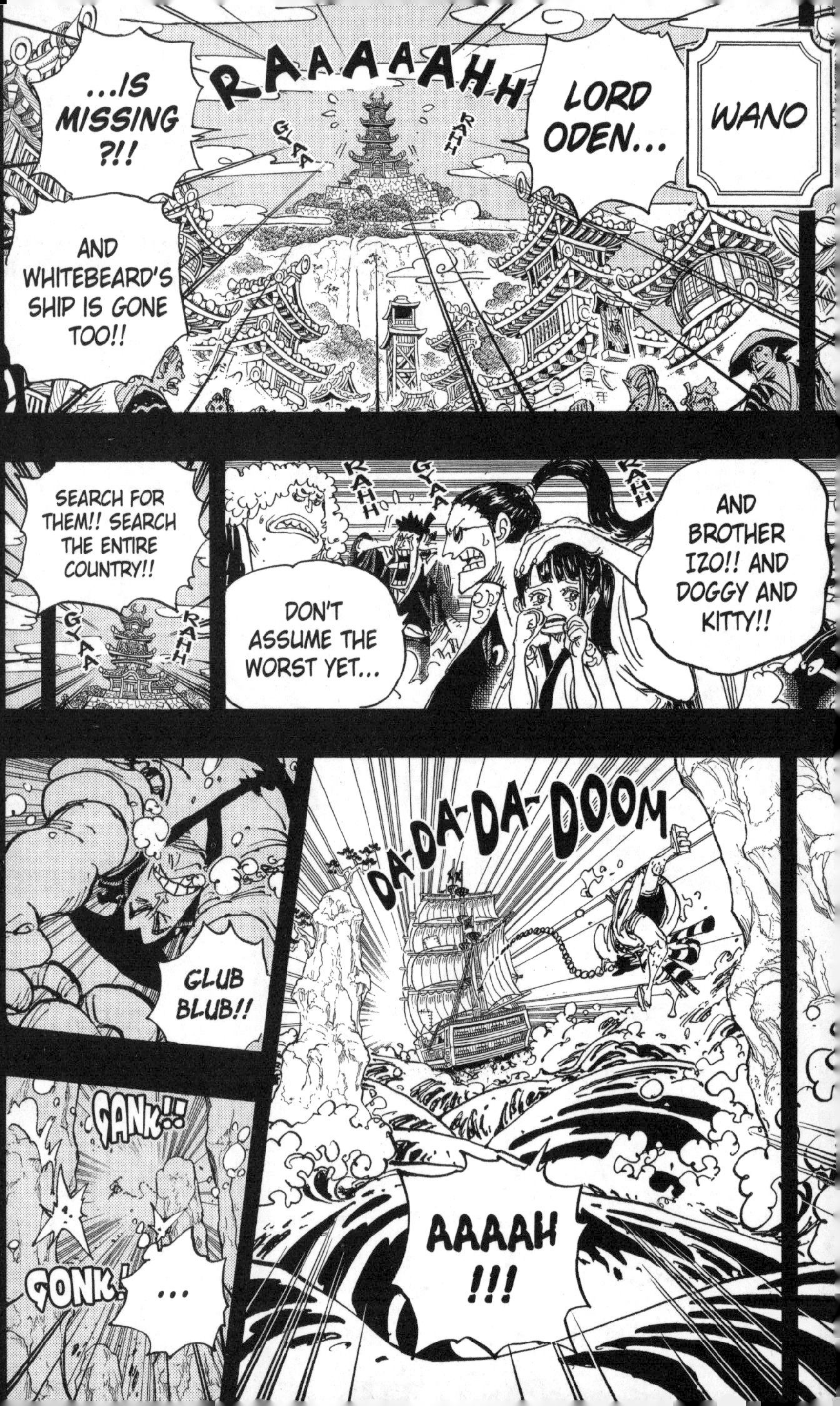
WANO
LORD ODEN...
RAAAAAAHH
RAHH
GYAA
...IS MISSING ?!!
AND WHITEBEARD'S SHIP IS GONE TOO!!
RAHH
AND BROTHER IZO!! AND DOGGY AND KITTY!!
GYAA
RAHH
DON'T ASSUME THE WORST YET...
SEARCH FOR THEM!! SEARCH THE ENTIRE COUNTRY!!
RAHH
GYAA
DA-DA-DA-DOOM
AAAAH !!!
GLUB BLUB!!
GANK!!
GONK!
...

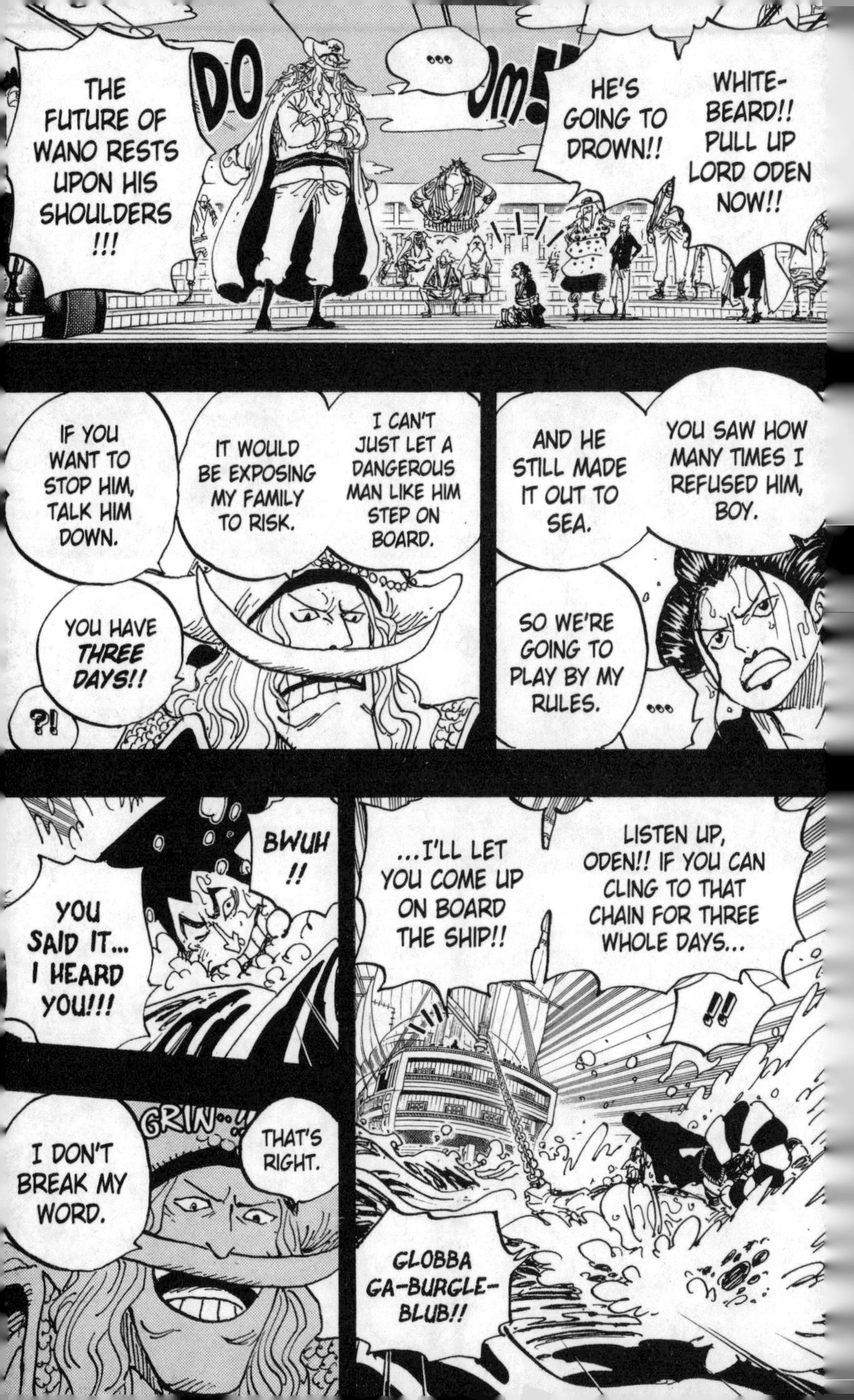
WHITE-BEARD!! PULL UP LORD ODEN NOW!!
HE'S GOING TO DROWN!!
DO
OM!
...
THE FUTURE OF WANO RESTS UPON HIS SHOULDERS!!!
YOU SAW HOW MANY TIMES I REFUSED HIM, BOY.
AND HE STILL MADE IT OUT TO SEA.
SO WE'RE GOING TO PLAY BY MY RULES.
...
I CAN'T JUST LET A DANGEROUS MAN LIKE HIM STEP ON BOARD.
IT WOULD BE EXPOSING MY FAMILY TO RISK.
IF YOU WANT TO STOP HIM, TALK HIM DOWN.
YOU HAVE THREE DAYS!!
?!
LISTEN UP, ODEN!! IF YOU CAN CLING TO THAT CHAIN FOR THREE WHOLE DAYS...
...I'LL LET YOU COME UP ON BOARD THE SHIP!!
!!
GLOBBA GA-BURGLE-BLUB!!
BWUH!!
YOU SAID IT... I HEARD YOU!!!
GRIN..
THAT'S RIGHT.
I DON'T BREAK MY WORD.

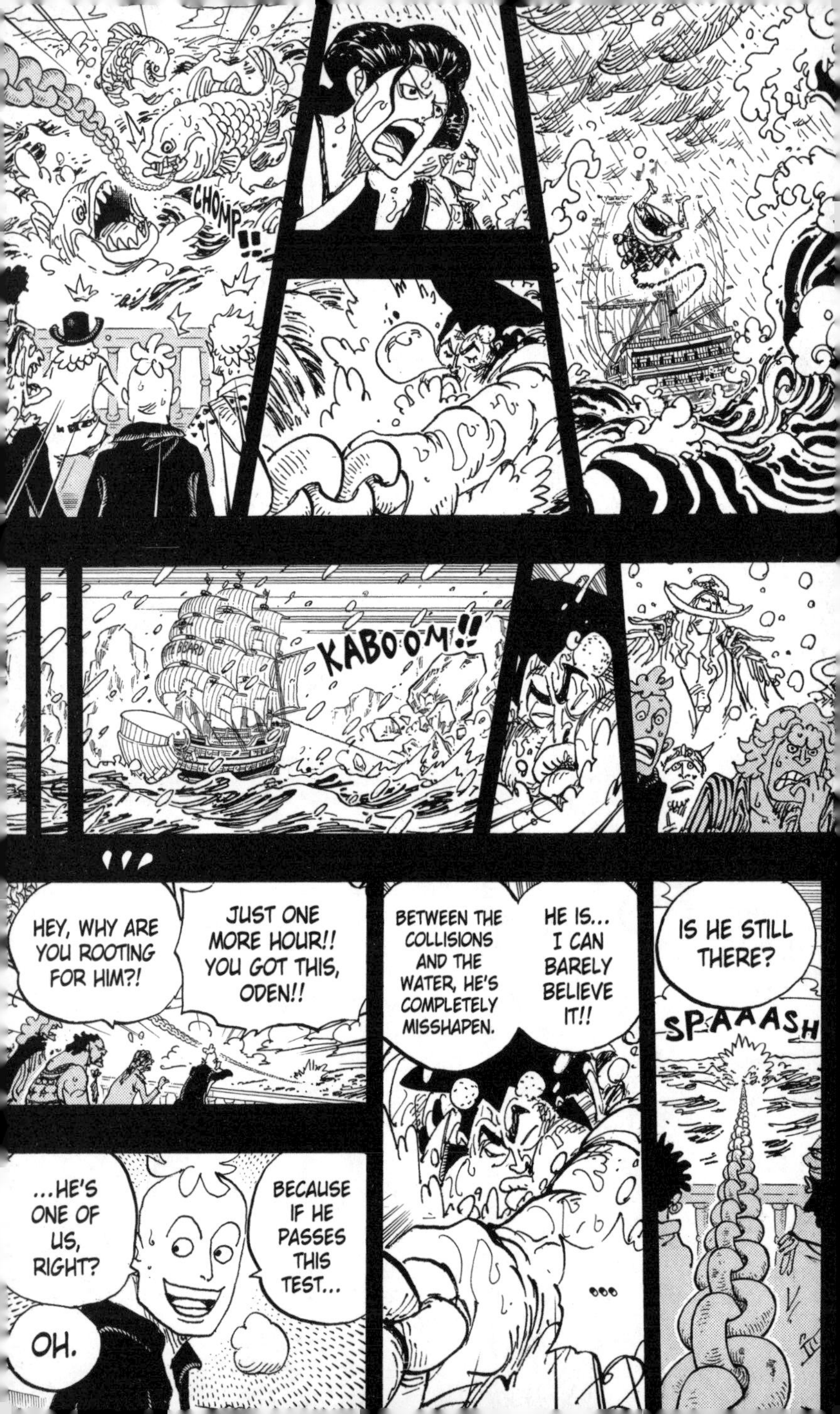
CHOMP!!
KABOOM!!
IS HE STILL THERE?
SPAAASH
HE IS... I CAN BARELY BELIEVE IT!!
BETWEEN THE COLLISIONS AND THE WATER, HE'S COMPLETELY MISSHAPEN.
...
JUST ONE MORE HOUR!! YOU GOT THIS, ODEN!!
HEY, WHY ARE YOU ROOTING FOR HIM?!
BECAUSE IF HE PASSES THIS TEST...
...HE'S ONE OF US, RIGHT?
OH.

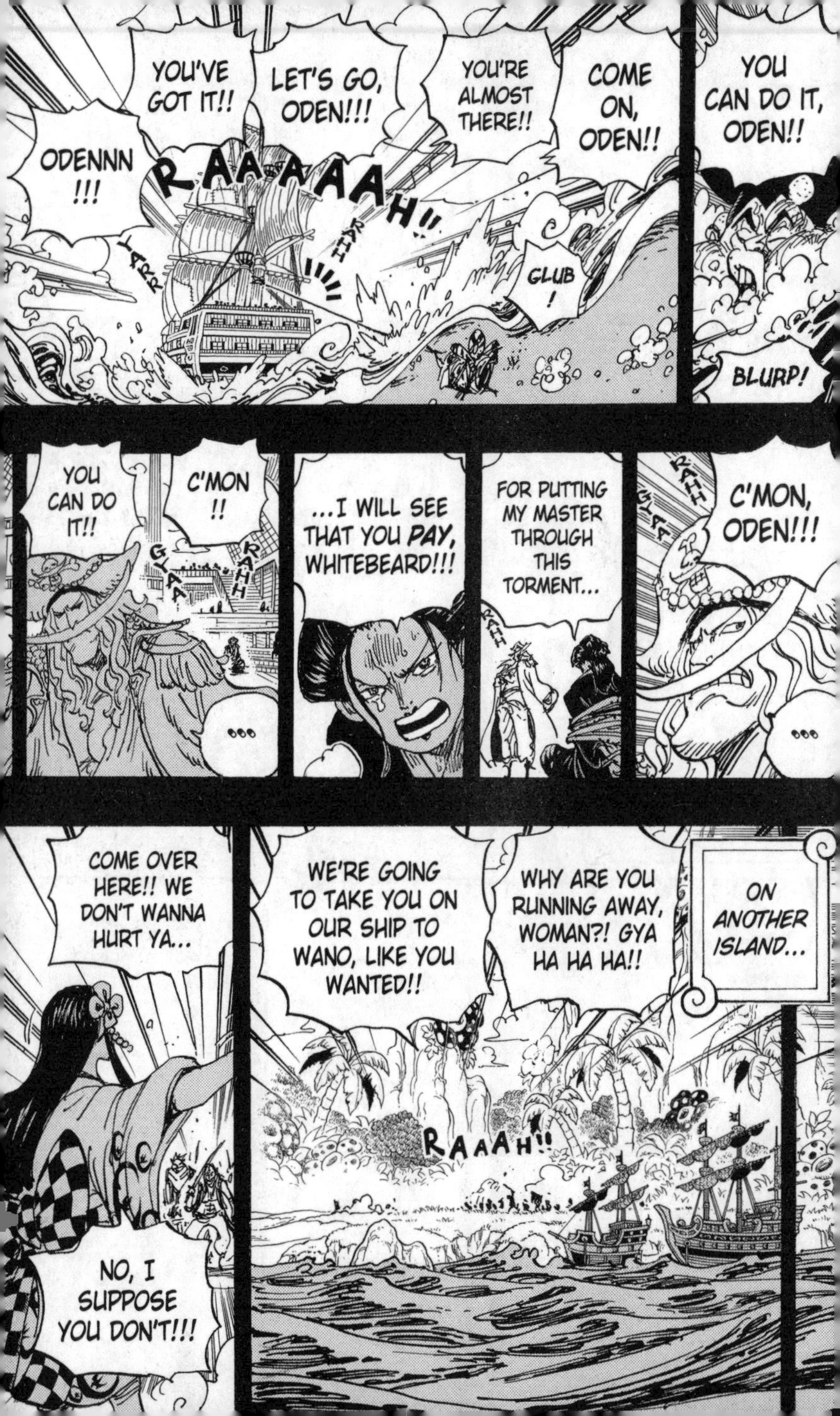
YOU CAN DO IT, ODEN!!
BLURP!
COME ON, ODEN!!
YOU'RE ALMOST THERE!!
LET'S GO, ODEN!!!
YOU'VE GOT IT!!
ODENNN !!!
RAAAAAAH!!
RAHH
GLUB !
YARR
C'MON, ODEN!!!
RAHH
GYAA
...
FOR PUTTING MY MASTER THROUGH THIS TORMENT...
RAHH
...I WILL SEE THAT YOU *PAY*, WHITEBEARD!!!
C'MON !!
YOU CAN DO IT!!
GYAA
RAHH
...
ON ANOTHER ISLAND...
WHY ARE YOU RUNNING AWAY, WOMAN?! GYA HA HA HA!!
WE'RE GOING TO TAKE YOU ON OUR SHIP TO WANO, LIKE YOU WANTED!!
RAAAH!!
COME OVER HERE!! WE DON'T WANNA HURT YA...
NO, I SUPPOSE YOU DON'T!!!

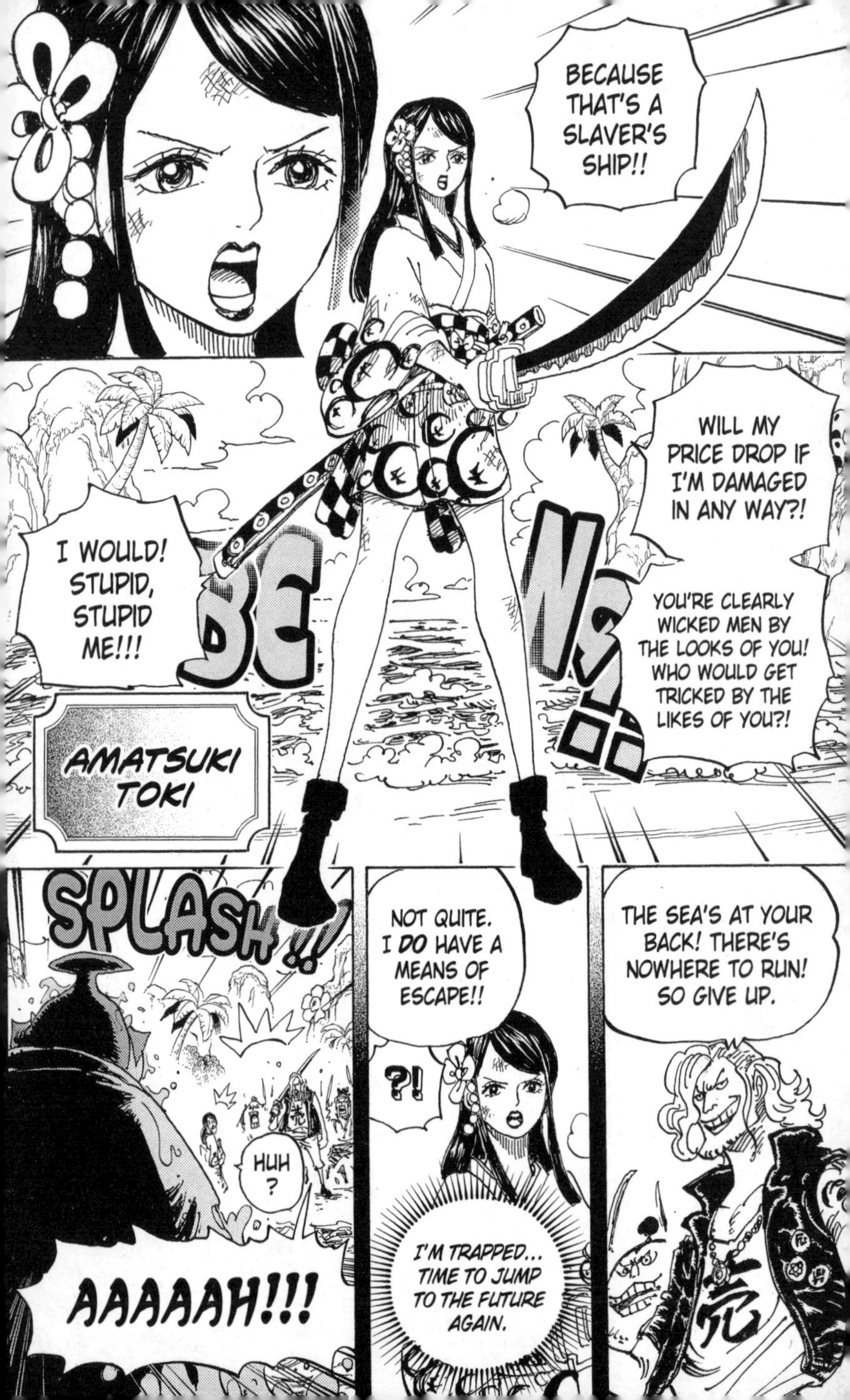
BECAUSE THAT'S A SLAVER'S SHIP!!
WILL MY PRICE DROP IF I'M DAMAGED IN ANY WAY?!
YOU'RE CLEARLY WICKED MEN BY THE LOOKS OF YOU! WHO WOULD GET TRICKED BY THE LIKES OF YOU?!
I WOULD! STUPID, STUPID ME!!!
AMATSUKI TOKI
THE SEA'S AT YOUR BACK! THERE'S NOWHERE TO RUN! SO GIVE UP.
NOT QUITE. I *DO* HAVE A MEANS OF ESCAPE!!
?!
I'M TRAPPED... TIME TO JUMP TO THE FUTURE AGAIN.
SPLASH!!
HUH ?
AAAAAH!!!

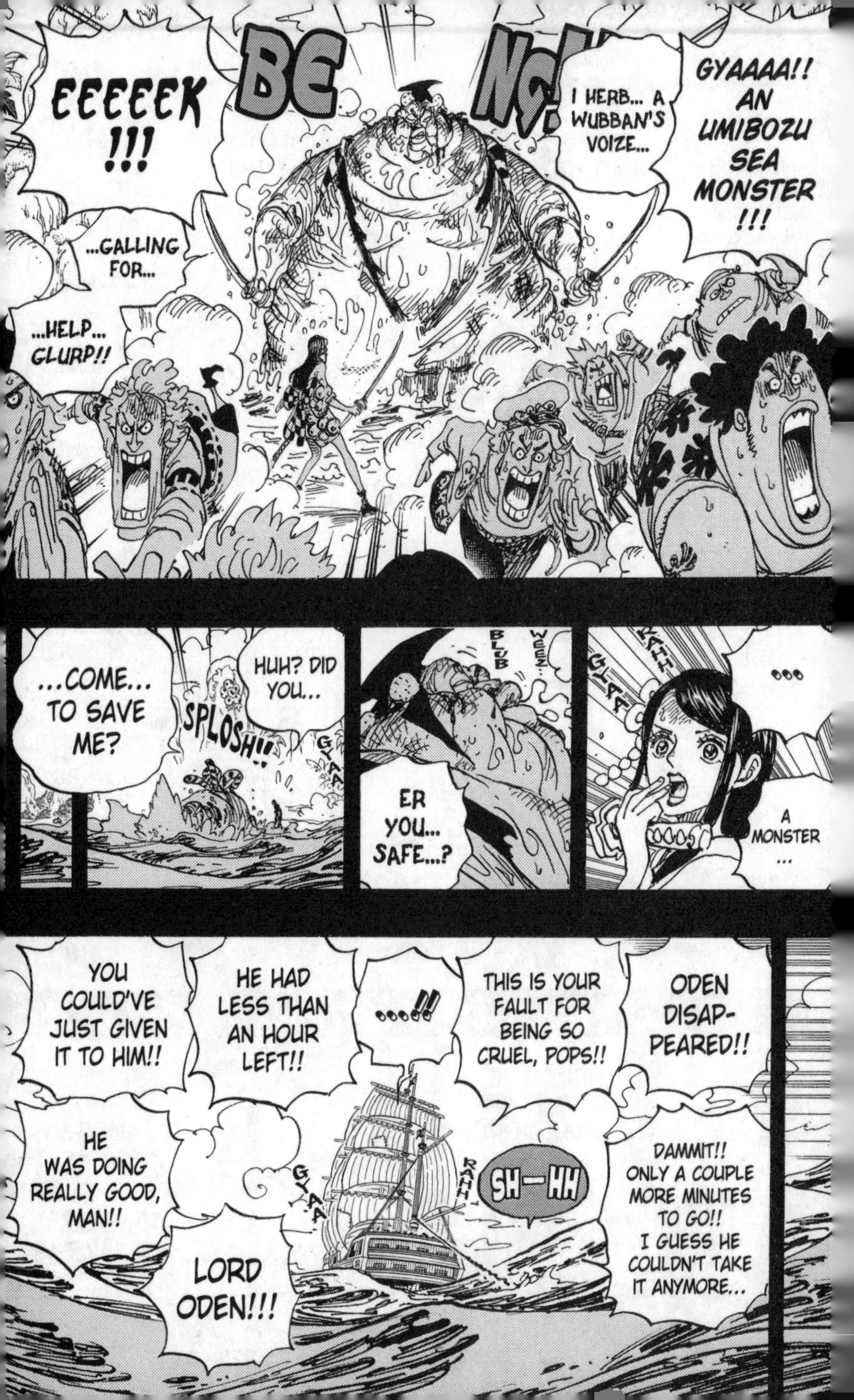
GYAAAA!! AN UMIBOZU SEA MONSTER!!!
I HERB... A WUBBAN'S VOIZE...
BE
NG!
EEEEEK!!!
...GALLING FOR...
...HELP... GLURP!!
...
GYAA
RAHH
A MONSTER...
WEEZ...
BLUB
ER YOU... SAFE...?
HUH? DID YOU...
...COME... TO SAVE ME?
SPLOSH!!
GYAA
ODEN DISAP-PEARED!!
THIS IS YOUR FAULT FOR BEING SO CRUEL, POPS!!
...!!
HE HAD LESS THAN AN HOUR LEFT!!
YOU COULD'VE JUST GIVEN IT TO HIM!!
DAMMIT!! ONLY A COUPLE MORE MINUTES TO GO!! I GUESS HE COULDN'T TAKE IT ANYMORE...
SH–HH
RAHH
GYAA
HE WAS DOING REALLY GOOD, MAN!!
LORD ODEN!!!

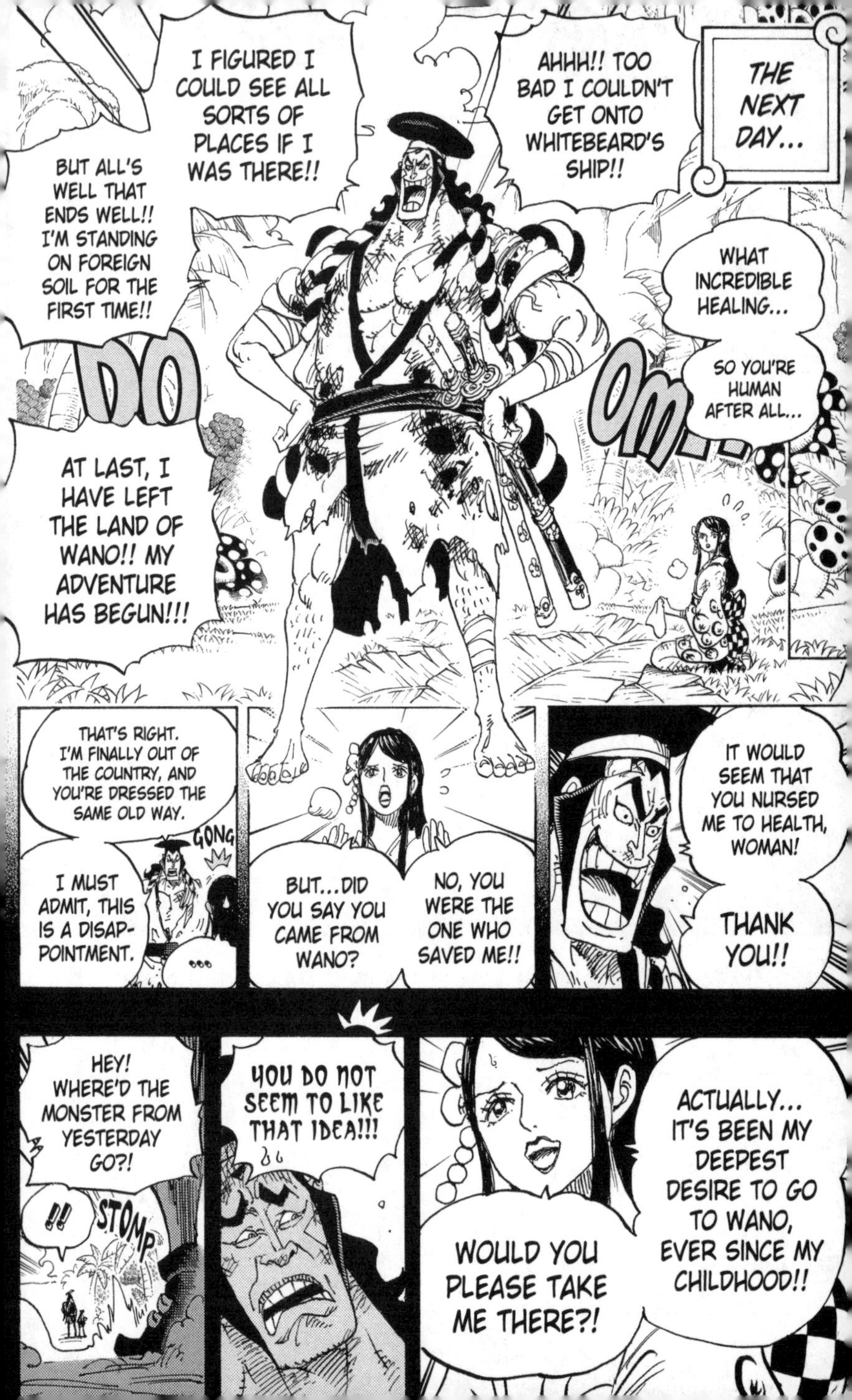
THE NEXT DAY...
AHHH!! TOO BAD I COULDN'T GET ONTO WHITEBEARD'S SHIP!!
I FIGURED I COULD SEE ALL SORTS OF PLACES IF I WAS THERE!!
WHAT INCREDIBLE HEALING...
BUT ALL'S WELL THAT ENDS WELL!! I'M STANDING ON FOREIGN SOIL FOR THE FIRST TIME!!
SO YOU'RE HUMAN AFTER ALL...
OM...
DO
AT LAST, I HAVE LEFT THE LAND OF WANO!! MY ADVENTURE HAS BEGUN!!!
IT WOULD SEEM THAT YOU NURSED ME TO HEALTH, WOMAN!
THANK YOU!!
NO, YOU WERE THE ONE WHO SAVED ME!!
BUT...DID YOU SAY YOU CAME FROM WANO?
THAT'S RIGHT. I'M FINALLY OUT OF THE COUNTRY, AND YOU'RE DRESSED THE SAME OLD WAY.
GONG
I MUST ADMIT, THIS IS A DISAP-POINTMENT.
...
ACTUALLY... IT'S BEEN MY DEEPEST DESIRE TO GO TO WANO, EVER SINCE MY CHILDHOOD!!
WOULD YOU PLEASE TAKE ME THERE?!
YOU DO NOT SEEM TO LIKE THAT IDEA!!!
HEY! WHERE'D THE MONSTER FROM YESTERDAY GO?!
!!
STOMP

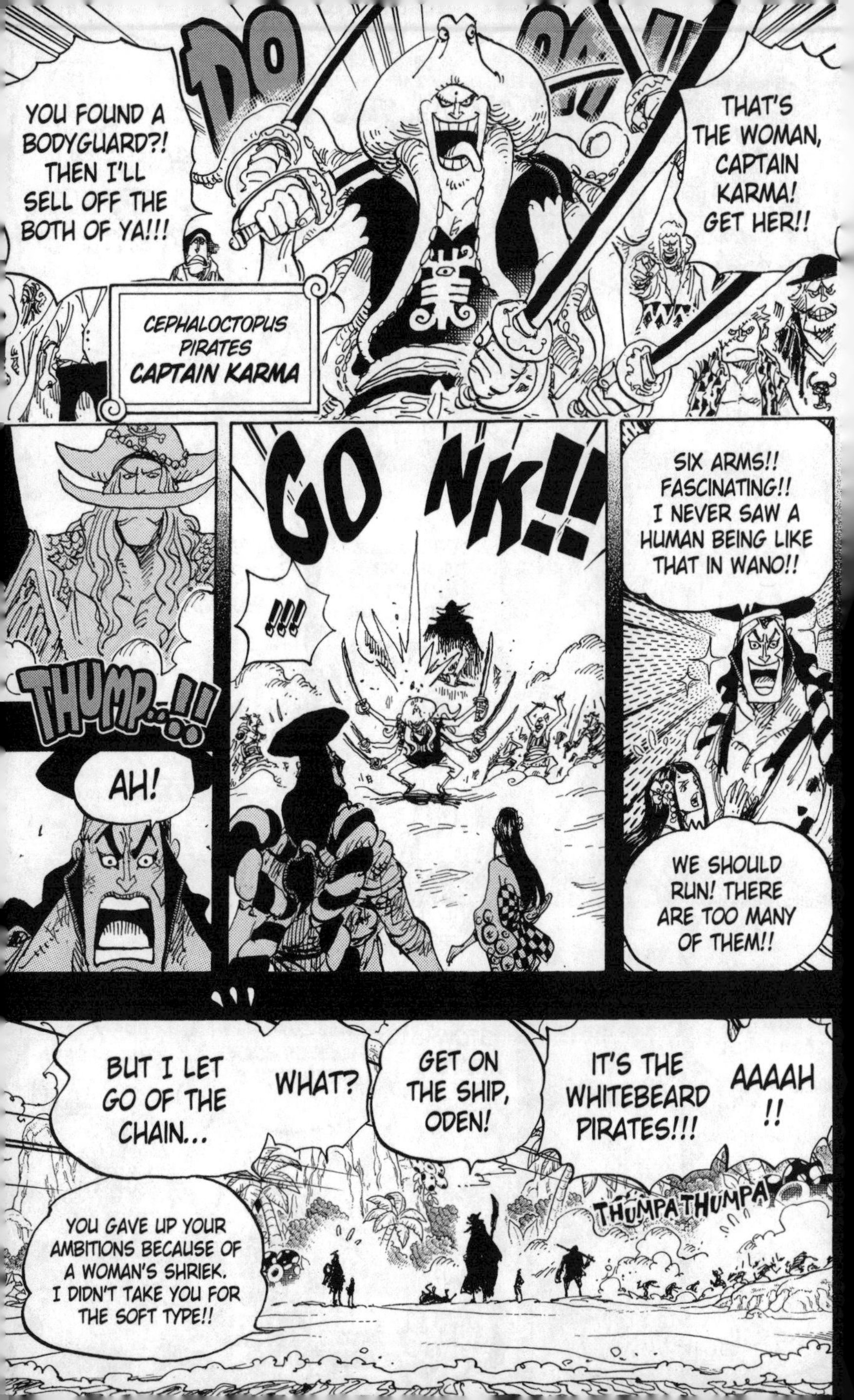

THAT'S THE WOMAN, CAPTAIN KARMA! GET HER!!
DO
YOU FOUND A BODYGUARD?! THEN I'LL SELL OFF THE BOTH OF YA!!!
CEPHALOCTOPUS PIRATES CAPTAIN KARMA
SIX ARMS!! FASCINATING!! I NEVER SAW A HUMAN BEING LIKE THAT IN WANO!!
WE SHOULD RUN! THERE ARE TOO MANY OF THEM!!
GONK!!
!!!
THUMP..!!
AH!
AAAAH!!
IT'S THE WHITEBEARD PIRATES!!!
GET ON THE SHIP, ODEN!
WHAT?
BUT I LET GO OF THE CHAIN...
THUMPA THUMPA
YOU GAVE UP YOUR AMBITIONS BECAUSE OF A WOMAN'S SHRIEK. I DIDN'T TAKE YOU FOR THE SOFT TYPE!!

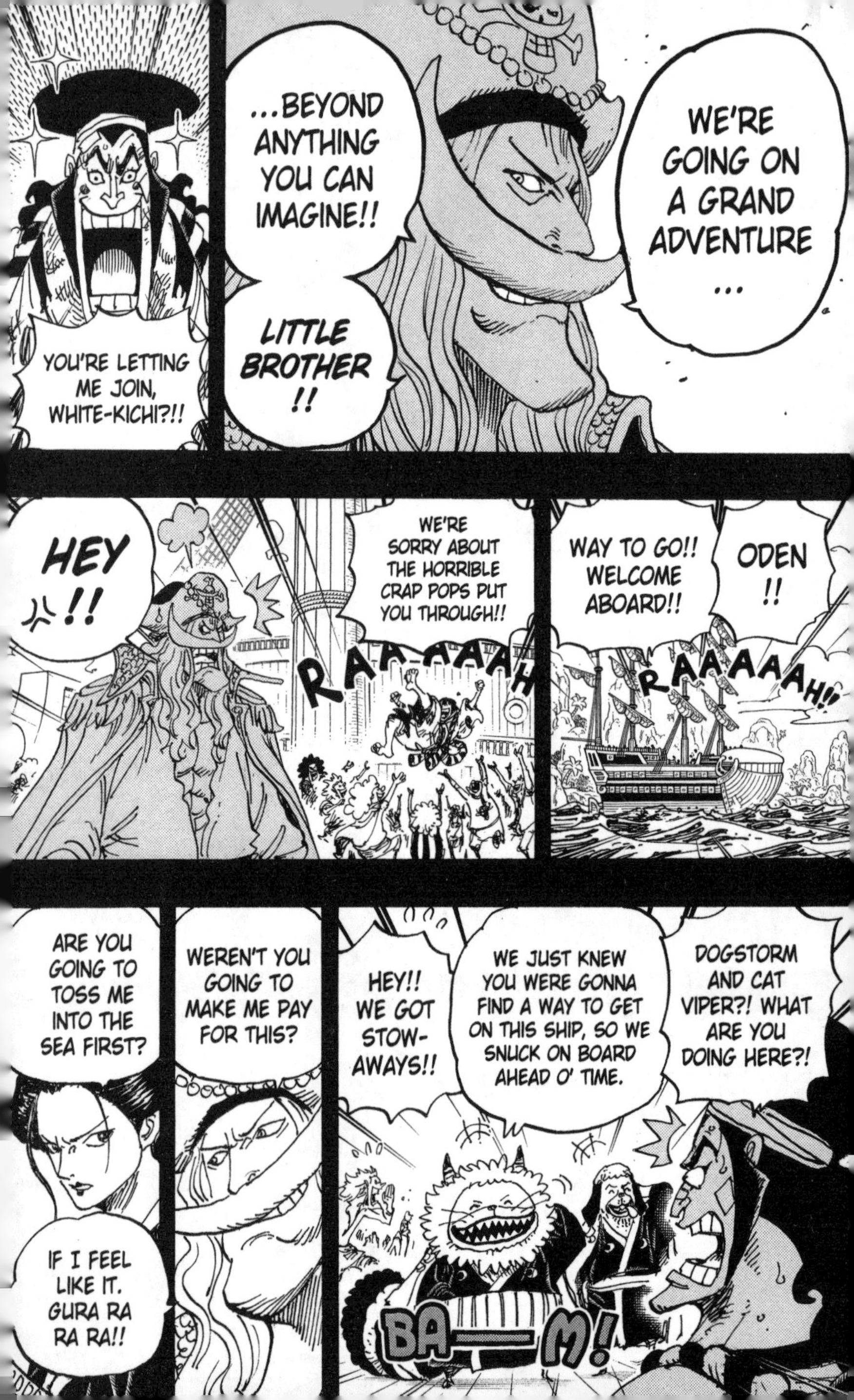
WE'RE GOING ON A GRAND ADVENTURE ...
...BEYOND ANYTHING YOU CAN IMAGINE!!
LITTLE BROTHER !!
YOU'RE LETTING ME JOIN, WHITE-KICHI?!!
ODEN !!
WAY TO GO!! WELCOME ABOARD!!
RAAAAAAH!!
WE'RE SORRY ABOUT THE HORRIBLE CRAP POPS PUT YOU THROUGH!!
RAAAAAAH
HEY !!
DOGSTORM AND CAT VIPER?! WHAT ARE YOU DOING HERE?!
WE JUST KNEW YOU WERE GONNA FIND A WAY TO GET ON THIS SHIP, SO WE SNUCK ON BOARD AHEAD O' TIME.
HEY!! WE GOT STOW-AWAYS!!
BA—M!
WEREN'T YOU GOING TO MAKE ME PAY FOR THIS?
ARE YOU GOING TO TOSS ME INTO THE SEA FIRST?
IF I FEEL LIKE IT. GURA RA RA RA!!

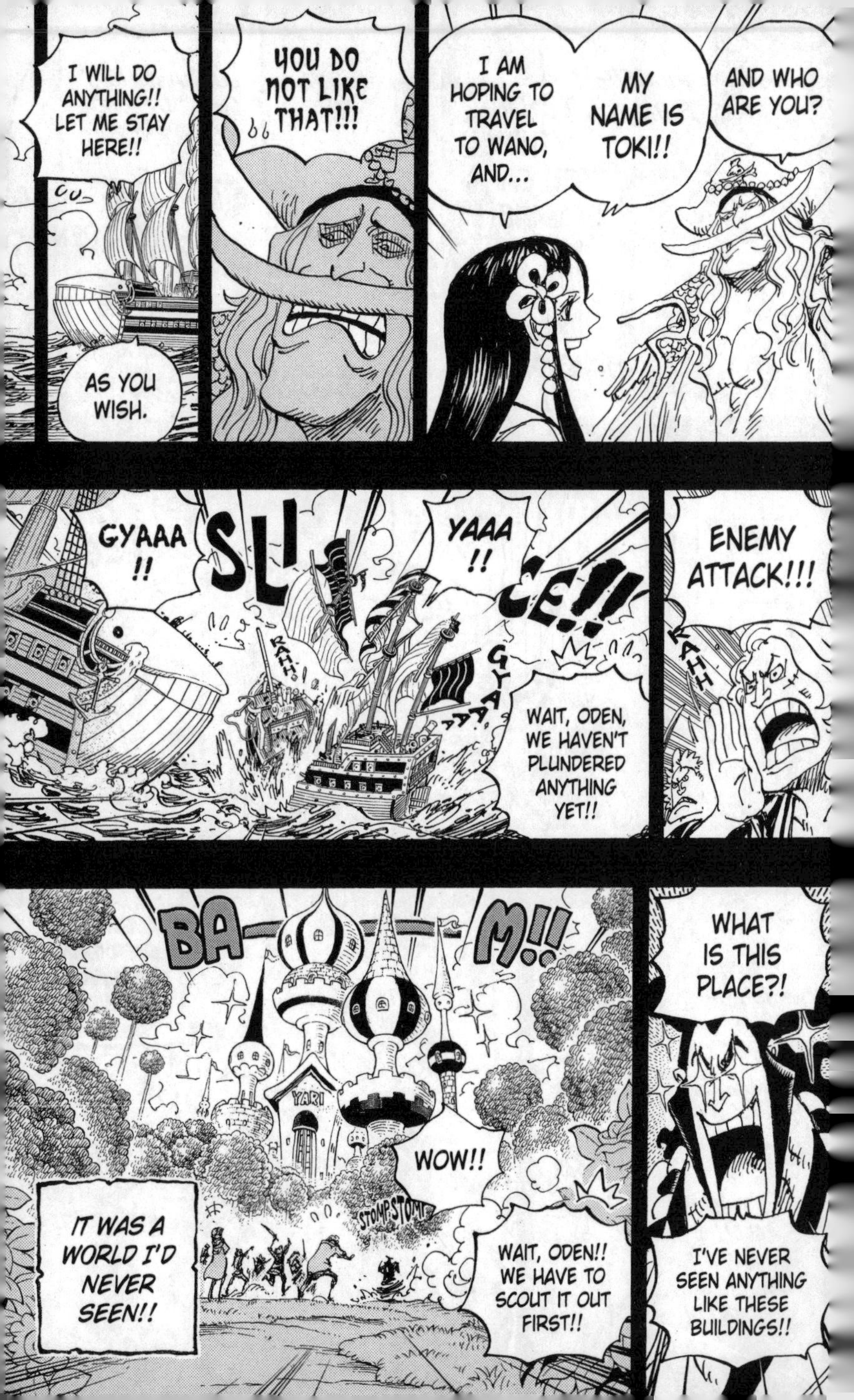
AND WHO ARE YOU?
MY NAME IS TOKI!!
I AM HOPING TO TRAVEL TO WANO, AND...
YOU DO NOT LIKE THAT!!!
I WILL DO ANYTHING!! LET ME STAY HERE!!
AS YOU WISH.
ENEMY ATTACK!!!
RAHH
YAAA!!
SLICE!!
GYAAA!!
RAHH
GYAAA
WAIT, ODEN, WE HAVEN'T PLUNDERED ANYTHING YET!!
WHAT IS THIS PLACE?!
I'VE NEVER SEEN ANYTHING LIKE THESE BUILDINGS!!
BA—M!!
YARI
WOW!!
STOMP STOMP
WAIT, ODEN!! WE HAVE TO SCOUT IT OUT FIRST!!
IT WAS A WORLD I'D NEVER SEEN!!

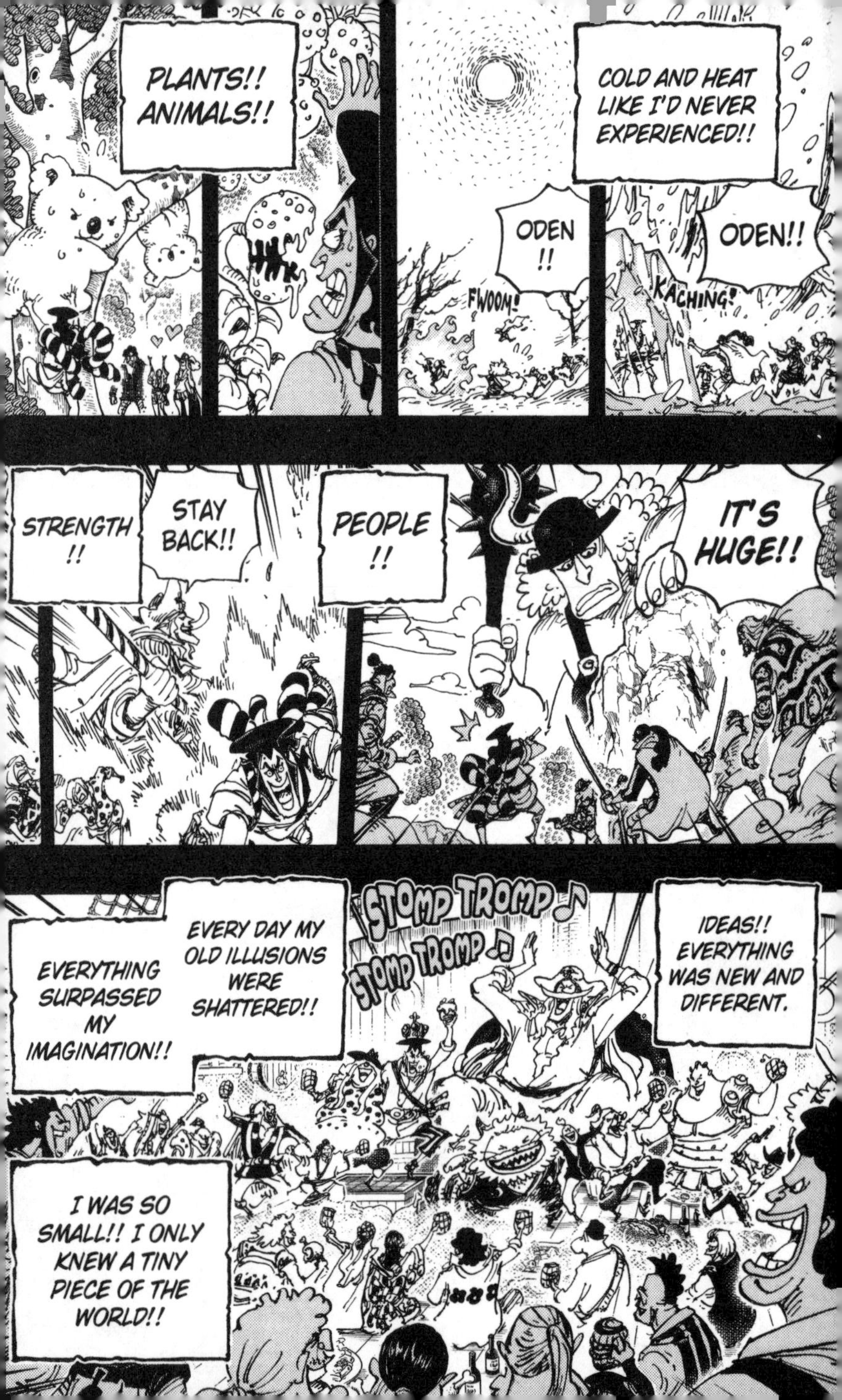
COLD AND HEAT LIKE I'D NEVER EXPERIENCED!!
ODEN!!
KACHING!
ODEN !!
FWOOM!
PLANTS!! ANIMALS!!
IT'S HUGE!!
PEOPLE !!
STAY BACK!!
STRENGTH !!
IDEAS!! EVERYTHING WAS NEW AND DIFFERENT.
STOMP TROMP ♪
STOMP TROMP ♫
EVERY DAY MY OLD ILLUSIONS WERE SHATTERED!!
EVERYTHING SURPASSED MY IMAGINATION!!
I WAS SO SMALL!! I ONLY KNEW A TINY PIECE OF THE WORLD!!

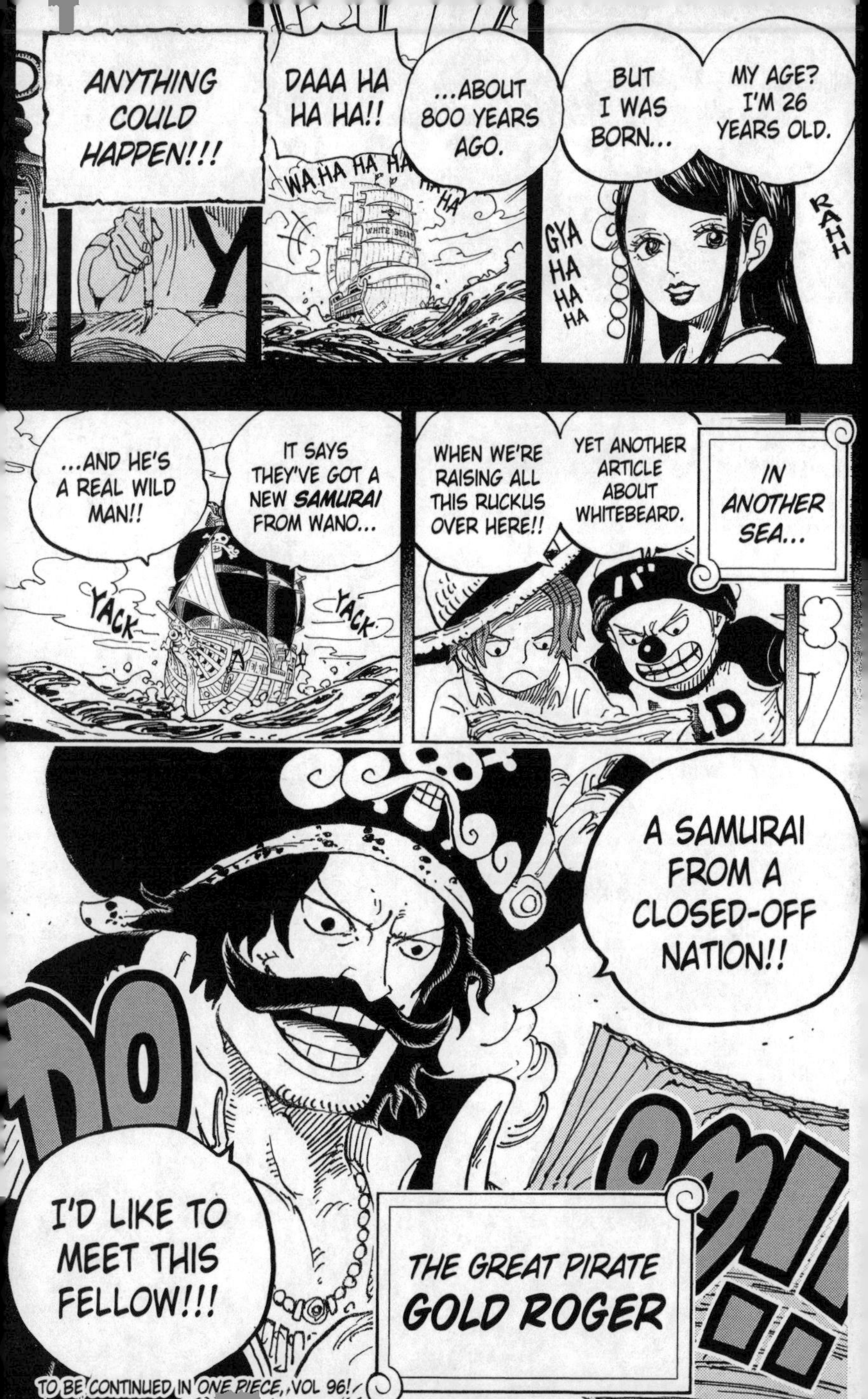
MY AGE? I'M 26 YEARS OLD.
BUT I WAS BORN...
RAHH
GYA HA HA HA HA
...ABOUT 800 YEARS AGO.
WA HA HA HA HA HA
DAAA HA HA HA!!
ANYTHING COULD HAPPEN!!!
IN ANOTHER SEA...
YET ANOTHER ARTICLE ABOUT WHITEBEARD.
WHEN WE'RE RAISING ALL THIS RUCKUS OVER HERE!!
IT SAYS THEY'VE GOT A NEW SAMURAI FROM WANO...
...AND HE'S A REAL WILD MAN!!
YACK
YACK
A SAMURAI FROM A CLOSED-OFF NATION!!
DO
OM!!
I'D LIKE TO MEET THIS FELLOW!!!
THE GREAT PIRATE GOLD ROGER

TO BE CONTINUED IN ONE PIECE, VOL 96!

COMING NEXT VOLUME:

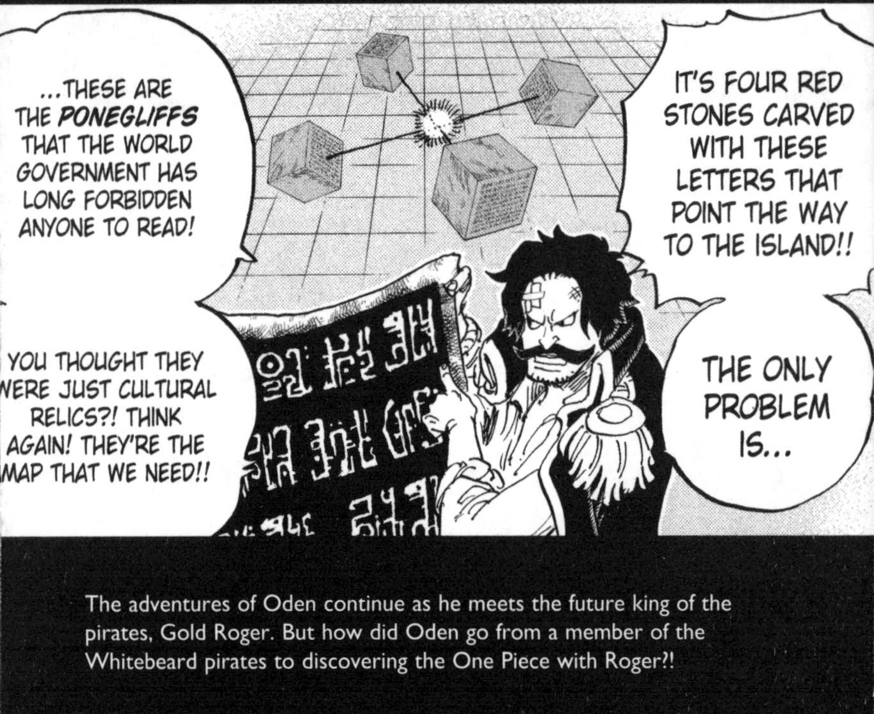
IT'S FOUR RED STONES CARVED WITH THESE LETTERS THAT POINT THE WAY TO THE ISLAND!!
...THESE ARE THE ***PONEGLIFFS*** THAT THE WORLD GOVERNMENT HAS LONG FORBIDDEN ANYONE TO READ!
THE ONLY PROBLEM IS...
YOU THOUGHT THEY WERE JUST CULTURAL RELICS?! THINK AGAIN! THEY'RE THE MAP THAT WE NEED!!

The adventures of Oden continue as he meets the future king of the pirates, Gold Roger. But how did Oden go from a member of the Whitebeard pirates to discovering the One Piece with Roger?!

ON SALE APRIL 2021!

尾田栄一郎

You know how you start cleaning one tiny corner of your room, and then it just never ever stops?!

Yeah. Nice. I always wanted to say that (but not actually do it). Well, now I'm done. But this adventure isn't done by a long shot!! Enjoy volume 95!!

-Eiichiro Oda, 2019

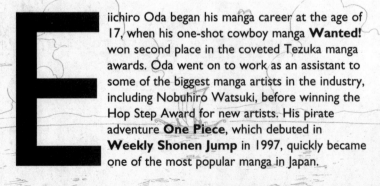

Eiichiro Oda began his manga career at the age of 17, when his one-shot cowboy manga **Wanted!** won second place in the coveted Tezuka manga awards. Oda went on to work as an assistant to some of the biggest manga artists in the industry, including Nobuhiro Watsuki, before winning the Hop Step Award for new artists. His pirate adventure **One Piece**, which debuted in **Weekly Shonen Jump** in 1997, quickly became one of the most popular manga in Japan.

ONE PIECE VOL. 95
WANO PART 6

SHONEN JUMP Manga Edition

STORY AND ART BY EIICHIRO ODA

Translation/Stephen Paul
Touch-up Art & Lettering/Vanessa Satone
Design/Yukiko Whitley
Editor/Alexis Kirsch

Printed in the U.S.A.

Published by VIZ Media, LLC
P.O. Box 77010
San Francisco, CA 94107

10 9 8 7 6 5 4 3 2 1
First printing, December 2020

viz.com

PARENTAL ADVISORY
ONE PIECE is rated T for Teen and is recommended for ages 13 and up. This volume contains fantasy violence and violence and tobacco usage.

ratings.viz.com
RATED T TEEN

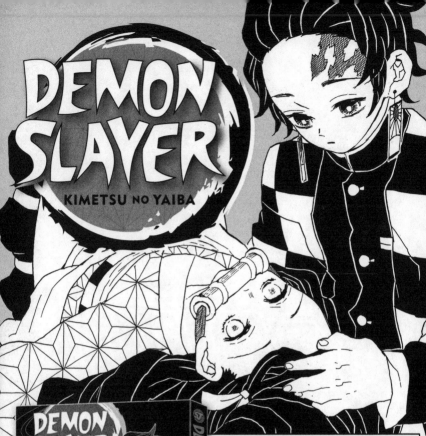

DEMON SLAYER
KIMETSU NO YAIBA

Story and Art by
KOYOHARU GOTOUGE

In Taisho-era Japan, kindhearted Tanjiro Kamado makes a living selling charcoal. But his peaceful life is shattered when a demon slaughters his entire family. His little sister Nezuko is the only survivor, but she has been transformed into a demon herself! Tanjiro sets out on a dangerous journey to find a way to return his sister to normal and destroy the demon who ruined his life.

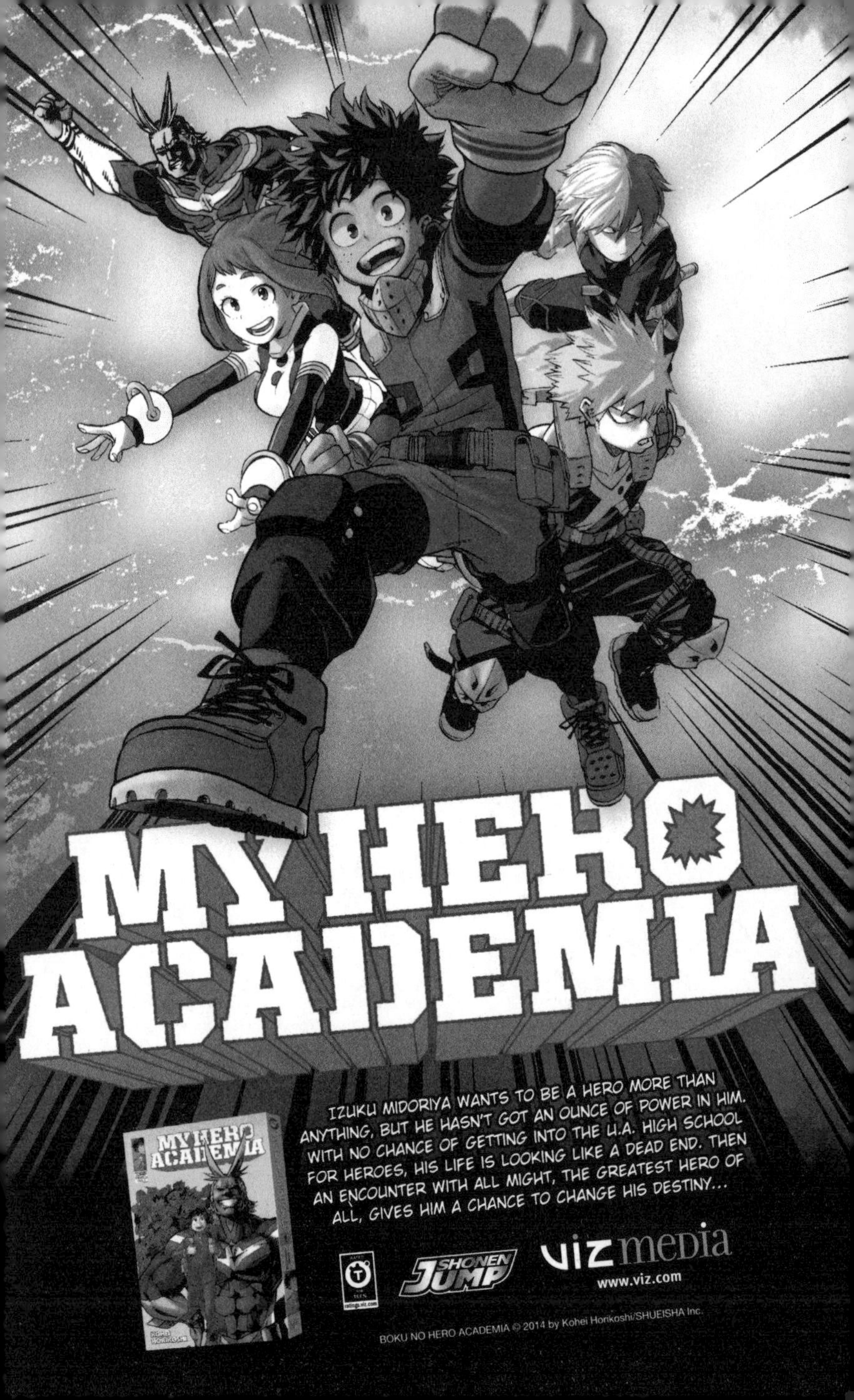
MY HERO ACADEMIA
IZUKU MIDORIYA WANTS TO BE A HERO MORE THAN ANYTHING, BUT HE HASN'T GOT AN OUNCE OF POWER IN HIM. WITH NO CHANCE OF GETTING INTO THE U.A. HIGH SCHOOL FOR HEROES, HIS LIFE IS LOOKING LIKE A DEAD END. THEN AN ENCOUNTER WITH ALL MIGHT, THE GREATEST HERO OF ALL, GIVES HIM A CHANCE TO CHANGE HIS DESTINY...
SHONEN JUMP
VIZ media
www.viz.com
BOKU NO HERO ACADEMIA © 2014 by Kohei Horikoshi/SHUEISHA Inc.

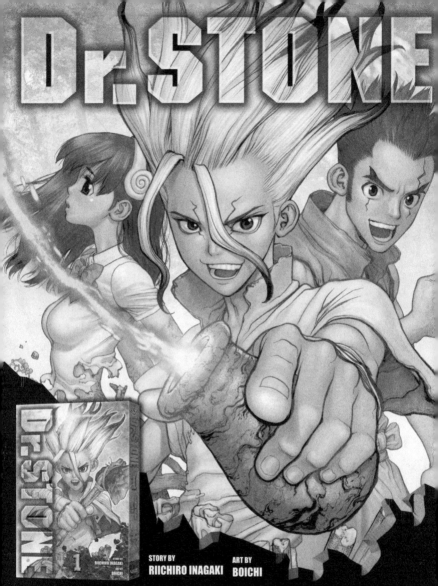

Dr.STONE

STORY BY
RIICHIRO INAGAKI

ART BY
BOICHI

One fateful day, all of humanity turned to stone. Many millennia later, Taiju frees himself from petrification and finds himself surrounded by statues. The situation looks grim—until he runs into his science-loving friend Senku! Together they plan to restart civilization with the power of science!

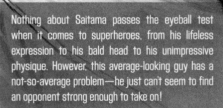

You're R
the Wro

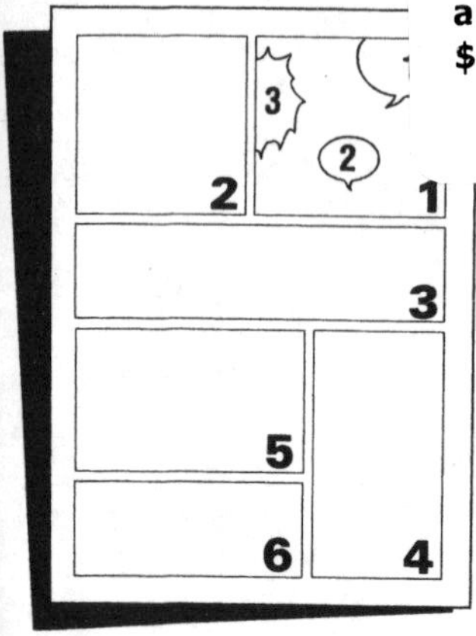
1
2
3
4
5
6

...it's true! In keeping with the original Japanese format, **One Piece** is meant to be read from right to left, starting in the upper-right corner.

Unlike English, which is read from left to right, Japanese is read from right to left, meaning that action, sound effects and word-balloon order are completely reversed...something which can make readers unfamiliar with Japanese feel pretty backwards themselves. For this reason, manga or Japanese comics published in the U.S. in English have sometimes been published "flopped"—that is, printed in exact reverse order, as though seen from the other side of a mirror.

By flopping pages, U.S. publishers can avoid confusing readers, but the compromise is not without its downside. For one thing, a character in a flopped manga series who once wore in the original Japanese version a T-shirt emblazoned with "M A Y" (as in "the merry month of") now wears one which reads "Y A M"! Additionally, many manga creators in Japan are themselves unhappy with the process, as some feel the mirror-imaging of their art skews their original intentions.

We are proud to bring you Eiichiro Oda's **One Piece** in the original unflopped format. For now, though, turn to the other side of the book and let the journey begin...!

—Editor

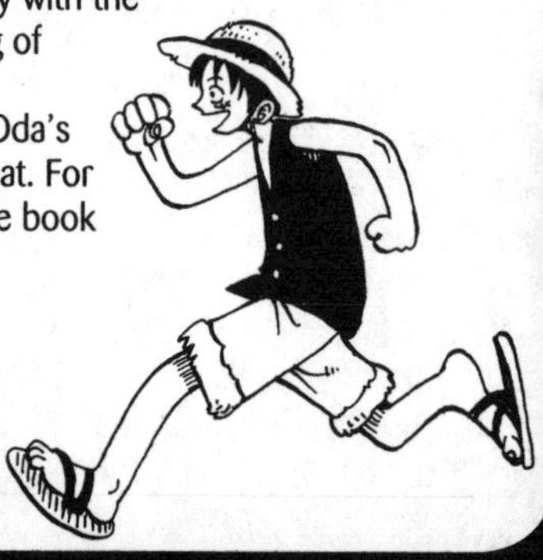